P9-DMV-184

WITHDRAWN

TRADITION AND TRANSFORMATION IN CATHOLIC CULTURE

TRADITION AND TRANSFORMATION IN CATHOLIC CULTURE

The Priests of Saint Sulpice in the United States from 1791 to the Present

Christopher J. Kauffman

MACMILLAN PUBLISHING COMPANY
NEW YORK

Collier Macmillan Publishers
LONDON

Macmillan Publishing Company
866 Third Avenue, New York, N.Y. 10022

Collier Macmillan Canada, Inc.

Library of Congress Catalog Card Number: 87-28235

Printed in the United States of America

printing number
1   2   3   4   5   6   7   8   9   10

Library of Congress Cataloging-in-Publication Data

Kauffman, Christopher J., 1936–
    Tradition and transformation in Catholic culture.

    Bibliography: p.
    Includes index.
    1. Sulpicians—United States—History.   2. United
States—Church history.   I. Title.
BX4060.Z5U64   1987   271′.75′073   87-28235
ISBN 0-02-917211-X

To Jane, Chris, and Katie
with loving thanks
for your joyful imprint upon my book of life

Contents

Preface

When I began research for this history, I had no idea that I would encounter such significant topics as Gallicanism, Americanism, Modernism, and the evolution of liberal Catholicism in France and the United States. I am very grateful to the many church historians, particularly John Tracy Ellis and Colman J. Barry, O.S.B., who introduced me to the Sulpicians. I owe particular thanks to the Lilly Endowment for its partial, but very significant, funding of this project. Robert Lynn, vice-president of the religion division of the endowment, and Frederick Hofheinz, his associate, expressed a strong and abiding interest in my work. It has been a stimulating, intellectual experience for me to have had the opportunity to share research discoveries and ideas on the history of Catholic theological education with Joseph M. White, a faculty fellow in the Cushwa Center for the Study of American Catholicism at the University of Notre Dame, a scholar whose work on Catholic seminary education is also sponsored by a grant from the Lilly Endowment.

I am deeply indebted to Vincent Eaton, the Sulpician archivist who designed and constructed a model for religious-community archives and who proofread my text with a keen eye for detail. His successor, John Bowen, has been a source of kind assistance and companionship over these last four years. Iréneé Noye, the Sulpician archivist in Paris, not only provided me with an abundance of rich material but also made arrangements for my family and me to live in the home of M. and Mme Forest, his niece, while they and their children were on holiday. White, Eaton, Bowen, and Noye were extraordinary proofreaders of the text and made valuable suggestions for improvements.

I am grateful to the Sulpicians for having established a blue-ribbon advisory committee for their bicentennial history project, which included John Tracy Ellis of the Catholic University of America; Sr.

Reginald Gerdes, O.S.P., of the Oblate Sisters of Providence; Robert
T. Handy of Union Theological Seminary in New York; and Dr. Henry
Tom of the Johns Hopkins University Press. I am indebted to each of
them for their careful reading of the text. The critical evaluations of
Ellis and Handy were particularly helpful in revising the manuscript.

Robert Robidoux, the Sulpician rector of the Canadian College in
Rome, provided me with comfortable quarters in an atmosphere of
warm hospitality during my visit to Rome for research in the Vatican
archives. The archivist of the Canadian Province of the Society of Saint
Sulpice, Bruno Harel, was very hospitable and helpful while I was in
Montreal on research. I am grateful to the two superiors general, Constant Bouchaud and Raymond Deville, who have been very supportive
of the history project. Edward Frazer and Gerald Brown, the American provincials, have been enthusiastic in their support of my work.
As the provincial's representative for the history project, William Lee
has been consistently available and vitally interested. I am indebted to
Louis Arand, James Laubacher, James Brennan, John Cronin, William
Morris, and to many other Sulpicians who shared with me their historical experience as Sulpicians. Another Sulpician, Robert Leavitt, was a
very hospitable president-rector of Saint Mary's Seminary; and Charles
J. Talar, priest, former faculty member of Saint Mary's, and scholar of
Modernism, lent me several significant books from his excellent library
and provided many stimulating conversations that relieved the tedium
of research. Lowell Glendon, a Sulpician scholar of Olier's spirituality,
and Robert Eno, a Sulpician church historian, were valuable resource
persons for this work. Thomas W. Spalding, C.F.X., historian of the
archdiocese of Baltimore, provided helpful suggestions for improving
the manuscript.

Many librarians and archivists have assisted me over the years:
Monsignor Charles Burns of the Vatican archives; Father Joseph Metz-
ler, O.M.I., then head of the archives of the Congregatio de Propaganda
Fide; David P. Siemsen, librarian at Saint Mary's Seminary, Baltimore;
Sister Felicitas Powers, R.S.M., of the archdiocese of Baltimore; the
Very Reverend Edward Granitch of the archdiocese of Saint Louis;
Drs. James O'Toole and Timothy Meagher of the archdiocese of Boston;
Dr. Jeffrey Burns of the archdiocese of San Francisco; Dr. Anthony
Zito and Sister Ann Crowley, S.N.D., of the Catholic University of
America; Dr. Wendy Schlereth of the University of Notre Dame;
Ms. Elizabeth Yaekel of the archdiocese of Detroit; Sister Marguerita
Smith, O.P., of the archdiocese of New York; Ms. Christine Bauer of
the archdiocese of Seattle; Kelly Fitzpatrick of Mount Saint Mary's
College Emmitsburg, Maryland; John Farina of the archives of the
Paulist Fathers, Washington, D.C.; Sisters M. Reparata Clarke, O.S.P.,
and Wilhelmina Lancaster, O.S.P., of the archives of the Oblate Sisters

of Providence; Sister Agnes Geraldine McGann, S.C.N., of the archives of the Sisters of Charity in Nazareth, Kentucky; and Fathers Delbert W. Robinson, M.M., and Robert E. Sheridan, M.M., of the Maryknoll archives, Maryknoll, New York.

Father Louis Reitz, Mr. Joseph Reynolds, Ms. JoAnn Cosden, and Ms. Barbara Kowalski of the staff of the U.S. Sulpician province were always available for assistance. Many thanks are due to Ms. Beverly Simpson, who to the surprise of many managed to read my rough and meandering handwriting in order to type several drafts of the manuscript.

I have been the grateful recipient of an abundance of concern for my work from my family. In my personal history I am proud to be the husband of Helen and the father of Jane, Christopher, and Kathryn Ann.

Introduction

In a study entitled "The Excellence of M. Olier," Henri Bremond focused on the spirituality of Jean-Jacques Olier. Whether one is referring to the richly cultivated interior life of the founder of the Society of Saint Sulpice or to the cultural manifestations of the Sulpician way of life, *excellence* is an appropriate descriptive term for the spirit of Saint Sulpice, to which thousands of alumni priests of Sulpician seminaries owe their religious formation.

The spirit of Saint Sulpice, derived from the charism of Olier, was manifested in a specific method of mental prayer, in the *haute culture* of an aristocratic concept of the priesthood, and in the Sulpician drive to model the interior and exterior ideals of the priesthood for those aspiring to the sacerdotal life. Institutionalized during the age of Louis XIV, this spirit became identified with the revival of religious idealism, the restoration of the nonregular clergy, and the reform of parish life. The Sulpician was a diocesan priest dedicated to the spiritual direction of those called to sacred orders. A community of diocesan priests with a superior general is a juridical anomaly, but in practice the directors of each house formed a collegial governance body authorized to make all policy decisions, including the initial call to ordination. The superior general and his council decided on matters relating to the life of a community that fostered a social individualism among its members.

The Sulpician system of spiritual direction—*pédagogie du Saint-Sulpice*—occurred within the context of the sacrament of penance, a context that tended to create strong bonds between the Sulpician priest and seminarian-penitent. Although this system was developed in an atmosphere influenced by the tradition of Augustinian austerity, the director–penitent bond was often characterized by a gentle personalism, as both priest and seminarian were striving toward a common goal. Because the director–penitent relationship tended to continue after ordination, the seminary became a permanent factor in the lives of many alumni priests and bishops. As the preeminent seminary in France, Saint-Sulpice was at the center of ecclesiastical life; when it was transplanted into the diocese of Baltimore, Saint Sulpice was a singular witness to the spirituality and dignity of the diocesan priesthood in the United States.

This history of the Sulpicians in the United States is a prism through which are refracted persistent patterns in the evolution of American Catholicism as well as in French Catholic culture. In the following study the prologue, "From Jean-Jacques Olier to the French Revolution (1600–1789)," traces the origins of the Sulpicians and depicts the central role of Saint-Sulpice in the development of post-reformation religious and social culture. During this period the charism of Olier was structured into a unique way of life. Although the Sulpicians were primarily spiritual directors of seminarians, they were also unofficial advisers of the leaders of the church in France. In a real sense Saint-Sulpice manifested itself as the spiritual and political conscience of the French church, and many French Catholics considered Paris to be the capital of Catholic culture just as Rome was the capital of the Catholic faith.

In part I, "The Sulpicians and the Formation of an American Church (1789–1850)," I cover how the Sulpicians reflected the patriotism of John Carroll, the first Catholic bishop in the new American republic, and Catholicism's adaptation to the unique religious conditions in the United States, that is, separation of church and state, religious liberty, and denominationalism. After the death of Carroll and throughout the remainder of this period, the Sulpicians dominated the religious life of the archdiocese of Baltimore.

As the most learned of the Catholic communities of men—most Sulpicians were educated at the Sorbonne—the Sulpicians staffed not only the first seminary in the United States but also the first college chartered in the state of Maryland. This adaptation to the new condition of religious freedom included the acceptance of religious pluralism. Saint Mary's College (1799–1852) symbolized this spirit, as Protestants were in the majority within its student body.

On the western frontier, French Sulpicians served as missionaries in Kentucky, Illinois, Indiana, and Michigan. Indeed the first frontier bishop, Benedict Flaget, was a Sulpician. These missionaries founded seminaries and colleges; Gabriel Richard, the Sulpician missionary in Detroit, was one of the three founders of the University of Michigan. The Sulpician response to the needs of the local church was derived from the society's moderate Gallicanism, that is, an ecclesiology that stressed the movement of the Holy Spirit in the *particular* national context rather than in the *centralized* authority structures of the papacy.

This French relationship to American Catholicism, so central to the understanding of the significance of the Sulpicians, requires an analysis of contemporaneous events in the history of the French church, which is given in chapter 3. During the first century of the society's history in the United States the vast majority of Sulpicians were born and educated in France; this part of the history, therefore, is based upon the Baltimore–Paris connection. Since no other major religious group, either Protestant or Catholic, was so strongly attached to its European roots for so long a period of time, the French-American character of this narrative constitutes a significant part of its uniqueness.

In part II, "Americanization in the Immigrant Church (1850–1911)," the French relationship plays a vital role. While the Anglo-American church (1790–1850) was cosmopolitan, the immigrant church was insular and preoccupied with nurturing its various ethnic components. Under the direction of authorities in Paris, the Sulpicians in Baltimore were told to close Saint Mary's College and to restrict their activities to the seminary. An American-oriented superior was replaced by a French traditionalist, and the Sulpicians turned inward. Ironically, as the Paris Sulpicians were subjected to papal harassment for their liberal Gallicanism, the Baltimore Sulpicians and their traditionalist superior were criticized by Archbishop Martin J. Spalding for their conservativism.

In the last two decades of the nineteenth century two Sulpicians greatly influenced the political and intellectual climate of the church and strengthened the cultural ties between Paris and Baltimore. Alphonse Magnien, considered the head and heart of the Americanist movement in the Catholic church, was a priest of the diocese of Orléans, France, and close to Bishop Felix Dupanloup, a liberal opponent (inopportunist) of the doctrine on papal infallibility as defined at the First Vatican Council. Just as Dupanloup was attempting to reconcile the church to contemporary society, Magnien (superior in the United States from 1878 to 1902) became a major figure in the attempt to reconcile the church with dominant trends in American culture that were perceived as paradigms of modernity. Magnien was also a seminary reformer who introduced many innovations in academic and social life. The tacit acceptance of religious pluralism inherent in Americanism prompted Magnien to permit qualified seminarians and Sulpicians to study at Johns Hopkins University and to encourage other liberal measures that would not become generally accepted features of seminary life until after the Second Vatican Council. During Magnien's tenure as superior, Sulpician seminaries were opened in Boston (1884), New York (1896), and San Francisco (1898). Under the leadership of an American superior, the New York institution became a seminary distinctively more modern than its contemporary counterparts.

The opponents of Americanism were those leaders who viewed

American society as materialistic, nativist, and anti-Catholic. They were the preservationists within the immigrant church, determined to separate themselves from the mainstream of American life. Magnien and the Americanists, on the other hand, were transformationists, that is, they believed that within the context of American freedom the church was being transformed and that Catholicism was in turn having a transformative effect upon American culture. Americanism was popular among the French liberal Catholics because the promulgation of the decree of papal infallibility marked the death of Gallicanism; Americanism filled the vacuum with a vital and particularist ecclesiology highly congenial to the tradition of French liberalism.

John Hogan, born in Ireland and trained in France, was an influential liberal intellectual in Paris before he became rector of the Sulpician seminary in Boston in 1884. As a quasi Modernist, John Hogan held Americanist sympathies as well. More an intellectual than an ecclesiastic, Hogan's ideas on scripture, on the development of doctrine, and on historical methodology vis-à-vis the predominantly ahistorical theology of neoscholasticism, mark him as a thorough transformationist. The struggles of Hogan and Magnien not only reflected the Catholic church's significant confrontation with modernity; because this confrontation was international in scope and occurred within many religious denominations, it also sheds light on the central religious questions of the modern era.

The nascent Modernist Hogan and the Americanist Magnien represented the Sulpician drive for a new apologetic suitable to the dynamics of the age and reflective of the advances in modern scholarship. Although Americanism was condemned in 1899 and Modernism in 1907, and although many of the liberal Sulpician innovations did not survive the oppressive climate of the pontificate of Pius X, the American Sulpicians who succeeded Magnien and Hogan remained strongly influenced by the Americanist ecclesiology. The evolution from Olier's spirituality to Magnien's ecclesiology is in accord with Charles-Pierre Péguy's remark that "everything begins in *mystique* and ends in *politique*."

The Sulpicians directly confronted anti-Americanism and anti-Modernism when Cardinal William H. O'Connell of Boston expelled them from the seminary. O'Connell perceived himself as a militant guardian of orthodoxy and identified "Sulpicianism" as a major source of the liberal conspiracy within the church. Part III, "From Romanization to the Second Vatican Council, (1911–1967)," opens with the Sulpicians establishing a seminary adjacent to the Catholic University of America, a move that was in accord with the elevation of Sulpicians in the United States to the status of an official province in 1922. Over the next thirty years the province expanded to include Seattle, Detroit, Louisville, and Honolulu.

Religious separatism continued during this period, but the immigrant church slowly became more American in its institutional structures and more modern in the professionalization of its personnel. The formation of the National Catholic Welfare Conference (NCWC), the work of second-generation Americanist Bishops and priests, represented a countervailing factor to the general trend toward increased Romanization of the American hierarchy. The Sulpicians were close to the leaders of the NCWC as well as to other religious communities that tended to be open to American culture, such as the Paulists and the Maryknoll missionaries. Although the Vatican imposed rigid regulations upon the seminary curriculum, the Sulpicians continued to preserve the unique features of their seminary tradition, which included personal spiritual direction and collegial governance.

During the 1950s, when both the church and the larger society were conservative, Sulpician seminaries, particularly Saint Mary's in Baltimore, developed a progressive intellectual climate that anticipated the dramatic breakthroughs of the 1960s. For example, in the mid-1950s the rector of Saint Mary's called for a revision of the curriculum according to such principles as the development of doctrine and the historical approach to scripture and theology. Although John Hogan had advocated the same revisionist principles in his 1901 book, *Clerical Studies*, the church had not been ready for his agenda in 1900, nor was it ready in 1955. Nonetheless, because of the legacy of Magnien and Hogan the Sulpicians were better prepared than most communities for the profound changes associated with the Second Vatican Council. Three Sulpicians theologians were advisers to bishops and several Sulpician scholars were influential in promoting a liberal agenda at this council. The Sulpician seminaries were in the vanguard of reform and renewal, and the student ferment of the times manifested itself in Sulpician institutions. The epilogue traces the ways in which the Sulpician leaders have responded to the many recent challenges brought about by the declining enrollment in seminaries and the ideological polarization within the American church.

To recapitulate, the theme woven throughout this study is that the Sulpicians were a major force in the liberal movements in the American church. When they transplanted Saint-Sulpice to Baltimore, the Sulpicians brought with them a particularist ecclesiology, a refined notion of spirituality and of theological education, and a tradition in which Saint Sulpice was at the center of the interaction between religion and culture. Sulpicians in France represented a voice of moderation in the struggle between religion and culture, so those trained in France and sent to the United States became active participants in opening the Catholic church to American culture. Although only about one hundred Sulpicians served the American community during their first century in the New World, their influence was enormous.

The history of the Sulpicians in the United States is best understood by allowing their most articulate and influential representatives to express themselves and, more particularly, by placing their experiences within the various cultural and religious contexts of the times. Since the Sulpicians form an elite in the church (regardless of their tendency to be self-effacing) and since the Sulpicians must necessarily avoid public notice, the major type of documentation for determining the historical topography of the Society of Saint Sulpice in the United States is the correspondence between members of the society and between Sulpicians and ecclesiastical and cultural leaders. It is impossible to document adequately the enormous spiritual influence of Sulpicians such as Anthony Vieban, Francis P. Havey, and Louis Arand.

In the epilogue (covering the years 1967–1986), the methodology of the historian gives way to that of the journalist. One's perspective on the recent past is necessarily two-dimensional, and the documentation is so uneven that the journalist has only a loose grasp of many relevant facts. However, whether I view this history through the lens of the journalist or the historian, one fact is clear: for nearly two centuries the Sulpicians in the United States were significant participants in the making of an American Catholic culture in accord with positive features of the modern world.

Prologue

From Jean-Jacques Olier to the French Revolution (1600–1789)

The priests of Saint Sulpice, unlike other groups of seminary priests founded in seventeenth-century France, the Vincentians and the Eudists, were not known as Olierists after their founder, Jean-Jacques Olier. Instead, they bear the name Sulpicians, a symbol of the predominance of Saint-Sulpice the place. Saint-Sulpice was not, of course, viewed as a unique holy place, as Carmel was for the Carmelites, but simply as the original locus of a dynamic reform movement in the religious formation of priests. The story of the foundation of the seminary community at Saint-Sulpice involves the story of the personal pilgrimage of Olier who abandoned the luxury he was accustomed to as an aristocratic Parisian in favor of the simple priestly asceticism of Vincent de Paul and the elaborate spirituality of Charles de Condren. Olier's life culminated, after a period of profound self-doubt, in a conversion experience that led to his creation of a method for the religious formation of priests.

1

Like the chiaroscuro tones of baroque art, the life of Jean-Jacques Olier was an intense struggle between the forces of light and darkness. Carl J. Friedrich's definition of the baroque is as apposite as most.

> Materialism vied with spiritualism, radical naturalism with extreme formalism, the most terrifying realism with the most precise illusionism. . . . Such an age, excited beyond measure by the potentialities of man, might well through some of its representatives, establish the foundations of modern science, while through others it would persecute old women as witches; for both presume an exaggerated belief in the power of man to think and to do, as with heightened powers he confronts a mysterious exciting world. God by his limitless will orders the universe; Satan by a comparable effort seeks to disturb this order.[1]

Olier experienced such internal and external polarizations; they are dramatically expressed in his religious experiences, in his writings, and, indeed, in his entire world view. Because he was also a vital participant in the evolution of Counter-Reformation France, in the French school of spirituality, in the early struggles with Jansenism, and in the general revitalization of the French priesthood, his biography represents in microcosm many of the trends in French religious culture as it passed through the age of the baroque.[2]

II

Jean-Jacques Olier was born in Paris on 20 September 1608, three years before Pierre de Bérulle introduced the Oratory into France and just a few months before Armand Jean de Richelieu took up residence as the bishop of Luçon. During the years that Bérulle was fashioning his spirituality of the Word Incarnate and Richelieu was developing the modern absolute state, the future architect of seminary reform was preparing for an ecclesiastical career according to the aristocratic norms of the day.

His father, Jacques Olier de Verneuil, was of an aristocratic family that had allied itself with the first Bourbon monarch, Henry IV, while his mother, Marie Dolu, dame d'Ivoy, also of an ascending aristocratic family, was a strongly religious woman who hoped that her son would secure a prestigious ecclesiastical position in the French hierarchy. Because of the family's connections at court and because the church had been virtually a department of state for more than a century, Mme. Olier's hopes for her son were not unrealistic. Indeed, his parents secured a benefice for him, and the young Olier was tonsured at the age of eight. It is typical of the age that several notable reformers were granted benefices as children. Mère Angélique, for example, became abbess of Port-Royal at the age of seven. Before Olier reached his majority, his parents obtained several other benefices for him: the Benedictine priory at La Trinité in Clisson, the abbey of Pébrac of the Canons Regular of Saint Augustine, the priory of Bazainville near Chartres, and the title of honorary canon of the chapter of Saint-Julien de Brioude.[3]

During his father's tenure as intendant of Lyons (1617–1624) Olier received his training in classics at the Jesuit college in Lyons, and upon his father's appointment to the Council of State by Cardinal Richelieu in 1624 Olier entered Harcourt College in Paris, where he pursued his studies in philosophy. Although he subsequently completed his theological studies at the Sorbonne, he did not immediately request ordination. According to all his biographers, the young aristocratic abbé was thoroughly immersed in the social life of Paris during the late 1620s. Nevertheless, because he had been an excellent student and was eager to achieve a reputation as a scholar, he was drawn to the study of Hebrew in Rome in 1630.

Shortly after his arrival in Rome, Olier's eyesight began to deteriorate. Medical treatment brought no relief, so the twenty-two-year-old cleric followed a traditional practice of popular piety of making a pilgrimage to a holy place by seeking a cure at the shrine of Loreto. He made the 200-kilometer pilgrimage on foot, and within a short time after his arrival at Loreto he was cured, not only of his strabismus, but of his spiritual apathy as well.

Upon the death of his father in March 1631, Olier returned to Paris. His father's legacy, estimated to have been more than 400,000 livres, provided the family with the means to continue to live luxuriously. The young abbé received over 1,200 livres annually from his benefices, which would have allowed him also to live in aristocratic comfort.[4]

Although his mother had high social ambitions for her son, his recent conversion experience at Loreto led him in the opposite direction. On Christmas Day 1631, apparently moved by his young cousin's entry into the Carmel, Olier publicly announced his conversion to a life of devotion to God and of service to the poor. Less than a year later he placed himself under the spiritual direction of Vincent de Paul, who by this time had founded the Congregation of the Mission and had established a regular series of preordination exercises at Saint-Lazare, the Vincentians' first house. These exercises lasted only three weeks, but they had a strong influence on the reformation of the nonregular clergy. After participating in one of Vincent's catechetical missions in rural areas, poorly served by the ill-trained priests, Olier prepared himself for ordination by undertaking the exercises. On 21 May 1633 the nearly twenty-five-year-old Olier was ordained, and on 24 June, the feast of his patron saint, John the Baptist, he celebrated his first Mass.

In 1634 he returned to the missions but this time in the area around his own abbey of Pébrac. Here he met Mother Agnes of Jesus, a Dominican who, he believed, had appeared to him in a dream and had recognized his own call to interior renewal and ecclesiastical reform. Mother Agnes died soon after this meeting, but one of her last letters was an introduction of Olier to Charles de Condren, superior general of the Oratorians and an influential exponent of the spirituality identified with Cardinal Bérulle.[5] Thus within three years Olier had moved from the ranks of the aristocratic clergy to the center of an intense movement for spiritual regeneration and religious reform. This movement was so deeply imbedded in French life and so widely spread throughout French society that it expressed itself in myriad cultural manifestations. One of Richelieu's biographers remarked that during the whole life of the cardinal, "France was being swept by a great tide of religious fervor."[6] The Catholic reformation of the sixteenth century, achieved by the renewal of the old and the rise of new religious orders, by the promotion of parish missions, and by the reform decrees of the Council of Trent (which held its last session on 4 December 1563), did not really affect France until the seventeenth century. This delay was caused by both religious wars and the lack of religious leadership, as well as by Gallicanism, which inhibited the implementation of the decrees of Trent.

Delayed for nearly a half-century by a generally demoralized religious climate, the reform spread rapidly in the early seventeenth century. By 1640 more than twenty new convents and monasteries had been opened in Paris alone. The old orders were revived under new leadership, while new congregations such as the Carmelites and the Capuchins represented the rise of asceticism. Francis de Sales, the bishop of Geneva, who promoted a humanist devotion to Jesus, was a popular figure even among the aristocracy; indeed, Madame Olier, a truly baroque blend of piety and ambition, had sought his confirmation of her decision to offer her son to the church. After blessing the fourteen-year-old, Francis de Sales indicated that the youth was one of God's chosen ones "to promote glory to Him and to do great service in the Church."[7]

The extent of de Sales's influence on Olier's spirituality has never been considered significant except as it was influential in Olier's later attachment to Bérullian piety. However, the mature Olier demonstrated his devotion to de Sales in 1649 when Olier was in the midst of the Jansenist controversy. Since Salesian spirituality was so positive, with its emphasis on God's love as opposed to the Jansenist emphasis upon human unworthiness of God's grace, perhaps Olier's public visitation to the tomb of de Sales in 1649 was his way of identifying with what, after Henri Brémond, has come to be known as the devout humanism of Saint Francis de Sales.[8]

Under Vincent de Paul's direction, Olier achieved a new sense of the high ideal of the priestly vocation. According to Henri Daniel-Rops the "decline of the clergy racked the truly priestly soul of Monsieur Vincent."[9] De Paul vented his deeply felt concern at the low moral and spiritual state of the clergy: "The church is going to ruin, in many places on account of the evil life of her priests; it is they who are ruining and destroying her . . . and the depravity of the ecclesiastical state is the chief cause of the ruin of God's church."[10] Adrien Bourdoise, founder of the community of priests of Saint-Nicolas-du-Chardonnet, who were in the vanguard of clerical reform in France, lamented that he knew of priests who "were so ignorant of the mysteries of our religion that some were even found who did not even know Jesus Christ and could not tell how many natures there were in him." De Paul was appalled with the liturgical ignorance among the clergy; "some began the Mass with the Pater Noster."[11] Olier did not join Vincent de Paul's Priests of the Mission, but he tacitly followed their formula: "to strive toward personal perfection by doing our best to practice the virtues which our Sovereign Master designed to teach us by work and example; to preach the Gospel to the poor, especially to the poor of the countryside."[12]

After his first renewal mission Olier became a devoted disciple of Charles de Condren (1588–1641). Although he did not know of Mother Agnes's letter to Condren, Olier was drawn to the superior general of the Oratory because of his reputation for holiness. Vincent de Paul, who had taken refuge in the Oratory during Bérulle's lifetime, understood Olier's attraction to the famous center of spirituality. Charles de Condren was also born of a noble family of Vauboin near Soissons. Although he was raised to be a soldier, Condren's health and sensitive disposition ultimately convinced his family to allow him to pursue philosophy and theology at the Sorbonne.[13] His scholarly brilliance and his personal piety became so well known that for three years Bérulle prayed that Condren would enter the Oratory.[14] After a brief retreat, he did so on 17 June 1617 and displayed such sublime piety that Bérulle appears to have been as deeply influenced by Condren as Condren was by Bérulle.

By the time he was introduced to Olier in late 1634, Condren had been superior general of the Oratory for five years and had been confessor and director to numerous persons of the social, political and spiritual elites of the day. Dedicated to exalting the priesthood, the Oratory cultivated a form of spirituality whereby the contemplative united himself to God through an identity with the priestly adoration of the Word Incarnate. Condren's contribution was to stress the need of the adorer to be emptied of all self-concerns, a process that he envisioned as vitally linked to the power of the Holy Spirit. Just at the time that Olier turned to Condren, Vincent de Paul was urging the young priest to accept the appointment of coadjutor to Sebastien Zamet, the bishop of Langres, who wished to resign in order to enter the Oratory. On the other hand, Condren preferred to see Olier cultivate a deeper sense of humility and detachment. In any case, because the negotiations in the matter were so protracted, Olier never accepted the see.[15]

During the period from 1636 to 1639 Olier engaged in two rural missions, both of which were terminated by his serious illness. In 1639, after Olier had regained a modicum of strength, Cardinal Richelieu urged him to accept a different appointment, this time as coadjutor bishop of Châlons. Once again, with the support of Condren, he refused ecclesiastical advancement. The conflict between a life of simplicity and service and a life of episcopal grandeur seems to have precipitated what Olier referred to in his *Memoirs* as the "great ordeal," a two-year-period characterized by bouts of deep scrupulosity, by utter helplessness in performing the simplest tasks of walking and talking, and by a sense of self-contempt, as well as by a sense of fall not only from divine grace but from social grace as well. Since his conversion experience Olier had been subjected to periodic illnesses and spiritual crises. Most biographers, following Olier's own interpretation, view the "great ordeal" as God's way of testing him for his future role as spiritual reformer. Certainly his almost obsessive drive to ascend the heights of spirituality under Vincent de Paul and Condren must have contributed to this deeply emotional crisis. Brémond has characterized the "great ordeal" as a battle between Olier the poet and Olier the neuresthenic:

> For two years a wild fear of falling into the sin of pride had made him appear proud. The more he felt depressed and wavering the more he felt called on to assert himself, to impose in any or every way, either on himself or on others. Now that these thoughts began to disappear, instead of imprisoning himself in the despairing contemplation of his ego, he joyously soothed himself by evoking another pose, another demeanor. This produced new reactions directly opposed to the lamentable obsessions that had so recently caused him to be taken for a maniac. His eye and heart were now filled with the lovely image . . . [of the Blessed Mother] and quite naturally he began to mold himself on the modest grace of the youthful virgin. No wonder that his astonished companions hardly recognized him.[16]

In a recent book on Olier, Michel Dupuy (a French Sulpician) stresses the maternal factor as a cause of the "great ordeal." Olier's conversion and his commitment to serve the poor represent his first break with the aristocratic design that his mother had planned so carefully for her clerical son; when he refused to become a bishop in 1636 and again in 1639, he was tacitly rejecting not only the design but also his mother. Dupuy implies that the many pious women who had such an influence upon Olier—Marie Rousseau, Mother Agnes, and later Marie Bressard, a Visitandine—were feminine authority figures who helped to counteract Olier's guilt at rejecting his mother. Similarly, Dupuy sees Olier's sudden attachment to the Mother of God, manifested in his pilgrimage to Loreto and carried on throughout his entire life, as symbolic of a shift from allegiance to his earthly mother to allegiance to the heavenly mother.

Dupuy seeks to substantiate his interpretation by pointing out that Condren initiated Olier's internal reconciliation by directing him to contemplate the infant Jesus, a process through which Olier unconsciously developed a deeper attachment to the Virgin Mother.[17] Such contemplation presumably led him to recapture the innocence of his own childhood, and this gradually had a healing effect upon him. Thus Olier wrote, "I feel that the child Jesus has given me the grace to be like a small child, without any will of my own. He has also given me the grace of joyful abandonment, and so abandoning myself to God, I place all of my trust in him."[18]

Lowell M. Glendon, S.S., who closely analyzed the "great ordeal" as Olier treated it in his *Memoirs*, which were written after he had recovered, does not try to interpret the major cause of Olier's period of intense mental imbalance but, rather, places it within the context of his articulation of his spirituality. Although Brémond, Dupuy, and others also stress the positive impact of the "great ordeal" upon Olier's self-awareness within the development of his religious formation, Glendon attempts to grasp it in Olier's own terms, which precludes a psychoanalytic understanding of the crisis.[19]

Condren died on 17 January 1641 shortly before Olier's crisis ended in the following summer. All of Olier's biographers suggest that the two previous years helped Olier, as Brémond writes, to incorporate Condren's "essential doctrine of our duty of self-effacement, of sacrificing and annihilating self, in order to give place to the spirit of God. . . . In some manner, and despite himself, he had become familiar with nothingness, the state of childhood, the victim state. . . ."[20]

During this critical period Olier was sustained by some of Condren's priest-disciples, who were committed to the evangelization of the poor. After missionary activity in the diocese of Chartres, the group resided in the home of one of the priests, located at Saint-Maur, near Paris. From September 1640 to the end of the following January, this small group of diocesan priests led a communal life dedicated to embodying the lofty Oratorian spirituality of the priesthood and ministry in their prayer. This ad hoc community of five or six priests was the precursor of the Society of Saint Sulpice. At the end of January 1641, the group returned to missionary work in Chartres and attempted to establish a seminary there in April. Although they were encouraged by the bishop, they failed to attract any applicants.

The Chartres experiment began only as a retreat house for ordinands and did not attach itself to a parish. In July the group abandoned its effort, but in late December they revived their experiment, after having experienced some encouragement in the town of Vaugirard on the outskirts of Paris. The following month, they accepted their first recruits, and the seminary became a reality. It was not until the community settled in Vaugirard in December 1641, however, that Olier fully recovered from his ordeal. He had been reluctant to join in the seminary project, but after several days of prayer he agreed to join Jean du Ferrier and François de Caulet (abbé de Foix) in a small house provided them by a Madame de Villeneuve. Three other members of the Saint-Maur group entered the community in early 1642: Charles Picote, Baltasar Brandon de Bessancourt, and Francois Houmain de Sainte-Marie. Soon they were directing the religious formation of eight clerics representing six different dioceses.

The young seminary attracted the attention of Adrien Bourdoise, founder of the community of Saint-Nicolas-du-Chardonnet, also dedicated to seminary work. Established in 1631, this community was at first concerned with instructing the younger clergy and providing retreats for priests. In 1644 Saint-Nicolas-du-Chardonnet was incorporated as a seminary.[21] Cardinal Richelieu, on hearing of the Vaugirard community, sent word to Olier through his niece, the duchesse d'Aiguillon, that the community could establish its seminary at his Château de Rueil, which would provide relief from the relatively impoverished conditions at Vaugirard. Olier graciously declined the cardinal's invitation, fearing that the seminary at the Château de Rueil would lose the asceticism present at Vaugirard. Such a move would have also detached the community from a parish in which the young clerics could gain practical experience to complement their theological and spiritual training at the seminary.[22]

In the spring of 1642 a series of fortuitous events led the pastor of Saint-Sulpice, a parish located in the faubourg Saint-Germain, to approach the Vaugirard community and ask it to assume the pastoral responsibility of his parish. Olier and his confreres accepted the offer because the community needed larger accommodations, because the parish was under the authority of the abbot of Saint-Germain rather than the bishop of Paris, and because its central location promised to attract more seminarians. As the most wealthy priest in the community, Olier assumed responsibility for the financial arrangements; he turned over his priory at Clisson to the retiring pastor and provided him with a sizable pension. Du Ferrier and de Foix successfully urged Olier to become pastor of Saint-Sulpice. On 11 August 1642, after most of the legal issues had been settled, Olier was installed as pastor. Four days later, on the Feast of the Assumption, the Vaugirard community of priests and seminarians moved to their new home.

Since the office of parish priest was considered the preserve of the lower classes, Olier's mother was extremely angry with her son's behavior, so much so that the family refused to attend the ceremonies installing him as pastor. Ironically, members of the most aristocratic families soon gravitated to Olier for spiritual direction, but even they could not reconcile mother and son.[23] The remaining fifteen years of Olier's life abound in such ironies. He was not only the source of spiritual solace to members of the royal court, as well as to the English king in exile, Charles II, but also the foremost exponent of a type of spirituality that ennobled the vocation to the priesthood. Saint-Sulpice became synonymous with the reform of the French clergy. Bérulle and Condren developed a sacerdotal spirituality within the context of their general spiritual world view. The practical threads of a revival and renewal of the diocesan priesthood were woven into a pattern. Bérulle elaborated his notions of the ideal priest:

> By its very nature the state of the priesthood calls for two things: first of all it demands a very great perfection and even holiness. For the priesthood is a state that is holy and sacred in its institution; it is an office that is divine in its operation and in its ministry; and it is moreover, the origin of all the holiness which must be in the church of God. In the second place, the priesthood calls for a very particular bond with Jesus Christ our Lord with whom we are joined in a special manner by our priestly ministry and through a power so elevated that our angels in their state of glory are not worthy of it.[24]

It appears that these notions on the character of the priesthood were elevated to heights inversely proportionate to the low levels of behavior in the actual lives of French priests in the seventeenth century. While Bérulle stressed the bond between priest and the priesthood of Jesus expressed within the eternal adoration of the Father, Condren focused on the bond in terms of the eternal sacrifice of Jesus as both priest and victim.[25] But Olier's dedication to the formation of priests was derived from his own personal reformation—the "great ordeal"—as well as from his predecessors in the French school. Although he held a highly idealized view of the priesthood, he consistently interpreted this view in practical terms. Perhaps this explains why the Sulpicians were so successful in establishing seminaries; their

founder bequeathed to them a methodology for spirituality, for community life, and for pedagogy.

When he became pastor of Saint-Sulpice, Olier thrust himself into
many practical tasks aimed at reviving the spiritual life of the parish,
which was one of the largest in France and was located in an area
considered to be a center of the grossest immorality. Because of its
size, he divided the parish into districts, with two priests assigned to
each district. He incorporated his experience at the missions into his
work, establishing catechism classes for children and adults. He insisted
that the workers' associations become truly religious organizations that
promoted frequenting the sacraments. Jean Gautier, a former rector
of the seminary of Saint-Sulpice, aptly summarizes Olier's pastoral
activity:

> He founded thirty-four parish schools and several libraries for circu-
> lation of spiritual books. He introduced preparatory retreats for en-
> gaged couples and those about to be married. He enhanced the splen-
> dor of church ceremonies . . . arranged for aid to be given discreetly to
> those who were ashamed of their poverty, restored several convents,
> erected suitable buildings for communities of priests and clerics, began
> the construction of a huge church [the present Saint-Sulpice], wrote
> rules of life for different social classes and commentaries in French
> for the more fruitful reception of the sacraments, [and] made good
> use of lay people.[26]

Impressive as this list of achievements is, it does not represent a
series of uninterrupted successes. Indeed, Olier suffered several very
painful experiences as the curé of Saint-Sulpice. During the summer
of 1645 a strange mixture of antagonists joined forces. These included
the former pastor, who was alienated over the settlement with Olier,
several noblemen in the faubourg who seem to have been jealous of the
new pastor's sudden rise to prominence, and several factions among
the common people who viewed Olier's reforms as interfering with
the pleasures that they had enjoyed or in which they had trafficked.
Vincent de Paul, women of the nobility, and several persons at court
and in the legal establishment came to Olier's defense. After experiencing a riotous attack upon the church and rectory as well as a violent
assault upon himself, Olier sought refuge in the home of a friend. Although his ecclesiastical colleagues urged him to resign, he maintained
a friendly attitude toward his enemies and accepted the tumultuous
situation as a cross to be carried with joy and gratitude. After four
months of legal and political maneuvering on the part of his allies,
which entailed satisfying the demands of the former curé, Olier was
recognized by civil and ecclesiastical authorities as the legal pastor.[27]

Olier's reform posture was in accord with the general asceticism
infused into French Counter-Reformation spirituality. In opposition to

the Jansenists, however, he defended the practice of frequent communion for those called to a high spirituality, extolled the notion of sufficient grace for penitents, and lashed out at the public penances prescribed by Jansenists as well as their "haughty and insolent zeal," which Olier said was characteristic of Saint Cyran, one of the major exponents of the doctrines of Cornelius Jansenius (bishop of Ypres in the Spanish Netherlands and author of the famous work *Augustinus*).[28] The pastor of Saint-Sulpice, spiritual director and confidant to many sensitive persons who were attracted to Jansenism, vigorously opposed the new theology and, in the process, alienated some powerful Parisian families. Jansenism was infused into the revolt of the Fronde, a series of noble uprisings against the regency of Anne of Austria and the power of Cardinal Jules Mazarin, Richelieu's successor as prime minister. Although Olier was almost entirely concerned with serving the needs of those parishioners who suffered from the social and economic consequences of the armed conflicts of 1648–1651, he was an opponent of Mazarin. He wrote the queen regent a long epistle on the relationship between Mazarin's disregard of his religious duties and the disastrous effects of the civil war on her realm, implying that the latter was the object of the divine wrath. Prince Louis de Condé, the most prominent of the military leaders of the Mazarin forces, was bitterly opposed to Olier during the uprising within the parish, and with characteristic baroque melodrama the Jansenist cause was also represented in the uprising of the Fronde.[29]

III

During the years 1645–1651, when Olier was in the center of several controversies, the seminary of Saint-Sulpice was developing its unique ecclesiastical character. The pastor of Saint-Sulpice depended upon the seminarians for catechetical work in the parish, a ministry that provided training for the priesthood. Since the level of religious knowledge was so low, the seminary community was engaged in a permanent mission in the parish. Besides their practical training, the seminarians attended classes in moral and dogmatic theology at the Sorbonne, but they took courses in scripture and the liturgy at the seminary.

Until the Council of Trent established directives for religious formation and theological training for the priesthood, episcopal residences, cathedral schools, monasteries, and universities were the training ground for aspirants to the priesthood. Several years before the opening of the Council of Trent, a papal commission concluded that ecclesiastical offices from the Roman Curia to the local parish had been

riddled with abuses of power and privilege. Bishops and abbots purchased their benefices, and it was common for them to have more than
one diocese or abbey and to be regularly absent from their cathedrals
and chapels. With such a lack of effective leadership it is no wonder
that the lower clergy had declined to cupidity and venality and that
the laity remained locked in ignorance. Luther, Calvin, and the An-
abaptists filled the religious vacuum until the Jesuits and other religious orders engendered reform inside and reconversion outside the
limits of Catholicism. Reformers within the hierarchy and older religious orders also contributed to the Counter-Reformation spirit, both
in the council and on the local level. The council fathers did not pass
legislation on clerical training until their last session in 1563. In the
meantime, the Jesuits had established two colleges in Rome under regulations composed by Ignatius Loyola, which were adopted by other
seminaries of religious communities. In 1556 Cardinal Reginald Pole
had successfully introduced new directives for seminary training in
England, which formed the core of those adopted at Trent seven years
later.[30]

John Tracy Ellis summarizes the conciliar legislation on clerical
training:

> Every Cathedral and metropolitan church was obliged to erect a spe-
> cial institution—or seminary [literally, seedbed] for the education of
> future priests. . . . In regard to entrance requirements, candidates
> should be at least twelve years of age, have a certain competence in
> reading and writing and possess the kind of character which would
> suggest a fit man for the ministry.[31]

The legislation stipulated that the curriculum include rhetoric, humanities, chant, scripture, theology, and rubrics. A seminarian's religious formation required daily Mass, monthly confession, communion
upon the advice of a spiritual director, and mandatory clerical garb. Ellis points out that there was no stipulation requiring candidates for
ordination to attend the seminary. The ordinary of the diocese was
given final authority over the training for the priesthood.[32] These reforms represented a considerable improvement, but they established
only a legal basis for training priests. However, Tridentine seminaries founded by Charles Borromeo in his archdiocese of Milan set the
precedent for the general implementation of the legislation. As noted
earlier, the Gallican drive to protect the prerogatives of the French
state and of the ecclesiastical authorities prevented the implementation of Trent's legislation. The cardinal of Lorraine did establish a Tridentine seminary at Rheims, but it never flourished and soon became
a choir school. One of the goals of Bérulle's Oratory was the foundation of seminaries, but those established at Lyons, Mâcon, Langres, and

Saint-Magloire in Paris were unsuccessful. The Oratorians, who represented, according to Daniel-Rops, the "flower of the priesthood" in France, gravitated to working in the missions, parishes, and colleges.[33]

During the first half of the seventeenth century many French bishops were interested in improving the conditions of ecclesiastical training, but they were obstructed by vested interests within the diocese, such as the cathedral chapters, whose members feared that a seminary would entail a loss of revenues. For example, when he was bishop of Luçon, Cardinal Richelieu established a seminary as a means of drawing candidates to the priesthood and of reforming his diocese. After two attempts, one of which included bringing the Oratorians in as faculty, the Luçon seminary failed to take root because of the opposition of the cathedral canons. When he became the dominant figure at court, Richelieu promoted the seminary projects of the three major reformers, Vincent de Paul, John Eudes, and Jean-Jacques Olier.

As we have seen, the precursor of the seminary movement of the 1640s was Adrien Bourdoise, who, with his community of priests dedicated to reform, settled in 1620 in the parish of Saint-Nicolas-du-Chardonnet in Paris. There he provided spiritual exercises and pastoral education for clerics and priests. He later established other parochial bases upon the nascent seminary model of the Paris parish. Bourdoise also provided retreats for ordinands.[34] It was Vincent de Paul, however, spurred on by the bishop of Beauvais, who became identified with this retreat movement. Beginning in 1631 the Vincentian motherhouse of Saint-Lazare offered Tuesday conferences for priests. Although these exercises provided only the rudiments of spirituality, they nevertheless became quite popular, and in 1659 they received official endorsement by the papacy.

The Lazarists were engaged primarily in mission work in the provinces. Bourdoise relates succinctly the ties between the missions and the seminary:

> The missions that are given up and down a diocese are something but a seminary is the most essential work of all. To give a mission is something like giving a poor starving man a meal, but to set up a seminary is to aim at feeding him all his life. . . . As no superior of religious orders can fill their convents with good religious if they have not good novitiates, so no prelate can fill his churches with good priests to carry on the good work wrought by the missions . . . unless he has an excellent seminary. On this basis Vincent de Paul established a seminary in 1636, the Collège des Bons Enfants, without departing from the mission character of his society.[35]

Little is known of this early seminary other than that it seems to have been an attempt to implement the Tridentine directives, particularly as they were interpreted by Charles Borromeo. Unlike the latter's seminary, however, the Lazarist college included students as young as twelve and others in the diaconate year. Because so few young students became priests, de Paul divided the institution into what is today referred to as minor (*petit*) and major (*grand*) seminaries. Sulpician historians point to the kernel of the Grand Séminaire planted at Vaugirard in late December 1640 as the first major seminary in France to have survived to the present, and they maintain that Olier, not Vincent de Paul, was the first to separate the theologians from the younger students.

John Eudes, an Oratorian priest whom Daniel-Rops calls "the Saint of the Seminaries of Normandy," also became convinced of the need to root his mission work in the education of priests. However, François Bourgoing, the Oratorian superior general, was unsympathetic. But after he received encouragement from Richelieu and Vincent de Paul in 1642, Eudes took steps to establish a religious community dedicated to this effort. On 25 March 1643, the Company of Jesus and Mary was dedicated to missionary work, to evangelization, and to the education of priests. The Eudist system stressed spiritual preparation over pastoral experience, and the seminaries, according to Daniel-Rops, were at first "more like novitiates than schools of theology." Only forty-two years old when he founded his religious community, John Eudes also became the foremost apostle of the devotion to the Sacred Heart, a piety grounded in the Bérullian emphasis on the Word Incarnate.[36]

Adrien Bourdoise, Vincent de Paul, John Eudes, and Jean-Jacques Olier were friends who had much in common. Although very different in personality, temperament, and family background, each had been touched by the Oratorian spirit of Bérulle and had been deeply immersed in the reform of parish life throughout France. They were all priests' priests, with strong drives to identify the calling to the sacerdotal life with the eternal utterance of the Incarnate Word. They expressed their personal vocation in the evangelical call to renewal and reform on the missions, which led them to the more fundamental reform movement, the training of priests. Shortly before Olier and his two companions established their seminary at Vaugirard, Olier made a solemn vow of servitude to Jesus Christ. Such specific personal vows were not uncommon to the spirituality of Bérulle and Condren, but they were to be made only after a period of prayerful reflection. Olier had wanted to make such a vow in January of 1641, but his confessor demanded that he wait a year. After he solemnly vowed to be the servant of Jesus he wrote:

> From the moment I made the vow I have been able neither to speak nor even to think of God save in dependence on the Spirit of my

Master, who possesses me and applies my soul to what he wills. . . .
The vow of servitude to the spirit of Jesus demands . . . an absolute
confidence and abandonment without reserve into the hands of this
blessed and fruitful master.[37]

The first seminary at Vaugirard was experimental, with an ad hoc
community of three diocesan priests as codirectors. When the seminary moved to Saint-Sulpice, the theologians attended the Sorbonne
not only for their own intellectual growth but also for the spiritual edification of those professors who would encounter the humble piety
of the students attached to a reform institution. Because Saint-Sulpice
was under the jurisdiction of the abbey of Saint-Germain-des-Prés, and
thereby exempt from French episcopal authority, it functioned as a national seminary that attracted students from many dioceses, most of
whom were attending the Sorbonne. Olier accepted ordained priests
into the community, but the vast majority were seminarians with no
fixed preordination program. Students lived at Saint-Sulpice for a few
months or several years, depending on previous academic training and
spiritual formation. By 1648, the student body had become so large
that new buildings were needed. Always on the brink of indebtedness,
Olier received large financial contributions from two wealthy students
and from Alexandre Le Ragois de Bretonvilliers, who was considered
the wealthiest priest in France and who became the second superior
general of the society. In 1651 a new seminary was completed, with
four connecting wings forming an inner courtyard. The architect was
Jacques Mercier, who had erected the Palais Royal, while Charles Le-
Brun, a notable baroque artist, decorated the chapel. Five years earlier
Olier had initiated construction of a new parish church; the queen regent, Anne of Austria, laid its cornerstone on 20 February 1646.[38]

The students' training was not limited to the Sorbonne; in the
seminary itself they attended classes in liturgy, homiletics, and chant.
Although the seminarians were drawn primarily from the ranks of the
aristocracy, those who were unable to pay for their food and lodging
were provided for by Olier and others. However, Olier insisted that all
seminarians adopt a simple way of life. Clerical dress was to be austere,
lace surplices were forbidden, students were instructed to perform
the housework and maintenance duties, and meals were adequate but
simple. Except at recreation and at holiday time, silence was observed
within the seminary buildings.[39]

While Olier emphasized the spirituality of the seminary, he also
stressed theological education, with particular focus on its practical
application:

In the confessional you are called upon suddenly, and without consultation or reference to give decisions on the most important questions,

decisions against which there is no appeal, and which will influence
your fellow man through all eternity. In the pulpit you have to deal
alike with the learned and the ignorant to maintain Gospel truth,
to combat against vice, to resist the force of public opinion, to re-
fute and expose heresy, so that the simplest can understand you,
all of which necessarily requires a more than ordinary amount of
knowledge—deeper and fuller than that men commonly acquire of
a stronger, more practical character.[40]

The religious character of the Seminary of Saint-Sulpice reflected
the spirituality of its founder. Olier's opening lines in his spiritual guide
for all seminarians, the *Pietas Seminarii*, read:

The first and ultimate end of this institute is to live supremely for
God, in Christ Jesus our Lord, in order that the interior disposition
of His Son may so penetrate the very depths of our heart, that each
may say what St. Paul confidently affirmed of himself . . . "I live, but
it is not I who live but it is Christ who liveth in me! Such shall be the
sole hope of all, their sole meditation, their sole exercise, to live the
life of Christ interiorly, and to manifest it exteriorly in their mortal
body."[41]

Olier identified the interior life of Jesus with the Incarnate Word,
as the mystery of the Incarnation includes all the mysteries—the birth,
passion, death, resurrection, ascension of Jesus—which are eternal
events manifested in history and liturgy. When Olier referred to interior disposition, he was echoing the French school's stress upon perpetual "states" of Divine Life in contrast to "acts" that were historical.
Bérulle elaborates on this principle:

The mysteries of Jesus Christ are in a sense over, and in another sense
they continue and are present and perpetual. As far as the execution
is concerned they are over, but in their power they are present and
their power never passes, nor does the love pass with which they
were performed. The spirit of God through which this mystery was
effected, the *exterior state* of the *exterior act*, the efficacy and the virtue
that makes this mystery living and operative in us, this state and
virtuous disposition, the merit through which he won us to his father
and merited heaven . . . even the *actual pleasure*, the living disposition
in which Jesus performed this mystery is *still living, actual and present to
Jesus*.[42]

Condren's mystical imagery stressed the priesthood and victimhood
of Jesus. Olier's own priesthood, his spirituality, and his view of clerical
training were influenced by such imagery. He wrote that the Christ
was the

King who being priest and victim altogether presents Himself to God,
His Father in heaven, and changes his throne into an altar, so that,

in the sacrifice which He offers may obtain the salvation of the world. The Church as the Mystical Body calls upon all Christians to incorporate themselves into the interior states of Jesus. However, those called to be priests are especially called to identify with the state of Jesus as eternal Priest-Victim.[43]

Olier describes the mystical role of the priest:

> As he offers the sacrifice the priest is in Jesus Christ; he offers it in unity with the power and the spirit of Jesus Christ, who is the same in this sacrifice as in heaven when he offers the sacrifice of Himself, and of all the saints with him. . . . Thus the priest is lifted in spirit into heaven, where Jesus Christ is offering Himself, and at the same time remains on earth making there the same offering he makes in heaven.[44]

The call to the priesthood is therefore literally the call to a life of perfection. The seminary of Saint-Sulpice was infused with what Brémond refers to as the "excellence of M. Olier." Although the sacraments formed the spiritual core of the seminary, they were buttressed by a highly refined method of mental prayer. Before one could assent to dwell in the interiority of Jesus, one was instructed to empty the self, to die to the world. Olier viewed the seminary as set apart from the world. The highly regulated life of the seminary was grounded in this ascetisim. He maintains that

> The seminary is the hedge which separates the Vineyard of the Lord from the World. This hedge is full of thorns, and the world ought not to approach it without feeling the prick of them; that is without being made sensible of the horror we have of its execrable maxims. This house ought to be so replenished with evangelical virtues as to inspire distaste, aversion and hatred for all contrary vices. We ought to strip ourselves of the world's livery and of its whole exterior and exhibit nothing in our bearing which can serve to attract its esteem.[45]

Olier's aceticism did not strongly stress physical mortification, for he believed there was a tendency toward pride in such behavior. Instead he established a highly structured regimen for the seminary day, one in accord with the asceticism of the French school. It began at 4:30 A.M. (5:00 in the winter) and ended at 9:00 P.M. and included attendance at Mass, meditation, spiritual reading, a particular examen (i.e., a directed reflection on a spiritual or moral theme), daily rosary, and portions of the divine office. He also encouraged a daily explication of scripture, a practice that placed him in the forefront of a new development. Although Olier's spiritual direction of those who had passed through several stages of development was highly mystical and grounded in an internalized asceticism, his basic principle for seminarians was obedience to the rule because students at Saint-Sulpice were apprentices in spirituality. Indeed, he views the seminarians as children:

> Obedience is the life of the children of the Church, the compendium
> of all virtues, the assured way to heaven, unfailing means for ascer-
> taining the severest, but at the same time, one of the sweetest of
> martyrdoms, seeing that it makes us perfectly conformable to Jesus
> Christ. He who faithfully obeys the rule is invulnerable; whereas he
> who lets himself follow his own caprices lays himself open to the as-
> sault of the enemy, and runs great risk of failing.[46]

Included in the spiritual exercises of the seminary was the principle that this way of life was the means by which one was separated from the world, was elevated to the dignity of the priesthood, and was prepared to return to the world fortified with a spirituality and outlook intended for the edification of the faithful.[47]

Essential to all spiritual direction was Olier's tripartite method of mental prayer: adoration, communion, and cooperation or, as Olier himself put it, "Jesus before my eyes, Jesus in my heart, and Jesus in my hands." In his letters to those who were advanced in religious formation and in some of his published works, Olier expresses a very refined mysticism, but the simple method just given was intended for initiates. This method, which was amplified by Louis Tronson, third superior general of the society, was intended to bring the seminarian into participation in the perpetual mysteries of Jesus, the Incarnate Word. It was a very flexible and practical method of meditation that concluded with a resolution to improve some aspect of one's spiritual life. The Seminary of Saint-Sulpice was designed to be a model for the French church, particularly in its struggle with Jansenism. Jansen developed a pessimistically Augustinian theology of grace and freedom, which Daniel-Rops describes as follows:

> According to Jansenius no one before him had discovered in the work
> of Augustine the synthesis of the demands of both grace and free will.
> Original sin created an abyss between man's first state and the fallen
> state that followed. Man was entirely free in his state of innocence,
> and his will tended naturally toward what was right. In his fallen state
> he was no longer free but a slave of sin . . . ; all that he did led him
> to the abyss of corruption. But argued Jansenius, God in his goodness
> offered humanity a chance to snatch itself from the abyss. Through
> Christ's merits He gave man efficacious grace, which ennobled the
> human will. Those who possessed it were indeed free . . . but nothing
> could be done for those who did not possess it; they were without
> hope. . . . Grace, however, Jansenius declared, was not given to all
> humanity. Many are called, but few are chosen. Only a few exceptional
> souls were capable of exercising free will in regard to salvation. As for
> the rest, God did not condemn them, but, because grace had not been

given to them, they remained *in massa damnata* as a result of original sin. The Jansenist synthesis, at best as far as the word is concerned, recognized free will in man, but limited it for those who received grace.[48]

The abbé de Saint-Cyran, Jean Duvergier (1581–1643), who was a close friend of Jansenius, incorporated doctrinal Jansenism into his own rigorous puritanical forms. Saint-Cyran wrote, "We have within, a perpetual source of sin flowing toward everlasting death, unless God places within us the fountain of life that flows into life eternal."[49] Saint-Cyran was the spiritual director of the Cistercian convent, Port-Royal, which was under the authority of Mother Angélique Arnauld. Dedicated to a life of severe austerity, the nuns of Port-Royal had developed an elitist tendency for which Jansen's *Augustinus* provided a theological base. Hence a moral puritanism became associated with Jansenism and assumed the forms of a Jansenist movement. Alienated by the court of the queen regent and her minister Cardinal Mazarin, by the influence of the Jesuits, and by the papacy, various groups drifted to the defense of the Jansenist cause and to the Fronde in the late 1640s and early 1650s.

Jansenism therefore became identified with a sect, but the movement maintained itself, with varying degrees of energy, throughout the next 150 years. The theological, moral, and sectarian forms of Jansenism were expressed in the controversy surrounding the 1642 publication *De la Fréquente Communion*. Written by Antoine Arnauld, the youngest brother of Mother Angélique and a priest under the commanding influence of Saint-Cyran, this pamphlet aimed at restoring what Arnauld considered to be the orthodox manner for the reception of the sacraments. Although he presents his views in a style with a strongly appealing sense of piety, Arnauld declares that the penitent should be directed to receive Holy Communion only after having experienced severe penances over a long period of time. Arnauld urges a revival of the spirit of the early church with its public penance.[50] It was as if only the elect could receive the Eucharist. Vincent de Paul and Jean-Jacques Olier publicly criticized Arnauld for placing the sacrament beyond the reach of ordinary penitents. Olier was therefore very remote from the doctrinal and sectarian manifestations of Jansenism.

The most representative of Olier's responses to Arnauld's Jansenism occurred on the feast day of Saint Sulpice in 1652, when the regent and her court, many priests, and other religious and civic dignitaries were present. The pastor of Saint-Sulpice, who was a reformer associated with a rigorous asceticism, approached the theological basis of penance in characteristically mystical fashion. He denied the Jansenist notion that pure contrition was a necessary condition for the sacrament of penance, which he said "does not demand a disposition so pure. Souls that have not perfect charity, having yet only the principle of love, receive through the sacrament of penance a participation in the perfect charity of Jesus Christ dying for us on the Cross." Olier concluded with a warning that a Jansenist "pretends to drive away abuses, but his object is either to abolish the use of sacraments altogether or lead men to dangerous extremes, contrary to the spirit of Jesus Christ."[51]

As a rejoinder to Olier's anti-Jansenist sermon, a pamphlet was published entitled (in English translation) *A Christian and Charitable Remonstrance Addressed to M. Olier*, in which the anonymous author accuses Olier of distorting Augustine's notion of grace.[52] The austere moral disposition and the intense piety associated with Jansenism were not totally alien to Bérullian spirituality. Indeed, Saint-Cyran and Condren were very close friends. Although there is some controversy over Condren's Jansenist inclinations, the two men certainly agreed on the need for rigorous self-abnegation and on an Augustinian theocentric basis for the spiritual life.[53] Perhaps it was these qualities that led several Oratorians into the Jansenist camp. Olier's two companions at Vaugirard, de Foix and du Ferrier, were also strongly attracted to Jansenism, even though Saint-Sulpice was rightly regarded as a center of anti-Jansenism.[54] Nevertheless, Saint-Sulpice and Port-Royal later shared the moral and spiritual climate of the Counter-Reformation. What distinguished Saint-Sulpice from Port-Royal was the fact that Sulpicians accepted the papal bull *Unigenitus* (1713) and that they never crossed the line that separated reformers from zealots. Ultimately the zealots placed their consciences above the laws of church and society.

In anticipation of the popular discussion of the role of Jansenism in the American church, it is necessary to point out that today's conventional wisdom about the Jansenist tendencies of the traditional seminary, particularly of the French model, are usually ahistorical judgements on puritanical rules that have little to do with Jansenism. The popular notion of Jansenism is actually closer to Manichaean dualism, which represents human drives, particularly those relating to the body, as manifestations of Satan and regards those relating to the spirit as the emanations of the divine. Such Manichaean tendencies crept into the rules governing seminary life, but they were not limited to seminaries of the Sulpicians nor to those of the French. Instead the priestly vocation was generally articulated in the style of puritanical idealism, the priesthood was a call to the life of perfection, and celibacy was a necessary condition of such perfection in order to promote the kingdom of God. Sexuality was a necessary evil of the life of imperfection in order to promote and increase human population.

The seminary movement originated within the Counter-Reformation, which included Trent's juridical affirmation of clerical celibacy in opposition to clerical marriage within the reformers' church, as well as a highly spiritualized ideal of the priesthood in opposition to the secularization of clerical life.

Bérulle, Condren, and Olier developed their spirituality not out of Manichaean dualism but rather out of the Patristic-Platonic tradition. The Incarnate Word is the Logos made flesh, mysteriously dwelling in a perpetual state from that of infancy to that of priest-victim. The flesh is not the dwelling place of evil, but evil lives in pride and love of self; danger lies in the pleasures of the body or in the opposite extreme of false asceticism. Just as Olier did not focus on the human physiological drives as synonomous with sin, neither did he stress contemplation of Christ's physical suffering as the means of achieving holiness. On the contrary, he emphasized the glorified Christ as the source of one's development to holiness.

Eugene Walsh, S.S., provided an analysis of Olier's views on the sacramentality of the priesthood, views that clearly illustrate his notion of how the call to perfection terminates in Holy Orders.

> Father Olier sums up [the] entire teaching of the French School on the dignity and power and glory of the priesthood when he calls a priest the sacrament of Jesus Christ on earth. The priest is the visible expression of Jesus Christ on earth. He is the efficacious sign of Christ and God. The priest is the mystery of Jesus Christ, just as Christ Himself was the mystery of God on earth, the primitive Sacrament of religion. . . . The sacramental character of Holy Orders constitutes the priest in a permanent and eternal state of religion and devotion toward God and the Church. . . . The character of Holy Orders confers, as it were, a new nature, a new personality upon the priest. He is drawn by ordination into the personality of Christ, and with Him becomes by state, by an ontological reality, an official person. Just as Christ by His subsistence in the person of the Word, by His possession of Divinity, became the New Adam, representative before God of all humanity, so the priest by the sacramental character of Orders becomes as it were a universal man.[55]

The spiritual exercises at Saint-Sulpice were intended to form the seminarian in his role as identical with Jesus as priest-victim. (They represent the Sulpician stress upon preparation for the *priestly state* rather than for the pastoral dimension so dominant in today's seminary.) These exercises and an ennobled ideal of the priesthood are the distinctive character of Saint-Sulpice. Just as the church of Saint-Sulpice represents the French restraint upon the baroque, Olier's design for the interior life of Saint-Sulpice and its insistence on a splendid liturgy symbolize the mystical exaggerations of baroque spirituality restrained and balanced by the exercises and the rule. There is, therefore, a certain stateliness to the spirit of Saint-Sulpice, analogous to the regal dignity that was manifested in Richelieu's model for absolute monarchy and later symbolized by the exterior structures and courtly life of the palace of Versailles.

The models for Olier's ideal priests were the directors at the Seminary of Saint-Sulpice, those clerics who aspired to become members of the community referred to as the inner seminary. Although Olier did not intend to establish a new religious community at Saint-Sulpice, by 1651 it became necessary to achieve some form of legal status within ecclesiastical structures. In 1649 Olier had reluctantly accepted a request from the bishop of Nantes to send priests to establish a seminary in that diocese. The following year he sent priests to Viviers to found another seminary based upon the model of Saint-Sulpice. Subsequently, he submitted the Rule of the Seminary of Saint-Sulpice to the General Assembly of the French Clergy as a model for all dioceses to follow. The assembly adopted the rule in 1651 but limited it to Olier's group and named the community Company of the Priests of the Clergy of France, shortened to Priests of the Clergy (or priests' priests), and because of the predominant role of Olier's disciples the people adopted the informal name Sulpicians.[56]

Organized according to the general plan of Philip Neri's Oratory, the company was composed of diocesan priests and was not, nor has it ever been, a religious congregation or order. Olier considered the life of the diocesan priest to be of such a high calling that the priesthood itself provided a basis upon which to build a community. Since the priesthood was instituted by Christ, Olier did not view himself as founder of a new society but rather of a new method of seminary education. The Sulpicians, therefore, have never taken vows; they have been incardinated within particular dioceses rather than in their communities. Since Sulpician seminaries in the provinces were under the authority of the local bishops, all the members of the company belonged to Saint-Sulpice, which as noted earlier, was under the abbot of Saint-Germain-des-Prés.

The spirituality of the Priests of the Clergy also marked them as the priests' priests. Olier defines the ideal Sulpician:

> These good priests, who in their ordinary life ought to be the models of their holy flock, must renew in themselves all that the church has ever demanded of what is most pure and holy for the perfection of the priesthood. They immolated and annihilated their own will, being assured that emptying themselves of self is the only disposition which will attract the Spirit of Jesus Christ.

Olier did not envision a large company, "as few are to be met who are willing to enter a life of self-denudation."[57]

Until practical circumstances necessitated changes, Olier's community was limited to a superior general and twelve assistants in accord
with the number of apostles, four of whom were elected as consultors
(four evangelists); there were also the ideal seventy-two associates not
required to give up benefices, reflective of the seventy-two disciples
of Jesus, ready to be sent along with one of the twelve, to establish
foundations in the provinces. Practical considerations, as well as his
mystical tendencies, prompted Olier to adopt the model of the apostolic church. The twelve were entrusted with authority over the seminary and parish of Saint-Sulpice and over the communities of priests
in the provincial seminaries. In accord with the centralizing tendencies of French political life, Olier centralized all authority in the superior general and his consultors; another practical consideration for
such centralization was derived from Saint-Sulpice's exemption from
the authority of the Ordinary of Paris. Even after the archbishop of
Paris assumed responsibility for the faubourg Saint-Germain in 1669,
Saint-Sulpice was not considered to be a diocesan seminary, and the
curé of Saint-Sulpice remained attached under the authority of the
abbot of Saint-Germain-des-Prés.[58]

Olier's mystical tendencies urged him to immerse himself deeply
in the life of the apostolic church, a tendency that was characteristic of the Counter-Reformation in France. Because Olier's mysticism
was influenced by Condren's directives, he expected *the twelve* to have
experienced self-annihilation and adherence to the Word Incarnate, a
condition that made them perceptive to any deviation from the character of Saint-Sulpice within the provinces. It seems that Olier did not
consider the seventy-two to be of inferior status. Indeed, he entrusted
them with the spiritual direction of those aspiring to be priests. It was
rather that the twelve were viewed as adepts at the Olierian way of
life: one of simplicity; of mental prayer; and of particular devotion to
the Blessed Sacrament, to the Virgin Mary, to Saint John the Baptist,
and to Saint Joseph. Since Olier's community was only in its tenth
year when it was recognized as the Priests of the Clergy, his concern
for stability and permanence is easily understandable. Those clerics
drawn to the life of the company were referred to as the inner seminary. A transition year from seminarian to Sulpician candidate was
spent in solitude. (Port-Royal attracted pious solitaires to its convent.)
The Solitude was first housed at the Château d'Avron, very near Paris,
and later moved to Issy. As mentioned earlier, all the seminarians were
trained in Olier's tripartite method of mental prayer: adoration, communion, and cooperation: One student of Sulpician spirituality provides a clear summary of Olier's notion of mental prayer:

> The first part (Jesus before our eyes) consists in watching Jesus just as
> the gospel, tradition and theology present Him to us. We contemplate

Him as our divine model and we pay Him our homage of adoration. The second part (Jesus in our hearts) consists in drawing into our soul, by the realization of our powerlessness and by repeated calls of grace. . . . The third part (Jesus in our hands) becomes the object of a resolution, because every consideration ought to be transformed into adoration and effective action. The hands are the symbol of activity. We must look at Christ, and live in Him, but we must also imitate Him.[59]

In his 1651 memorial to the Assembly of the Clergy, Olier wrote,

As the seminary is the seedplot, in our Lord, of the ecclesiastical spirit, the first and principal care of the Directors [the Sulpicians], who ought themselves to be men of prayer, must be to make their subjects, as far as possible, interior men, by showing them the importance of doing all things, in union with the Spirit of our Lord. . . .[60]

To ensure that the "Spirit of the Lord" animates the seminarians throughout their day, Olier and his successors placed great emphasis upon the *esprit ecclésiastique*. This spirit became synonomous with the propriety of the priesthood and included all the activities of sacerdotal life.[61] *Esprit ecclésiastique* stands in bold relief against the backdrop of the ignorance and immorality of clerical life in mid-seventeenth-century France. Simultaneous with the evolution of Saint-Sulpice, Vincent de Paul and John Eudes had developed seminary education with a similar emphasis upon the interior life. Also, each of the founders departed from the Tridentine model by limiting the Grand Séminaire to those preparing for orders.[62] However, the Sulpician tradition was a unique blend of the French school of spirituality and the *esprit ecclésiastique*.

As models for those who aspire to the priesthood, Olier's priests were instructed by their superior to live a common life with the seminarians, that is, in chapel, refectory, and recreation there was to be no official separation between priests and seminarians. Familiarity with dedicated priests, rather than fear of superiors, has been one of the foremost marks of Sulpician seminary life. Collegiality is embedded in the governance structure, and the superior is expected to reach a consensus within the community prior to indicating a new policy. Although this principle was not made explicit until after Olier's death when the first constitution was written, it is implicit in his writings. These characteristics have been etched into the tradition and, when joined to Olieran spirituality and the stress upon the *esprit ecclésiastique*, form the charism or special quality of the Sulpicians.

A year after the Assembly of French Clergy had approved the establishment of the Priests of the Clergy, Olier's health compelled him to retire as pastor of Saint-Sulpice. Although his condition improved in 1653, he never again experienced good health.

Nevertheless, during the last five years of his life (1652–1657) he founded two more seminaries, preached a mission, wrote several devotional and catechetical works, corresponded with those dependent upon his spiritual direction, and contended with Protestants and Jansenists. Included in the *Memoirs* (composed from 1642–1652) and in his correspondence were many references to mystical experiences, revelations, and prophetic utterances, which mark him as one of the holy men in this century of saints. He frequently expressed the desire to evangelize the peoples of the Far East as well as the natives of New France, and shortly before he died he approved the project to establish a Sulpician mission in Montreal, the story of which will be included in another chapter.[63]

There is an epic, if not heroic, quality to the life of Jean-Jacques Olier. Ever haunted by deep feelings of inadequacy, he nevertheless struggled against the moral pessimism and theological elitism of the Jansenist view of nature and grace; confronted with the depravity of the clergy, he established a seminary infused with the highest ideals of the priesthood; led to the heights of mysticism, he was nevertheless a practical parish reformer and an author of books on methods of mental prayer, meditations for apprentices as well as masters of the spiritual life; and though he was remote from the world he was active in many of the ecclesiastical and civil conflicts of the times.

IV

Olier's successor as superior of the Priests of the Seminary of Saint-Sulpice was Alexandre Le Ragois de Bretonvilliers. One of the wealthiest clergymen in France, Bretonvilliers provided money for the construction of the new mission of Saint Sulpice in Montreal, for the purchase of the property that later became the Solitude at Issy, and for numerous charitable projects of various ecclesiastical institutions. With Louis Tronson, who succeeded him in 1676, he codified the traditions of Saint Sulpice into a constitution in 1659. Approved at the first meeting of the General Assembly, the constitution included thirteen chapters and formed the basis for the society's development until 1921.[64]

As we have noted, the society was composed of a superior general, twelve assistants (of whom four were elected as consultors), and seventy-two associates. The superior general possessed an enormous amount of authority but was mandated to seek the approval of his four consultors and in certain instances of all the assistants. The associates could be appointed superiors, directors, and professors of the society's provincial seminaries, but they neither possessed voice or vote in the affairs of the society nor were required to renounce all benefices. They were, however, expected to limit their pastoral ministry to the needs of the seminary. In the eighteenth century the proliferation of Sulpician seminaries engendered constitutional changes providing for the expansion beyond seventy-two members for full memberships in the society. However, the peculiar authority of the twelve assistants, the four consultors, and the superior general remained intact until the twentieth century. All the members retained rights to their worldy possessions but promised to live in the spirit of poverty, self-mortification, and obedience to the rule.

Louis Tronson, third superior general, is known as the legislator because he modified the rules of the seminary and because he routinized the charism of the founder. Tronson is best known among seminarians for his work *Examens particuliers*, which was required reading in seminaries for three centuries until the reforms following the Second Vatican Council. Although the tradition of struggling against specific faults as impediments to spiritual growth may be traced back to the Desert Fathers, Ignatius Loyola is viewed as the foremost advocate of the method. In the spiritual exercises Ignatius focused on the role of the method within the scope of the Jesuits' spiritual journey, and later he remarked, "The practice of the particular examen after the Exercises are over ought to be for life."[65] Tronson's method for the particular examen was influenced by Loyola as well as by Olier. Lyman A. Fenn, a twentieth-century Sulpician author of a book of particular examens, remarks, "The form he [Tronson] gave to the particular examen was an abridgement of the Sulpician method of mental prayer [i.e., adoration, communion, resolution]. . . . Typical of the Oratorian spirituality, God is the starting point."[66] Following a prayer of adoration, the examen's second point includes a series of questions that focus on ways in which the seminarian may have fallen short of the ideal. The third or concluding point is a prayer seeking divine aid on the road to "perfection." Tronson's examens include nineteen topics for meditation under the heading of "'Examen pro Clero." Among the topics is that of the "Priestly Spirit," which again reveals the Sulpician's stress upon the need for an *esprit ecclésiastique*.

> The gift of the Priestly Spirit enables us to share more abundantly in the Spirit of Our Lord Jesus Christ, the Great High Priest. This Spirit causes us . . . to reverence our sacred calling, and makes us strive after the virtues more especially belonging thereunto; it gives us a great love for the duties of our office, and imparts the grace through which we discharge those duties in a fitting manner.[67]

Among Tronson's interrogations are several references to the ideal priest, such as, "Have we duly reverenced the great dignity of our

office, the highest and holiest on earth. . . ?"[68] Tronson also includes
a meditation "of the warfare which priests are bound to maintain
against the world."[69] Since the original drive of Saint-Sulpice was to
combat the worldly character of the priesthood, such a meditation
was grounded not only on theology but also on the culture. "Have we
loved and esteemed all which the world hates and despises, shunning
what it seeks, and seeking what it regrets?"[70] Influenced in part by the
Jesuit tradition, Tronson emphasized the role of the will in overcoming
faults, while Olier stressed the dissolution of the individual will in
union with God. Hence, Tronson also represents a retreat from the
mysticism of the founder, a move that was in step with the spiritual
and psychological trends of the late seventeenth century. While Olier's
battles were in baroque chiaroscuro, Tronson's place him closer to the
clear light of the classical age, symbolized by the *esprit géométrique* of
which "Descartes was the shining prophet and Fontenelle the high
priest." The latter proclaimed, "The geometric spirit is not so attached
to geometry that it cannot be disentangled and carried over into other
areas of knowledge."[71]

Unlike Olier, Tronson did not directly confront Jansenist hostility,
but during the papal-Jansenist truce, the so-called Peace of Clement
IX, he did dismiss a seminarian who had sided with the Jansenists. The
Sulpician superior general also proscribed books that were critical of
the Holy See's condemnation of Jansenism. Although as a theologian
and as a confessor, he seems to have shared the gloomy pessimism of
the Jansenists, Tronson held to a moderate position on grace and freedom along the lines enunciated by Olier. In the quietist controversy,
ignited by the publication of Madame Guyon's work on the true love
of God, Tronson also took a moderate stand. In deference to Fénelon,
his friend and former penitent and seminarian at Saint-Sulpice, and in
defense of mystical prayer in general, Tronson abstained from a condemnation of quietism. Indeed, he was the moderator of the famous
meeting of Fénelon and Bossuet on the quietist controversy, which
was held on the grounds of the Sulpician Solitude at Issy. However,
when the Holy See issued its decision condemning quietism, Tronson
issued his submission to the decision.[72]

By the end of Tronson's administration the society had six provincial seminaries and had established the so-called Petit Séminaire, particularly designed for those students who could only afford one-half
the cost of the Grand Séminaire, and had assumed responsibility for
the Maison des Philosophes, geared toward students preparing for entrance into theological studies. Under Tronson's successor, François
Leschassier, the society assumed control over a small community of
seminarians in Paris known as the Robertins. In 1708 the Sulpicians
received a legacy to sustain that community, which housed nonaris-

tocratic students who qualified for scholarships. The first superior in Baltimore, Father François Nagot, was a graduate of the Robertins.

The Grand Séminaire, which was a national seminary, attracted students from the aristocracy, but as long as the spirit of Olier prevailed, life within each of the four Sulpician houses in Paris was characterized by simplicity and a strong adherence to a routine of prayer and study. The Sulpician tradition also emphasized spiritual direction, communal life among priests and students, and conferences at least once a week.

During the middle third of the eighteenth century the society drifted away from rigid adherence to the original rule. Deterioration was particularly rapid under the administration of Jean Cousturier, superior general from 1731 to 1770. Cardinal André Hercule de Fleury's residence in the Sulpician house at Issy, which originated during the administration of Cousturier's predecessor, appeared to have compounded the problems, as ambitious aristocrats were frequently drawn to Louis XV's prime minister. In general there was a distinctive relaxation of the rules; careerism, rather than pastoral ministry, tended to be the major motivating factor among the students at the Grand Séminaire. For example, the aristocratic students of Saint-Sulpice were so attached to their wigs that they nearly rioted when confronted with a rule prohibiting them.[73]

Saint-Sulpice also reflected current trends within the church in Paris. For example, in 1765 twenty-eight monks of Saint-Germain-des-Prés appealed for a change in the rules governing night services and fasting; such practices allegedly prevented them from useful study.[74] Although this group represented a minority, the incident illustrates the dissension within an ecclesiastical community close to Saint-Sulpice. According to one church historian familiar with this period of decline in the Sulpician way of life, the major seminary in Paris was most seriously affected by the wave of worldliness, unlike the Petit Séminaire, the Maison des Philosophes, the Robertins, and the provincial seminaries. Such a view has been somewhat substantiated by John McManners' research: "In Paris under Cardinal Fleury's unlucky patronage the [Sulpician] motherhouse became a haunt of graceless young aristocrats, while in the provinces there was greater propriety."[75]

The intellectual climate in Paris during this period was charged with excitement. The publications of Diderot's *Enclycopédie*, of Voltaire's biting satire, and of Rousseau's essays on the state of nature, along with the salon life of the *haute culture*, no doubt found expression among some students at the Grand Séminaire. Although the seminaries in the provinces (numbering nearly twenty on the eve of the French Revolution) adhered to the rules, the education they provided, according to McManners, was

narrow and clericalist. From the first, the sacramental and mar-
ial devotion of Saint Sulpice and its infallibilist theology had been
anti-Jansenist in flavor, and the use bishops made of the seminaries as
instruments against Jansenism led to a concentration upon orthodoxy
which discouraged independent thought. Certainly this was the view
of the *Nouvelles ecclésiastiques* [the Jansenists' journal], whose commen-
tators throughout the eighteenth century referred to the Sulpiciens
[sic] of Angers as purveyors of superficial instruction.[76]

As will be noted in the next chapter, Jacques-André Emery initiated
the intellectual and spiritual renewal of the society on the eve of the
French Revolution. During the 150-year period from its beginning
in Vaugirard (1641) to the passage of the Civil Constitution of the
Clergy (1790), the society had a deep impact upon the church in France.
Although they were few in number (never exceeding 150 members),
the Sulpicians had enormous influence. By 1700 fifty French bishops
had been educated by the Sulpicians, a number that increased to 200
during the next century. Saint-Sulpice was at the crossroads of the
ecclesiastical life in France.

V

Sainte-Beuve described Olier as possessing "more charity and zeal
than breadth and stability of intellect; [he] was full of ceremonies
and imagery, a mystic, even a visionary."[77] John Carroll Futrell, S.J.,
provides a theology of charism that he applies to founders of religious
communities. He notes that "a founder's specific charism is given at
certain moments in the history of the church to a person whose
manner of reading the multi-dimensional gospel portrayal of the life
of Jesus brings him to focus on some particular aspect of Jesus's life
leading him to follow Jesus and to serve others for his love in a
particular way."[78] Olier focused on Jesus the priest-victim, and after
passing through his "great ordeal" Olier took his vow of servitude to
the will of Jesus. He simultaneously incorporated his prayer life and
his mission life into the religious reform of the priesthood through
the establishment of the Seminary of Saint-Sulpice and the "inner
seminary," the priests' priests: the twelve original Sulpician followers
of Olier.

In a sense, Tronson routinized the founder's charism, provided stability to his vision, structured the prayers and meditations through his
particular examens, and provided a constitutional basis for the seminary and the society. *Esprit ecclésiastique* is the term that most closely

captures the essence of the Sulpician imprint. It can note a concordance between the call to the sacred character of the priesthood and the profane behavior of the individual seminarian, between interior piety and external posture, and between the priest-victim state of holiness and the clerical status of an ecclesiastical servant. The Sulpician was an individual model for the *esprit ecclésiastique*, but because his spiritual ideals were grounded upon the denial of self, the Sulpician clerical model represented the dignity of the priesthood embodied in the refined style of clerical life. Olier's interpretation of the modeling role was etched into the tradition of Saint-Sulpice, where priests and seminarians shared the communal life in chapel, refectory, and recreation room. So strong was the Sulpician drive to represent the excellence of the priesthood that, even when the society experienced a decline in the observance of the rule, it seems to have maintained a sense of style, particularly derived from its aristocratic background but also from its loyalty to at least the exterior manifestation of the *esprit*. The history of the Sulpicians in America is in a sense the story of the development of New World forms for this *esprit*, a development that originated in Olier's unique rendering of the life of the priests' priest.

PART ONE

The Sulpicians and
the Formation of the
American Church
(1789–1850)

The 1791 foundation of the Sulpician seminary in Baltimore was contemporaneous with the revival of Olier's charism, with the threat to
the church in France, and with the optimism of the new republic. Thus,
the Sulpicians were driven by the missionary idealism of their original
spirit and by a practical realism to escape from the anticlericalism of the
French Revolution. However, the Baltimore seminary was no mere
missionary outpost but a replica of Saint-Sulpice, with its *haute
spiritualité*, its tradition of learning, and its Gallican ecclesiology. During
this entire period, the Sulpicians were not only seminary directors but
parish priests, vicars-general, and archbishops in Baltimore; founders
of, and collaborators with, communities of sisters; and missionary
priests and bishops along the western frontier of the United States.
Their blend of idealism, realism, and Gallicanism was congruent with
the Enlightenment Catholicism of John Carroll, and by the time of
Carroll's death in 1815 most Sulpicians had internalized the traditions
of the Anglo-American church and integrated them into their world
view. Indeed, many Sulpicians became identified as Americanizers.

To understand the Sulpician participation in the formation of the
American church, one must explore the French Sulpician experience
and developments in the French church. These developments, particularly in ecclesiology, are integral to the larger story of Saint Sulpice
in America.

31

1

American Foundation

Jacques-André Emery, the ninth superior general, is so identified with the revival of the Society of Saint Sulpice that he may be viewed as embodying the original charism of Olier. However, his leadership during the French Revolution was so vital to the survival of this tiny community of seminary priests that he may also be considered as the founder of the modern Sulpicians. Just as Olier's life represented the baroque culture of the early seventeenth century, so Emery's was expressed in a style akin to the neoclassical: whether he was engaging in subtle polemic against the deist and agnostic writers of the Enlightenment, rebuking aristocratic seminarians for their departure from the traditional austerity of Saint Sulpice, extolling the mystical qualities of the Spanish Carmelite Saint Teresa of Ávila, advising French ecclesiastical leaders to accommodate themselves to the liberal climate of the first phase of the French Revolution, establishing a code of behavior for the Sulpicians in America, or candidly informing Napoleon that he had contradicted himself in his policies governing the church in the empire—in all these enterprises Emery was the personification of balance, clarity, harmony, and judicious restraint.

Jacques-André Emery was born in Gex in the diocese of Geneva on 16 August 1732. After attending the Carmelite college there, he completed the course in humanities at the Jesuit college in Mâcon.

He began philosophy at the Sulpician seminary at Lyons, and at the end of the first year he successfully competed for a burse at Les Robertins, one of the four houses attached to Saint-Sulpice in Paris. Since Les Robertins was limited to students who had passed a difficult entrance examination, a strong academic spirit prevailed in the house, in contrast to that found in the Grand Séminaire, which, as noted above, housed the sons of the aristocracy and which experienced a decline in religious observance in the mid-eighteenth century. At the completion of the course in theology at the Sorbonne, Emery entered the Sulpician Solitude as a deacon, and on 11 March 1758 he was ordained. After teaching at the seminary in Orléans, Emery received the doctor's degree from the University of Valence in 1764, whereupon he was appointed professor of moral theology at the Sulpician seminary of Saint-Irenée in Lyons.[1]

During the last half of the eighteenth century the Jansenist publication *Nouvelles ecclésiastiques* frequently associated the Sulpicians with a "Molinist conspiracy,"[2] as if they represented a tendency to stress easy access to divine grace. The anti-Jansenist tradition established by Olier was manifested in Emery's life at Orléans and at Lyons. In both instances he defended the orthodox position with the diplomatic skill of a statesman rather than the impassioned strategies of an ambitious ecclesiastic.

At Lyons he confronted followers of Olier's contemporary Saint-Cyran and of Pasquier Quesnel, a Jansenist of the late seventeenth century. Indeed, the archbishop of Lyons was so enamored of Jansenist theological, moral, and ecclesiastical writings that "the theology of Lyons" is an eighteenth- and nineteenth-century code word for Jansenism.[3] To illustrate Emery's tact in dealing with this strain of heterodoxy, he presented a lecture to a clergy conference in Lyons in which he explored the heresies of the early church, drew analogies to current heretical doctrines, and concluded that the allegedly new theology was a mere shadow of earlier ideas previously condemned by the church. He did not have to refer to the anti-Jansenist bull *Unigenitus;* thus he avoided a politically explosive issue. In his dealings with the Jansenists among the Oratorians at Lyons, he gained a reputation for his moderation, for his restraint, and even for his sense of humor.[4]

While he was at Lyons, Emery wrote *Esprit de Leibniz* as an indirect response to those savants of the Enlightenment, the *philosophes*, who attacked Christianity as irrational.[5] In his study of the religious controversies of eighteenth-century France, Robert R. Palmer notes that Leibniz was seldom incorporated into the debate on the philosophical basis of religion.[6] Indeed, the common defense of religion was that it could be explained only within the context of faith and mystery.

Hence, Emery's work was an exception in the religious polemics of the day. He thus explains his motivation for selecting the topic:

> It seemed that religion might draw some advantage from such work, and that the name Leibniz might influence a great number of the enemies of religion. Some of them, indeed, push fanaticism so far as to maintain incredulity is necessarily that portion of the brain that thinks, and then are satisfied with opposing to the blows that are aimed at them the name and authority of the philosophers. It is well to knock this weak defensive instrument out of their hands, and to show that . . . the Christian religion . . . would . . . be sure of victory if men would examine her case and decide it on . . . [Leibniz's and other philosophers'] authority.[7]

The significance of Emery's collection of the writings of Leibniz extends beyond his debate with the critics of religious belief. In fact, developing the philosophical basis of religion (which included not only Leibniz but Bacon and Descartes as well) in order to counter the anti-Christian critique became the core of the apologetic identified with seminary training at Saint-Sulpice well into the nineteenth century. As will be explored in the later chapter, Félicité de Lamennais worked out his romantic apologetic in opposition to what he considered to have been the ineffective, inadequate, and all too coldly rationalistic approach of the Sulpicians.[8]

In 1774, two years after the publication of his work on Leibniz, Emery's *Esprit de Sainte Thérèse* was published.[9] Because mysticism was associated with quietism, eighteenth-century spirituality avoided mysticism and concerned itself with asceticism and devotionalism. Like his book on Leibniz, Emery's work on Saint Teresa is a collection of her writings prefaced by his introduction. He responded to two currents in contemporary intellectual life: the secular savants' sarcasm toward anything that smacked of the mystical, and the believers' opposition to the allegedly heretical tendencies of the mystics. Emery's portrait of Teresa, intended to dispel the antimystical prejudices of the Enlightenment, was one of the first to show her humanistic qualities and psychological insights. To edify his fellow believers he selected those writings of Teresa that could be easily understood by the general reader.[10] In a sense Emery's *Saint Thérèse* was in the tradition of Olier who, after passing through his "great ordeal," tended to translate the mystical into practical guides for novices in the spiritual life.

Emery closely identified himself with the spirituality of Olier. He spent several hours a day at prayer and was very ascetical. At his death several instruments of physical self-penitence were found in his room. When he was appointed superior at Angers, the largest seminary in France (it had over 300 students), he continued to be moderate in tone, but in substance he was dedicated to the rigorous pedagogy of the original Sulpician spirit, with its stress upon mandatory attendance for both priests and seminarians at all the daily spiritual exercises. John McManners, who studied the ecclesiastical life at Angers, concludes that Emery "was a rigorous and unsparing man who would tolerate no slackness—not even from his bishop, whom he turned out of bed to take an ordination service."[11]

Upon the resignation of the superior general, M. Le Gallic, in 1782, Emery was elected to the highest office in the society, which meant that he also became superior of the Seminary of Saint-Sulpice. As previously noted, the Grand Séminaire was limited to aristocratic aspirants to the priesthood. While the other houses attached to Saint-Sulpice had observed the traditional rule, the aristocratic residence had deviated from the Sulpician exercises, a condition that reflected weak leadership within the community. Poor attendance at Mass and at spiritual conferences, a general disregard for the rules governing the religious decorum of the house, and a strong interest in the antireligious writers of the day characterized the spirit of the Grand Séminaire. In short, it had become a place where "aristocratic young men destined for high position in the Church were sent to acquire a smattering of theology."[12] These young aristocrats had many models for their behavior. Loménie de Brienne, archbishop of Toulouse and first minister to Louis XVI, was more closely associated with secular affairs than with sanctuary and altar. When his name was proposed for the archbishopric of Paris, Louis XVI remarked that "at least the archbishop of Paris should believe in God." Similarly the bishop of Le Mans was known for his attachment to loose women, hunting, and rich clothing, as well as for his disdain of his religious duties. There were only a dozen or so such scandalous bishops, but equally there were only a few ecclesiastical leaders who led ascetical lives, such as the bishop of Perpignan, who frequently prayed on his knees for an entire night. According to Adrien Dansette, most of the 135 French dioceses were led by bishops who "were neither scandalous nor edifying but simply more influenced by the attraction of this world's pleasures than by the prospects of eternal happiness in the next."[13] From all available evidence, this remark could also be applied to the vast majority of the students at the Grand Séminaire.

These young aristocrats did not welcome Emery as their superior. Indeed, in retaliation for Emery's restoration of discipline, particularly his prohibition of elaborate hairstyles, on one occasion several seminarians set off fireworks and other explosives in the dead of the night. Emery pursued the perpetrators with characteristic zeal, and before long he had expelled over twenty seminarians, several of whom were from the leading families of the realm. Emery also restored the traditional Sulpician pedagogy among his own community of priests by insisting that they follow the same rule as the seminarians. His own asceticism and piety were strong factors in reviving the spirit of Saint Sulpice, and as a testimony to his effective leadership not one Sulpician left the community during the French Revolution, though in that troubled time many religious communities experienced heavy losses. One of the seminarians viewed Emery as a prophet of the Old Testament:

> He was not an innovator; he altered nothing, conserved all; he knew how to unite and speak as well as our secular philosophers; he had a well organized head, was able to sustain and long maintain a painful work of the mind; he was versed in the knowledge of history, he was a disinterested soul, really poor in spirit, rich in virtues and the gifts of Heaven.[14]

Emery's statesmanlike qualities were never more in evidence than during the French Revolution. Although his sympathies were royalist, he was never a rigid defender of the *ancien régime*. Once it was dismantled he attempted to maintain a moderate position. For example, he accepted the first oath drafted by the national assembly: "I swear to be faithful to the nation, to the Law and to the King; and with all my power to support the National Assembly."[15] His advice to priests to take the oath marked him as a leader of the center in contrast to the Gallican-Jansenist Bishop Paul Grégoire on the left and to the ultramontane intransigent Cardinal Jean-Siffrein Maury on the right. Like the intransigents, Emery did not condone the oath to support the Civil Constitution of the Clergy, an oath that denied practically all ecclesiastical authority of Rome; he attempted to chart a middle ground. Because he was neither active in pastoral ministry nor a member of a religious order, he was not required to take the oath to the civil constitution. Instead he had to swear his loyalty to the principles of liberty, equality, and fraternity, an oath that the intransigents rejected. While the latter fled, Emery remained in Paris, and as vicar-general of the archdiocese he was responsible for its ecclesiastical administration in the long absence of the Ordinary.[16]

By the summer of 1792 the revolution had entered its radical phase. Emery had prepared for the impassioned anticlericalism endemic to the far left by closing the seminaries and by establishing a Sulpician seminary in Baltimore. During the September massacres, when anyone who appeared to smack of disloyalty to the revolution was summarily executed, eight Sulpicians were among the hundreds of victims.[17] This situation and the subsequent Reign of Terror led Emery to disperse the Sulpicians, many of whom emigrated. Yet Emery remained in Paris and continued to defend the legitimacy of the oath to liberty, equality, and fraternity as so general and vague as to lack any substantive relation to sound theological principles.

Cardinal Maury disputed with Emery on this issue. He not only viewed the oath as tantamount to capitulation to the diabolical forces of the revolution but also predicted that the oath would result in the permanent destruction of Catholicism in France. Pope Pius VI did not explicitly condemn the modified oath, but he was personally opposed to it.[18] Despite his defense of the oath, Emery was imprisoned twice during the Reign of Terror (1793–1794), the second time for nearly a year. Narrowly escaping execution, the superior general became a strong source of spiritual strength for his fellow prisoners. Finally released during the Thermidorean reaction to the terror, Emery resumed his position as leader of the moderate group of French clergymen. Indeed, he was the leading French ecclesiastic residing in France and loyal to Rome during the decade between the crisis over the Civil Constitution of the Clergy (1790) and the Napoleonic concordat with the papacy (1801).[19] During that period a number of Sulpicians took refuge in other countries. Those who went to Germany operated, from 1796 to 1814, a seminary at Walsau near Würzburg in the castle of the saintly Prince Alexander-Leopold von Hohenlohe, a bishop who became renowned, even in America, for his intercession for miraculous cures. Unlike the Baltimore seminary, however, Walsau was not regarded as a permanent foundation. The Baltimore seminary had opened in 1791 in the episcopal city of the only diocese in the United States.

II

The decision to found a Sulpician house in Baltimore was made in the summer of 1790. The French Revolution had not entered its radical phase, but virulent anticlericalism was prevalent among the majority of the revolutionaries. Within this atmosphere, Emery, in consultation with his council, considered establishing an American refuge from the imminent storm of antireligious outbursts. Aware of recent French emigration to Gallipolis, Ohio, he sought the advice of the papal nuncio, Archbishop Antonio Dugnani, who persuaded him to reject Gallipolis in preference to Baltimore.[20] He told Emery of the recent appointment of John Carroll as first bishop of Baltimore and of his consequent visit to England for consecration. On 14 August, the eve of Carroll's consecration at Lulworth Castle, Emery's plan to approach the bishop received the approval of the Sulpician assembly, convened primarily to discuss the American venture. Emery viewed the prospect of a Baltimore seminary not only as a refuge but also as a means for members of the society to carry out their vocation in the infant republic.[21]

Ten days later Archbishop Dugnani wrote to Carroll informing him of the Sulpician proposal and of the "zeal, wisdom and principles of the house of Saint Sulpice."[22] The following day Emery also wrote to Carroll about the plan and asked him to visit Paris for a general discussion of the proposal. Carroll's immediate response to the proposal was cool. He was grateful for the Sulpicians's offer to establish a seminary, but, as he told his friend Father Charles Plowden, "We certainly are not ripe for a seminary; it will take some years before we have scholars far enough advanced to profit by this generous offer."[23] The scholars to whom Carroll was referring were those of the prospective Georgetown College, which had for one of its purposes the preparation of young men for seminary education. Carroll also told both Dugnani and Emery of the poor prospect of a seminary in Baltimore. He indicated to Emery, however, that he would welcome Sulpicians to serve the French missions along the Wabash River and to assist him in his duties in Baltimore until they would be needed as full-time directors of the seminary. If Emery would agree to these conditions, the bishop invited him or his representative to explore the prospects with him in London where Carroll was busy preparing for a return to his diocese within the month.[24]

In mid-September Emery sent his confrere François Charles Nagot to London for a meeting with Bishop Carroll. With the bishop in desperate need of priests (there were only about thirty-five priests serving over thirty thousand Catholics in the United States) and with the Sulpicians eager to establish a seminary in America, Carroll was well disposed to achieving an agreement. Through his emissary, Emery posed seventeen questions to Carroll, ranging from inquiries on the climate and the suitability of wearing clerical garb to questions about the number of priests to be sent on mission and the economic security of their future. The Sulpicians agreed to pay for their own voyage, to maintain the seminary, and to supply the priests and three or four French seminarians who could adapt to the American language and customs.[25] Carroll promised to seek advice from the Society of Priests Incorporated (i.e., the Maryland clergy, most of whom were former Jesuits) as to the purchase of land, the rent from which would provide for the subsistence of the Sulpicians. He also agreed to provide them with "books, apparatus for the altar, the Church and Professors of Philosophy and Divinity." The bishop said that only two Sulpicians would be sent to the missions in Illinois and on the Wabash.[26]

Carroll was very pleased with the prospect of having Sulpicians in his diocese. He told Dugnani: "For myself, I can not help regarding the proposition of the gentlemen of Saint Sulpice as a signal mark of providence and proof that it [sic] wishes to dwell upon the faith in the States."[27] Carroll hoped to locate the Sulpicians close to his cathedral that "they may be, as it were, the clergy of the church and contribute to the dignity of divine worship." Appreciative of "the great auspicious event for our new Diocese," Carroll was well aware of the irony that Baltimore was to gain "so great a blessing [because of] the lamentable catastrophe in France."[28]

The following March, Carroll informed Emery of the needs of the missions in the regions of Vincennes and Kaskaskia.[29] On 21 March he "engaged a house" for the Sulpicians, but that news never reached them, for on 8 April 1791 four priests and five seminarians embarked from Saint-Malo on a chartered ship destined for the port of Baltimore.[30] It is evident from the background of the four Sulpicians that Emery placed great significance upon the venture in the diocese of Baltimore. For superior he chose Nagot, who at that time was vice-president of the Grand Séminaire. Five years after entering the society, Nagot received his doctorate in theology at the University of Nantes and served as director and professor at the Sulpician seminary in that city. In accord with Emery's policies aimed at reviving the spirit of Olier, the superior general asked Nagot to write a biography of the founder, but the French Revolution precluded its publication.[31] As a superior of two seminaries from 1768 until he was appointed to the Grand Séminaire in 1789, Nagot had implemented the reform policies of the superior general.

Jean-Edouard de Mondésir, one of the seminarians who traveled to Baltimore, recalled some personal qualities of Nagot:

> He then possessed and always retained as long as I knew him the fervor of the most fervent novice. Father Nagot seldom put aside his serious and reserved manner—as soon as he perceived that he had, he quickly came back to it . . . at the Seminary of St. Sulpice I often heard that Father Emery sought to calm his *directeur du*, who had the fire of a young man. On All Saints' Day, in particular, Father Nagot . . . sang the magnificent preface with so much strength and joy that Father Emery could not help congratulating him on it after the service. . . . He was a man of [the] rule by taste; by need he loved solitude and prayer. His face was red when he prayed. . . . He fatigued himself much at mental prayer, which he made on his knees for hours at a time, and with much contention of spirit. As a result he was nervous and needed to be ceaselessly occupied. He did in an animated way whatever he did, whether it was tending the orchard or translating into French the supplement we have to the *Lives of the Saints* of Butler under the [pen] name of Godescard.[32]

Antoine Garnier (1762–1845) was the foremost scholar in the original group of Sulpicians. He too was awarded a burse at Les Robertins.

He was an excellent student of Oriental languages and was the associate of the leading professor of "sacred languages" at the Collège de France. When he returned to Paris in 1803, he taught scripture, Hebrew, and Arabic at the Seminary of Saint-Sulpice. According to Jean Edouard de Mondésir, Garnier was "open, communicative and a good talker. One had the impression that Father Garnier was taking him into his confidence and was glad to tell him what he knew. Never, no, never did Father Garnier make me feel that he was my superior." Mondésir concluded by stating that his relationship with Garnier was characteristic of the director–student relationship of Saint-Sulpice: "Esteem and friendship, such is the bond of union between master and disciple." Mondésir compared Garnier with other administrators: "Father Nagot appeared to be, as it were, led by the rule; Father Emery appeared to make the rule and be dominated by it; the rule did not encumber Father Garnier."[33]

Jean-Marie Tessier (1758–1840) was a director and professor of theology at the Sulpician seminary in Viviers before embarking for America. Tessier became Nagot's assistant for administrative matters and, after Levadoux departed for the west, he was appointed treasurer (*économe*) of the seminary. He subsequently became second superior of Saint Mary's Seminary from 1810 to 1829.[34]

Before his appointment to Baltimore, Michel Levadoux (1746–1803) was a director and professor at the Bourges seminary. He was appointed treasurer, but of the original four Levadoux was destined to become the only missionary. In 1792 he was sent to Cahokia in the Illinois Territory, and in 1796 he took up residence as a missionary in Detroit.

The five seminarians were Francis Tulloh from England, who remained in Baltimore for just over one year; John Edward Caldwell, an American adopted by General Lafayette who later left the seminary and rejoined his family; Joseph Perinault of Montreal who in 1793 returned to Canada, where he was eventually ordained; John Floyd, another Englishman, who was ordained in 1795 and subsequently served as pastor of Saint Patrick's Church in Baltimore from 1795 to 1797, when he died of yellow fever; and Jean Edouard de Mondésir of Chartres, who spoke English and was a gifted student. Because his studies were interrupted by a teaching assignment at Georgetown College, Mondésir was not ordained until 1798; he returned to France in 1801.[35]

During the 104-day journey to Baltimore, the little seminary community lived according to the rule of Saint Sulpice: Mass, private mental prayer, conferences, and spiritual reading. One of their fellow passengers was François René, viscount de Chateaubriand, who had been born in Saint-Malo. Only twenty-three at the time, he had yet to establish himself as the leading writer of the new sensibility later referred to as Romanticism. Mondésir recalled that Chateaubriand "willingly assisted . . . at Spiritual Reading, which was made in common. . . . Now the effervescent Chateaubriand preferred reading out loud to listening in silence, so it was often his turn. Father Nagot one day observed to him that an ascetical book should not be declaimed in a tone which befitted a tragedy. The reader answered that he put his soul into everything he did."[36] In his *Memoirs*, Chateaubriand mentions his Sulpician "traveling companions [who] would have been more to my liking four years earlier: from being a zealous Christian I had become 'a man of strong mind,' in other words a man of weak mind."[37] His only other recollection of note was his friendship with the seminarian Tulloh, who seems to have kept in contact with the famous writer.

When the seminary group arrived in Baltimore on 10 July 1791, it was met not by Carroll who was in Boston, but by Father Charles Sewall, rector of Saint Peter's procathedral. The community's first residence was at 94 Market Street. Eight days later they moved north to the western edge of the city and into a large building called the One-Mile Tavern (one mile from the town center). Perhaps this is the property Carroll had "engaged" for the Sulpicians as early as 21 March of that year. At first, however, they paid rent—500 pounds a year. On 16 September 1791, Carroll purchased the property for 850 pounds and then sold it to the Sulpicians on 21 October for the same amount. Over the years the community expanded beyond the tavern's original four acres. The original 850 pounds represented a little over one-third of their assets of 2,400 pounds.

When John Carroll was consecrated bishop in 1790, his Baltimore diocese encompassed the entire nation: thirty-five priests ministering to some 30,000 Catholics, the vast majority of whom lived in Maryland and Pennsylvania. The arrival of the four Sulpicians considerably augmented the clergy in Baltimore, while their seminary was the first fully developed American institution exclusively devoted to theological education in the United States. Protestants prepared for the ministry at Harvard and Yale, but the first independent Protestant divinity school was not founded until 1808 when Andover Theological School broke away from Harvard to establish a separate school of divinity.

On 3 October 1791, the Seminary of Saint Sulpice, later known as Saint Mary's Seminary, was officially opened. Before the directors departed from Paris, the superior general had provided them with a sixteen-point document called "Counsels and Rules of Conduct for the Priests of the Seminary of Saint Sulpice Sent in April, 1791, to Found a Seminary at Baltimore in the United States." Although the original motive for the foundation was to provide a refuge from the French Revolution, Emery's counsels indicate that he intended it to be a permanent Sulpician seminary, one which "will be for a long time the only one in the United States of America."[38] He envisioned for the future a Sulpician preparatory seminary. Emery did not intend to establish a mission seminary, a frontier institution, but rather an extension of the original Saint-Sulpice. "They [the American Sulpicians] will often recall that they are destined to perpetuate the spirit and the name of their Society in the new world, and they will keep before their eyes the rules and practices of St. Sulpice, in order to be guided by them as much as possible."[39] The superior general underscores the principal characteristics of the Sulpicians' way of life, such as separation from the world, daily prayer (particularly one hour of mental prayer), deference to the bishop, the celebration of the major feasts, (i.e., the interior life of Our Lord, the Blessed Virgin, Saint Joseph, Saint John, and Saint Sulpice). Emery tells them that their first duty was the education of the clergy, but he also noted the unusual circumstances that compelled the priests to do mission and parish work. He reminds them that when they found themselves "out of their element," they should not "be satisfied until they return to their special mode of life."[40] The nonessentials of the rule, such as "hours for meals, rising and retiring," should be in accord with the customs and climate of the country. Because Emery viewed Americans educated in their seminary to "be less emotional and less frivolous than French boys," and because the American seminarians had to be prepared for a more "laborious ministry," he authorizes a daily hour of mental prayer for all students.[41]

The superior general encourages the priests to give lessons in mathematics and French to groups of boys of Baltimore. This way they would be making "themselves agreeable to the citizens of the town by being useful to their children." He also tells them "to render the same service to the sons of Protestants, avoiding, however, speaking of religion, in order not to offend the parents. . . . But nothing can be set down concerning this article until after actual conditions are known and the advice of the bishop is had."[42] In a final article Emery stipulates that the directors should acquire a piece of property, the revenues from which would provide for their needs. They should seek the advice of the bishop and the consent of the superior general.[43] Composed with characteristically French thoroughness, with an accent upon centralized authority and a unified rule, these directives were also a reflection of Emery the reformer, statesman, and defender of the original spirit and of the traditional piety embedded in the rule and in the religious culture of Saint-Sulpice.

Throughout the 1790s gradual changes were introduced into the nonessentials of the rules, such as a reduction of mental prayer from an hour to a half-hour and a restriction of wearing the soutane to the seminary grounds. Generally, however, the routine in Baltimore was the same as that in Paris: meditation, daily Mass, spiritual conferences, particular examen, night prayers, recreation—with a seasonal *grande promenade*—classes, study, and general silence. In the early years Tessier taught moral theology and Garnier dogmatic theology. There were no textbooks since the professors taught from notes based upon their own reading.

The seminary was the first Catholic institution of higher education in the United States. Georgetown, "a school for studies in humane letters," though conceived earlier than Saint Mary's, did not come into being until 22 November 1791.[44] As an enclave of French culture, the seminary added to the stature of the church in Baltimore. John Carroll describes the situation for Cardinal Leonardo Antonelli at the Propaganda Fide:

> It is truly remarkable how these [Sulpician] priests conduct them-
> selves; they are highly praised for their piety; their example arouses
> and stimulates all of us who have been called to work in the vineyard
> of the Lord. Since their arrival there has been notable improvement
> in conducting ecclesiastical functions and in the celebration of divine
> worship. To such a degree is this the case that while the church in
> Baltimore is scarcely worthy of being considered a Cathedral if one
> merely regards its size and external appearance, it can be regarded as
> such if one contrasts present conditions with the extreme simplicity
> of our beginning."[45]

The Sulpicians contribution to the liturgical life was matched by their general influence upon education in the diocese. The best English-speaking seminarian, Jean Edouard de Mondésir, was sent by John Carroll to Georgetown College where for nearly five years he taught several courses in "humane letters."

Toward the end of 1791 when French seminaries were being closed, Emery sent another group to Baltimore. On 29 March 1792, Jean-Baptiste Chicoisneau, Jean-Baptiste David, and Benoit Flaget, accompanied by two seminarians, Stephen T. Badin and N. Barrett, arrived in Baltimore. A little less than three months later, three more Sulpicians arrived: Ambrose Maréchal (1778–1828), Gabriel Richard (1767–1832), and François Rousset-Ciquard (1754–1824). Chicoisneau had been sent "to found an establishment of Missionaries of St. Sulpice in the Illinois country," but Nagot appointed him treasurer of the seminary and sent Levadoux to Kaskaskia, where he was later joined by Gabriel Richard.[46] Flaget went to Vincennes, while Rousset-Ciquard journeyed to Maine, where he served the Penobscot tribe, until 1794 when he moved to the diocese of Quebec to work with the Saint John's River tribes.[47] David and Maréchal were appointed to the Maryland missions. By this time (1792) Garnier had founded Saint Patrick's

Parish in the Fells' Point section of Baltimore. This second church of the diocese was two miles from Saint Peter's and served a growing community of Irish and of French refugees from the West Indies.[48] Hence by the end of 1793 nine Sulpicians were engaged in seminary work, secular education, and parish frontier ministries scattered throughout Carroll's vast diocese. Although few in number, they nevertheless represented over one-fifth of the clergy in the infant diocese.

With only a handful of seminarians, the directors of the seminary gradually gathered together young boys of the city for classes at the seminary in order to supplement their income, but because this represented a threat to the fledgling Georgetown Academy, Bishop Carroll had it discontinued. To help defray expenses, the Baltimore community appealed to their Canadian confreres for funds. Although the confreres in Canada generously sent 25,120 francs and a 6,000-franc gift from a private source, such amounts did not provide long-term security.[49]

As early as November 1792, the Maryland Chapter of the Clergy (the former Jesuits in assembly), under the leadership of Bishop Carroll, resolved to sell a piece of property, a part of the revenue from which would be given to the Sulpician superior as the first of a series of annual payments "as long as the Chapter shall deem it necessary to continue the same."[50] However, before the sale of this property was consummated, Carroll received a letter from Nagot informing him of the poor financial condition of the Baltimore Sulpician community, a condition that was caused not only by the paucity of students and the cost of improving the facilities but also by the discontinuance of financial aid from Paris after the revolution had reduced the society to penury.[51]

On 28 January 1793, Carroll communicated the contents of Nagot's letter to the Select Body of the Roman Catholic Clergy (the former Jesuits had incorporated themselves under that name on 23 December 1792). Rather than provide the Sulpicians with a portion of the revenue from the sale of the property, he proposed to allow the Sulpicians to manage the estate called Bohemia Manor, 1,700 acres in Cecil County on the Eastern Shore of Maryland, with the entire revenue going to the support of the seminary. A Sulpician would replace the estate's clergyman-manager and would also minister to the small community of Catholics in the vicinity.[52] On 3 May 1793, the corporation of former Jesuits passed a resolution reflecting the wishes of Carroll with the stipulation that the Sulpicians assume the debts of the estate "to the amount of four hundred pounds currency." This resolution was in the form of a contract signed by Nagot and Robert Molyneux, secretary general of the chapter.[53]

Ambrose Maréchal was appointed administrator-chaplain at Bohemia Manor. During the next six years the Sulpicians at Bohemia Manor borrowed 1,900 pounds for construction of a suitable house for the farm and for repairs and spent nearly 900 pounds for indebtedness and capital investment; receipts amounted to only 950 pounds for the same six years. Although by mid-1799 the seminary had yet to receive any income from the estate, the investment promised to yield profits in time.[54] In this six-year period there were disputes between the Sulpicians and the corporation over financial responsibilities. The tensions were exacerbated by Sulpician-Jesuit conflicts concerning Georgetown College.

William DuBourg, an emigré priest who had been an administrator of the newly formed Sulpician Petit Séminaire at Issy and who had joined the society in Baltimore, was appointed president of Georgetown by Carroll in 1796. Assisted by his Sulpician confrere Flaget, DuBourg, a strong character and at times an impulsive person, soon alienated the "Jesuit" faculty. There were even rumors among the faculty that the Sulpicians were planning "to take the college from us."[55] DuBourg was forced to resign in December 1798; Flaget had resigned earlier that year. Carroll was unsure of just who was at fault "in this untoward business," but he concluded that "national attachments [were] the bane of all communities . . . [and] the original cause of the mischief. He [DuBourg] was too fond of introducing his countrymen into every department; and the ["Jesuit"] Directors had too strong prejudices against everything which was derived, in any shape, from France. . . ."

Carroll seems to have maintained a basic objectivity toward the situation; he told Charles Plowden that DuBourg was a man of great merit and admirable accomplishments.[56] There appears to have been a general fear among the former Jesuits of a Sulpician conspiracy to undermine their prominence in Maryland. Anti-DuBourg sentiment developed, and reports circulated that the Sulpicians were "being enriched at the expense of Bohemia."[57] Then, on 30 April 1799, a number of the trustees of the Clergy Corporation informed Nagot of their decision to resume command of the administration of Bohemia Manor in order to pay the debts of Georgetown College.[58] For the sake of harmony within the diocese the Sulpicians did not forcefully contest this decision, but they did point out that they had never achieved a full return on their investment and that they were just beginning to make a profit when the estate was taken away from them. Later they succeeded in gaining some compensation for their 1799 investment in the form of produce and two slaves who had originally belonged to the corporation but who had been working at the seminary.[59]

By the time of the final legal resolution of this issue on 9 October 1799, the "Jesuit"-Sulpician conflict had intensified. As Carroll pointed out, national prejudices formed the basis of the conflict, but the central figure in the rivalry remained Louis William DuBourg, whose administrative style was "genial and popular" in contrast to the rigid system imposed upon the students by his "Jesuit" successor, Leonard Neale.[60] On 18 December 1798, shortly before DuBourg resigned as president of Georgetown, representatives of the student body expressed their "grief" at the loss of the popular French Sulpician. "Beloved sir," they wrote,

> as no treasure on us can be compared to a faithful and beloved friend, to a virtuous and tender father (permit us to call you by that endearing name), so no loss whatever can be compared to what we now sustain, and we dare venture to assert that grief is proportionate to our misfortune.

Eight faculty members echoed the sentiments of the students and referred to DuBourg as "our dear, our worthy friend, our Benefactor."[61] DuBourg's enemies fed the suspicions of those former Jesuits who feared a Sulpician attempt to take control of Georgetown College. It seems more than coincidental that three months after the forced resignation of DuBourg the corporation demanded the return of Bohemia Manor.

The entire future of the Sulpicians in the United States was very doubtful at this juncture. Income from the manor, which was estimated to have been almost 900 pounds in 1799, was cut off; the society was still in debt; and there was only one student at the seminary in Baltimore. Only a few seminarians had successfully pursued ordination in Baltimore by 1799. Stephen T. Badin, the first priest of the United States, was ordained in 1793 and in 1799 was doing mission work in Kentucky. Demetri A. Gallitzin, the famous convert son of a Russian diplomat at The Hague, was ordained in 1795, joined the Sulpicians that year, and became a missionary in southeast Pennsylvania. Jean de Mondésir, ordained in 1798, returned to France in 1801.[62] Meanwhile three Sulpicians—Babad, Flaget, and DuBourg—were in Havana, desperately attempting to establish a Sulpician academy in Cuba.

DuBourg, who was born on the island of San Domingo (an early name of the Dominican Republic) but grew up in France, had had prior experience in the instruction of young boys at the Petit Séminaire at Issy. In 1796, he started a catechism class in Baltimore for freed black refugees who had fled political disturbances in San Domingo. This Sunday catechism class was continued by Tessier and ultimately led to the formation of a black ethnic "parish" at Saint Mary's.[63] Although only thirty-four years old when he joined Babad in Havana, DuBourg had a rich background in dealing with youths of diverse cultures. The Cuban venture was dependent upon approval by the Spanish government in Madrid. DuBourg and Flaget returned to Baltimore in August of 1799 with three students of Spanish families in Cuba. Officially opened on 20 August 1799, "DuBourg's school" immediately attracted three French-speaking students from San Domingo refugee families.[64]

On the basis of one of Emery's instructions, which called for the establishment of a school for boys that would help support the seminary, Nagot and the Sulpician assembly in Baltimore agreed to allow DuBourg's school to be housed in the seminary. They also hoped the school would eventually provide students for the seminary or at least provide funds to aid seminarians unable to meet the cost of their education. While Carroll did not oppose the school, he did stipulate that it should limit its enrollment to foreign boys rather then those from the local community so that it would not pose a threat to Georgetown.[65] However, the Georgetown's administration lodged complaints against the school that caused Carroll to remain ambivalent toward DuBourg's venture.[66] Emery was also ambivalent. He told Carroll of his concurrence in Nagot's decision to approve the school, but he also promised Carroll that, if he were opposed to the school, then the superior general would also withdraw his support; to defy the will of the ordinary would, he said, "be altogether contrary to the spirit of our Society, which can do nothing except in dependence on the bishops."[67]

The anti-Sulpician attitude on the part of local clergy was generated also by disputes over tuition for their seminarians. Moreover, the former Jesuits accused the Sulpicians of attempting to recruit among the aspirants to their society. During the spring of 1800 Nagot attempted to ease tensions by meeting with Carroll and Leonard Neale, the president of Georgetown and Carroll's coadjutor-elect. Nagot reported the details of this meeting to his assembly, which made the following decisions:

1. Not only have we never accepted into our Society any subject of his [Carroll's] diocese without permission but we do not believe we have the right to.
2. That we desire to receive here gratuitously the seminarians who will come here from the college [Georgetown] and who cannot pay for their board themselves.
3. That we shall limit the number of scholars [enrolled at St. Mary's College] to twenty-five without taking a single subject born in the diocese, provided that on his part, the bishop will . . . regard us always as his seminary and confide to us the philosophy and theology of his clerics or at least the theology. In case he refuses this we hold ourselves free from limits on the number and quality of the boys of our school.[68]

Nagot's attempt at reconciliation was unsuccessful. By August of 1800 there was not one student of Saint Mary's Seminary, though there were seven students at Georgetown ready to pursue a course in philosophy at Saint Mary's. Rather than turn them over to the Sulpicians, the former Jesuit directors resolved "to open a course in philosophy at Georgetown with the purpose of keeping these young students." Carroll told Nagot that this was done "without my approbation and contrary to the will of the agents of the clergy," namely, the representatives of the corporation.[69] Hence, it does not appear to have been entirely a "Jesuit" versus Sulpician conflict, but rather one of Georgetown versus Saint Mary's. On the other hand, Carroll traced the conflict to "national prejudices, in my opinion, very ill founded, against the worthy priests of St. Sulpice and the system of education pursued in the Seminary,"[70] as he told his old friend Charles Plowden. An anti-French spirit may indeed have been at the origin of the conflict, but DuBourg's ill-fated presidency of Georgetown and the foundation of his school appear to have exacerbated affairs. For example, Carroll told Emery in January of 1801 that the Georgetown directors refused to send the seven students to Saint Mary's Seminary because "they will be too distracted by their mingling with the pensioners at DuBourg's academy, and also that Father DuBourg (for it is primarily against him that their temper is directed) will attract to himself the best subjects [i.e., students] and get them to serve as regents [i.e., instructors] at his college."[71]

In the midst of this crisis Nagot received word from Emery that the Sulpicians were to be recalled to France if Carroll did not furnish students and did not treat Saint Mary's as his diocesan seminary.[72] Carroll responded with alarm. He wrote to Nagot, "I well see and I deplore the future which opens before me. But, in heaven's name, do not make it more sorrowful still by being discouraged and painting your situation to Father Emery in such colors as will make him strip my diocese of its best and most able directors."[73] When Carroll received word from Emery that he intended to recall the Sulpicians to France, the bishop replied, "I declare to you . . . that I have never seen or known anywhere men better able by their character, their talents and their virtues to form ecclesiastics . . . than the Fathers of your Society." He told Emery that a Sulpician departure from his diocese would be "one of the greatest misfortunes which could happen. . . . I earnestly beg you to banish the idea from your mind."[74]

Six months later Napoleon's concordat with the papacy, signed in July 1801, officially reestablished seminaries in France. Hence, Emery needed directors for Sulpician seminaries. While he was waiting for the appropriate time to recall his confreres from Baltimore, Emery reminded DuBourg that he could not declare his college "a work of

St. Sulpice" because it "was an obstacle to the seminary and to the peace which ought to reign among the clergy." Therefore, he advised DuBourg, "take charge of the college in your own name."[75] With apparent knowledge of the anti-Sulpician attitude of Leonard Neale, the coadjutor bishop of the diocese, Emery considered it to "be absurd to attempt further to establish a seminary in a country where the ecclesiastical superiors believe that we are not suitable to the work."[76] However, he did allow DuBourg to remain in Baltimore and even permitted Babad and Flaget to remain as faculty members of Saint Mary's College.

As late as October of 1801 the Sulpicians were attempting to resolve the conflict with Georgetown. The assembly (the official name of the Sulpician faculty meetings) approved a request by Carroll that Maréchal be appointed to teach philosophy at Georgetown so that "this could become a means of reconciliation with the Gentlemen of the Clergy whom our academy has so greatly offended."[77] According to the minutes of this meeting of the assembly, Carroll proposed that DuBourg's school be moved to New York or to Charleston. The Baltimore Sulpicians opposed the latter because of the hot climate but considered New York favorably if the United States were divided into two dioceses with New York named the second see city.[78] Because they were waiting for Emery's decision as to whether to recall the community altogether, the Sulpicians postponed a decision on possible relocation of the school.[79] It appears that Maréchal's appointment did not reduce the hostile sentiment toward the college. In a January 1802 letter to DuBourg, the superior general places the question of the college within the context of the Sulpician presence in the United States and its revival in France.

> But I believe that Providence has shown me enough evidence to make me judge that we can no longer think of establishing a seminary conducted by French priests. I am giving Father Nagot a summary of my reasons for such a statement. You see at what a price we undertook the education of ecclesiastics! It is necessary even that the college which indeed did not enter into my plans,—a college which should not be objectionable to these gentlemen of Georgetown especially since it limited itself to French and Spanish boys,—it is necessary that that college be moved into another State. I see a depth of rivalry and jealousy which I did not at all conceive, which I did not even suspect, but which, once perceived, demands infinite consideration. They write that we are not proper for educating young Americans, and that may be the truth. Perhaps it is fitting that Americans be educated by Americans? However that may be, it would be absurd to wish to force, so to speak, those upon whom it depends, to confide the education of the young clergy to us, while our own country whose needs are just as great as those of America calls us

back, and while we are helpless here because of lack of subjects to fill our old institutions which are revived by the reestablishment of seminaries in France.[80]

Emery's pessimism did not extend to the future of the college, whose success he attributed to the qualities of its founder. In this letter to DuBourg he gives his consent to the continuation of the institution: "Since God has given you great talents for the education of youth, since He has given you such relish for it, since there are contracted engagements which cannot honorably be left unfulfilled, since your academy is flourishing, follow your attraction, continue your work."[81]

Once again, Carroll urged Emery to reconsider the recall of the Sulpicians and noted that if the seminary would close the only testimony "which the Society of St. Sulpice would leave behind in the United States was a college."[82] This comment elicited an angry response from Emery:

> I come to the root of the matter: surely in the whole course of the French Revolution, there has been nothing like that which we did for you and your diocese. A small Society like ours, in fact the smallest of all Societies, makes you the offer of establishing a seminary in your new diocese. It sends a considerable number of subjects and even adds seminarians with which to start the exercises at once. It sends these at its own expense; it undertakes to support its subjects, and in fact, it has always supported them since. It sacrifices for this establishment the greater part of its savings and gives nearly a hundred thousand francs. What is the result of all this? At the end of the ten years we are no farther advanced than in the first days. There is no question at this moment of abandoning the Seminary of Baltimore, since in fact it has never existed; it is only question of abandoning the project of a seminary. It has been promised from time to time to send subjects there; this was pictured as a favor and a grace: but it was never accomplished, and obstacles have arisen where they ought to have been the least expected. You tell me, My Lord, that the Society will have left no other monument than a college. I hope that you would hold as something, all the services which its members have rendered you during the space of ten years. If there were any complaints to be made, it seems to me that I have the right to make them, since at the end of a ten years' stay and after very many promises we have nothing done or nothing possible to do of all the objects we have in mind on entering your diocese. However, My Lord, I am far from imputing blame to you. We know that you have not been the master of the situation and we shall live always very grateful for all the goodness which you have shown us.[83]

Emery began to recall the Baltimore Sulpicians in early 1803. Carroll had pleaded with him not to recall Garnier. "Although all of your gentlemen merit my esteem," he said,

> I should do injustice to the distinguished merit of Father Garnier, if I
> did not add that his talents, viewed from every side, his modesty, his
> love of peace, his sane and solid judgement, and the facility with which
> he accustomed himself to the usages of the country, have obtained for
> him the attachment, the respect and confidence of everybody.[84]

Despite this appeal, Emery recalled Garnier on the basis that he "was
destined for teaching and to honor Catholic teaching" and therefore
should return to Paris. Emery seems to have merely tolerated Garnier's parish work at Fells Point, for he maintained the exercise of
external ministry "weakens the spirit peculiar to [his] vocation" as a
Sulpician teacher and spiritual director. Although Emery recalled him
"definitely," he told Garnier, "I do not wish to force you."[85]

Carroll was somewhat encouraged by the latter, but Garnier informed the bishop that despite his "repugnance for returning to
France," and despite the "desire I have remaining with you, [I have]
determined to leave without delay." He explained to Carroll that Sulpicians take no vows and "our Superiors are not accustomed to use
terms of command."[86] However, once Garnier knew the will of his
superior, he identified it with the guidance of Providence. In May
1803, Maréchal, Levadoux, and Garnier departed for France. Just as
the three Sulpicians were preparing to leave, DuBourg received official notice from Havana that because of a change of policy in Madrid,
Cuban boys would not be permitted to study outside of their native
country, a policy that decimated the enrollment at his college.[87] With
characteristic éclat and with the consent of the Sulpician assembly in
Baltimore, DuBourg decided to open the college to students of all nationalities and religious denominations. Only after the new policy had
been announced did DuBourg seek the approval of Carroll and Emery.
While the bishop reluctantly gave his approbation, the superior general
concluded that this time DuBourg had departed too drastically from
the tradition of Saint Sulpice. Although Emery considered DuBourg's
"French college . . . [as] a sort of hors d'oeuvre" in America, he found
it "impossible to approve" of the change from a French Catholic college
to an American mixed college.[88] In fact, the superior general was so
shocked by DuBourg's boldness that he doubted DuBourg's vocation
as a Sulpician:

> You have all the qualities necessary for a good Sulpician, but you
> have others which a Sulpician ought not to have. You have a taste
> and talent for governing and for grand enterprises, and that in a high
> degree. To these you join such a great aptitude for dealing with men
> of the world that I believe that if you had to be limited to live within
> the four walls as a *solitaire* [i.e., a candidate for the Society who spent
> a year in the Sulpician solitude] solely occupied with prayer and study
> you would never have lived at St. Sulpice—you would have left and

I believe I would have given you such counsel because such rare and interesting talents as you possess were not meant to be hidden.[89]

Emery told DuBourg that he had consulted with Pope Pius VII, who was in Paris for the coronation of Napoleon as emperor; when the superior general mentioned the mixed character of Saint Mary's College the pope "gave a sign of disapprobation by turning his head."[90] Emery also informed DuBourg that Cardinal Antonelli of the Propaganda Fide, the papal congregation responsible for the administration of all mission countries, had also "crisply disapproved of what you were doing in Baltimore. . . . I made the point to Cardinal Antonelli of the [economic] advantage which will result from our establishment for the support of the seminary. He was not at all moved by that consideration on the ground that one may not do an evil for the sake of procuring a good."[91] Nevertheless, DuBourg's college was a success, with over 125 students enrolled by 1805.

To strengthen the college and to enhance its status, DuBourg successfully sought a charter from the state of Maryland (19 January 1805) that allowed the college to grant academic degrees. Emery received a letter from Carroll saying that, though he was disappointed with the abrupt way that DuBourg initiated the new policy, he saw "nothing wrong" in admitting Catholics and Protestants to the same college.[92] In early 1806, Emery decided not to consult Rome for approval of the college.[93] Carroll's endorsement of the new Saint Mary's was in accord with his genuine concern for good relations between Catholics and Protestants. Although the Georgetown-Sulpician feud continued, Carroll—perhaps relieved that the Sulpicians seemed committed to remain in his diocese—did not represent Georgetown's position to the Sulpicians.

Emery had intended to recall all his confreres from the United States, but he did not carry out his stated policy. Reopening of Sulpician seminaries in France prompted him to recall Garnier, Maréchal, and Levadoux (only poor health prevented Nagot from making the transatlantic voyage), but Emery seems to have been uncertain about the prudence of deserting the infant diocese of Baltimore. When Pius VII came to Paris, he presided at a liturgy at Saint-Sulpice (in late December of 1804), which was followed by a two-hour audience with the superior general. As noted earlier, during this meeting Emery reported on the state of the society, including his plans to abandon the seminary at Baltimore in order to better provide for the needs of the church in France. Pius responded with the prophetic remark, "My son, let it remain; yes, let that seminary exist; for it will bear its fruit in time. Recalling the directors to employ them at other houses in France would be to rob Peter to pay Paul."[94]

Emery followed the direction of the pope; subsequently Saint Mary's Seminary began to take on new life, and in the first decade of the nineteenth century enrollment increased rapidly. Between 1800 and 1810 forty-six students were admitted, of whom twenty-three were ordained. Although that figure appears small, it represented a significant proportional increase in clergy for the Catholic community in the United States. Meanwhile this tiny group of French priests had had a strong impact on the city of Baltimore. Not only were they educating young aspirants to the priesthood and the sons of prominent Protestant and Catholic families but they were also providing missionaries in Michigan and teaching catechism classes to blacks, acting as theological advisers to Carroll, extending themselves to the French families in the area, and representing an enclave of European culture in a city proud of its growing sophistication. With several new buildings and with its growing religious, intellectual, and cultural influences, One-Mile Tavern had been transformed into Saint-Sulpice in America.

2

Influence of French Ecclesiastical Developments

Once the Society of Saint-Sulpice was transplanted to Baltimore, it was nurtured with the nutrients of French religious life, derived from the experiences of the Sulpicians during the period of the French Revolution and of Napoleon. Because the society was at the center of the ecclesiastical life in France and because it was identified with the development of a moderate form of Gallicanism, the Sulpicians who were sent to the mission church in the United States throughout the nineteenth century were strongly influenced by the religious culture and ecclesiology of Saint-Sulpice. Ironically, the Gallicanism of the Sulpicians in Baltimore was manifested in strong loyalties to the particular church and was especially evident in those priests determined to Americanize their institution and to identify with the liberal Americanist vision of the last half of the nineteenth century. The ecclesiology of Saint-Sulpice experienced profound developments in the French church.

Jacques-André Emery bequeathed to the postrevolution Sulpicians a strong blend of ecclesiastical realism and priestly idealism that allowed Saint-Sulpice to preserve its traditional identity and at the same time

55

accommodate itself to the trends of modernity. Emery's idealism, as expressed in his restoration of the charism of Olier, was dramatically manifested in his ministry to his fellow prisoners during the Reign of Terror. During the period of the Directory (1795–1799), when there were sudden shifts between moderation and extremism, Emery's ecclesiastical realism was evident in his role as vicar-general of the archdiocese of Paris, which continually put him in communication with émigré priests and bishops. It was during the Napoleonic period, however, that both his idealism and his realism were severely tested. By his coup d'état of 18 Brumaire (9 November 1799), Napoleon replaced the Directory with the Consulate, and within a matter of a few months the Corsican "child of the revolution," as he styled himself, had begun to consolidate his dictatorship. Then in June of 1800 he announced his plans to reach an agreement with the papacy. By this time Pope Pius VI had died (as a prisoner of the French) and a Benedictine monk had been elected as Pope Pius VII.

Encouraged by the new policy, Emery planned to reopen the Seminary of Saint-Sulpice. After the parish church and the old seminary buildings had been seized by the government, he had established an "unofficial seminary" located in the house on the rue d'Enfer occupied by Antoine Duclaux, former superior of the Grand Séminaire at Angers and of the Solitude. With about thirty students, the seminary opened in September 1800. Duclaux presided at prayer and spiritual conferences. Emery appointed the following directors: Marie-Nicolas Fournier and Jean Montaigne for moral theology; Denis-Luc Frayssinous for dogmatic theology; Pierre-Denis Boyer for philosophy; Arnaud La Brunie for scripture. Emery himself taught canon law and church history.[1]

In mid-January 1801 Emery and the other vicars-general of Paris met with Napoleon to encourage him to conclude a concordat with the papacy. With characteristic diplomatic skill, the seventy-year-old Sulpician suggested to Napoleon that he allow the publication of the peace overtures of the prior June. Although the suggestion went unanswered, Napoleon's silence implied that he would not oppose publication. One biographer of Emery notes that Napoleon remarked that if Emery did publish the June speech then he should "beware of the Minister of Police," Joseph Fouché. Without revealing any of his motives, Fouché did arrest Emery in July 1801 while negotiations over the concordat were at an intense point. Charged with illegal collusion with émigré or "unsubmissive clergy," the superior general was placed in a local city jail along with common criminals. Three weeks later, however, he was suddenly released, an act that would seem to indicate that Fouché had been subjecting the old priest to harassment. Ironically, within a short time Emery was instrumental in garnering support for the concordat among the émigré bishops. For his efforts he was nominated bishop on three occasions, refusing each time on the grounds that his primary vocation was to the Sulpician way of life.[2]

The concordat signed in July 1801 reestablished the church in France. The government recognized Catholicism as the religion of the great majority of Frenchmen. The 136 sees were reduced to 60, whose ordinaries were to be nominated by the government and canonically instituted by the pope. Bishops appointed parish priests, but, as both bishops and priests were paid state salaries, the government reserved the right to approve the appointments. The papacy accepted the alienation of the church's property seized during the revolution and agreed to respect the religious and political consciences of the French people. Those churches that were still free and needed for worship were placed "at the disposition of the bishops."[3] The Organic Articles, attached to the concordat by the Corps Législatif when it approved that document in 1802 included provisions that allowed the government to control the publication of official statements of the pope, of his representatives, of foreign synods, and of general councils. It also stipulated that the government must grant permission before any ecclesiastical council could hold a meeting. If any of the above measures was violated, the Council of State had authority to take the necessary punitive action. Also included in the Organic Articles was the mandate that seminary professors instruct their students in the Gallican Articles of 1682,[4] which in abbreviated form were

1. St. Peter and his successors, Vicars of Christ, and likewise the Church itself have received from God power in things spiritual—but not in things temporal and civil. . . . Consequently kings and princes are not by the law of God subject to an ecclesiastical power . . . with respect to their temporal government.
2. The plenitude of power in things spiritual which resides in the Apostolic see . . . is such that at the same time the decrees of the Ecumenical Council of Constance . . . remain in full force and perpetual obligation.
3. Hence the exercise of the Apostolic authority must be regulated by the canons enacted by the Spirit of God. . . . The ancient rules, customs and institutions received by the realm and Church of France likewise remain inviolable.
4. The Pope has the principal place in deciding questions of faith and his decrees extend to . . . all Churches: but nevertheless his judgment is not irreversible unless confirmed by consent of the Church.[5]

The promulgation of the Organic Articles, contrary to the wishes of the pope, indicated that Napoleon wished to exercise authority comparable to that of the old regime. A semblance of peace between pope and emperor was maintained until shortly after Pius VII's visit to Paris for the coronation of Napoleon. In September 1806, French troops occupied a part of the Papal States. When Pius VII protested, Napoleon stated, "In the temporal sphere your holiness will have for me the regard that I have for [you] in the spiritual. Your holiness is sovereign of Rome but I am the Emperor and all my enemies must be [yours]."[6] After three years of conflict over the pope's temporal authority, Napoleon annexed the Papal States to the kingdom of Italy, and in July 1809, after Pius VII announced the excommunication of those responsible for the seizure, the pope became a prisoner of French troops in Rome. Because the pope's excommunication decrees related only to the temporal power of the papacy, the French episcopate decided not to enforce them. However, when Pius retailiated by not investing bishops appointed by Napoleon, the French bishops respected the papacy's spiritual authority, and thus from 1808 to 1810, twenty-seven of the sixty dioceses were without authorized ordinaries.[7]

Emery's involvement in French ecclesiastical life during the ten-year period (1801–1811) reflected the general trend in relations between the French and the papacy, namely, a swing from a condition of relative peace to one of hostile impasse. In the period of rapprochement the superior general negotiated his society's return to nine of the twenty seminaries that it had staffed before the revolution; in addition, he took on for the society the administration of the seminary at Saint-Flour, formally staffed by Lazarists. Emery was able to retain the property at Issy, but there was no seminary there until much later. He was particularly interested in returning to the old seminary adjacent to the parish church of Saint-Sulpice, but the civil authorities had commenced a thorough renovation of the area to form a public square. Emery was nevertheless determined to move from the seminary on the rue Saint-Jacques (which he referred to as *un séminaire bourgeois*) and finally decided to settle in the former quarters of a house of Christian Instruction, which was situated on the rue du Pot-de-Fer (today's rue Bonaparte). The property not only included gardens, chapel, and suitable living accommodations but was also located near the original Séminaire de Saint-Sulpice.[8]

Emery's moderate Gallicanism was in accord with the articles of 1682 and was expressed in the introduction to a work he published in 1807 entitled *Les nouveaux opuscles de Fleury*. Claude Fleury (1640–1723) was the foremost church historian of his time, and in his twenty-volume work he strongly supports Gallicanism. The new tracts published by Emery include a concise reiteration of Fleury's ecclesiology, while his introduction is a nuanced defense of the 1682 articles. Indeed, Bossuet introduced Fleury into the court of Louis XIV, where he was highly regarded both as a learned priest and a pious confessor. However, he was also close to Fénelon, and during the quarrel on quietism Fleury remained a friend to these two dominant figures in French ecclesiastical life.[9] As Joseph P. Chinnici points out, Fleury, despite his Gallicanism and selective use of sources, "recognized the tools of proper scholarship, linguistics, the study of chronology, and the use of scientific criticism to judge facts, authors and sources."[10] Chinnici also notes that Fleury's Gallican ecclesiology, particularly the primacy of the church council in defining articles of faith, was popular among the enlightened Catholics of the late eighteenth century.[11]

Emery may be viewed as on the fringes of Catholic liberalism because, like the liberals, he developed an "enlightenment" in his work on Leibniz and because he was in the tradition of Claude Fleury. As previously noted, during the first two years of the French Revolution, Emery represented a position of moderation between the counterrevolutionary intransigents and the revolutionary constitutionalists. He believed that the church was never to be used as a political means but rather a cherished end. Hence he quietly pursued any rational or just means to reconcile political reality to the church.[12] Emery's moderate Gallicanism veered away from Erastianism and stressed the rights of the episcopate, the prerogatives of an ecumenical council to define doctrine, and the authority of the papacy to enunciate and defend the faith. Because of the strong Sulpician deference to the authority of bishops over their seminaries, Emery's episcopal Gallicanism possessed a practical as well as a theoretical basis. During the early years of the Napoleonic era, Emery had persuaded many émigré bishops to accept the concordat and to return to France. Joseph Fesch, Napoleon's uncle, was a constitutionalist priest who renounced his clerical state in 1793. Before officially reentering the priestly life in 1800 he made a retreat under Emery. Later appointed archbishop of Lyons and French ambassador to the Vatican, Fesch remained close to Emery throughout the remainder of the Sulpician's life.[13]

Under the old regime, episcopal Gallicanism was expressed in collaboration with the French monarchy. But the polarization between emperor and pope was based upon Napoleon's extreme Erastian form of Gallicanism, which viewed the episcopacy as merely a bureau of the state. Hence, the only consistent policy for Emery and other moderate Gallicans to follow was to support papal authority. Within the context of Napoleon's Erastianism, Emery appears as an advocate of papal authority. Indeed, as Jean Leflon points out, the publication of Emery's *Les nouveaux opuscles de Fleury* "marked his orientation toward ultramontanism."[14] Joseph Fouché, the infamous chief of police, had never trusted the Sulpicians, particularly their superior general. Hence when the Fleury book was published, Fouché brought Emery in for questioning on the absurd grounds that Fleury was an ultramontanist. Emery replied that Fleury's view of papal authority—the power of the pope is sovereign and above all—was incorporated into the concordat of 1801, and therefore it was the law of the land.[15]

In 1809 a supplement to Emery's book, which was intended to soften the tone but not alter the moderate Gallicanism of the church historian, was "denounced to the Emperor." Napoleon responded to the charge by inviting Emery to the palace at Fontainebleau to defend himself. After waiting for a week, Emery finally received an audience. Napoleon remarked, "I have read your book and though it is true that the preface contains one point that is not quite to my liking, there is not enough in that book to whip a cat for."[16] The emperor then elaborated on the conflicts between himself and his prisoner Pope Pius VII. Emery's responses were so concise and candid that the emperor named him to the ecclesiastical commission, composed primarily of bishops and archbishops.

Napoleon had been impressed with the old Sulpician superior before their confrontation at Fontainebleau. As early as 1808 Napoleon had appointed Emery counselor for life of the Imperial University, which was responsible for the educational system throughout the empire. After consulting with several friends, Emery accepted the position.[17] Had Saint-Sulpice not been struggling for survival, Emery would never have accepted a post on the ecclesiastical commission. The commission was charged with approving the nullification of Napoleon's marriage to Josephine and his marriage to the Austrian archduchess Marie Louise. Emery's conscience did not allow him to sign the commission's report, which he considered to be a capitulation to Napoleon's design to make the pope his spiritual and temporal vassal. In June 1810, two months after his marriage, Napoleon retaliated against Emery by announcing his intention to turn Saint-Sulpice into a diocesan seminary, to dismiss the Sulpician directors, and to expell Emery as superior of the seminary. Only the last measure was immediately implemented.[18]

The superior general moved to a small apartment, located on the rue de Vaugirard, where he tended to the affairs of the society with characteristic austerity and simplicity. Although he had succumbed to Fouché's strongly anti-Sulpician bias, Napoleon nevertheless continued to admire the unpretentious Sulpician superior general. In February 1811, Napoleon formed an ecclesiastical commission composed of three cardinals, two archbishops, three bishops, and Emery. Confronted with the dilemma that either acceptance or rejection of the appointment could endanger the very existence of the society, Emery decided to accept the dubious honor. The commission was charged with improving relations between emperor and pope. Emery's worst fears were realized

when the commission was instructed to ratify Napoleon's policy of ecclesiastical autonomy regarding episcopal appointments and to justify
the emperor's behavior toward Pius VII. In response to these instructions, Emery wrote to Cardinal Fesch, a member of the commission,
that there was no legitimate justification in Gallican tradition for such
a usurpation of papal authority.[19] Ultimately Fesch and the majority of
the commission were in sympathy with Emery's position. The conflict
culminated in a confrontation between the commission and Napoleon
at the Tuileries, amid a grand assemblage of civil and ecclesiastical dignitaries, including Talleyrand, Fesch, and Cardinal Jean-Siffrein Maury
(the former intransigent had by this time become Napoleon's ecclesiastical tool.) The drama of the occasion was recorded in Antoine Garnier's
"Notice sur M. Emery" and in the memoirs of others present on the occasion. An English account based on these sources captures the event
in late Victorian prose:

> It was to be the final and the grandest scene in M. Emery's public life,
> so far as earthly grandeur goes; and unwittingly the Emperor had
> prepared a stage for what was to prove to be their last interview and
> an open display of the mysterious attraction between these two men
> of extraordinary interest in their separate spheres. . . .
>
> [After the] illustrious assemblage waited two hours, the Emperor
> appeared. A deep silence succeeded to the resounding acclamations
> that hailed his entrance. He opened the session by a violent harangue
> against the Pope, whom he accused of unjustly opposing his plans.
> He enumerated his grievances, enhancing them by threats; and his
> words were so violent, they betrayed so plainly the bitterness and
> vehemence of his wrath, that he seemed openly to defy any of those
> who heard him to dare to contradict him or to defend in his presence
> the dignity of conscience and the honor of the Church. . . .
>
> All present, with one exception, kept silent. "That one, a simple
> priest, arose" (so writes Cardinal Consalvi) "to save the honor of his
> priestly state, and dared to tell the truth to the most formidable of
> the Caesars. This priest was the Abbé Emery, a man equally to be
> respected for his learning and his years, who had lived through the evil
> days of the Revolution without their leaving upon him the slightest
> taint."
>
> When the Emperor had finished his diatribe against the Pope's au-
> thority, of which, he said, the bishops had no need for the govern-
> ment of their churches, he suddenly exclaimed: "M. Emery, what do
> you think of all that?" . . . M. Emery, being so directly questioned,
> glanced first at the bishops, as though asking their permission to act
> instead of them; then, turning to the Emperor, he spoke. . . .
>
> "Sire," said the priest, answering the abrupt, positive question,
> what do you think of that? "I can have no other opinion on this point
> than that which is contained in the catechism taught by your orders
> in all the churches of the empire. We read, in several places of this

catechism, that the Pope is the visible head of the Church, to [whom] all the faithful owe obedience as to the successor of St. Peter, and according to the express institution of Jesus Christ. Can, then, a body do without its head, that is, without him to whom by divine right it owes obedience?"

"Continue," said the Emperor, briefly; and M. Emery spoke again. "We are obliged in France," he said, "to sustain the four articles of the Declaration of 1682, but it is necessary to receive the entire doctrine as a whole (literally, *La doctrine dans son entier*). Now, it also says, in the preamble of this declaration, that the primacy of St. Peter and of the Roman pontiff was instituted by Jesus Christ, and that all Christians owe him obedience. Moreover, it is added that the four articles have been decreed, in order to prevent, under pretext of the liberties of the Gallican Church, any attack upon that primacy." Hereupon he entered into some developments to show that even though the four articles might limit the Pope's power on some points, they preserved to him so great and so eminent an authority that no important matter could be determined upon, in regard to dogma or discipline, without his participation; whence he concluded that if a national council were assembled, as the emperor was proposing, this council would have no true value if it were held without the approbation of the Pope. . . . [After a discussion on the relevance of Bossuet's views on Gallican privileges, Napoleon remarked] "And I have not the right," demanded the Emperor, "to declare to the Pope that if he does not give canonical instruction to the bishops I will do without him, and avail myself of a provincial council?"

"Never, sire," was the firm response. "The Pope will not make this concession. It would turn his right to institution into a mockery."

Napoleon cast a severe and scornful glance upon the members of the commission. "You were willing, then," he said to them, "to let me commit a gross blunder, persuading me to ask from the Pope a thing that he has no right to grant me!"

Thus ended the session, during which it was noticeable that the old superior of St. Sulpice was almost the only one to whom the Emperor spoke. Rising to retire, he bowed graciously to him, without appearing to pay any attention to the others who were present. He asked one of the bishops, however, if what M. Emery had said about the instruction contained in the Catechism concerning the Pope's authority was actually to be found there. The bishop could, of course, only give an affirmative reply, so that M. Emery afterwards remarked to M. Garnier that he had taught the Emperor his catechism, which he did not know.

As Napoleon was about to leave the salon, some of the prelates, fearing that he might be displeased with M. Emery's frankness, implored him to excuse the venerable man on account of his advanced age. "You are quite mistaken, gentlemen," said the Emperor. "I am by no means angry with M. Emery. He has spoken like a man who knows what he is about, and that is the way I like men to speak to me. It is true that he does not think as I do, but everyone ought to have the right to his own opinion here." Cardinal Fesch took advantage of the Emperor's favorable dispositions to ask leave for M. Emery to return to his seminary, but Napoleon simply answered, "We shall see."[20]

Emery left the Tuileries with deep apprehension that the emperor would retaliate for his bold behavior by suppressing the society. He even considered transferring the central authority of the society to the United States and naming Father Nagot vice-superior. Before he could execute this plan, however, he became ill and after a short time died on 28 April 1811, one month and eleven days after the meeting at the Tuileries. When Napoleon heard of his death, he reportedly told Cardinal Fesch, "I am very sorry; he was a wise man and an ecclesiastic of distinguished merit. We must provide him with a grand funeral and he must be entombed in the Pantheon."[21] The emperor's uncle reported that a burial site that was more in accord with Emery's austere simplicity had already been arranged in the cemetery of Issy.

Napoleon's reverence for Jacques-André Emery had prevented the enforcement of the order of suppression. A few months after the superior general's death, letters from seminarians and one anonymous letter attributed to a Sulpician were intercepted; each letter included comments critical of Napoleon. This evidence was magnified into treasonous conspiratorial behavior at Saint-Sulpice. Upon the direct orders of the emperor, the Society of Saint-Sulpice was officially dissolved on 11 December 1811. Friendly bishops appointed the Sulpicians to various posts, while diocesan priests became directors of their former seminaries and in general maintained the Sulpician spirit and traditions. Thus Emery's strongly enduring legacy guaranteed the survival of Saint-Sulpice, even though the society was legally extinct.[22]

II

With the fall of Napoleon and the restoration of the Bourbon monarch Louis XVIII in the spring of 1814, the Sulpicians returned to their seminaries. On 5 September 1814, Antoine Duclaux was elected superior general. It was not until 3 April 1816, however, that the legal reconstitution of the society occurred by an ordinance of Louis XVIII.[23] The moderate Gallicanism of the Sulpicians was in accord with the views of the French episcopacy. Antoine Duclaux and his successor Antoine Garnier (1826–1846) were never called upon to play such a large part in ecclesiastical life as was Jacques-André Emery, but they were deeply influenced by the latter's revival of the traditional charism of Jean-Jacques Olier. After such a tumultuous period as the French Revolution, Sulpicians settled into their familiar patterns—Gallican ecclesiology, Cartesian apologetics, and Olierian-Tronsonian spirituality. The major challenge to Sulpician tradition came not from the state but from Félicité de Lamennais, a thinker whose writings and struggles had a profound effect upon French ecclesial life in the nineteenth century. (Note that the traditional spelling of de La Mennais was changed during the revolution.)

Simon Bruté, a young Sulpician and later a major figure in the American church, had introduced Jean and Félicité de Lamennais to M. Emery in 1809. Alec Vidler reports that Emery approved Lamennais' manuscript, which was published in 1809 as *Réflexions sur l'état de France pendant le xviiie siècle, et sur sa situation actuelle*.[24] After linking the agnostic individualism of the *philosophes* with the "terror of liberty" of the Jacobin dictatorship, Lamennais outlines a plan for ecclesiastical reform that extolls principles of collegiality and calls for more religious societies that, like the Sulpicians, are dedicated to elevating the level of clerical education. Emery, whom Vidler refers to as "the moral leader and arbiter of the French clergy,"[25] also asked Jean Lamennais to explore the origins of the installation of bishops and the part played by the papacy in this process.[26] However, the Lamennais brothers did not complete the three-volume work *Tradition de l'Eglise sur l'institution des évêques* until 1814, long after Emery had died and the conflict between Napoleon and Pius VII on the installation of bishops had been obviated by the forced exile of the emperor. Lamennais' work was an ultramontane manifesto that asserted almost all papal prerogatives to be of divine right,[27] an approach that ran directly counter to the moderate Gallicanism of Saint-Sulpice, which held that until the thirteenth century metropolitans had usually installed suffragan bishops. After that time a bishop was instituted by a papal bull, a matter of church discipline rather than of divine right. But contrary to Napoleon's wishes, the Sulpician position was that a return to the pre-thirteenth-century practice could be decreed only by a universal council, rather than by a national synod.[28]

The Gallicanism of Saint-Sulpice was most clearly enunciated by Pierre-Denis Boyer (1776–1842), a director of Saint-Sulpice and a professor of moral theology who became a strong anti-Mennaisian.[29] No doubt Boyer had some personal contact with Lamennais, just as the young intellectual had frequent contacts with several Sulpicians, particularly Simon Bruté, who had encouraged Lamennais's vocation to the priesthood. In the mid-1820s Boyer defended Gallicanism in a polemical pamphlet aimed at Lamennais' ultramontanism to which Lamennais responded with his own published defense.[30] However, the conflict between Lamennais and Boyer was not limited to Gallicanism but also included apologetics. The current apologetic was founded on the Cartesian methodology popularized in the manuals of the seminaries, "and the seminary of St. Sulpice was . . . [this methodology's] venerable guardian in the Church of France."[31] The Cartesian method was evident in Emery's work on Leibniz, which had attempted to deal with unbelievers on their terms by proving that human reason could achieve certitude on the truths of natural religion that formed a rational bridge to the understanding of revealed religion. The distinctive apologetic of Saint-Sulpice was an attempt to demonstrate that the world of natural religion and that of revealed religion were not inherently incompatible. Boyer succinctly defended this apologetic: "Religion is the combination of man's duties towards God. And since these are made known by reason and revelation, religion has long been divided into natural religion and supernatural religion."[32]

In the first two volumes of his four-volume work, *Essai sur l'indifférence en matierè de religion* (1817, 1820, 1823), Lamennais contends that there is no division between natural and supernatural religion and that the individual is not dependent upon reason but rather upon tradition, in which is embedded divine revelation. Tradition, he maintains, is alive with the "general reason" of humanity, the *sensus communis*, the "common consent."[33] Vidler explains Lamennais' notion of tradition thus: "Because tradition is ultimately derived from the testimony of God or from revelation it proves firm ground for human certitude. The primal revelation has 'an infinite certitude' and is 'infallible,' since it is the testimony of God himself. Unlike the individual reason, the general reason of the *sensus communis* cannot err."[34] Lamennais explained to Bruté that the second volume of the *Essai*, which introduces the notion of *sensus communis*, would be the most significant because "it would develop a new system of defending Christianity against all unbelievers and heretics."[35] He did indeed develop a new system, one that unified individual and society, reason and faith, tradition and revelation. Gradually, this evolved into a general critique of French society in which Lamennais embraced democratic principles for society, the principle of separation of church and state, and a progressive social agenda based upon a radical notion of common consent.[36]

Lamennais' liberal political ideas were branded erroneous in 1832 in the encyclical *Mirari Vos*, while his notion that tradition and revelation are embedded in the *sensus communis* was condemned two years later in *Singulari Nos*. Ironically, the dedicated ultramontane was condemned by the papacy on grounds developed by the Gallicans of Saint-Sulpice. Prior to the publication of *Singulari Nos*, the French hierarchy met at Toulouse, where three Sulpicians presented them with a catalog of errors found in the *Essai sur l'indifférence*, particularly as the *Essai* related to the apologetic of the *sensus communis*. Prepared at the instigation of the archbishop of Toulouse, this list of errors was approved by many of the

French bishops and has been referred to as the censure of Toulouse. Sent to Rome in July of 1832, the censure was a catalyst in the papacy's condemnation of Lamennais.[37] The three Sulpicians were well known for their Gallicanism, but they based their case on theology rather than ecclesiology. One of the three Sulpicians at Toulouse was Joseph Carrière, who became superior general from 1850 to 1863. Another Sulpician at Toulouse was Pierre-Denis Boyer, who, as noted earlier, was an ardent opponent of Lamennais. In response to the latter's political liberalism, Boyer wrote a lengthy treatise in which he placed Lamennais in the modern Carbonari movement.[38]

The Mennaisian movement, which reached its peak in the 1830–1831 period with the publication of L'Avenir, identified liberal Catholicism and ultramontanism with religious reform. These reformers viewed Gallicanism as a corrupt alliance between a self-serving state and a defensive episcopate, both of which were incapable of reading the signs of the times. L'Avenir was born in a hopeful period immediately following the revolution of 1830. However, as Alec Vidler notes, "Lamennais' liberalism ceased to be a strategy for an age of revolution and became a fundamental element of faith as a Catholic. Political freedom became for him part of the liberty wherewith Christ had come to make all men free."[39]

The conflict between Saint-Sulpice and the Mennaisan movement was not only a clash of strategies but also an opposition of world views. Jacques-André Emery revised the original Sulpician charism; he melded Olier and Tronson's seventeenth-century reformism, Berulle's spirituality, Bossuet and Fleury's Gallican ecclesiology, and a Cartesian-inspired apologetics. For Emery these were the basic elements of faith, and his revival of their spirit, combined with his own charisms, assured the survival of the Sulpicians during a period of profound upheaval. Hence, liberal Catholic ultramontanism of the Mennaisian movement appeared as antithetical to the spirit and traditions of Saint-Sulpice. In the Sulpician seminaries in France, as well as in the United States, students were nurtured on the religious culture of the second half of the seventeenth century; works emanating from the Mennaisian movement were proscribed as inimical to the piety and order of Saint-Sulpice.[40]

During this period when Saint-Sulpice was struggling to maintain the virtues of French religious culture, there were fewer than two hundred Sulpicians in the community. Indeed, between 1791 and 1852 only thirty-five Sulpicians had served the American church. This disproportionate relationship between size and significance has been a traditional mark of the Sulpician character, one that was consciously cultivated by Olier and his successors. Few diocesan priests were suitable for the life of Sulpician spiritual direction, teaching, and participation in the tightly structured schedule of the seminary. The small size and the large significance of the society were also evident in its centralized structure; the establishment of the American province is a twentieth-century development. Hence, throughout the nineteenth century most of the aspirants spent their Solitude in the vicinity of Paris, where they could experience at first hand the legacy of Olier and Emery and the vast cultural significance of Saint-Sulpice, which was at the crossroads of French ecclesiastic life.

3

Expansion in the New Nation

In the first half of the nineteenth century the Sulpicians maintained Saint Mary's Seminary, founded a short-lived preparatory seminary in southwestern Pennsylvania, sent the students of the latter to Emmitsburg to establish Mount Saint Mary's College, and supplied nine members to missions in Pennsylvania, Indiana, Illinois, Missouri, Kentucky, Ohio, and Michigan. Several Sulpicians and former Sulpicians became archbishops, bishops, and vicars-general of the pioneer American church. No other community of priests could count among its members such notable historic figures as DuBourg, Maréchal, Flaget, David, Bruté, Richard, Dubois, and Eccleston. Besides their involvement in diverse apostolates, the Sulpicians played a vital role in the foundations of three communities of women religious: Saint Elizabeth Seton's Sisters of Charity, Elizabeth Lange's Oblate Sisters of Providence, and Catherine Spalding's Sisters of Charity of Nazareth, Kentucky.

A statistical summary of the Sulpicians in the United States from their origins in 1791 to the closing of Saint Mary's college in 1852 clarifies the society's historical significance. During that period a total number of thirty-five Sulpicians served the church of the United States. Of these only eight were born in the United States. Ten Sulpicians became archbishops and bishops, five left the society but remained priests, and many served as official and unofficial advisers to several bishops at the seven provincial councils of Baltimore. Sulpician history is so intertwined with the major strands of institutional development that one may refer to this period prior to the formation of the immigrant church as one of Sulpician dominance in the making of American Catholic culture.

This chapter deals with the Sulpician response to the diverse needs of the American church, while the next chapter focuses upon the society's work in Baltimore. Both chapters, however, reveal the common character of the society as it expanded beyond the traditional hedge enclosing seminary life and influenced the flow of events within the general religious and cultural streams of the nation.

II

The religious situation in the infant American republic was unprecedented in modern history. Never before had the principles of church-state separation and religious freedom been legally incorporated into the constitution of a nation. Although a few states maintained an established church for a time, gradually there developed an acceptance of denominationalism. The latter entailed an unwritten code whereby each religious group agreed that it should not attempt to directly influence public policy as it had once been customary under the rules governing the privileges of an established church. Religious creed became almost entirely privatized, and religious groups tended to foster a general morality of democratic behavior, later to be known as *civil religion*. Although various sects that behaved contrary to the general consensus, such as the Mormons, did arise, denominationalism is still prevalent today. Because the Catholic church had been, at best, a tolerated minority, it developed its own tradition of privatization, and under the leadership of John Carroll, American Catholics asserted a strong patriotic spirit that embraced the new political principles as a positive factor in the evolution of American Catholicism. Indeed, American Catholics tended to display excessive patriotism in order to dispel any suspicions of their loyalty.[1]

John Carroll was from an aristocratic Maryland family that had supported the American Revolution. He had accompanied Benjamin Franklin, Samuel Chase, and his cousin Charles Carroll of Carrollton on a diplomatic mission to Canada in 1776 to promote support for the American cause. John Carroll was "a reluctant diplomat" who, as a priest, did not feel comfortable on a political mission.[2] Later he applauded the denominationalism and the general impact the revolution had upon religion in America:

> Thanks to the genuine spirit of Christianity, the United States have banished intolerance from their systems of government, and many of them have done the justice to every denomination of Christians which ought to be done to them in all, of placing them on the same footing of citizenship and conferring an equal right of protection in national privileges. . . . Freedom and independence, acquired by the united efforts and cemented by the mingled blood of Protestant and Catholic fellow citizens should be equally enjoyed by all.[3]

Carroll's ecclesiology was a blend of moderate Gallican principles and American experience. In a pamphlet written in response to an anti-Catholic publication by Charles Wharton, a former Maryland Jesuit turned Anglican, Carroll defends papal infallibility, but he places it in the context of conciliarism. He then explains "that there are some divines . . . [who] hold the pope, as Christ's vicar on earth, to be infallible without a council; but with this opinion faith has no concern, every one being at liberty to adopt or reject it, as the reasons for or against may affect him."[4] Carroll's view of episcopal authority also places him in the tradition of moderate Gallicanism: "The body of bishops every where claim a divine right in virtue of their ordination to interpret the *decrees* of councils, and the *ordinances* of the popes."[5] This was akin to the Gallicanism of Bossuet and should not be construed as an attack upon Roman authority but as a defense of the rights of the episcopacy.[6]

Carroll's American experience led him to propose the formation of a national body of clergymen authorized to nominate bishops. He also advocated the use of the vernacular in the liturgy in order to dispel prejudices among Protestants and to provide for a readily understandable worship service for nonliterate Catholics, particularly black slaves and freedmen. He himself was nominated bishop by a body of clergymen in 1788, but his previous appointment as head of the mission in the United States (1784) was actually opposed by several clerical groups and came about primarily through the intervention of Benjamin Franklin. Carroll's plan for a strongly autonomous American church hinged upon the development of a native clergy imbued with the principles of the new republic and adapted to the needs of the infant church. Georgetown College figured prominently in his plans; Saint Mary's Seminary, as noted, was initiated by the Sulpicians. Carroll was receptive to the coming of the Sulpicians only if they would be available to serve in his missions. In the church of John Carroll, twenty Sulpicians, seven of whom became bishops, ministered in diverse ways: in seminaries, colleges, parishes, and in frontier missions.

It was a distinctive period in the history of Saint Sulpice in America, for never before had the society ventured beyond its traditional seminary ministry. But wherever the Sulpicians served, they shared a common ecclesiological perspective with John Carroll. Like their bishop, the Sulpicians were loyal to the papacy, but they moderated that loyalty with a strong conciliarist tradition and deep ties to the national episcopate and to the spirit of a particular culture. Yves Congar notes that such openness to a particular culture is a dimension of the Gallican tradition.

Politically, Bishop Carroll sympathized with the Federalists and abhorred the violence of the leftist factions in the French Revolution. For the most part the Sulpicians had been sympathetic to the monarchy, but they easily adapted to George Washington's American republic. Although the Sulpicians in France opposed the separation of church and state, which was championed by Lamennais, on the grounds that it would mean a return to the religious persecution of the revolution, they accepted the principle in the United States, apparently on the same grounds, namely, that a return to established churches would mean the persecution of the minority nonestablished Catholic church.

The earliest and most dramatic expression of Sulpician American patriotism occurred in Detroit in 1797, the year following the British surrender of the town to General Anthony Wayne. Carroll had appointed Father Michael Levadoux vicar-general of the Michigan Territory and pastor of the parish of Sainte-Anne de Detroit. Up to this time he had ministered to French Catholics in Kaskaskia, Cahokia, and Prairie du Roche. Shortly after his arrival at Detroit, Levadoux, with the permission of the military authority, offered a Te Deum for President Washington on 15 August 1796, the Feast of the Assumption and, perhaps not uncoincidentally, the day upon which John Carroll was consecrated bishop in 1790. Levadoux wrote to Carroll that he and his parishioners sang the Te Deum "in thanksgiving for our union with a free people, and at the same time . . . [to] pray heaven to preserve the hero who so wisely presides over the United States, and who by his victories has delivered us from the fury of a barbarous people. . . . I thought, my Lord, that you would approve of this action on my part."[7] Levadoux's patriotic zeal offended several pro-English Catholics in Detroit and Canada. In February of 1797, he told Carroll that his critics had denounced him to his Sulpician confreres in Montreal "as an enemy of royalty and a veritable *sans-cullotte*."[8]

Levadoux responded to his critics with a eulogy on George Washington's birthday, 22 February 1797. His address, presented at the request of the military authority, was delivered on the Sunday following the president's birthday. Levadoux's hour-long tribute was an impassioned account of Washington's genius as a military and political leader.

With references to scripture and to history, he portrayed the roles of the president in providential terms: Washington "triumphed solely to bring happiness and to win for his people that independence and liberty which are the chief treasure of mankind. How deeply the country is in his debt. How gladly and how devoutly we should gather to thank Heaven for granting us a share in the blessings of the wise government which owes its freedom to this great man!"[9] Levadoux justified his speech to Carroll:

> I confess that I was much perturbed, realizing that the royalists of whom the country is full would not fail to find fault, but I knew that my confrères in Montreal continually sound the praises of the English King and government, and I consider that in similar circumstances I also might speak in favor of the President and government of the United States.[10]

John Carroll's eulogy of December 1799, on the death of George Washington closely resembled Levadoux's of 1797. "We have every reason to expect his glorious memory will be transmitted. . . ; after ages [it] will in some measure never be extinct."[11] Carroll also wrote a special letter on the occasion of the president's death in which he urges his priests to "observe the day [of official mourning] with a reverence expressive of . . . [their] veneration for the deceased Father of this country and founder of its independence. . . ."[12] However, the bishop instructs the clergy to avoid references to scripture "but rather compose an oration, such as might be delivered in an academy, and on a plan bearing some resemblance to that of St. Ambrose on the death of the young Emperor Valentinian who was deprived of life before his initiation into our Church. . . ."[13]

III

Except for that brief period (1801–1804) when Emery seriously considered abandoning the American venture, the Sulpicians viewed their role in the United States as permanent. During the first half of the nineteenth century, Saint Mary's Seminary never had the enrollment to qualify as a major institution of theological education, at least not in the European sense of the term. However, as the first and only seminary exclusively dedicated to training for the sacerdotal life for over forty years, Saint Mary's was indeed highly significant in the history of the Catholic church.

It has been noted that the seminary was a replica of Saint-Sulpice in Paris. The daily routine was detailed down to the minute. The traditional emphasis upon spirituality, particularly mental prayer, seems almost rigorous in contrast to the loose character of the pioneer American church. However, with its stress upon the spiritual exercises, supported by individual spiritual directors and confessors, the Sulpician system was considered extremely important as it provided an internalized spiritual structure for priests called upon to minister in an otherwise unstructured society. Because there were seldom more than twenty-five students enrolled at Saint Mary's during this period prior to mass immigration, its rigid program was tempered by the family-size community of priests and seminarians.

François C. Nagot, superior from 1791 to 1810, was well known for his deep piety. His life of Olier and his translation of a volume of Butler's *Lives of the Saints* illustrate his interest. His "Rule of Life for the Seminary" was a handwritten document that includes schedules for the daily routine and for retreats for seminarians and priests, as well as maxims for the spiritual life.[14] Hence Saint Mary's, like its French model, was not limited to intellectual and spiritual formation of seminarians but was also viewed as a continuous source of spirituality for the American priests throughout their lives.

Nagot's daily schedule provided for only two one-hour classes a day, one in "Scholastique" (dogmatic) theology and one in moral theology. Twice a week there were two conferences on scripture and two on the Roman ritual; three nights a week there was a brief conference on ascetics.[15] Since conferences were designed for the spiritual edification of the seminarians, these subjects were not in the educational curriculum; scripture was not treated scientifically until late in the century. There were no textbooks, but the theology classes were dependent upon the multivolume work of Louis Bailly, which was strongly Gallican, and emphasized the four articles of Bossuet. An 1811 list of new books requested for the library at Saint Mary's reveals an interest in the classic works on scripture, patrology, canon law, and church history; among the authors of the last, the Gallican Claude Fleury was prominent.[16] Individual Sulpicians had their personal libraries shipped to Baltimore; Simon Bruté possessed nearly 5,000 books, and the libraries of Gabriel Richard and Benedict Flaget were also renowned for their size and diversity. John Tracy Ellis includes these Sulpicians among the "highly culturated French priests who exercized a strong and uplifting influence upon the intellectual life of the small and beleaguered Catholic Body."[17]

Because Nagot was never very robust, during the last ten years of Nagot's life (1806–1816), Jean-Marie Tessier became solely responsible for teaching both theology courses to the twelve students enrolled at the seminary. Bishop Carroll, who was critical of Tessier's pedagogical style, told Antoine Garnier, a close friend and confidant, that Tessier was "fully competent to the task of forming them in the principles of sound morality and doctrine," but because he possessed a "narrow range . . . of litterary [sic] pursuits" and because he was immersed in the "temporal concerns" of the seminary Tessier was unfit to inspire "that love and ardor for study and general information which is requisite for young men to hold converse with and be employed amongst the great variety of nations, languages, religions and characters, so observable in this country." Carroll also told Garnier that Nagot was still presiding as a spiritual director: "the excellent and respectable Mr. Nagot enjoys his solitude, and seems to be himself once more."[18] Carroll appears to have captured the contrary characters of Tessier and Nagot; the former has been consistently portrayed as an unimaginative, practical man with an eye for minute detail, while the latter's aloofness and mystical qualities were the subject of frequent contemporary commentary.

The dominant personality among the Baltimore Sulpicians was Louis William DuBourg. Carroll was deeply impressed by the founder and president of Saint Mary's College. He wrote to Charles Plowden,

> One of the Sulpician priests, who is a man of very pleasing manners, of an active and towering genius, named DuBourg, has formed a college in this town. . . . It contains far more Protestants than Catholics. Some of the rigid Sulpicians shake their heads at this (to them) seeming departure from their Institute, but I believe that the general effect will be beneficial.[19]

In an earlier letter, Carroll notes that Nagot was apprehensive about DuBourg's "enterprises and taste for expense," but he adds that the Sulpician superior had become "fully convinced of the merits of St. Mary's College and his other pursuits."[20]

Saint Mary's College achieved a high enrollment after it had opened its doors to students of all nationalities and creeds. In October 1804, a new college building, which symbolized the college's separate existence from the seminary, was completed, and a year later the Sulpicians received Emery's permission to sell some of their Baltimore property to fund the construction of a chapel. Designed by Maximilian Godefroy (c. 1765–c. 1845), a French émigré and professor of civil and military architecture and fine arts at Saint Mary's College,[21] the chapel was the first neo-Gothic ecclesiastical building in the United States. Benjamin Latrobe, the architect of the Cathedral of the Assumption in Baltimore and an associate of Godefroy, praised the chapel's "exquisite beauty."[22] Seminarians and students of the college attended liturgy in the upper chapel, while the French-speaking whites and blacks used the lower level as a parish center. Bishop Carroll consecrated the chapel on 16 June 1808, and Elizabeth Seton recorded the experience: "The organ's solemn peal, then the burst of the choir. This is the moment of consecration of Mr. DuBourg's chapel. We entered without a word; prostrate in an instant. Human nature could scarcely bear it. Your imagination can never conceive the splendor—the glory of the scene."[23] For the next year Carroll, DuBourg, and the Sulpicians figured prominently in Elizabeth Seton's transition from struggling widow and schoolteacher to the founder of the first American community of women religious.

Mrs. Seton came from a notable Episcopalian family in New York. She was drawn to Catholicism in 1803 when she and her family were in Italy in the vain hope that her husband's health might improve. The widowed Mrs. Seton came into the church in New York on 4 March 1805. By the time DuBourg met her (November 1806), she was groping for ways to regularize her prayer life and to earn a living to support herself and her five children. Within a short time DuBourg encouraged her to move to Baltimore. In the spring of 1808 he submitted a detailed proposal to Mrs. Seton. In a letter to a friend she describes the plan: "Mr. DuBourg . . . has offered to give me a formal grant of a lot of ground situated close to the College, which is out of the town and in a very healthy situation. . . ." DuBourg also promised to provide her with students and to enroll her two sons—then in attendance at Georgetown—at Saint Mary's College at a reduced tuition.[24]

Elizabeth Seton desired to live a vowed religious life but had to balance that desire with her duties as a mother. The move with her three daughters to Baltimore where she could be close to her two sons in Washington, D.C., appeared to satisfy both needs. Within three weeks of her arrival, she wrote, "You would scarcely believe the change I experienced in my manner of life since I am in my new home, after so long a period of trouble and confusion to lead a life of regularity and comparative repose."[25] She was deeply grateful to the Sulpicians, who "received [the Seton family] as their adopted charge." She was also grateful to be so near to the chapel, which she viewed as "the most elegant in America," and where there was "Mass from daylight to eight . . . Vespers and Benediction every evening."[26] Her spiritual director was the Sulpician Pierre Babad, whom she referred to as her patriarch. One of Elizabeth Seton's biographers remarks on the relationship between Babad and Mrs. Seton: "His temperament was like hers, romantic, poetic and tender; and like all souls that have disciplined such a temperament, he burned as it were with a pure white flame of divine love."[27] Babad apparently possessed what has been called "the gift of tears," held to be symbolic of a deeply mystical state. On one occasion when Seton witnessed his tears as he "dispensed the Sacred Passover" to first communicants, she was so moved that she too sobbed aloud.[28]

Shortly after Mrs. Seton took up residence in the shadow of Saint Mary's chapel, she attracted four other women to join her in a life of prayer and schoolwork. Encouraged by Father Babad, Father DuBourg, and Bishop Carroll, she and her little band professed to Carroll, for the first time on 25 March 1809, their vows of poverty, chastity, and obedience. Some weeks later, on 2 June 1809, dressed in religious garb, they attended the liturgy in the college chapel. The brave band, self-sacrificing as they were, were very much aware that their place of residence was inadequate; they were aware, too, that their financial resources were even more inadequate. In this crisis, Samuel Cooper, a wealthy convert who had entered Saint Mary's Seminary in 1808, presented Mother Seton with $10,000 for the purchase of property suitable for a convent and a school. Much to the dismay of DuBourg and Carroll, Cooper insisted that the property be located in Emmitsburg, a mountain village fifty miles north of Baltimore. Once again the story of Mother Seton converges with a Sulpician institution; a few months after the Seton community established Saint Joseph's of Emmitsburg, the Sulpicians opened Mount Saint Mary's College just two miles down the road.

At the origin of Mount Saint Mary's was the Sulpician desire to establish a proparatory seminary to nurture vocations among the Catholic youth in Maryland and Pennsylvania. In his written "Counsels . . . for the Baltimore Sulpicians," Jacques-André Emery envisions the time when it would be necessary to establish a community of philosophy and classics students "separated from the community of theologians."[29] The foundation of the first Sulpician preparatory seminary received its impetus from Joseph Harent, a French émigré and a close friend of the Baltimore Sulpicians who had provided them with the use of his 250-acre farm in Adams County, Pennsylvania, during the time when he was in France on family business. Harent had used the house on the farm as a small boarding school for boys and had called the house Friendly Hall. The farm was located in an area known as Pigeon Hill. In September 1803, shortly after Harent's departure for France, thirty-two members of the community of La Trappe—priests, brothers, novices, and aspirants to the Trappists—arrived at Saint Mary's Seminary in Baltimore. The superior, who had remained in France, was a former penitent of Father Nagot; the Sulpician superior arranged for them to live at Harent's farm. After nearly two years it became apparent that Pigeon Hill could not support so many monks, so they moved to a site about forty miles from Bardstown, Kentucky, a Catholic settlement on the frontier.[30] With the Harent property vacant and with DuBourg's college producing few vocations, Nagot decided to establish a preparatory seminary at Pigeon Hill.

After recruiting ten students from the area, Nagot opened the seminary on 15 August 1806, the sixteenth anniversary of the consecration of Carroll as the first bishop in the United States. Nagot assured Carroll that his seminary was not in competition with Georgetown as the families of his students "either would not or could not place them in any other institution."[31] The bishop wrote to Ambrose Maréchal,

> Undoubtedly you know that the venerable Mr. Nagot, no longer being able to bear the heat of Baltimore, nor the attention necessary to the government of the Seminary, has retired to the farm of Mr. Harent near Conewago, where he has formed an establishment for a dozen pupils, destined after this to complete their studies at the seminary in Baltimore. He enjoys there a health and tranquility which sweeten his last days. . . .[32]

With the revenue from the farm and a $1,600 subsidy from the Sulpicians of Baltimore, the new institution could meet expenses. For a short time Father Jean Dilhet, a Sulpician with mission experience, assisted Nagot; he also relied upon two seminarians from Saint Mary's for his faculty. Nagot describes his hopes for the new seminary to a young Sulpician at Baltimore:

> Rejoice with me, you who are not so much the pupil as the flower of our seminary. May all you confreres who flourish in our spiritual orchard while awaiting the abundant harvest in the holy garden of the Church of Baltimore, rejoice with me over the prospect of seeing born, first tender children, then youths who, blessed by God and aided by all the efforts of our zeal, will enter our seminary after being nourished here on the milk of piety and the honey of pure doctrine. According to the hope I nourish in my heart, they will find there models of science and sanctity according to which they will attempt to form themselves. And so they will be rendered worthy to be called by our venerated and illustrious Prelate his joy and crown, which he does not hesitate to term you yourselves.[33]

During the first year (1806–1807) at Pigeon Hill, DuBourg visited Emmitsburg, where Father Jean Dubois had purchased and developed property for a retreat house for missionary priests. In April 1807 this property was, at the suggestion of DuBourg, given to the Sulpicians for a preparatory seminary; at the same time Dubois, who had for two years desired to become a Sulpician, was accepted into the society. Jean Dubois was a Parisian, born in 1764 and ordained by special dispensation at the early age of twenty-three. Trained by the Oratorians, Dubois's first and only assignment was to the parish of Saint-Sulpice, where sixty priests ministered to ninety thousand communicants. However, his primary ministry was chaplain to the Daughters of Charity, who ran a hospital for both the mentally and physically ill.[34]

Sympathetic to the ideals of the French Revolution, Dubois would not take the oath in support of the Civil Constitution of the Clergy of 1791. To provide for safe emigration to the United States, he appealed to the Marquis de Lafayette, whom he had met at Saint-Sulpice, where the marquis' wife frequently attended services. After receiving a letter of introduction from her, Dubois fortunately happened upon the leading Jacobin, Maximilien de Robespierre, a former classmate of his at the Collège Louis-le-Grand. Robespierre proved loyal to his friend and supplied Dubois with the necessary papers for his safe emigration from France. When he arrived in Norfolk, a letter from Lafayette gave him entrée to several prominent Virginian families, including those of James Monroe and Patrick Henry; the latter instructed Dubois in English.[35] Carroll appointed him to missions in Norfolk and Richmond. Later he established a church in Frederick, Maryland, from which he served the neighboring villages. He had been drawn to the Sulpicians, with whom he shared many mutual friends in Paris, and at Saint Mary's he made several retreats. He had sought entrance into the society as early as 1805, but Nagot and his assembly deferred to the superior general for permission to accept Dubois. DuBourg wrote to Emery on Dubois's behalf, to which the superior replied, "You tell me, my dear DuBourg, a propos of Father Dubois' vocation to St. Sulpice, that he is more fit than you? I do not know him, but this is a fact: that the life of a Sulpician in his strict and ordinary melieu is certainly not for you."[36] However, Emery approved Dubois on the condition of final approval by the assembly in Baltimore. No action was taken until April 1807, after DuBourg and Dubois had made the arrangement for establishing a preparatory seminary in Emmitsburg. Dubois later recalled that he had agreed to DuBourg's plan "on the condition that I would not have to conduct it [i.e., the seminary] and I promised to give the land to St. Sulpice of which I hoped then to become a member."[37]

After Dubois received word of his acceptance into the society, he was directed to return to Emmitsburg to develop the property for the seminary, acting as the "agent of Father DuBourg who was to furnish the funds and give the orders."[38] By the time Elizabeth Seton arrived in Emmitsburg in June 1809, DuBourg, with characteristic financial mismanagement, had incurred heavy indebtedness—he had promised to pay a large annuity to a Catholic couple who had turned over their farm, with its slaves and all its equipment, to the nascent seminary. Moreover, Harent had returned to his farm in the spring of 1809, which meant that the eighteen students at Pigeon Hill had to be transferred to Emmitsburg before accommodations were ready. DuBourg had also sent Mother Seton to Emmitsburg before a proper facility was completed. DuBourg's interest in the construction of Mount Saint Mary's Seminary gave way to his concern for Mother Seton's little community, to whom Dubois had given his own log cabin until their new home was completed. While Dubois and the students were boarders in the Catholic homes of Emmitsburg, DuBourg became involved in a growing conflict with the Sisters of Charity.

From their origins, the sisters had been under the authority of the bishop and the superior of the Sulpicians. Nagot, who had accompanied DuBourg and Cooper to Emmitsburg prior to the arrival of the community, was, in the words of Mother Seton, "going to take charge of our community and reside in Emmitsburg."[39] However, poor health prevented the move, and DuBourg was appointed superior. One of his first directives was to prohibit the sisters from any correspondence with Father Babad, who had been Mother Seton's former spiritual director and confessor.[40] In response to an appeal from DuBourg's directive, Carroll supported DuBourg. Earlier he had noticed that Babad was unfit "for the regular routine of a seminary" and that he possessed "a proneness to oppose the views and measure of the heads of the Seminary and the College. . . ."[41] In September 1809, shortly after this incident, DuBourg resigned as superior of the convent; his resignation, as he later recalled, was probably his excessive sensitivity, which made incompatible his roles as confidant and as superior. To replace DuBourg, Nagot appointed Jean-Baptiste David, who had been confessor to two of the recently professed sisters.

Father David (1761–1841) had spent seven years in the missions in Maryland and had taught philosophy at Georgetown before his appointment as superior of the Sisters of Charity. David's stern style of authority rankled Mother Seton (he interfered with internal affairs of the school), but some of the sisters, who had him as a confessor, preferred him to Babad or DuBourg. With divisiveness threatening the community, there was speculation that Elizabeth Seton would be replaced as mother superior.[42] The conflict subsided, however, as more pressing matters occupied the attention of the pioneer community, and in September 1810 Carroll notified Mother Seton that David would be leaving for Kentucky. The following summer, Dubois was appointed superior. At the request of Carroll, Dubois translated and adapted the rule of Vincent de Paul's Daughters of Charity for the new American community and clarified the lines of authority. Shortly after he received the pallium as archbishop, Carroll expressed to Mother Seton his satisfaction with the rule and his desire that "every allowance . . . be made, not only to the Sisters generally, but to each one in particular, which can serve to give quiet to their conscience." He was also gratified that a spirit of charity, rather than of rigid legality, prevailed within the Daughters of St. Joseph and the Society of St. Sulpice; I mean that their interests, administration, and government are not the same, not at least under the same control. Only their designated Sulpician superior possessed any authority, except (on very rare and uncommon occasions) the Superior of the Seminary in Baltimore, [could intervene] but not his society.[43]

Since the American sisters limited themselves to schools while the French Daughters of Charity were primarily involved in hospital ministry, Carroll did not envision a union between the Daughters of Charity and the Seton communities for at least a century. Actually a little less than forty years were to pass before the union was consummated.

Previous to her arrival in Emmitsburg, Mother Seton did not have a high regard for Dubois, but by 1811 she was gratified to have him as a superior. He did not meddle in school affairs, and his many other concerns precluded undue interference of any sort. According to Seton, Dubois was "an economist and full of details dictated by habits of prudence," and his spirituality reflected his character.[44] However, Simon Bruté, another Sulpician who, like Babad, was a kindred soul to Mother Seton, had arrived in Baltimore in 1810 and made his first visit to Emmitsburg in 1811; the following year he was assigned to assist Dubois at Mount Saint Mary's.

As noted earlier, Simon Bruté was raised in Saint-Malo (1779), where he developed close friendships with the Lamennais brothers. After studies in Rennes and Paris he was awarded a degree in medicine in 1803. Although he received the first prize from the medical faculty in Paris, he turned aside a career in medicine and entered the seminary the year of his graduation. Ordained in 1808, he taught philosophy at the seminary in his home diocese, of Rennes. Eager to serve in the American mission, Bruté was assigned to Baltimore in 1810. Although few of his confreres shared his sensibilities, no Sulpician was so thoroughly immersed in the romantic spirit of the age as was Simon Bruté.

With a blend of tender piety and strong intellectual acumen, Bruté appealed to sensitive spirits such as Mother Seton and to deeply scholarly men such as Francis Patrick Kenrick. When Bruté was assigned to Mount Saint Mary's, Bishop Carroll feared that Bruté would become too absorbed in the needs of the Sisters of Charity. In that regard Carroll informed Tessier:

His tender piety will deservedly beget . . . confidence in him: insensibly the Sisters will multiply their prayers and intreaties to confer with him on their spiritual concerns. . . . If . . . [I] or other Superiors deny the indulgence, discontents will ensue. Mr. Bruté himself, from the purest of motives, may become their advocate. His talents, now so useful, and promising . . . will be diverted from those principal objects, which have hitherto engaged . . . [him] to fill the office of a director of some devout women.[45]

Carroll referred to the dignity of that calling and alluded to Francis de Sales and Vincent de Paul, but, in his pioneer archdiocese, he particularly appreciated intellectual abilities. "Mr. Bruté should go to the Seminary [i.e., Mount Saint Mary's] . . . [but I hope] that he may never be employed with the sisterhood without necessity."[46]

Bruté did indeed become a spiritual director for Mother Seton, but it was based upon mutual needs: "You whom I like to call mother . . . you have so well helped me better to know, yes, better still, a priest of his as I am to know my happiness and desire, but alas, [I] so vainly desire to impart the same to others to know and love and say Jesus. . . ."[47] Bruté and Mother Seton remained close until her death in 1821. He viewed her as a saint and once remarked, "There could not be greater elevation, purity, and love for God, for heaven and for supernatural and eternal things, then were to be found in her."[48]

During Bruté's first year at Emmitsburg, relations between Dubois and the Sulpicians in Baltimore became critical. This ultimately led to dissolution of the relationship and the separation of Dubois and Bruté from Saint Sulpice. The 1812 crisis was primarily financial; Dubois could not liquidate the debts, particularly the $1,000 annuity owed to the Elder family, that had been brought on by DuBourg's cavalier spending. In November 1812, Dubois wrote a long report to Ambrose Maréchal, whom the Sulpician assembly had appointed to investigate the situation at Mount Saint Mary's. Baltimore decided to help Dubois but placed several restrictions upon him. Tessier, who officially became superior upon the resignation of Nagot in 1810 (he had been superior in all but name since Nagot's departure to Pigeon Hill in 1806), seems to have treated Mount Saint Mary's as at best a probationary institution that had to prove itself as a loyal daughter of Saint Sulpice. On the other hand, Dubois, who had never been a director at a Sulpician seminary and who, as a missionary, had been completely autonomous for many years, viewed his superior at Baltimore as unappreciative of the needs of Mount Saint Mary's, particularly of the need for a Sulpician faculty at Emmitsburg. Tessier was adamant that the mountain school must limit its enrollment to students aspiring to the priesthood.

From the outset Dubois had accepted a few nonseminarian students, the sons of Emmitsburg families or orphans placed in his care. The general economic depression of the nation, brought on by a severe drop in foreign trade during the war between England and France and then the War of 1812, certainly exacerbated the conflict between Baltimore and Emmitsburg. Both were attempting to pay off debts incurred by DuBourg, who in 1812 was appointed administrator of the diocese of Louisiana (and bishop in 1815). Saint Mary's College was still heavily in debt, but according to the legislative act (1807) providing for a public lottery to raise funds for the college, it was required to remain open for thirty years. With the Emmitsburg debt increasing because of a building program to accommodate a growing enrollment, and with Dubois's refusal to limit enrollment to seminarians, the Sulpicians of Baltimore decided in 1818 to suppress Mount Saint Mary's, but negotiations continued.[49]

Over the years, the unavailability of Sulpicians or other priests to teach at the college compelled Dubois to employ the older boys as teachers; he himself taught them philosophy and theology rather than send them immediately to Baltimore for their studies. In effect Mount Saint Mary's became a mixed college rather than a seminary for exclusive clerical education; more importantly, it became an ad hoc major seminary, though for several years some of the seminarians at Emmitsburg spent their last years at the Baltimore seminary, and some even went to Saint-Sulpice in Paris. Tessier never condoned Mount Saint Mary's retention of candidates, while Archbishop Maréchal only tolerated it as a temporary measure (1820) for those poor students for whom there was no free bursary at Saint Mary's in Baltimore. The practice continued, however, and in 1824, when Antoine Garnier, the new superior general, received detailed accounts of the situation, he and his council issued a mandate to Dubois that Mount Saint Mary's must return to its stated purpose as a minor seminary; Saint Sulpice would not support two major seminaries and two colleges in the archdiocese of Baltimore. Bruté, who had left the presidency of Saint Mary's College in 1818 to join Dubois without Tessier's permission, went to France to plead the case of Mount Saint Mary's. There he argued that to liquidate the debt it would be necessary to appoint qualified older students as teachers who would be taught philosophy and theology by Dubois and himself. Paris rejected the proposal, and in January 1826, Mount Saint Mary's was removed from the rolls as a Sulpician institution, and Dubois and Bruté were dismissed from the society. However, that same year, Maréchal, with the acquiescence of Tessier and three of his confreres, permitted Mount Saint Mary's to remain open for five years as a major seminary and a mixed college.

Over the next several years there were attempts to reconcile the two communities. Bruté was particularly persistent in these efforts and never really considered himself spiritually separated from Saint Sulpice. In August 1826, Dubois was appointed bishop of New York, and Bruté became bishop of Vincennes in 1834. By this time, Mount Saint Mary's had been incorporated by the state of Maryland and was fairly well established as both a seminary and a college. Even the Sulpician archbishop, Samuel Eccleston, recognized the permanent status of Mount Saint Mary's. Established as a Sulpician *petit séminaire* to feed candidates to Saint Mary's in Baltimore, the college proved to be a feeder for its own seminary. In 1829 there were seventeen seminarians studying philosophy and theology at the mountain, while in Baltimore there were only ten theologians.

From the vantage point of Baltimore, the creation of the new seminary was an act of defiance, but from Dubois's point of view it was an absolute necessity for survival. Both Tessier and Dubois were very practical and stubborn men, but whereas Dubois developed a pragmatic attitude as a missionary priest, Tessier's attitude was imbued with attachment to the Sulpician rule. According to Dubois, Tessier was "only a shuttle in the hands of those who make him act." Dubois wrote to Garnier that the "whole trouble comes from the fact that there is not a firm head as leader, and that he who makes the loudest outcry, is the one who prevails."[50]

At times the conflict between the two institutions filtered down to the students. For example, Charles Constantine Pise (1801–1866), who was to become a prominent educator, editor, and historian, was sent from Mount Saint Mary's to the Baltimore seminary, where he felt subjected to what he termed the "prejudiced junta." He wrote to Bruté of his

> disgust with the conduct of the gentlemen of Baltimore; . . . one of them was heard to say the Mountain [Mount Saint Mary's] was a *good tavern* for young men while it was impossible for discipline . . . ; another called it the congregation of *outcasts* . . . ; [Such behavior] deserves our most feeling commiseration, and while they insult we must revenge ourselves with a polite and Christian disregard for them.[51]

Although Tessier and others considered Dubois an embarrassment to the society and urged Garnier to expel him, Dubois nevertheless made a retreat with his former confreres immediately prior to his consecration as bishop of New York. He also sent his seminarians to Saint Mary's (Baltimore) where they would be free of the distractions so characteristic of the mixed college-seminary at the mountain. Dubois wrote to Tessier regarding one of his student's education at Saint Mary's that the Sulpicians should instruct him in "plain chant as will enable him to sing Mass and Vespers with decency when at the altar. It is a remarkable circumstance that the Jesuits neglect altogether that part of ecclesiastical education so that I can get no service for High Mass from any of them."[52] Dubois and the Sulpicians had achieved a reconciliation; the bishop obviously respected the Sulpician stress upon the *esprit ecclésiastique*.

IV

Benoit Joseph Flaget (1763–1850), the first bishop of Bardstown, Kentucky, was very close to Bruté and Dubois and sympathized with them in their struggle with Baltimore. He too had experienced the kind of problems endemic to the relations between missionary and central authority, but he was a seasoned frontier priest by the time he was appointed bishop in 1808.[53] Flaget was from the farming district in Auvergne. After he decided to enter the Sulpicians in 1785, he spent three years in the Solitude because he was too young for ordination. He developed a deep loyalty to Saint Sulpice that endured throughout his many years on the mission. A few months after Flaget's arrival in the United States, Carroll assigned him to the French community at Vincennes. For nearly three years he remained in that post on the banks of the Wabash River. Flaget appears to have had a joyful disposition and a keen practical sense. At Vincennes he purchased a farm, taught young boys various trades, built a loom for the domestic production of cloth, acted as a probate judge, and nursed the sick. Gradually, through his catechism classes and his example, attendance increased substantially. He was also active among the Indian tribes, particularly the Miami. In 1795, Carroll recalled him to become professor and vice-president of Georgetown College. Three years later Flaget joined Babad and DuBourg in Havana, where they unsuccessfully attempted to establish a Sulpician college. Sickness, and later a commitment to tutoring, prevented him from returning to Baltimore until 1801. When he did return, he brought three Cuban students for Saint Mary's College, where he taught until he was appointed bishop of Bardstown on 8 April 1808. Fearing that his acceptance of the office would preclude his remaining a Sulpician (the society had a rule against its members accepting ecclesiastical dignities), Flaget resisted his appointment. He even traveled to Paris to enlist the aid of his superiors in his struggle against the appointment. However, Emery told him to accept the position on the grounds of obedience but allowed him to remain a Sulpician. As a symbol of Emery's high regard for Flaget, he presented him with Olier's chalice.

Upon Flaget's return to Baltimore, he was consecrated bishop by Carroll on 4 November 1810. In his letter nominating Flaget as bishop, Carroll remarks that the forty-four-year-old Sulpician was "sensitive in his devotion to God, gracious in manner, and sufficiently versed in theological learning."[54] Carroll mentioned that Stephen Badin, who had resided in Kentucky since his ordination in 1793, was considered too severe a confessor to be consecrated. Moreover, his severity had antagonized the Dominicans. Carroll told his old Sulpician friend Antoine Garnier that only Flaget

> will so effectually reconcile all and put an end to the heartburnings in the State. . . . You are too well acquainted with his amiable character, his piety (and) humility . . . not to believe that he [i.e., Flaget] would contribute wonderfully to the increase of religion, and sanctity of manners; and that by his exertions, spiritual assistance would be obtained for the numerous and destitute flocks of Fort Vincennes, the Illinois and the immense country between the Ohio and the Lakes, which is now filling with inhabitants.[55]

Of the four suffragan dioceses established in 1808—Philadelphia, Boston, New York, and Bardstown—only Bardstown encompassed such a vast area.

In May 1811, Flaget, Jean-Baptiste David; Guy Ignatius Chabrat, a French seminarian who had spent his subdiaconate year at Saint Mary's Seminary; and two other seminarians recruited from France left Baltimore for Bardstown. In a letter to Bruté, David describes the foundation of the Kentucky seminary-community on board a flatboat floating down the Ohio River from Pittsburgh to Louisville.

> The roof is high enough not to oblige anyone to stoop. Imagine on this confortable Ark Monsignor Flaget, who is its life and delight, together with three priests; for you must know that Father Edward Fenwick joined us at Pittsburgh, and in giving us a pleasant, useful travelling companion, he has freed us of the discomfort (which they say is extreme) of having a horse on board since he sent our horse over land by two of his nephews who are taking his own horses. You know the three others who are accompanying us and the three servants. Imagine, then, this family living in the greatest harmony (with a good-natured pilot who speaks little, but who is always in a good humor and very obliging, etc.), performing our regular exercises; edifying one another, cheering one another, and not refusing to put our hands to work, all knowing how to man the oars; keeping watch in turn; with book in hand marking all the places we pass; counting faithfully the hundreds of miles passed and the hundreds still to go; making guesses as to the probable hour of our arrival in Louisville, and so on and so forth, and you will be able to form some idea of our present situation.
>
> You might, perhaps, like to know the life we lead and the rule we follow on board. I shall satisfy your charitable curiosity on that subject. The Bishop and I rise at four o'clock, the Community at four thirty. We have prayers and meditation, as at the Seminary. Then we say Mass, each in turn, having found it too inconvenient to say four, one after another. Sundays, however, having gone to confession, each of us says Mass. After Mass we read, row, study, etc. At eight o'clock we eat a little cracker and drink something. About nine we recite the

Little Hours in choir. It is the very young Cathedral of Bardstown that is beginning as the mustard seed. . . . At noon we say the Regina Coeli and make our particular examen. Then, Vespers; at four o'clock, the Rosary; at five, Matins and Lauds; at six, spiritual reading for half an hour, then supper; at eight thirty, prayers and reading of the subject for meditation, and then to bed and perfect sleep until it is time to rise again. I shall not tell you that the hours marked out above are always exactly observed, but the exercises are not at all neglected. . . .

All this, dear friend, doesn't make us forget our dear friends in Baltimore. In spirit we are often at the Seminary, and our conversations turn frequently to that dear home—At this hour they are doing such and such a thing at the Seminary.[56]

After receiving this letter, Bruté reported to Emery:

Our Kentucky missionaries have reached Louisville, after a most happy and holy voyage on the Ohio. What letters from Monsignor Flaget and M. David! You would think you were reading Chateaubriand, but here is a delightful reality. A chapel permanently erected in the boat, Mass every day and four on Sundays and all communicate, on the waters in the midst of the forests! Here and there as they pass on, the beginnings of civilization appear, now a few homes, again a small village and occasionally towns already half built with sign of industry and greater activity. All hearts are full of hope in that ark of safety, the regular exercises are held as in a seminary, hour by hour, from rising until retiring. Behold from Ascension Day, when they embarked from Pittsburgh until the 4th of June, when they landed in Louisville, the life and preparation of our modern Apostles![57]

Flaget's presence quieted a controversy between the Dominicans and Badin, one that entailed conflicting attitudes toward social morality, with Badin the rigorist. Within a year after his arrival, Flaget and Badin were locked in a struggle over property rights, a conflict that was never fully resolved until Badin left the diocese to return to France in 1819. He returned to the United States in 1828, after a brief stay at the Dominican novitiate in Rome. For the next twenty-five years he was a missionary in Michigan, Illinois, and Indiana. (His property in South Bend was given to Father Edward F. Sorin, C.S.C., for Sorin's college of Notre Dame.) Badin died in 1853 in Cincinnati, sixty years after he was ordained by Bishop Carroll.[58]

Flaget's mission journeys which often lasted a year or more, mark him as the episcopal Daniel Boone, blazing trails of evangelization throughout the Midwest and old Northwest. In his first report to Rome in 1815, Flaget notes that in Kentucky there were ten priests and nineteen churches, most of which were log cabins.[59] When he died in 1850, there were fifty-five priests and forty-six churches, two of which were cathedrals (Bardstown and the newly completed cathedral in Louisville).[60] Flaget's pride was his seminary, which was headed by Father David whom he described as "a priest of the Society of St. Sulpice (of which I too am happy to be a member) who, on account of his zeal for ecclesiastical discipline which he imbibed from that Society, is very commendable and dear to me."[61]

Saint Thomas Seminary, housed on the plantation where Flaget lived until it was moved to the town of Bardstown in 1819, was, in the words of Flaget, "a small miserable log house."[62] In the Sulpician tradition, Flaget and David both shared in the community life of the seminary. In September 1821, Francis Patrick Kenrick arrived from Rome, where he had been a student at the Urban College of the Propaganda Fide. In 1830, he was appointed coadjutor to the strife-torn diocese of Philadelphia, where he remained until 1851 when he succeeded to the see of Baltimore. Shortly after Kenrick arrived at Bardstown, David wrote to Bishop Joseph Rosati, C.M. of Saint Louis:

> We have received in the seminary a young Irish priest, who was sent to us by Propaganda, a model of sweetness, of humility, and an excellent theologian, knowing both Greek and Hebrew. We have retained him in the seminary where he has charge of the class of theology and of several classes in the college. His instructions are very solid, very apostolic, very enjoyable, and very impressive.[63]

Over the years Flaget was deeply disappointed that his superior general, Antoine Duclaux, seemingly influenced by Tessier and Maréchal, would not recognize his seminary as belonging to Saint Sulpice. David, assisted by Chabrat (until 1814), adjusted the seminary routine in accord with the frontier way of life. Besides the regular Sulpician exercises and hours of classes, each seminarian did manual work for three hours on each weekday afternoon. Instead of the traditional recreation, which Flaget referred to as "walking or jostling . . . [the students gathered] around M. David, who translates for the young men the most interesting parts of letters, after listening to the edifying bits each one contributes freely and gaily by voicing his own reactions."[64] This practice of manual labor and informal spontaneous discussions were such drastic departures from the rule that the Sulpician authorities could not embrace Saint Thomas as a daughter seminary. Flaget admitted that the piety of the seminary was "not on a par" with the level of its academic studies, telling Bruté, "The Americans, in general are cold; to try to find in them the French fervor would be to ask a miracle. . . ."[65]

The seminarians of Kentucky had had little or no previous education. They were too poor to pay for their clerical training. Hence, they blended general and theological education in their frontier seminary. Yet in a letter to Garnier, Flaget defends his pioneer institution. "You tell me, finally with M. Maréchal, that St. Sulpice will never adopt as a seminary one where are taught at the same time the doctrines of the Incarnation and the *Fables of Phaedrus*."[66] Although the separation of profane and sacred in the Plato curriculum was the tradition in Paris, Flaget remarks, "I scarcely know whether this will hold much force *for America*." The bishop was willing to compromise; he would establish a preparatory seminary for rhetoric, history, languages, and so on and combine philosophy and theology into an enlarged *grand séminaire*, which was roughly equivalent to the six-six program later adopted at the Third Plenary Council of Baltimore.

Flaget's letter predicts that "in a few years our men of Baltimore . . . will be animated by the same spirit [of adaptation to American ways] and will follow the same plans of operation." He urges Garnier to consider this plan and to confer with Duclaux. If the seminary were approved, Flaget would either adopt the rule of the Canadian Sulpicians, which allowed for diverse Sulpician apostolates, or devise a rule specifically for the American frontier, one founded, he said, "on our own experience and adapted to the places and customs of the peoples with whom we live. This rule would be sent to you so that you could add or curtail what seems reasonable to you. Then, after you sanction it, it would become the Constitution of the [Sulpician] missionaries of Missouri."[67]

Flaget's plans were not approved for several reasons. The expansion of Saint Sulpice into Emmitsburg was at this time (1816) entering a precarious phase; Saint Mary's College was heavily in debt; Sulpicians were reopening seminaries in post-Napoleonic France; Sulpician Superior General Duclaux was a cautious leader; and, perhaps most importantly, there was a strong consensus that the rule was sacred and that to deviate drastically from it would be "non-Sulpician." During these years Flaget was extremely dependent upon his Sulpician confrere Jean-Baptiste David, not only as director of his seminary, but also as a confidant and adviser. Thus when Tessier attempted to recall David to Baltimore, or when there were rumors that David was to be made bishop of Philadelphia, Flaget responded with vigorous opposition.

David's brief experience as superior of the Sisters of Charity and his generally strong interest in spiritual direction led him to preach on the beauties of the religious life with the hope of stimulating vocations and ultimately establishing a religious community. By June of 1813, six women had entered what later became the Sisters of Charity of Nazareth; the title derived from David's devotion to the "hidden life of Jesus."[68] The Nazareth group gave some thought to joining Elizabeth Seton's community, but the latter was still too young to spare someone to go to Kentucky as novice-mistress. Hence, the Nazareth community views Jean-Baptiste David and Mother Catherine Spalding, one of the first sisters, as its founders.

David was also Flaget's major defender against attacks by various Protestant ministers. Besides writing polemical and apologetical works, David engaged in public debate on the truths of the Catholic faith. Moreover, he wrote a catechism that became popular throughout the church in the United States.[69] To assure that David would remain in Kentucky and to provide episcopal presence while Flaget was on journeys, Flaget had his friend appointed his coadjutor, and in the fall of 1817 Flaget received word that David had been elevated to the rank of bishop. Flaget told Garnier, "I shall no longer fear that I may be deprived of this excellent friend, that my diocese will be ruined by a misdirected zeal. We will not cease, for that, to be Sulpician."[70] David was consecrated by Flaget in the new cathedral in September 1819.

Bardstown was subdivided into many dioceses during Flaget's long life. A period of great confusion ensued when Flaget retired to Europe in 1835, only to return as bishop four years later because David could not adequately administer the diocese and because the new coadjutor, Guy I. Chabrat, was neither a good administrator nor a very popular prelate. Flaget outlived both David and Chabrat and was ultimately succeeded by one of his early students, Martin John Spalding. Over the years, Flaget saw many new bishops: Louis William DuBourg; Edward Dominic Fenwick, O.P.; John B. Purcell of Cincinnati; Joseph Rosati, C.M., of Saint Louis; and Flaget's old friend Simon Bruté of Vincennes. Two former students of the Bardstown seminary became bishops during Flaget's lifetime: Ignatius A. Reynolds of Charleston and John M. Henni of Milwaukee.

During the last part of his life, Flaget seldom mentioned his status as a Sulpician. When he did so, it seems to have been with a feeling of ambivalence. For example, during the 1829 visitation of Joseph Carrière, the superior general's representative, Flaget lamented Carrière's decision not to visit Bardstown.[71] Flaget remained on the periphery of Saint Sulpice, but DuBourg was even more remote. He was appointed administrator of New Orleans in 1812 at a time when the Sulpicians in France were suppressed. Hence there was no superior general to extend permission to receive ecclesiastical dignities. Given Emery's views of DuBourg, one doubts whether the latter would have remained in the society had he been able to seek permission. In September 1815, DuBourg was consecrated at Rome as bishop of Louisiana, and after two years of recruiting priests and raising funds he returned to the United States. However, because of the clerical dissension in New Orleans, which he had confronted upon his appointment in 1812, DuBourg settled in Saint Louis. In 1826, two years after having consecrated Rosati his coadjutor, he resigned his diocese. The immediate cause of his resignation was another wave of clerical discontent.[72] He was then appointed bishop of Montauban, and shortly before he died in 1833 he became archbishop of Besançon.

One of DuBourg's most significant contributions was participation in the origin and development of the Society for the Propagation of the Faith, founded in Lyons in 1822. He remained very close to his Baltimore, Bardstown, and Emmitsburg confreres, even though he was officially outside the community. The New Orleans experience left a cloud over DuBourg's capacity as a leader. In a letter to Rosati shortly after DuBourg's death, Flaget refers to him as a "super genius," one who will be maligned by the many "miserable critics and virulent carpers. . . . There is not a Catholic one in a thousand who will be heard to say that it is to Msgr. DuBourg that we owe the Sisters of Charity of Emmitsburg, the College of the same place, the Madames of the Sacred Heart, etc." He places DuBourg within the context of the "European gentlemen [who had given] the most honor to our religion and [who] contribute the most effectively to extend it."[73] He consciously excludes the Irish from that group of gentlemen, describing the latter as "those who do not speak English naturally."

Perhaps the most brilliant of these European gentlemen was Simon Bruté. Francis P. Kenrick wrote in opposition to Bruté's appointment as bishop of Vincennes only because he had the reputation of being a poor administrator. However, Flaget and David were ardent proponents of Bruté's appointment and eagerly urged him to accept the position in spite of his scruples and self-doubt.[74] As the "patriarch of the hierarchy," Flaget proudly consecrated Bruté at the new Saint Louis Cathedral, which had been designed by a Vincentian brother from the seminary at the Barrens in Missouri. Flaget's Sulpician identify, though ambiguous at times, was strengthened by his ties with David and Chabrat. As mentioned earlier, the Bardstown missionary Sulpicians identified more with Montreal than with Baltimore. However, it was Gabriel Richard who was the closest to Montreal's model, both geographically and in his missionary life.

V

The story of the Sulpicians in Canada begins in 1657 when four members of the society embarked for New France, where they joined the Jesuits and the Recollects in the evangelization of the native Indians. The pioneer group was granted the deed to the island of Montreal, and the superior held civil as well as ecclesiastical authority. The "seminary" they established in Montreal was actually a Sulpician residence rather than a theological college and it was not until 1840 that the Grand Séminaire of Montreal was founded.[75] When England absorbed Canada in 1763, twenty-eight Sulpicians were permanently serving in missions and parishes in the French districts. The British government allowed the Sulpicians in Canada to remain in control of their properties, but it was only in 1839 that their property rights were officially recognized. Since the British prohibited the Canadian Sulpicians from being legally tied to their French superior general, Canada became an independent Sulpician province, with the superior of the seminary elected by a council that was appointed by the superiors; hence the election was by co-optation.

When Flaget referred to the Canadian model for his own constitution, he was, of course, seeking juridical approval from Paris for his missionary seminary on the basis of 150 years of tradition in Canada. Michael Levadoux, and later Gabriel Richard, ministered to the Indians in Michigan, including the Ottawa Indians along the Saint Joseph River and along the Straits of Mackinac. Blackbird, the chief of the Ottawa, was educated by the Sulpicians in Montreal, and his son was a seminarian in Rome's Urban College, where he died in 1833.[76]

Richard was born in the city of Saintes on 15 October 1767. He studied at the Sulpician Seminary at Angers, entered Saint-Sulpice in 1790, and was ordained in October 1791. Immediately afterward, he was sent to Baltimore with three other priests who were in flight from the revolution and who were to make a significant contribution to the American church: Ambrose Maréchal, who would become third archbishop of Baltimore; François Ciquard, a missionary to Indians in Maine and Canada; and François Antoine Matignon, a secular priest who became a missionary in Boston. After laboring in the missions of Kaskaskia and Prairie du Rocher, Richard was assigned to Detroit in 1798. John Carroll had also assigned another Sulpician, Jean Dilhet, to Michigan. From 1798 to 1804, when he was recalled to Baltimore, Dilhet served the mission parish of Saint Anthony, which encompassed hundreds of miles in the Ohio Territory south of Detroit.[77] Richard served Detroit and northern Michigan from his arrival in 1798 to his death in 1832. He was associated with the foundation of several institutions; he was one of the two founders of the University of Michigan and founded several schools for white settlers and Indians. He brought the first printing press into the Ohio Territory and started one of the first Catholic newspaper in the United States, and during one brief period he had hoped to establish a Sulpician seminary.

Gaunt and ascetic, Richard possessed the blend of religious idealism and social practicality so necessary for a successful missionary. Joseph

Octave Plessis, bishop of Quebec, noted in his journal after visiting
Richard,

> This ecclesiastic is . . . thoroughly estimable on account of his reg-
> ularity, the variety of his knowledge, and especially of an activity of
> which it is difficult to form an idea. He has the talent of doing al-
> most simultaneously ten different things. Provided with newspapers,
> well informed on all political matters, ever ready to argue on religion
> when the occasion presents itself, and thoroughly learned in theology,
> he reaps his hay, gathers the fruits of his garden, manages the fish-
> ery fronting his lot, teaches mathematics to one young man, reading
> to another, devotes his time to mental prayer, establishes a printing
> press, confesses all his people, imports cording and spinning wheels
> and looms to teach the women of his parish how to work, goes on sick
> calls at a very great distance, writes and receives letters . . . preaches
> every Sunday and Holy Day both lengthy and learnedly, enriches his
> library, spends whole nights without sleep, walks for whole days, loves
> to converse, receives company, teaches catechism to his young parish-
> ioners, supports a girls' school under the management of a few female
> teachers of his own choosing whom he directs like a religious commu-
> nity, while he gives lessons in plain-song to young boys in a school he
> had founded, leads a most frugal life, and is in good health, as fresh
> and able at fifty as one usually is at thirty.[78]

Richard did not limit his ministry to Catholics but also conducted a
weekly nondenominational service on Sunday afternoons for Detroit
Protestants, who were without a resident clergyman. He explained to
John Carroll that these services originated at the request of the "Governor and some other gentlemen." The nondenominational character
of his speeches reflected the *apologétique* of Saint Sulpice, with its emphasis upon the relationship between natural and revealed religion.

> I have chosen for the subject of my Discourses to establish the General
> Principles of the Christian Religion, that is to say the Principles used in
> the discovery of truth, the several causes of our errors, the existence
> of God, the spirituality, immortality of our souls, the Natural Religion,
> and the several evidences of the Christian religion in general.[79]

Richard's ecumenism even entered the area of popular Catholic devotionalism. It became his custom to lead through town the Corpus
Christi procession, to which he invited Protestants of all denominations. On several occasions a military honor guard escorted the sacrament while Protestant civic dignitaries were assigned to hold the rib-
bons of the canopy under which the monstrance was carried.[80]

Richard is also known as the first priest to serve in Congress. Two
French-speaking parishioners requested him to stand for election in
September 1823. Although he had taken a moderate interest in politics,
Richard had never become a U.S. citizen. Encouraged by his assistant,

Francis V. Badin (the brother of Stephen), Richard gradually realized the advantages the office would have for his work among the Indians. The salary of eight dollars a day was also very attractive because it could be used to build the parish church of Sainte-Anne's. After consulting with Bishop DuBourg, who viewed Richard's nomination within the context of Providence's design for the improvement of the church in Michigan, and after applying for citizenship, Gabriel Richard accepted the nomination. It was an extremely close election; the opposition unsuccessfully contested the results. However, since Michigan was a territory, Richard, though a delegate to Congress, was unqualified to vote.[81]

Richard entered Congress during the so-called Era of Good Feelings, characterized by nationalism, westward expansion, and road and canal building—all of which affected Indian life. Richard wrote Joseph Rosati, "The principal reason why I have accepted this charge is to work more effectively for the good of religion and particularly for the poor Indians."[82] During his two-year term he had several meetings with President James Monroe, Secretary of War John Calhoun, and others who could lend support to his Indian policy, which involved federal support for Indian schools and missions. Ultimately, such support was included in legislation, but it was small compensation for the harsh policy of resettlement of tribes. For example, in 1838 the Catholic Potowatomi tribe was forced to migrate from the Michigan-Indiana area to Sugar Creek, Kansas. In general, Richard's term was uneventful. The only bill that he successfully guided through the House of Representatives was one for the construction of a road from Detroit to Chicago.[83]

During the congressional recess of the summer of 1824, Richard was convicted and imprisoned for libeling a parishioner whom he had excommunicated for an illicit remarriage. (This was not his first stay in a prison; during the War of 1812, his strong display of American patriotism had led to a prison term in Canada.) Released on bond by Wayne County officials, he claimed congressional immunity and went to Washington, but for the remainder of his life he never set foot in Wayne County for fear of returning to prison. He unsuccessfully stood for reelection in 1825.[84]

Richard was originally subject to Bishop Carroll, but with the establishment of new dioceses in 1808 and then in 1821, he was under Flaget and Edward Fenwick of Cincinnati respectively. Flaget, Maréchal, and Fenwick urged the Congregatio de Propaganda Fide to establish a diocese in Detroit and to appoint Richard as bishop. Richard was aware of these efforts on his behalf and his reports to Propaganda Fide indicate the need for a diocese. Finally, in 1827, Rome approved the diocese and appointed Richard. However, the bulls announcing the appointment were postponed because of Richard's heavy indebtedness and his threatened imprisonment. When these embarrassments were supported by other testimony that shed doubt on the need for establishing a diocese, Rome rescinded its 1827 decision. It was not until 1833, a year after Richard's death, that the diocese of Detroit was created when Frederic Résé, a German priest recruited by Fenwick in 1824 and one of those who had provided testimony against Richard, was appointed bishop.[85] By this time Michigan was part of the old West, as migration under the banner of Manifest Destiny had already begun. Flaget, David, Richard, and other pioneer Sulpicians, who brought the rudiments of civilized life to the frontier, could see the product of their labors in such forms of institutional growth as churches, schools, seminaries, and colleges.

4

The Sulpicians
in Baltimore

John Carroll's presence dominated the church in the new republic from its infancy to his death in December 1815. From the time he was appointed superior of the mission in 1784, he pursued an enlightened ecclesiastical policy characterized by the high regard for individual and institutional freedom that was in accord with his deep appreciation for American pluralism. He was particularly mindful of the cultural role of the Catholic church in a land desperately in need of educated leaders to raise the infant nation to the level of European sophistication. He was proud of Georgetown College (which was declared a university shortly before he died), of the way in which the Jesuits maintained their unity during the period of suppression (1773–1814), and of the institutional growth that followed the population expansion to the West. Although he never fully appreciated the Sulpician stress upon religious formation and doubted Jean-Marie Tessier's ability to inspire his students with a love of learning, Carroll was nevertheless very close to the society and held such Sulpicians as Louis William DuBourg, Benoit J. Flaget, Gabriel Richard, and Simon Bruté in high esteem.

A few years before he died, Carroll remarked to his close friend Charles Plowden, "Too much praise cannot be given by me to the priests of St. Sulpice here for their zeal and sacrifice to the public cause. They now maintain and educate at their own expense twenty-two seminarians for the ministry."[1] Yet, as he was approaching eighty years of age, he found himself a bit impatient with one characteristic of the French priests in his archdiocese: "Amidst the many advantages which this diocese had derived from the example, zeal and labors of the French clergymen employed in it, I have to lament one inconvenience arising from them, and that is, their overloading me with increasing letters on subjects which they might terminate as well as [i.e., instead of] by referring them to me."[2] This tendency may have derived from the French penchant for frank expression of opinions, but it more likely stemmed from the Sulpician deference to the bishop as the superior of the seminary.

As noted earlier, the Sulpician closest to the archbishop was Antoine Garnier, the affable pastor of Saint Patrick's, a gifted Hebrew scholar, and a charming gentleman. He frequently expressed his hope that Garnier would return to Baltimore. Ambrose Maréchal, who had also been recalled to Paris, was also close to Carroll. Before his return to France, Maréchal had taught at Georgetown College and at the seminary, had administered the plantation of Bohemia Manor, and had been chaplain for Charles Carroll of Carrollton. John Carroll told Maréchal how deeply affected he was by his departure from Baltimore:

> You know how earnestly I endeavored to keep you here and how heavily I grieved at your separation from us: my grief was not only for a loss personal to myself; and which was indeed a most grievous one; but a loss extending itself perhaps to the whole diocese, and whose effects are yet severely felt.[3]

Maréchal, returning the sentiment, wrote to Carroll, "My heart yearns to dwell in the country I adopted and which I left with regrets."[4]

Upon the suppression of the French Sulpicians in 1811, Maréchal, who had been a director at the seminairies in Saint-Flour, Aix-en-Provence, and Lyons, immediately planned to return to Baltimore. During the eight-year interval in France he had kept himself informed of events in the American church and had been an adviser to Richard Luke Concanen, O.P., the bishop-elect of the diocese of New York. Maréchal so impressed Concanen that the latter confided to him his intention of appointing him coadjutor, with right of succession. In June 1810, however, Concanen died in Italy. The see remained vacant because of the pope's imprisonment in France. As late as January 1815, Carroll wrote to Cardinal Lorenzo Litta at the Propaganda Fide, "A rumor prevailed that the Pontiff intended to name as Bishop . . . Reverend Mr. Ambrose D. Maréchal, a professor of theology in the Sulpician seminary of this city. Born in Orléans, France, he is a member of the Order of St. Sulpice, about 42 years old, of understanding piety, skilled in sacred and profane sciences, and endowed with a most gracious personality."[5] Apparently the Irish Dominicans at the Minerva College in Rome had more influence than did Concanen's last testament, for just about the time of Carroll's letter to Litta, John Connolly, O.P., was appointed bishop of New York. (The diocese of New York contained only three churches and four priests in 1815; Boston, under Bishop Cheverus, had but two priests.)[6]

When Carroll died in December 1815, Leonard Neale, S.J., his coadjutor since 1800, immediately succeeded to the office of archbishop. A native Marylander who had been a missionary in British Guiana (now Guyana), Neale was sixty-seven years old and not in good health when he became archbishop.[7] Hence, he at once sought a coadjutor, naming Cheverus at the top of his list, followed by Maréchal. DuBourg had already suggested Maréchal as the replacement for the deceased bishop of Philadelphia, Michael Egan, O.F.M., Maréchal struggled vigorously against all episcopal appointments. Rome actually appointed him to Philadelphia (a bull dated 26 January 1816), but that appointment was rescinded because Cheverus successfully struggled against being appointed to Baltimore, which left Maréchal as the choice for the unofficial primatial see.

On 24 January 1817, before receiving confirmation of Maréchal's appointment from Rome, Neale appointed Maréchal vicar-general. The archbishop died the following June, before Maréchal's letter urging the appointment of someone else to Baltimore had arrived in Rome. Propaganda Fide had issued a bull naming him coadjutor, but it was not until 10 November that the bull reached Baltimore. Maréchal maintained his membership in the Society of Saint Sulpice and, symbolic of that affiliation as well as of his close association with his confreres on episcopal matters, frequently spent several days at Saint Mary's, where he maintained his own room. The new archbishop was a traditionalist on the question of ministries outside the seminary. Just as he had struggled to preserve his role as a spiritual director and a professor at the seminary, so he opposed others becoming engaged in nontraditional ministry. Before his elevation to the episcopacy, he even suggested to Garnier that the Bardstown and Detroit missionaries be reassigned to seminary teaching and that enrollment at Baltimore's Saint Mary's College and at Emmitsburg's Mount Saint Mary's College be limited to candidates for the priesthood. Although as archbishop he never attempted to press for the implementation of these suggestions except as related to Mount Saint Mary's, there is evidence that Maréchal, unlike Bruté, Flaget, David, and Richard, did not perceive the Sulpician missions within the plan of divine providence.

Maréchal's strong loyalty to the seminary was never more evident than in his petition to Rome that Saint Mary's receive the status of a pontifical university, which the Propaganda Fide granted on 1 May

1822. From that time to the present the seminary has been allowed to confer the degrees of doctor of sacred theology (S.T.D.) and licentiate of sacred theology (S.T.L.). On 25 January 1824, Maréchal conferred the S.T.D. on Louis Deluol, who had been a Sulpician professor of theology at Saint Mary's since 1817; on Edward Damphoux, Sulpician president of Saint Mary's College; and on James Whitfield, a student of Maréchal's in Lyons who came to Baltimore upon his mentor's appointment as archbishop. Deluol recorded the event in his diary:

> 1824, January 25—Received the Doctorate, at the Cathedral, with M. Whitfield and M. Damphoux. The Mass started at 11:15, and ended at 1:45. M. Eccleston preached for an hour, and the ceremony began immediately afterwards, and lasted a quarter of an hour. M. Tessier read the document from the Holy See making us Doctors. Then, in the name of all three, I read the Profession of Faith of Pius IV, in front of the Archbishop's throne, and facing him. Then the Archbishop pronounced the form, and gave us rochet, shoulder-cape, and doctor's cap.[8]

Archbishop Maréchal confronted many problems, most of which were the result of the blurred lines of authority in the American church. For nine years he struggled with the Jesuits over his (i.e., the archbishop's) right to a regular (annual) stipend from them. His claim was based on the annual grant that Bishop Carroll had received from the Corporation of Roman Catholic Clergymen of Maryland. The grant had been established during the time of the suppression of the Jesuits, but Maréchal claimed that it remained in effect after the 1814 restoration of the Society of Jesus. This complex conflict entailed many appeals to Rome, to the general of the Society of Jesus, and was ultimately resolved in Maréchal's favor in 1827. Although it absorbed an inordinate amount of time and effort, Maréchal viewed it as not only a battle for funds but also a struggle for the principle of episcopal authority over a clerical corporation, one that owned most of the ecclesiastical property in Maryland. The conflict was seldom viewed in terms of Sulpicians versus Jesuits, but the two groups never had a warm relationship.[9] Over the years suspicion of Maréchal lingered as the "Maréchal ordination myth" was woven into the lore of the Maryland Jesuit province. In 1827, according to the myth, Maréchal, motivated by vindictiveness, "withheld his interior intention while ordaining five Jesuit scholastics to the priesthood."[10] The story's apocryphal nature has been well established and was evident in Maréchal's cordial relations with several American Jesuits while he was engaged in the struggle with what he considered to be a small minority within the Society of Jesus.

The most vexing problem in the American church during Maréchal's administration was parish trusteeism. The trustee contro-

versy originated in the ad hoc character of church organization. A congregation of the laity could purchase property and build a church without a resident priest. Parish congregations held title to the property,
which was administered by trustees elected by the congregations.[11]
As long as congregations were satisfied with the priests assigned
to their parish (generally true of a majority of the parishes), there
was no conflict between congregation and pastor or congregation and
bishop. When conflicts occurred, they frequently originated in disputes between Irish congregations and French pastors. (Few canonical parishes in the United States had irremovable pastors; instead,
chapels of ease were under the authority of missionary priests.) Carroll respected the trustee system but struggled against its abuses. He
confronted trustee rebellions in New York, Baltimore, Philadelphia,
and Charleston. Maréchal's major problems centered on Saint Mary's
Church in Philadelphia (where national difference did not play a role)
and the churches in Charleston, South Carolina, and Norfolk, Virginia, which entailed Irish-French conflicts. To go into the details of
these struggles, which included visits and appeals to Rome, is beyond
the scope of this work. Nonetheless, the trustees in these two towns
formed a strongly anti-French and, at times, an anti-Sulpician coalition,
and this aspect of the struggle deserves attention.[12]

Father Thomas Carbry, O.P., a classmate of Bishop Connolly of
New York, complained to Propaganda Fide that the French minority dominated the American church at the expense of the majority
of Irish-American laity, who at great sacrifices were building churches
throughout the land. In his first report to Propaganda Fide after his
visitation of the archdiocese, Maréchal refers to those Irish priests who
"most recently . . . tried by means of writings to persuade these ignorant peoples [of their parishes] that the Bishops of Boston [Cheverus],
Bardstown [Flaget], and myself intended secretly to establish a French
hierarchy in these provinces and to expel the Irish priests. They did
not hesitate to broadcast this absurd calumny at Rome." To under-
score his lack of prejudice toward the Irish clergy, the Sulpician archbishop reports that he had granted faculties to ten Irish priests and that
the majority of students at Saint Mary's Seminary were Irish. Indeed,
he states, "The Irish, who are moved by the spirit of God and imbued with truly ecclesiastical habits, serve religion faithfully. For they
are prompt in their work, speakers of no mean ability, and outstand-
ing in the zeal for souls." However, Maréchal continues, "there are so
many priests who have come hither from Ireland [who are] addicted
to the vice of drunkenness . . . [that] I cannot place them in charge
of souls without a mature and thorough examination." He writes that
the "drunkard priests" flee from the American, English, and European
parish communities but have an enormous influence "among the lower

classes of their race . . . [because] these consider drunkenness only a slight imperfection [and] they defend their profligate pastors, associate with them, and enter into and remain with them in schism."[13] Hence, Maréchal implies that the rebellious trustees in Charleston and Norfolk were led by alcoholic Irish priests. After reporting on the details of the trustee problem, he urges Propaganda Fide to establish an episcopal see at Charleston. Maréchal says that he knows of no native-born clergyman to recommend for the post and suggests the appointment of a French-speaking English priest rather than either a French or an Irish priest. Maréchal's suggestions were rejected, and John England, a priest of the diocese of Cork, Ireland, was appointed first bishop of Charleston in 1820. Patrick Kelly and Henry Conwell, two other Irish priests, were appointed bishops of Richmond and Philadelphia, respectively. The trustee controversy continued to preoccupy Maréchal, but John England's leadership in particular was a direct challenge to the Sulpician archbishop.

Shortly after his arrival in Charleston (December 1820), England wrote to Maréchal and suggested that the metropolitan call a provincial council "for the purpose of having established some uniform system of discipline for our churches and of having common counsel and advise upon a variety of important topics regarding the causes and remedies of the disastrous contests [of trusteeism] which have torn and do still agitate this afflicted Church."[14] Certainly the Philadelphia trustee problem—which included election contests, schismatic alignments, the excommunication of schismatic pastors, and Rome's recall of Bishop Conwell—illustrated the need for ecclesiastical discipline. In support of his views, England refers to a decree of the Council of Trent that calls for provincial council meetings every three years. Maréchal, however, refused to call a council because he preferred that problems be solved locally and because he seems to have feared that England, with the support of the new Irish bishops, would dominate the council. Had England, Kelly, and Conwell not been appointed his suffragans, Maréchal might have carried on the tradition of John Carroll by convening a council.

Even though England was frustrated in his promotion of a provincial council, he did develop a constitution for his diocese that provided for clerical and lay participation with consultative and administrative authority in local and general conventions. Implemented in 1822, the constitution forms a unique chapter in the story of the American church. Although based upon solid ecclesiastical tradition and articulated in the popular democratic notions of the Era of the Common Man, England's constitution never moved beyond Charleston and died with him in 1842. Maréchal believed that England's constitution worked well in Charleston, where the strong bishop allowed lay involvement but prevented lay ownership and lay election of pastors, yet he considered it dangerously democratic and a drastic departure from sound episcopal policy. Rome neither approved nor prohibited the constitution's implementation in Charleston.[15]

Not all of Maréchal's Sulpician confreres supported his anticouncil, anti-England position. Bruté and Flaget, for example, promoted the provincial council. In 1827 Flaget confided to Bruté, "Monsignor [Bishop] David and I are beginning to think that a National Council would be very useful in these deplorable circumstances [i.e., the trustee conflicts in Philadelphia]. This is our opinion and that of some of our other friends [i.e., Bishop Dubois of New York], not less wanting of respect because of their talents as well as of their piety."[16] For obvious reasons Flaget suggested Pittsburgh as the site of the council. Flaget wrote that he had corresponded with England and that together they wanted to hold a council not only to resolve the trustee crisis in Philadelphia, but, he added, "also to prove to the Catholic world that there is now a hierarchy in the United States and that the bishops are assembled there to establish general rules of discipline and to prove that they take to heart the interests and the glory of our religion."[17] Despite the support he received from Bruté and Flaget, England viewed his conflict with Maréchal as an indication of the inability of French priests to discern the needs of the American church and to read the signs of the times. On the other hand, England viewed his own experience in Ireland, his command of the language, his understanding of ecclesiastical history, and his appreciation of the American character as having prepared him (and, by implication, the Irish clergy in general) to adapt more readily to the needs of the church in the United States.

In the meantime, Maréchal's anti-Irish prejudice grew stronger. Even Bruté noted this attitude when the Sulpician archbishop visited Rome shortly after the 1820 appointments of his three Irish suffragans. According to a note in Louis Deluol's diary, Bruté said that Maréchal's trip to Rome "was harmful because it was a declaration of war against the Irish." Deluol then paraphrased Bruté's defense of the Irish American priests. "To want to establish the French system in America is ridiculous. Actually, the French clergy in America had given just as much scandal as the Irish; we owe them a lot, we must appreciate the worth of our Irish subjects."[18] In fact, Maréchal did not attempt to impose a "French system" but, rather, stayed clear of the Irish-French conflict and aligned himself with the Anglo-American and English clergy. In short, England was pro-Irish but Maréchal was not, as an archbishop, pro-French. For example, when the New York diocese was open, he favored Benedict Fenwick over Jean Dubois and asked Rome to appoint an Englishman, James Whitfield, or an American Sulpician, Samuel Eccleston, as his own coadjutor.

Hence, Maréchal represents the continuity of the predominance of the Anglo-American culture of the church of Carroll, a patrician minority subculture, very patriotic and privatistic, in contrast to the Irish-American subculture, which, though patriotic, was very assertive and at times confrontationist. Given the rise of nativism and anti-Catholicism in the 1820s and the increase in Irish immigration, England's views and policies appear, in hindsight, to have been prescient. To place the Maréchal-England conflict in political terms, the former represented the oligarchic tendencies of the Federalist while the latter clearly articulated a strong republicanism. Both were moderate Gallicans, but whereas England blended the liberalism of the later Lamennais with the conciliarism of Gallicanism, Maréchal represented the traditional blend of episcopal Gallicanism with *ancien regime* culture. As Gallicans, both held to an ecclesiology that stressed the unfolding of Providence within the local church; Maréchal's perspective was formed by the aristocratic spirit of Saint Sulpice, while England's was formed by the Irish struggle against the tyranny of the British.

Maréchal's Sulpician spirituality and his own relatively reserved personality led him to pursue his objectives behind the scenes. England, in contrast, published his own periodical, the *United States Catholic Miscellany;* spoke before Congress and other gatherings of religious and civic dignitaries; and seemed to thrive on controversy.

In a letter to Samuel Eccleston, who was then in the Solitude at Issy, Maréchal expresses his Sulpician loyalty and his view of the needs of the American church:

> The principal object that ought before everything occupy you during your sojourn at the Solitude is to penetrate yourself well with the Spirit of St. Sulpice; and be well persuaded, my dear friend, that if you come here having imbibed all that, this immense advantage will be for you and for the Church in the United States, infinitely preferable to all the knowledge you can acquire during your sojourn in Europe; and as Theology is taught in the house you are living in, profit by the lectures that are given in that science. As for Canon Law [which Eccleston wished to study] its use is so rare in this country, that I regard its study as a thing only secondary and ornamental . . . our good missionaries [i.e., the clergy in the United States] are not at all associated with the government of the church. . . . But the grand object that the good of religion in this country demands that you have principally under your eyes, is sacred eloquence . . . capable of announcing the word of God in a noble, simple, pious and touching manner.[19]

These last four adjectives—noble, simple, pious, and touching—may be viewed as representing the Sulpician ideals for reconciling the piety of Saint Sulpice to the American church. As he attempted to reconcile the Church and American democracy, John England was thoroughly engrossed with constitutionalism, with political and ecclesiastical governance, and with the rights and duties of the church's membership.[20]

During Maréchal's administration, England appears to have been merely anti-French, but during the administration of James Whitfield (1828–1834), Maréchal's successor, England became distinctively anti-Sulpician. Whitfield was not himself a member of the society, but he had attended Saint-Irénée Seminary in Lyons, where he had been under the spiritual direction of Maréchal. Immediately after Maréchal's elevation to Baltimore (10 December 1817), Whitfield emigrated from England and settled in the cathedral parish. At the outset, Whitfield alienated England by not inviting him to his consecration in May 1828. Although the new archbishop explained that he did not wish to impose an expense upon the bishop of Charleston, the lack of any invitation caused bad feelings between them. However, because there was a growing consensus among his suffragan bishops in favor of a provincial council, Whitfield ultimately fulfilled one of England's most persistent goals by convening a council in October 1829.[21] Among the priests present at the council were six Sulpicians: Edward Damphoux as assistant secretary of the council; John J. Chanche as master of ceremonies; Jean-Marie Tessier as vicar-general of the archdiocese; Louis R. Deluol as a theologian for Whitfield (Tessier and Damphoux were also listed as his theologians); Michael Wheeler as theologian for Father William Mathews, administrator of the diocese of Philadelphia; and Joseph Carrière, official visitor from Paris, as an observer.[22]

Although the minutes of the thirteen sessions have not survived, historians have concluded from the council's decrees and preparatory correspondence that its major concerns were trusteeism, Catholic education, the publication of an English edition of the Bible, the problems of nativism and anti-Catholicism, the establishment of a publishing company to promote Catholic literature, and the need for uniformity in diocesan discipline, particularly the relationship between clergy and their ordinaries. The most immediately significant decrees were those touching on trusteeism and discipline; of more lasting import was the very fact that the American hierarchy, representing several nationalities, had met and discussed common problems. In 1830, with only 318,000 Catholics out of a total white population of 10,500,000 the first Provincial Council of Baltimore did not attract attention from the general public.[23]

Archbishop Whitfield's attachment to the Sulpicians led him to propose Saint Mary's as the central seminary in the United States. He told Antoine Garnier of the motivation behind his proposal and of its reception by the bishops:

> I have expressed to him [Carrière] my rooted friendship for your good Sulpicians and my determination to patronize to the utmost of my power, the Seminary and College of St. Mary's of Baltimore. It was with the greatest sincerity of heart and would to God I was as able as willing to promote your holy institution. The Rev. Mr. [Carrière] will inform you that the other bishops give but little hope of their cooperation of rendering this a central Seminary. They complain of want of money to pay the moderate sum required for board.[24]

John England strongly opposed Whitfield's suggestion. England affirmed that the clergy in the United States must be well "acquainted with the nature of our republican government, and attached to its institutions,"[25] with the implication that such attitudes would not be cultivated in the French-dominated seminary in Baltimore.

Although the first Provincial Council decreed that such a council should be held every three years, Whitfield refused to convoke another. He explains his reasons to England with a singular emphasis upon the strategy of privatization so earnestly cultivated by Maréchal and so characteristic of the Anglo-American Catholic minority:

> The good effects of the council are yet to be seen. . . . I not only see no necessity for one but have good reason to apprehend injurious effects from such a convocation. But whatever may be the opinion of yourself or others I am fully determined to convoke none in 1832. It is my opinion, also, that every diocese being so very extensive each bishop will be much better employed at home.

Whitfield then implies that Maréchal's restrained aristocratic tone was far preferable to Bishop England's confrontational approach:

> For my part I am quite adverse to unnecessary agitation and excitement; experience seems to prove, that walking silently in the steps of my predecessor, doing what good Providence puts in our way and publishing it as little as possible has with God's blessings promoted Religion more and made it more respectable in the eyes of Protestants than if a noisy stirring course had been pursued.[26]

Bishops England, Dubois, and Francis P. Kenrick (appointed bishop of Philadelphia in 1830) urged Whitfield to abide by the 1829 decree for another council. But after the archbishop refused, they agitated within the Catholic press for a council. Ultimately England brought the issue to Rome when he visited there in the winter 1832–1833. In May of 1833, Propaganda Fide notified Whitfield of Pope Gregory XVI's desire that a council be convoked, and Whitfield dutifully responded by announcing a council for the following 20 October.

Sulpicians were once again well represented. By this time Louis Deluol had replaced Tessier as vicar-general of the archdiocese. The decrees of 1833 dealt principally with uniform discipline, the delineation of new dioceses, the selection of bishops, and Catholic education. England and Whitfield differed on substantive and on procedural issues. For example, when the archbishop appointed Bishop Fenwick and Father Deluol promoters for the council, England responded with a proposal that these appointments be subjected to a vote from the bishops. Peter Guilday, England's biographer, describes the archbishop's reaction to this proposal: "Dr. Whitfield opposed this, declaring that it was his right to make the appointment if he wished, and warned Dr. England that he was not the Archbishop of Baltimore."[27] Indeed, the council fathers decided that England was not even to be considered as a successor to Whitfield when they submitted the names of three Sulpicians for the appointment as coadjutor: John J. Chanche, Samuel Eccleston, and Louis Deluol, with Eccleston receiving the most votes. They also voted against two of England's proposals touching on missions to Native Americans and the new black American Republic of Liberia, both of which he had advocated in Rome the previous May.[28]

A few days after the council, Deluol attended a dinner in honor of many of the visiting prelates, including England. Deluol recorded the evening's events in his diary:

> On the way there and on the way back . . . [England] spoke at length to M. Chanche and M. Eccleston about the lack of unity in the council, about the fact that, because of [this lack of unity] . . . little had been accomplished. He complained bitterly about that, as he did about the attitude of Archbishop Maréchal towards him, and the attitude of the people around the archbishop [i.e., Deluol, Tessier, and other Sulpicians]. . . . In a word, he seems to be suffering cruelly. Actually what he had so positively affirmed in Rome was repudiated to Rome by the Acts and Decrees of the Council. If it is true that he had his eyes set on the See of Baltimore, his hopes were now dashed by the nomination of M. Eccleston; anyone would be vexed at less than that.[29]

England was so distressed by the results of the council that he even considered resigning as bishop of Charleston. No other prelate had developed such a creative approach to the challenge of reconciling Catholicism to the new republic. Nor had anyone responded so strongly and so eloquently as he to the anti-Catholic animus expressed during the 1830s in the strident sermons of the Reverend Lyman Beecher, in the stump oratory of former priests, in the bogus memoir of Maria Monk, and in the burnings of convents in Charlestown, Massachusetts, and in Philadelphia.[30] England had hoped to be appointed to a major see, such as Baltimore or New York, to be fully effective. He believed that the Sulpicians had frustrated his aspirations and, indeed, had conspired to obstruct his programs. Although he respected Eccleston more than he had respected Eccleston's two predecessors, England commented bitterly in 1835 that Eccleston's Sulpician vicar-general, Louis Deluol, was virtually "the regulator of the American Church."[31] England notified the authorities at Propaganda Fide that "the progress of the faith was being hindered by the administrative methods of the Baltimore group. . . . The Sulpicians should be replaced by secular priests either born in America or belonging to a race more easily adaptable to American ways than the French."[32]

Some months after the Second Provincial Council, England confided to his close friend, Paul Cullen (1803–1878), then rector of the Irish College in Rome and later Cardinal Archbishop of Dublin, how the Sulpicians had thwarted his plans for the American Church.

> I am under the impression and no doubt exists in my mind of its correctness, that the Archbishop, without being aware of it, is completely the tool of the Sulpicians, who have for a number of years created a government of faction and intrigue, instead of honest, open, strong administration, based upon the convictions, and sustained by the affections, of the Catholic body. The consequence is that the great body of the priests and the great body of the people are in secret opposition to the great body of the Hierarchy and their adherents; and on the other hand the power of administration being lodged in this few is regarded with jealousy and distrust by those who ought to support authority. . . This faction, for in truth I can give it no better name, instead of sustaining itself by the force and by the provisions of the law, standing upon firm ground, prefer a miserable course of evasion . . . which fosters a spirit of intrigue, is more congenial to their habits and modes of thinking, and whenever we are forced into Court not only exposes us to defeat but to ridicule, and keeps up the impression that the Catholic religion is hostile to our political and legal institutions. These causes render an [anti-French trustee] schism here very formidable; it might be created by the most chuckle-headed priest, and it would require more than I can easily find here to extinguish it. That [trustee conflict] in Philadelphia, which continued ten years, could by any other administration have been stifled at its birth; frequently I could alone have done it, but now I know and have the proofs abundant that at that very time it was not desired to have it cease, until by its means Irish influence should be destroyed. The history is melancholy; I hope I shall never be forced to give it to the printer.
>
> Upon all these grounds I feel that I can do no good by interfering in American concerns. I do not now blame Rome as I formerly did, but I lament that whilst she imagines herself doing good, she has thrown an incubus upon the energies of the Catholic Church in America. . . . I

repeat; the fault is not at Rome, except that Propaganda is led by the whisperers. But I have no right to complain of that, for they are more numerous and more adroit than I am.[33]

It appears that this 1834 letter marks the end of England's hopes to preside over a see worthy of his broad vision. Although he was close to bishops F. P. Kenrick and John B. Purcell, England apparently failed to gain their full confidence. Neither of these two bishops was in accord with his anti-Sulpician animus; indeed, during the anti-Catholic riots in Philadelphia, Kenrick took refuge in Saint Mary's Seminary. Purcell, who had been trained at Saint-Sulpice and spent a year in the Sulpician Solitude, kept in close contact with several Sulpicians in Paris and Baltimore. There is evidence of Maréchal and Whitfield's antipathy to Bishop England, but there are no extant letters that verify a Sulpician anti-England conspiracy. Nonetheless, Maréchal, Whitfield, and their Sulpician vicars-general, Tessier and Deluol, were in opposition to what they regarded as England's liberalism. They viewed his constitutionalism as dangerous and abhorred his confrontational style of leadership as one that would only inflame anti-Catholism and nativism.

Intertwined in the struggle between the archbishops and the bishop of Charleston was the strong suspicion that England was excessively ambitious. For example, when he was in Rome in 1833 promoting the cause for a second provincial council, John Chanche, a Sulpician on the faculty of Saint Mary's College, told Samuel Eccleston that England "was bound and determined to go to all the length of his power" to pressure Rome for a council because "he will be the cock of the hill."[34] Regardless of his motivation, England acted at times as if the nation was his diocese. Even without the other, more significant issues dividing Bishop England and the archbishops of Baltimore, the conflict in styles of episcopal leadership alone might have been enough to place obstacles in the way of England's advancement in the United States church.

By the time Eccleston became archbishop in 1834, England's influence among the hierarchy was on the decline, and the young American Sulpician prelate did not hesitate to fulfill a decree of the second provincial council that called for a council every three years. At the third and fourth provincial councils, England's talents as preacher and writer were in evidence; he was assigned a prominent place as homilist and the role of author of the pastoral letter at the conclusion of the councils. Yet he seems to have been resigned to the fact that because of the dominance of the Sulpicians in Baltimore he would remain in Charleston, where, in fact, he died in 1842. Although he was consistently cordial and respectful in his relations with Eccleston, England knew that the archbishop was deeply influenced by his former professor and spiritual director, Louis Deluol.

The Sulpician superior appears to have been relatively unconcerned about constitutional or other structural ways of reconciling Catholicism to American democracy. Deluol's own experience may provide insight into his views of Catholicism in America. His American patriotism was so strong that while aboard a ship leaving the United States for Canada, he climbed to the deck at 2:00 A.M. and sang the "Star-spangled Banner" and recited the De Profundis.[35] He also noted that "in America, we must doubtless respect national pride and feelings," but he felt that it was appropriate for the Sulpicians in Baltimore to honor the memory of Louis XVI on the anniversary of his birthday by offering a requiem Mass as requested by the French ambassador to the United States. Deluol remarks in his diary, "It was . . . said that the Americans would be up in arms for all that [i.e., requiem Mass] for a King. A king he certainly was, but it was largely due to . . . [his support of the American army during the War for Independence] that Americans have this liberty of which they are rightly jealous."[36] Contrary to England's view of the Sulpician, Deluol possessed a keen insight into the American character. As a superior, Deluol had been referred to as an Americanizer by one of his opponents among the Baltimore Sulpicians. Moreover, as will be discussed in a subsequent chapter, Deluol's accommodation to American customs and his immersion in the practical affairs of the community ultimately led to his recall to France.

Deluol was an utterly practical man. His diary, which in translation totals some 1,000 typed pages, includes not one long passage of theoretical significance. This is particularly disappointing because one cannot clearly discern from it the philosophical basis of his opposition to John England's views. As noted earlier, England considered Deluol his archenemy and held him responsible for obstructing England's appointment to a see more important than that of Charleston, South Carolina. Deluol did indicate his views of England in a letter to a confrere in Paris, he said that "for several years, Msgr. England has sought the Archiepiscopal mitre . . . his many compatriots believe he would transform the . . . [Archdiocese of Baltimore] into a terrestrial paradise."[37] Deluol accused England of intrigue in Rome and told of England's conspiracy to have Eccleston appointed to the diocese of New Orleans in order to remove any competition for England's own appointment to Baltimore.

The conflict between Deluol and England was more than a clash of strong personalities; it was also a struggle between opposing ecclesiologies. Although England viewed Deluol as hopelessly French and therefore oblivious to the American ethos, both men held Gallican ideas on the nature of church governance and were influenced by their American experience. England, however, as may be seen in his numerous theoretical writings and in his progressive diocesan constitution with its provisions for lay participation, incorporated American republicanism into his Gallicanism. Deluol tended toward liberal Gallicanism, which veered away from its traditional ties to monarchy, and accepted American principles of civil liberty and of representative government; he held fast to the supremacy of a general council in ecclesiastical government. Deluol viewed England's republicanism and constitutionalism as utopian, as fostering illusions of a "terrestrial paradise."

After Deluol returned to Paris in November of 1849, he notes in his diary his strong adherence to the views of Lacordaire and his antipathy to the new ultramontanism, which had led to the condemnation of the Gallican theologian Louis Bailly. He also corresponded with Isaac Hecker during the foundation of the Paulists. Although Deluol did not leave a well-developed ecclesiology, several remarks in his letters and his diary form a liberal Gallican pattern, strongly influenced by his thirty-two-year experience in the United States. In contrast to what might be called the Jacksonian Gallicanism of England, Deluol appears to have held to a sort of Whig Gallicanism; he feared egalitarianism in political life and the participation of the laity in ecclesiastical life.

England's Irish experience had contributed to his readiness to adapt republicanism to Gallican ecclesiology and had certainly prepared him to battle the anti-Catholicism of the host Anglo-Saxon culture. Deluol seems to have adapted to the new republic because separation of church and state allowed for a freer development of the faith than existed in France, where the polarization of the revolution remained the dominant dynamic of religion and culture. John England's arrival in the United States marked a new phase in a continuum of development, while Deluol experienced deep discontinuity in his passage from the intense church-culture conflict of France to the relative calm of religious freedom in the United States. Because he mediated his passage through the Anglo-Catholic milieu of Baltimore, Deluol reflected the "old" Catholic alliance with American culture that had been formed by John Carroll and developed further by Maréchal, Whitfield, and Eccleston. As *éminence grise* to Eccleston, Deluol was, in the words of John England, the "regulator of the Church" in the United States.

5

American Innovations

The diverse ministries of the Baltimore Sulpicians were not limited to missionary and diocesan activity but also included various kinds of pastoral work in Baltimore. Jean-Marie Tessier, who became de facto superior in 1807, when Nagot left for Pigeon Hill, was responsible for the daily spiritual exercises and discipline of the seminary, presided over meetings of the Sulpician assembly, and assigned the priests to parish work on Sundays and holy days. There were always Sulpicians and seminarians in attendance at the Sunday Eucharist and vespers at the cathedral. As superior, Tessier was also the protector of the Sisters of Charity. According to a report of 1829, Tessier had 200 penitents, many of whom were drawn from the French-speaking community that attached itself to the seminary chapel.[1]

As mentioned earlier, in 1794 Louis William DuBourg began a catechism class for the children of black refugees from the revolution in San Domingo. When DuBourg left in 1796 to become president of Georgetown, Tessier took over the class. In 1809 the class moved to the lower part of the new chapel and met after Sunday Mass, which was attended by both black and white San Domingans and other French-speaking Catholics. On 1 September 1827, Tessier stated that he "handed over to Father Joubert the duties of Catechist for the Negroes which I had performed every Sunday since September 20, 1796."[2] James Hector Joubert de la Muraille, born in France in 1777, had been a tax collector in San Domingo. Forced to flee the island during the revolution of 1793, Joubert, accompanied by his uncle, eventually settled in Baltimore, and in 1805 he entered Saint Mary's Seminary. Ordained in 1810, he joined the Sulpicians and was on the faculty of Saint Mary's College as well as its chief disciplinarian. Joubert was a keen administrator and a deeply sensitive priest. Within a few weeks after his appointment as catechist to the black community he noted that the children's knowledge of the faith would remain minimal unless they learned to read. On 27 September 1827, he recorded in his diary:

> Then I thought that if a school could be opened for the colored girls where they might learn to read, it would be possible to have them recite the Catechism on Sunday. A school would be a work most pleasing to God and useful to the children. I talked the matter over with M. Tessier, who approved of it, but the lack of funds seemed to him an insuperable difficulty. I saw Archbishop Maréchal who approved the idea but offered the same objections.[3]

In March of 1828, Joubert took his plan to James Whitfield, then administrator of the diocese, who also gave his support for the project. Joubert then sought the help of two black women who told him "that for more than ten years they wished to consecrate themselves to God for this good work, waiting patiently that in His own infinite goodness He would show them a way of giving themselves to Him."[4] Until this time Joubert had only been concerned about the school, but with the promise of such support from these two women and with the hope of finding others who would join them, he "thought of forming a kind of Religious Community. . . ." Joubert wrote in his diary: "Hence, it was that I conceived the idea of forming the Sisters of Providence. . .; vows would keep these teachers together and a religious community would secure better results for the colored people."[5] On 13 June 1828, Elizabeth Lange (a native of Cuba) and Marie Rosine Boegue and Marie Magdaleine Balas (both from San Domingo) took possession of a house that they rented on Saint Mary's Court just opposite the seminary chapel. To raise funds for the community, Joubert turned to two prominent Catholic women, a Mrs. Chatard and a Mrs. Ducatel, who became a continuing source of support. By the end of the following November, this small community had attracted twenty-four girls, nine of whom were boarders, to its school. Board and tuition paid by the girls' families amounted to five dollars a month.

The community's first year was an ad hoc novitiate for which Joubert composed a rule of life derived from that of Saint Benedict. Then, on 2 July 1829, four black women (Marie Thérèse Duchemin had joined the community on 29 June) took the three vows as Oblate Sisters of Providence, which became the first black community in the church and the first to be in charge of a black school in the United States. Joubert, who was appointed director of the Oblates, conducted the ceremony at their home. Deluol recorded in his diary that Joubert "said Mass in their house, to which he had brought beautiful vestments and candelabra; they had music and they pronounced annual vows. There were twenty-two communions of persons of all colors."[6]

Prior to the ceremony, Joubert and the Oblates were frightened by rumors that a group of irate white Catholics was planning to stage a protest against the "profanation of the religious habit." Joubert visited Whitfield, who strongly encouraged him not to fear such rumors.[7] Gradually the Baltimore community came to tolerate the Oblates and, as a result of their heroic service during the 1832 cholera epidemic, gave the sisters a public commendation. Whitfield was very proud of this new community. He petitioned Rome for papal approval of their rule and received it in 1831. Also, during the First Provincial Council (October 1829), he introduced several bishops to the Oblates, who by this time had moved to a new home on Richmond Street.[8] Bishop England visited the community in November 1829 and was so impressed that he planned to establish a convent school for blacks in Charleston. When he did begin a school in 1835, however, it created such alarm and near riot that it proved a short-lived experiment.[9]

In October 1834, when news reached Baltimore that anti-Catholic riots had culminated in the burning of the Ursuline convent in Charlestown, near Boston, Joubert received word "of planned raids on the Carmelites and the colored sisters."[10] He went to see the mayor and the archbishop, and as a security measure he and two seminarians spent the night in the Oblates' convent. Violent anti-Catholic protest did not occur, but fear of such violence persisted throughout this period. Meanwhile the Oblates and their school continued to grow and flourish. Seminarians and Sulpician faculty frequently visited the school while Joubert continued to act as its spiritual director and superior. The governance of the community reflected Sulpician collegiality: the superior, responsible for the internal administration, was required to call an assembly of all the sisters on important matters.

When Joubert died on 5 November 1843, no Sulpician took his place as superior of the Oblates. As the superior of the Sulpicians, Deluol appears to have played a kind of juridical role; he was present at the election of a new Oblate mother superior in December 1844. Without an official tie to the white culture and to the ecclesiastical structure, the community floundered. In 1847, when the situation reached a critical stage, Thaddeus Anwander, a Redemptorist priest who took a strong interest in the sisters, became the superior of the Oblates. The black Catholic community, the vast majority of whom were apparently descendants of the refugees from San Domingo, continued to attend the liturgies in the lower chapel at Saint Mary's until the Oblates built their new convent on Richmond Street in 1836. There the black

Catholics of Baltimore worshiped for the next two decades. In 1857 the basement of Saint Ignatius, the Jesuit church, was renovated as a chapel for the Baltimore black Catholics and dedicated to Blessed Peter Claver. In 1863, the year of the Emancipation Proclamation, a large building, some four blocks from Saint Ignatius, was purchased, which became Saint Francis Xavier Church, the first independent black parish community in the United States. By this time the Oblates had expanded beyond Baltimore.[11]

Since Sulpician support for Joubert's role as founder and superior of the Oblates was strong and consistent, it is difficult to explain Deluol's reluctance to appoint a successor to Joubert. (Apparently John Chanche, a young Sulpician whose parents had emigrated from San Domingo in 1795, was unsympathetic to Joubert's work with the Oblates.) As vicar-general of the archdiocese and as a confidant of Eccleston, Deluol certainly had the influence at least to urge the archbishop to appoint a successor. The likely explanation is that the authorities in Paris were determined to limit Sulpician ministry to its traditional seminary context and, therefore, Deluol was restrained from maintaining the strong pastoral association with the Oblates. For example, in the 1847 *Catholic Almanac*, the Oblates' chapel is listed as "occasionally attended from St. Mary's Seminary."[12] Perhaps the four-year hiatus between Joubert's death and Anwander's appointment may be best explained by the lack of motivation on the part of the few priests in the city to transcend racial barriers by making a long-term pastoral commitment to the Oblates.

The diverse ministries that characterized this expansive period in American Sulpician history were of primary concern at the official visitation of Joseph Carrière (1795–1864) as the representative of Superior General Antoine Garnier. However, it was a deep personality conflict that had led the Baltimore Sulpicians to request the visitation. The central figure in the conflict was Jean-Baptiste Louis Edward Damphoux, the president of Saint Mary's College. Born in the diocese of Nîmes in 1788, he entered Saint-Sulpice in 1810 and was ordained a deacon in 1812, the year the Sulpicians were suppressed in France. He wished to enter the society and received permission to accompany Maréchal upon his return to Baltimore. Damphoux taught classics at the college while he completed his theology and undertook his solitude. Ordained in 1814, he was appointed president of the college in June 1818.

Damphoux seems to have possessed all the qualities necessary for academic leadership, but he was so mercurial that he lacked the emotional stability to foster confidence. On two occasions he resigned the presidency, only to insist later that he be reappointed; Tessier capitulated in each incident. One may piece together a record of Damphoux's quixotic behavior. Shortly before Damphoux's first resignation, Deluol recorded that at an Ascension Thursday liturgy (16 May 1822) one of the instructors was unable to keep the college boys orderly. "At that M. Damphoux became very angry and said that he hates ceremonies so much that, if it were not a crime, he would become Protestant for that reason."[13] The following July Damphoux resigned the presidency because Tessier had told him he could not dismiss five students for misconduct. Deluol was selected to replace him; Damphoux expressed a desire to return to office, but a carriage accident later that month prevented the fulfillment of his desire. In September 1823, however, Tessier reappointed him president. During the next four years Damphoux had several serious conflicts with Joubert, his vice-president; with Deluol; with Tessier; and with two young American Sulpicians, Michael F. Wheeler and Samuel Eccleston. Deluol considered Damphoux utterly unstable and refers to Damphoux's "attack of nerves."[14]

In June 1827, Damphoux resigned again after a display of temper; Tessier appointed Michael Wheeler as president and John Chanche as vice-president. Then in February of 1828, Tessier reappointed Damphoux, in turn alienating Wheeler and Chanche. Eccleston was appointed vice-president for a short period, but at Damphoux's insistence Tessier dismissed him. Tessier's removal of Chanche so distressed the latter that he unofficially left the society. Wheeler blamed his forced resignation on Deluol, who from the beginning had been opposed to Wheeler's appointment as president. Joubert appears to have been as indecisive as Tessier; nevertheless, he joined Damphoux and Wheeler to form an anti-Deluol faction. According to Eccleston, who wrote to the superior general, Antoine Garnier, these three were "an uncountable league [and] M. Tessier . . . does whatever they prescribe."[15] By this time Deluol had managed to convince the entire community to appeal to the superior general for an official visitation. Dated 15 July 1828, Eccleston's letter refers to "an extremely critical year in the life of the house in Baltimore" and mentions that there was "a tendency toward ruin."[16]

Four days later, Joubert wrote to Garnier, indicating that there was also a minority position that was sympathetic to Tessier and in opposition to Deluol. In effect Joubert told the superior general that Deluol wished to succeed Tessier as superior and that was why he (Deluol) had been uncooperative in resolving the problems of the house. Joubert said that if Deluol achieved his goal he would appoint young Americans to positions of power and thereby become "absolute master of the community and its institutions."[17] He then described Deluol's external ministry, which by implication disqualified him as a spiritual leader of the community.

Garnier's letters to Eccleston indicated a clear understanding of the crisis. In one letter the superior general refers to Damphoux's 1828 return as president as "the second revolution."[18] Eccleston had sent him a Baltimore newspaper that had reported the confusing behavior of the Sulpician administration. Garnier understood that in this crisis it was almost impossible to augment the declining enrollment in the college. With his own experience in Baltimore and with his appreciation of the personalities involved, he was very sympathetic to the majority opinion represented by Deluol and his penitent, Samuel Eccleston. In contrast to Deluol's self-confident, cosmopolitan character, Tessier was almost a diffident recluse. However, the leadership conflict was between Damphoux and Deluol, two very strong willed individuals, the latter commanding the support of the younger American Sulpicians.

After John Chanche abruptly left the community in late 1828, Deluol represented his own case to Tessier. He told the superior that "the house was suffering because of his absence and that people are talking against us throughout the city on that subject, and we have already become rather odious."[19] Despite Deluol's intervention, Chanche did not return until Joseph Carrière opened his official visitation on 29 August 1829. The visitation resulted in the resignation of Tessier and Damphoux, the appointment of Deluol as superior, of Eccleston as president, and of Chanche as vice-president of Saint Mary's College. Carrière's official report contains a list of the diverse activities of the Baltimore Sulpicians. It records that Jean-Marie Tessier had about 200 penitents, was adviser to the archbishop, and assumed all the responsibilities attached to the role of superior. James H. Joubert taught French and was in charge of discipline at the college; was head of the French congregation of the *chapelle basse* (i.e., the basement chapel), which was "composed primarily of colored people"; was director of the Oblates; and had 100 penitents. Louis Deluol was a professor of theology and teacher of Hebrew and was in charge of chant at the seminary and responsible for the financial affairs of the community; he was superior-general of the Sisters of Charity and had 140 penitents. Edward Damphoux, besides his position as president of the college, was director of a pious confraternity of men entitled the Association of the Blessed Virgin and had only 2 penitents. John Chanche taught at the college, gave weekly catechetical instructions, and had 4 penitents. Michael Wheeler, who like Chanche was a native of Baltimore and an alumnus of Saint Mary's College, taught at the college and was spiritual director of the Sisters of the Visitation. (His health deteriorated in 1826; he died in 1832 at the age of thirty-six.) Alexis Elder, an alumnus of Mount Saint Mary's College, was confessor of the Baltimore convent of the Sisters of Charity and had 90 penitents. Francis Lhomme, who had arrived from France in 1827, taught at the college and was in charge of the library. John Hickey, an alumnus of Saint Mary's College, remained in Emmitsburg after Mount Saint Mary's separated from the society.[20] (Upon his appointment as superior, Deluol was ordered to resign as superior of the Sisters of Charity, whereupon Hickey was named superior.)

Garnier appears to have been very influential in forming Carrière's attitude toward the Baltimore community. Although Carrière stressed the need to focus on the traditional seminary ministry, he was open to alternative pastoral expressions. For example, he gave the local superior the authority to decide on the priority of "external ministry." Since Deluol was by far the most active Sulpician in the United States, this provision was an implicit endorsement of various ministries. Carrière, who was concerned with the declining enrollment in the seminary, was told by the Baltimore community that the reason for the higher enrollments earlier was that the seminary had admitted many Irish applicants. However, the Irish students gave "little satisfaction" and tended to view the seminary only as a *pied-à-terre*, a "temporary home," and left the seminary as soon as they found a place in the city.[21] The Anglo-American students were, according to the visitation report, reserved and discreet. The principal reason for the enrollment of only eleven seminarians in 1829 was that the "spirit of the country [among] the upper and middle classes little disposed them to the ecclesiastical life." The poor classes could augment the enrollment, but this increase would entail a large expense for the house, particularly since students from these classes would require so much pretheology education. Because there was little hope of recruiting seminarians from Mount Saint Mary's, the report concluded that the Baltimore Sulpicians should increase the enrollment of Saint Mary's College, where they should create an atmosphere of "piety, and theology, scripture and preaching"; they should also strengthen the ecclesiastical studies at the seminary in order to attract more seminarians from the various dioceses.[22] As mentioned earlier, at the provincial council of 1829 Carrière and Whitfield unsuccessfully sought to make Saint Mary's the national seminary for the Catholic church in the United States.

In response to Carrière's question on the decreasing enrollment in the college, Damphoux presented five major causes: with the termination of the War of 1812 and the opening of the seaports, many French families sent their children to schools in France; the king of Spain prohibited his subjects in Latin America from sending students to the United States because of the prevailing "republican spirit"; the French families in Louisiana that had previously sent their students to Saint Mary's now had them educated in the increasing number of colleges at home; American Protestants harbored many prejudices against the Catholic clergy; and Saint Mary's did not have the library or science facilities to compete adequately with other colleges.[23] Since enrollment had increased considerably under Eccleston's leadership and since none of these five conditions had changed substantively, they appear to have been Damphoux's way of rationalizing the erosion of public confidence in Saint Mary's College during the critical years prior to the visitation.

Carrière discovered two abuses of Sulpician tradition that called for reform. Without citing the persons involved, he noted that there was a custom of allowing women (both parents and penitents) to enter the priests' offices, which were attached to their rooms in the college. Since Carrière perceived a situation of potential scandal he ordered that suitable parlors be constructed outside the living area for conducting the business of the college. Because women penitents should be counseled in the confessional, only rarely should such spiritual direction occur within these parlors.[24]

The second abuse was far more serious as it pertained to the essence of the Sulpician vocation, the spiritual direction of seminarians, which, since the time of Olier, had occurred within the context of the sacrament of penance. Carrière stated that he was "shocked that a Sulpician and a good priest [would] search for penitents in order to have a great number and . . . when one [seminarian] . . . changes confessors, [the former director openly reveals] . . . his discontent." Carrière admonished the entire community to reflect on this deviation and make the necessary individual reforms.[25] As an illustration of this abuse, Deluol referred to Tessier's tendency to shepherd jealously his own flock of penitents.

The transfer of authority from Tessier to Deluol represents a watershed in the history of the American Sulpicians. Deluol's cosmopolitan character, his expansive openness to the vitality of American cultural life, his own diversified "exterior ministries," and his closeness to the prominent families of Baltimore, both Catholic and Protestant, were in marked contrast to Tessier's introverted, rigorous, and narrow-minded views on the Sulpician apostolate in the United States. Immediately after Deluol became superior, Damphoux asked him if he should resign as president of Saint Mary's College. Deluol responded, "I told him 'yes'! [Then] he told me we [sic] were all wrong and that I was a heretic but invincible ignorance would excuse me."[26]

Damphoux wrote to Garnier that he had been the victim of prejudices and that Carrière had acted impulsively in appointing Deluol superior. Opposed to the new developments within the community, Damphoux severed himself from the society and went to live with Archbishop Whitfield, who admired Damphoux's keen grasp of theological issues. Later he moved to Saint Peter's Parish, but he remained as a valued adviser to both Whitfield and Eccleston and was a *peritus* at the seven provincial councils of Baltimore.

Michael Wheeler, also disturbed by Deluol's appointment as superior, wrote to Garnier that Deluol had not earned his confidence, that he tended to ignore the opinions of "his inferior," and that Carrière had acted prematurely in the appointment of superior.[27] For reasons of health, Wheeler moved to Georgetown, where he was superior and spiritual director of the Visitation Convent. Because of his strong attachment to the spirit of Francis deSales and Jane de Chantal, the foundress of the Visitation Sisters, Wheeler brought four sisters from France to Georgetown and thereby prevented the sisters from joining the Ursulines.[28] Wheeler was a very sensitive priest with a strong call to the interior life. His brief tenure as president of Saint Mary's College during a critical period resulted in what was reported as a breakdown in his health but was apparently an emotional as well as a physical malady. Joubert also seems to have been frightened by the direction of Deluol's administration. He wrote to Garnier that he and Tessier were "on the watch" because the "new government" represented a "very independent [or free] style of authority."[29]

Tessier, Wheeler, Damphoux, and Joubert stressed the need for the traditional barrier separating the Sulpician seminary from the life of the world. In their view, Deluol threatened to dissolve this barrier because he stressed the need to bend to American informality. He did not reform the rule and was rather loose in interpreting it. Deluol allowed the seminarians and college students privileges to dine out with parents and to attend special civic affairs. It was not coincidental that Garnier supported Deluol; the superior general had also been a loose constructionist in contrast to his predecessor Antoine Duclaux. One should recall that Garnier had been the affable pastor of Saint Patrick's Church in Fells Point, while Duclaux had been head of the Sulpician Solitude. Garnier, Deluol, Duclaux, and Tessier were all traditionalists deeply touched by Emery's revival of the spirit of Olier. Although they agreed on the substantive issues of the Sulpician way of life, their styles of leadership differed. Deluol's appointment represented a new stage in the development of Saint Sulpice in America. He presided as if Saint Mary's Seminary was clearly at the crossroads of the ecclesiastical life in the United States, and by his presence at the seven provincial councils of Baltimore and his influence upon Samuel Eccleston, the only archbishop in the United States, the crossroads metaphor was very close to reality.

Eccleston had been Deluol's protegé since the former's seminary days. When Eccleston was doing his Sulpician Solitude in Paris (1825–1827) Deluol frequently wrote to his "dear Brother Sam." (Such informality reveals the extent to which Deluol had became Americanized.) As mentioned earlier, Deluol appointed Eccleston president of the college with the hope that an American would improve the morale of the students and restore the institution's reputation. Since enrollment went from fewer than 100 students in 1829 to 195 in 1833–1834, it seems evident that Eccleston was indeed a very successful president.[30] His leadership earned him the respect of Archbishop Whitfield and other members of the hierarchy. Although Eccleston was a mediocre administrator, he was an excellent speaker and preacher, frequently called upon to address important civic and religious gatherings. These were the qualities that led Archbishop Whitfield to nominate him as his coadjutor. When he became archbishop, Eccleston felt utterly unprepared; he retained Deluol as his vicar-general and strongly relied upon the advice of his mentor. Indeed, from the many references in Deluol's diary, it appears that the archbishop referred to his vicar-general much of the detail work of the administration.

The fifth archbishop of Baltimore suffered severe emotional and psychological strain in 1843. In late July of that year, shortly after the close of the Fifth Provincial Council, Deluol and Bishop Fenwick accompanied Eccleston on a tour of the western states. Although he had complained of anxiety and exhaustion in preparation for the previous council, it was while he was on this trip that Deluol recorded Eccleston's bizarre behavior, which included tormented hallucinations and paranoid fears of persecution.[31] At the end of the trip, Deluol notes in his diary that he talked with the archbishop "about his situation, and his need of abstaining from wine, especially Spanish wines, or strong wines."[32] Since this is the only reference to Eccleston's intemperate indulgence in wine and since Eccleston's abnormal behavior often occurred in situations where no alcohol was served, the periodic overindulgence may have been symptomatic of his emotional condition rather than the cause of his hallucinations and paranoia. Nevertheless, rumors about his drinking problem circulated, particularly after a fall in which "nearly half his cranium [was] stripped."[33] Eccleston recovered, but complaints about his competency reached Rome. In November of 1846, Propaganda Fide authorized Francis P. Kenrick, the bishop of Philadelphia, to investigate the complaints of such reports. Kenrick concluded that Eccleston was indeed competent but nevertheless agreed to consider the appointment of a coadjutor.[34] Other than the above reference to Eccleston's hallucinations and his drinking problem, Deluol does not remark on the archbishop's general condition or on particular instances revealing his psychological health.

When Deluol became superior he was immediately confronted with the issue of the establishment of a Sulpician preparatory seminary. With few vocations from Saint Mary's College and the loss of Mount Saint Mary's College, Superior General Antoine Duclaux encouraged Archbishop Maréchal to pursue the foundation of another Sulpician *petit séminaire* in the United States. Maréchal had made the initial request for land, upon which to erect the college, to the granddaughter of Charles

Carroll of Carrollton. However, she did not convince her grandfather to donate the land until late 1829 after the death of Maréchal and after the visitation of that autumn had led to Deluol's appointment as superior. Toward the end of January, the Sulpicians received 250 acres of land immediately north of the Fredericktown Road beyond what is today Ellicott City, some fifteen miles west of Baltimore.[35] The following month Saint Charles' College was incorporated with authority vested in the board of trustees, which was composed of John Chanche, Jean-Marie Tessier, Louis Deluol, Alexis Elder, and Samuel Eccleston. The articles of incorporation stipulated an essential aspect of the Tridentine character of the college as "exclusively for the education of pious young men of Catholic persuasion for the ministry of the Gospel."[36] Charles Carroll also donated fifty shares of stock in the United States Bank to help in the costs of construction. The Sulpicians named the college in honor of the patron saint of Charles Carroll, and for the college seal they intertwined the Carroll coat of arms with that of Saint Sulpice. Although the ground breaking occurred in 1831, completion of the college was delayed until 1848 for a variety of reasons. There was a lack of funds, a condition compounded by general economic distress in the nation during the 1830s; there were too few Sulpicians to staff the college; and there seems to have been some ambivalence about Saint Charles' because of the Sulpician involvement in Saint Mary's College, which had regained its prestige and had an average enrollment in excess of two hundred students.

Deluol's opinions on the feasibility of maintaining both colleges appear quite confusing. In 1837, the year after the termination of the thirty-year period that the state had required Saint Mary's to stay open or return the money raised by public lottery, Deluol was convinced that when St. Charles' "was in full operation, St. Mary's College of Baltimore would be suppressed or at least the boarding part of it . . . retaining the externs or day scholars."[37] He said that even with high enrollments the college had never paid for itself because of the need for costly capital improvements. Deluol wrote these reflections because of the death of the young Sulpician vice-president of the college, John H. Hoskyns. Hoskyns, like Chanche, Eccleston, Wheeler, Hickey, and Elder, was an alumnus of Saint Mary's College. Ordained at the age of twenty-four and entering the society two years later, he was only twenty-nine when he died in 1837. Deluol was conscious of the demands placed upon the vice-president and president of the college and of the fact that few Sulpicians were equal to the task.

The religious reasons for suppressing Saint Mary's were that the college had produced few vocations and that the Protestant majority dominated the student body. Since Protestant students were "more wealthy and therefore far more influential than Catholics . . . the

Catholic boys frequently [lost] confidence in their religion." Saint Charles' would enroll only Catholic boys who "seeing nothing but Catholicity, their ears hearing nothing but what is right, they would acquire the habit of thinking what is right. Protestantism would be mentioned, no doubt, since they would have to live in a Protestant community. But at least, there you could explain to them [the errors] of Protestantism." Deluol hoped that by appointing American Sulpicians to positions of authority at Saint Mary's College he would foster strong loyalty among the alumni.

But by 1837 he was disappointed with the poor response. In contrast "St. Charles bids fair to be popular with Catholics."[38] Although the *Catholic Almanac* (the predecessor of the *Catholic Directory*) carried an advertisement for Saint Charles' every year from 1839 on, the building program was far from complete, and even in 1843 Eccleston solicited funds from the Society for the Propagation of the Faith at Lyons:

> One of the things that I desire most, is the formation of a national clergy accustomed from infancy to the manners and language of the country, and at the same time pious, instructed, and sufficiently numerous. On the other hand, the vocation of our young Americans is too liable to be lost in colleges, where they necessarily come in contact with Protestants and other fellow-students, whose heads are already filled with ideas of money, of speculation, commerce, etc. We should have here, as you have in France, a Petit Séminaire, where we might train separately those who have piety and show some dispositions for the clerical state. This is the purpose of a building which we have about 16 miles from Baltimore. It looks as if it were ready to receive students, but we have not the funds required either to complete it, or to procure and support the personnel necessary for such an institution, so that, after expending much money, I cannot obtain the object that I have in view. I find it equally impossible to procure the number of priests strictly necessary to attend missions where several Catholic families are scattered and deprived of the ordinary services of religion.[39]

In the meantime, Saint Mary's College was flourishing. In 1837, the very year that Deluol penned his pessimistic notes on the college, members of the faculty and student body of the medical school at the University of Maryland, alienated by policies established by their board of trustees, sought to establish a medical school at Saint Mary's College. Although heartened by the confidence placed in the college, Deluol, on behalf of the faculty, explained that they did not wish to absorb a portion of the medical school and thereby "take advantage of the misfortune of a sister university." If the University of Maryland suppressed the medical school, then Saint Mary's "might think itself called upon to establish a school of medicine so that the city and state would not be deprived of such a vital component of university education."[40]

When John Chanche was named bishop of Natchez in 1840, Deluol appointed Gilbert Raymond (1809–1881) president of Saint Mary's College. A native of the Auvergne, Raymond entered Saint Sulpice in 1835 and was assigned to Baltimore in 1837. Although regarded as a good teacher at Saint Mary's, he was not a good disciplinarian. Nevertheless, the college thrived during his administration (1841–1849).[41] By the time of Raymond's appointment, several Sulpicians had been added to the faculty. Jean Blaise Randanne (1793–1864) was ordained in 1817 and almost immediately sailed for Baltimore. After a brief stay at Mount Saint Mary's he was assigned to teach at the college. However, for reasons unknown, he did not officially enter the society until after Carrière's visitation. Randanne wrote a Latin textbook that was used at Saint Mary's and other colleges for many years. Pierre Frédet (1801–1856), ordained about 1825, arrived in Baltimore in 1831 and was immediately assigned to the college. His books on church history were standard texts in Catholic schools throughout the nineteenth century. Augustin Vérot (1805–1876), a classmate of Félix Dupanloup, bishop of Orleans, and of Henri Lacordaire, the equally famous Dominican preacher, was destined to be one of America's most remarkable bishops. In 1830, two years after his ordination, Verot reluctantly accepted an assignment to Baltimore. He taught mathematics and several scientific subjects at Saint Mary's College, where he earned a reputation as a serious scholar and teacher. Edward Knight (1806–1862), a native of Baltimore, attended Saint Mary's College, where he converted to Catholicism. Prior to his ordination in 1830, he taught at the college, and in 1833 he entered the society. A teacher of Greek and botany, Knight was very much influenced by Deluol. Oliver Jenkins (1813–1869), from one of the most distinguished Catholic families of Baltimore, was also an alumnus of the college. Jenkins entered the society in 1846 but had been teaching at the college since his seminary days in 1842. He later became the first president of Saint Charles' College.[42]

The prosperity of Saint Mary's College and the prospect that Saint Charles' College would be ready to receive students by the end of 1848 appears to have placed Deluol in a quandary. To maintain two boarding colleges would have strained the resources of the community. To close Saint Mary's College would have entailed suffering the loss of public confidence, particularly since the college had brought great prestige to the Baltimore Sulpicians. Although Deluol understood that St. Charles' College would eventually be opened and that at least the boarding school component of St. Mary's would be closed, he seems to have wanted to delay this as long as possible because he was unsure of the enrollment potential for a *petit séminaire*. However, events occurred rapidly and were determined by the will of Archbishop Eccleston and by the authorities in Paris. Deluol's position became untenable.

As early as 1838 the Jesuits of Georgetown had indicated their interest in buying Saint Mary's College and opening their own college on the site. Deluol did not entirely discount their interest, but he never received an attractive offer. In early 1848, the Jesuits renewed their interest and were supported by Eccleston. On 28 February of that year, Deluol recorded in his diary that the archbishop was "very anxious" to see the issue resolved.

> He insists on the fact that the reputation of St. Mary's College, as far as its discipline is concerned, is lost, and that it is morally impossible for us to rehabilitate it with what we have. I said that we would not give up the college for a piece of bread; that, if the Jesuits could not or would not give us a fair price, we could just as well as they make a day school out of it; our only difficulty arose out of our managing the boarding school.[43]

Two days later he recorded that Eccleston again approached him "about the college and the Jesuits. I believe nothing will come of it."[44]

The major conflict between the superior and the archbishop occurred when the latter surprised everyone by announcing in late September that he had decided to open Saint Charles' College. On 26 September, Deluol wrote that Eccleston came to see him about opening Saint Charles'. "I don't believe it will succeed, but, since the archbishop wants it, it will be done."[45] Three days later Eccleston appointed Oliver Jenkins president of the new *petit séminaire*; included in the letter was a check for $250. Since the archbishop had not sought permission from Deluol for the appointment, Jenkins could not in conscience accept the office. He told the archbishop, "I cannot, because of the respect and obedience I owe my superior, take any steps in the undertaking . . . before being aware of M. Deluol's wishes nor without having been appointed by him."[46] Eccleston was so furious that he immediately sent a copy of this letter to the superior general, Louis de Courson (1799–1850), with the note, "Will you have the kindness to tell him what [his duty] is?"[47] Both letters were premature, as just a few hours after Jenkins's letter to Eccleston, Deluol told Jenkins that "although he had great doubts as to the success of the scheme, yet he thought it was the will of God that I [Jenkins] should undertake the charge which the archbishop wished confided in me."[48]

On 31 October 1848, Oliver Jenkins, Edward Caton, a deacon, and four students commenced classes at the pioneer "minor seminary," Saint Charles' College in Ellicott City. Jenkins was president, treasurer, disciplinarian, and teacher, while Caton assisted with teaching and studied theology under Jenkins. By 1 March of the following year there were seventeen students enrolled; "our number is full" recorded Jenkins on that day.[49] In the meantime there was pressure to close Saint Mary's College. On 21 April 1849, however, Etienne-Michel Faillon (1800–1871) and Constant Guitter (1810–1873), official Sulpician visitors representing de Courson, arrived in Baltimore. From that time until the following November, the major questions were related, not to Saint Charles' or to Saint Mary's College, but to the Sulpician way of life in Baltimore.

Unlike the 1829 visitation, that of 1849 did not originate with a community appeal. De Courson, who was elected superior general upon the death of Garnier, had planned to visit Baltimore personally, but the revolution of 1848 rendered his visit impossible because Republican sentiment threatened the very existence of seminaries in France. Particularly disturbed by reports of the extent to which the Baltimore community was engaged in external ministry, de Courson sent the two visitors.[50] Guitter, director of the seminary at Nantes, appears to have played a secondary role to Faillon, a powerful figure in the society primarily known for his research and writing on the life and spirituality of Olier. Unlike Carrière's 1829 visitation, which lasted only a few weeks, that of Faillon, which was interrupted by a visit to Canada, lasted for more than a year. Since the visitors' major goal was to restrict the Baltimore Sulpicians to their primary ministry as directors of aspirants to the sacerdotal life, and since Deluol was engaged in a variety of nonseminary activities, anti-Deluol sentiment swelled into a movement to remove him as superior. Vérot and Frédet expressed their discontent in letters to de Courson. Just over a month after the visitors arrived, Frédet wrote that Deluol should resign and that Paris should appoint someone from France, perhaps Guitter or Faillon, who would preside as a "directeur du," a Sulpician of traditional piety commanding the respect of his confreres.[51] Vérot forcefully stated the case against Deluol.

> During the twenty years that he has been superior, he has governed the house in a totally absurd manner, never bothering himself about the rules, acting by worldly caprice, and working always with a vanity as silly as it is intolerable. Nevertheless, he has a good heart, he is affable on many occasions; he cheers people in conversation, and he has dealt fairly in the temporal administration of the house and in the handling of house funds. . . . On the other hand, as superior, he is absolutely incapable of giving any instruction whatever to seminarians. Although customarily he does not criticize at the reading, and although he no longer preaches (because of his throat, as he repeats ceaselessly), still he does explain the rule at present, and also the method of prayer. Eh bien! It is my duty to tell you that he speaks inanities without end.[52]

Deluol did not express his reaction to the visitation of de Courson until August of 1849 because, as he wrote, he "wished to . . . understand the purpose of the visitation before writing and, [until recently] all has been surrounded in mystery." He notes the brevity of Carrière's visitation in contrast to the current one. However, the entire letter reads as a blend of sarcasm and rage. After stating that he understands that the visitors have the confidence of the superior general and therefore have authority over "my life," he tells de Courson that Faillon and Guitter had charged him "with flagrant violation of thirty different points of the Constitution of St. Sulpice, violations so flagrant that they have shocked the eyes of everybody! I ask you honestly can one find oneself in a more damnable situation?" He then pleads to be recalled to France since the visitation was a powerful statement of no-confidence in the Baltimore superior. However, he says that he had been "faithful to the spirit of St. Sulpice as it was embodied in Emery, Duclaux and Garnier and he had been particularly supportive of their desire to extend the Catholic Church in this country."[53] He implies in this letter, and is explicit in subsequent correspondence, that the three previous superiors general had permitted the Baltimore Sulpicians to engage in external ministry because of the mission character of the church in the United States. In another letter he boldly asks, Why is the commitment to "external ministry so meritorious in Montreal and so damnable in Baltimore?"

Deluol tells de Courson that it was the "triple authority of Msgr. Maréchal, of M. Garnier and of M. Tessier who directed me to take charge of the Sisters of Charity." And despite his reluctance he fulfilled his duty and contributed to the general welfare of the sisters. He then notes that over the years Vérot, Frédet, and Lhomme had just a handful of penitents in the seminary, while he himself with all his outside ministry was also confessor to the vast majority of the seminarians. Hence, it was ironic that Vérot and Frédet should have accused Deluol of being lax in his duties at the seminary when the superior had fulfilled his duty as a director with more effectiveness than his accusers. Indeed, Deluol points out that during his time as superior, forty-two priests had been formed at the seminary, and of those only three or four were "the creation of Tessier." To substantiate the fact that the seminary had the confidence of the hierarchy, Deluol notes that Saint Mary's seminarians represented the dioceses of Richmond, Natchez, Dubuque, Albany, and Pittsburgh. Since his accusers were "wrong in fact and in principle," he concludes that Vérot and Frédet are "two excellent inquisitors, because they have such great zeal against the slightest irregularity in others but believe themselves to be entirely innocent and blameless." Deluol tells de Courson that he "regarded M. Frédet as fanatical, M. Raymond as ambitious and M. Vérot as both."[54]

According to the letters from de Courson to Deluol, the latter had exaggerated his case and should develop a spirit of cooperation with the visitors. Ultimately the superior general took the advice of Faillon and Guitter; he recalled Deluol to Paris and appointed Lhomme as temporary superior. In the meantime, Eccleston was very disappointed with the visitors' insistence that the Baltimore Sulpicians remove themselves from all external ministry. He wrote to de Courson that he appreciated the need for the Sulpicians to live according to their rule, which prohibited members to be confessors for nuns. Yet he considered the needs of his archdiocese to require, according to tradition, suspension of the rules.

> But, after having for so long a time taken charge of the Sisters of Charity, of the Baltimore house of the Visitation, of the Carmelites, of various duties of the Mission, have you authorized the Rev. Messers Faillon and Guitter to throw the whole business upon me, unprepared as I am to meet it? Have you authorized them to assign the times within which I must do impossibilities under the penalty of having the Sulpicians withdrawn from Baltimore? . . . But, if you knew the importance of St. Sulpice in this magnificent country, you would not, on light grounds, deprive us of your venerable and noble Society. You might be inspired to pay us a visit yourself or to send over M. Carrière, whose presence would give us all courage.

In a postscript to this letter of 9 August 1849, Eccleston tells de Courson that he has just received word "that the Lazarists have consented to take charge of our Sisters of Charity."[55] This meant Deluol would be relieved of his duties as superior because the sisters were to be united with the French Daughters of Charity. Ironically, Deluol was relieved of his major external ministry, whereas his replacement, Lhomme, did not leave his post as confessor for the Visitation nuns until a year after Deluol had left the United States. Lhomme was a dedicated traditionalist, and Deluol was regarded as an Americanizer who, in the name of pragmatic adjustments to the varied needs of the church in the United States, had compromised the principles of Saint Sulpice. Although Deluol and Eccleston disagreed over the matter of the two colleges, they remained in accord on the need for the Sulpicians to be open to the pastoral needs of the church.

On 4 November 1849, the seminarians presented Deluol with the following testimonial, an implicit rejoinder to those who doubted his effectiveness as a spiritual director.

> Beloved Father,
> Silence on the present mournful occasion would perhaps better express the deep affliction of your children, than any words could do; yet we would fain not to forbear this last tribute of our duty and affection, when about to be deprived of you. We had cherished the fond

hopes of remaining yet many more happy years under your paternal tutelage, of being directed in the path of virtue by your wise counsels, and of being cheered on in the difficult path of our undertaking by your virtuous example. Nay more, we had hoped that, in after years, when exercising the duties of the holy ministry, we might be able to look to you for advice and consolation in our difficulties. These hopes have now fled and we bow, in humble submission, to the will of God. The unwelcome goodbye is about to break the links of love that unite fond children to the dearest of Fathers.

Many of us have, for several years, enjoyed your paternal care. When we reflect that, in our troubles, we had recourse to you and received joy; when, in the hour of temptation, we received, through you, strength from on High to resist the storm; when we consider, in a word, your diligent care to render us happy, both spiritually and corporally, oh! how our souls heave with emotions of gratitude.

Yes, beloved Father, we are grateful to you for all the kindness which you have manifested toward us, and language is not sufficiently strong to convey to you the deep and unfeigned grief which we feel at this moment. We form but a part, Beloved Father, of those to whose hearts your departure will send a deep pang. But, amidst this great affliction, we have one consolation: the knowledge that though time and space may separate us, they cannot break the ties of memory and affection which with the virtues which have characterized your life, have sealed a union which time will not disturb, nor eternity destroy.

Be assured then, Beloved Father, that we will not forget you until gratitude ceases to be a virtue; till well-regulated love ceases to animate the heart, our prayers shall be unceasingly offered up to Heaven, for your temporal and spiritual happiness. Need we urge the request that you will give the memory of us a place in your paternal heart, and that when you stand at the Altar of the living God, you will still breathe the fervent prayer for the welfare of your separated yet devoted children? Farewell then, Beloved Father, and, if not during life, may we all meet in Heaven to enjoy that eternal union, the too early interruption of which we now lament.[56]

Although these words convey the distinct impression that Deluol would not be returning to Baltimore, his future had not been decided at this time. He was to discuss it with de Courson. Eight days after his arrival in Paris, Deluol wrote to Eccleston that "as soon as I was in . . . [M. deCourson's] presence I went on my knees to beg his blessing; he fell on his knees also. He received me most affectionately, and, I may add, with a kind of veneration. He has continued so ever since. . . . Now what shall be done with respect to Baltimore? It is more that I can tell you, and, I believe that Mr. de Courson is at a loss what to think of it." When the superior general did broach the topic, Deluol "answered him with a great deal of moderation, but still without deviating from the truth. He was mortified but it was evident to me that if the visitors had tried to follow the substance of his instructions, they had gone wide from the *modus agendi*. He acknowledged to me that he had written to them to that effect."[57]

De Courson became ill and died on 10 June 1850 before making a final decision on Deluol's future. Deluol's last letter to Lhomme indicates that he understood that, if he did return, there was little for him to do in Baltimore. On 12 July Carrière was elected superior general, and in September the general council decided that Deluol could not return to Baltimore. Deluol wrote to Alexis Elder that he was in agreement with the decision but was opposed to the rationale behind the action.

> M. Deluol cannot return to Baltimore for three reasons; 1) because his presence in St. Mary's would be incompatible with the prosperity of the establishment; 2) because he would disturb the peace of the inmates; 3) because he would mar their happiness. . . . Dog it all, if I were not afraid of sin, I'd be tempted to compare them [i.e., those in authority] to snarling dogs who have got a bone which they are gnawing, ready to snap at anyone who comes near them. . . . I'm not going to sit down before them and sing psalms. They need not growl so much, I don't want their bone. They may gnaw in peace.

Deluol noted that nearly a year after he had left for France, Michael Feller (who had entered the society in Baltimore in 1848) and Edward Knight had left the Sulpicians. "I was not in Baltimore to disturb the peace and mar the happiness of Mr. Feller. What has driven him from Baltimore to Mount Saint Mary's? Again, I was not in Baltimore to disturb the peace of Mr. Knight. . . . What has torn him from his home of 30 years. . . ?"[58] Lhomme, who had been appointed permanent superior that September, was authorized to close Saint Mary's College. It has been assumed that Feller and Knight left the community because of that decision. However, it seems evident from the correspondence that Lhomme's appointment was the overriding factor in their departure.

In a 6 January 1851 letter to Carrière, Vérot provides us with an insight into Lhomme's character. He says that "all the reforms that have been made [by the visitors and by the appointment of Lhomme] may be reduced in the last analysis to a matter of economics and money; that in this view you have given us a merchant for a superior."[59] The following September, Vérot told Carrière that Lhomme was "dry, incisive, surly and there is no one who can associate with him."[60] Ironically, Vérot, who was an impassioned opponent of Deluol, was allowed to devote himself entirely to external ministry after the closing of Saint Mary's in 1852 until he became vicar apostolic of Florida in 1858. At the first Vatican Council he was an ardent opponent of the promulgation of papal infallibility.

Subsequently Deluol was appointed director at the Seminary of Saint-Sulpice in Paris, where he taught theology and Hebrew. His diary includes many references to the steady flow of visitors from the United States, including several bishops. He seems to have embraced French liberal Catholicism; he greatly admired Lacordaire, but he had no respect for the radical social ideas of F. de Lamennais. His Gallicanism was evident in his struggles against the Holy See's 1852 condemnation of the Gallican theologian Louis Bailly, who was identified with the Sulpicians almost as deeply as Olier or Tronson. Deluol was also close to Isaac Hecker. He wrote to him during Hecker's 1857 break with the Redemptorists and his foundation of the Paulist Fathers. He compared his own ordeal in Baltimore to Hecker's expulsion from the Redemptorists, though the latter "grieves me ten times more than my own affair has done."[61] In 1829, he had been dubbed by his enemies within the community as the "Americanizer."

The visitation of 1849–1850 may be viewed as the de-Americanization of the Baltimore Sulpicians in the sense that it was a repudiation of a style of leadership that was both pragmatic and cosmopolitan. The visitors, Faillon and Guitter, were traditionalists who regarded Deluol as too absorbed in the affairs of the world. For his part, Deluol viewed his detractors, Frédet, Vérot, and Raymond, as excessively French in spirit. In many of his letters to de Courson, Deluol says that the three of them were assigned to Baltimore against their will. Although they became naturalized citizens, they did not open themselves to American culture and, indeed, treated American students as if they were French. Hence, as mentioned earlier, they had very few penitents in the seminary, while Deluol had many. As vicar-general of the archdiocese, as a confidant of Eccleston, as confessor and counselor to numerous lay people, religious, clergy, and bishops, and as superior, Deluol was in the mold of M. Emery. Like Emery, Deluol was drawn onto the center stage of ecclesiastical life, but in characteristic Sulpician style he preferred to remain behind the scenes directing and influencing the leading characters and the flow of events.

PART TWO

Americanization in the Immigrant Church (1850–1911)

The dialectic of expansiveness and constriction, that took place within the Sulpician community with the shift from American adaptation to French separatism was in accord with the general trends within the immigrant church. The church of Carroll, Maréchal, Whitfield, and Eccleston was distinctively open to American culture. It tacitly accepted religious pluralism and denominationalism and consciously cultivated an *American* Catholic identity. Among the French Sulpicians in the United States, DuBourg, Flaget, David, Richard, Bruté, and Deluol were the most ardently pro-American.

The period of French separatism (1850–1878) was concurrent with the constricted character of the immigrant church with its emphasis upon nurturing the various ethnic roots of Catholicism. By the late 1880s a conflict had developed within the church in the United States, one that posed the Americanist transformationists, championed by Archbishop John Ireland of Saint Paul, against the separatist preservationists, with Archbishop Michael A. Corrigan of New York as one of their major proponents. The Sulpicians emerged from their own isolationist enclave in the 1880s with the appointment of the liberal Gallican Alphonse Magnien (1878) as superior of the Baltimore seminary and of the liberal theologian John Hogan as superior of the new seminary in Boston (1884). Magnien and Hogan were in the vanguard of the Americanist and the nascent Modernist developments in the late nineteenth-century church.

During the 1890s American-born leaders Charles Rex, Edward Dyer, and James Driscoll held distinctively progressive ideas on the American character of the seminary and on theological studies and scriptural exegesis. The condemnation of Americanism (1899) and Modernism (1907) and the Romanization of the American church marked the temporary frustration of seminary reform and of the attempt to reconcile religion and modern culture.

This section opens in 1850 with the Sulpicians restricted to Saint Mary's and Saint Charles' seminaries; develops through their expansion into Boston, New York, and San Francisco; and closes in 1911 with the Sulpicians expelled from Boston by the militant ultramontane cardinal, William H. O'Connell. In 1850 there were twelve Sulpicians in the United States; in 1911 there were forty-five, the majority of whom were French. During this same period the Catholic population grew from 1,200,000 to over 15,000,000. Once again the Sulpician influence was extraordinarily disproportionate to the size of the community.

6

Restoration of the French Tradition

The repudiation of Deluol's expansive style of leadership and his Americanist administration entailed a revival of the traditional separatism in Sulpician life and of rigid interpretation of the rule. Alexis Elder and Oliver Jenkins were the only Americans within the Sulpician community during this period (1849–1878). As president of Saint Charles' College from 1848 to his death in 1869 (except for a two-year term as president of Saint Mary's College) Jenkins was the only American in a position of authority. The dominant figures during this period were the two superiors, Francis Lhomme (1849–1860) and Joseph Dubreul (1860–1878). Concurrent with the revival of the rigor of the Sulpician rule was the rise of the immigrant church, symbolized by the passage from Anglo-French leadership to that of Irish-Americans within the American hierarchy.

The death of Samuel Eccleston, the appointment of Francis Patrick Kenrick as his successor, and the convocation of the First Plenary Council of Baltimore (1852) mark the emergence of new trends in the American church. Eccleston died on 21 April 1851, without a coadjutor. At one time he had mentioned Jenkins as a possible successor, and to avert such an eventuality the Sulpician superior general, Joseph Carrière, intervened through the apostolic nuncio in Paris. John Chanche, the Sulpician bishop of Natchez, was at the top of Eccleston's list, discovered a month after his death. Although Anthony Blanc, C.M., the ordinary of New Orleans, also supported Chanche, Kenrick opposed him because Chanche's "mind was seriously affected years ago, and also is most exclusive in his national feelings [i.e., anti-Irish] and not at all distinguished for learning or zeal." Kenrick regarded Gilbert Raymond, another Sulpician who was on Eccleston's list, as unfit for the honor, particularly because his French accent marked him as a foreigner.[1]

Kenrick considered John Timon, C.M., bishop of Buffalo and moreover a native of Baltimore, the most worthy candidate. Eventually Kenrick himself received strong support and was appointed archbishop of Baltimore in August 1851.[2] In Paris, Deluol recorded in his diary that indirectly he had heard "that Pius IX, upon learning of the death of Archbishop Eccleston, had said that for a long time he had wanted to see F. P. Kenrick in the See of Baltimore, and that the time had come to fill that wish."[3] A native of Ireland educated in Rome, Kenrick represented the dominant trend of the immigrant church. From the time of Maréchal to the accession of Kenrick, Baltimore had been dominated by the Sulpicians and was the preserve of the Anglo-American Catholic culture and its genteel tradition. Kenrick, who was the American church's foremost scholar-theologian, was dispassionate in contrast to John Hughes of New York ("Dagger John"), but to the staid Archbishop James Whitfield, Kenrick was a "warm headed" Irishman.[4]

Since Kenrick's first American experience was in Bardstown at Flaget and David's seminary, he was familiar with the spirit of Saint Sulpice. Kenrick was relatively close to Eccleston, as mentioned earlier, and when rumors of Eccleston's problems with alcohol reached Rome after the archbishop had suffered a fall from his carriage (1845), Kenrick was assigned to investigate the matter. Deluol had admired Kenrick over the years, and after his appointment to Baltimore he wrote to Lhomme from Paris that Baltimore had a "holy and learned archbishop."[5]

The day of Kenrick's arrival in Baltimore to assume episcopal authority (10 October 1851) he visited the seminary, where he received the Sulpician pledge of loyalty and bestowed his blessing upon the entire seminary community.[6] Three days later he returned to the seminary to discuss with Lhomme and Ignatius Brocard, S.J., the provincial of the Jesuits, the closing of Saint Mary's College and the opening of a Jesuit college in Baltimore. As mentioned earlier, Deluol had considered closing the college as early as 1837. At this same time Eccleston had invited the Jesuits to negotiate with the Sulpicians for the purchase of the property of Saint Mary's College, but Deluol had considered their offer far too low. Perhaps the economic panic of 1837 had an impact on the negotiations, but Deluol's reluctance to close the institution was probably the predominant factor.

Eleven years later the issue surfaced again when Eccleston decided to open Saint Charles' College and to invite the Jesuits to open their own institution in Baltimore. Deluol's attachment to Saint Mary's and his pessimism regarding the future of Saint Charles' appeared in the eyes of his superior general a lack of commitment to the traditional Sulpician ministry and proved to be strong causal factors in his recall to Paris. Lhomme was eager to fulfill the mandate, and he welcomed Kenrick's role as broker in a settlement with the Jesuits. The 13 October meeting concluded with a commitment to establish a Jesuit school in Baltimore, but it was not until 12 June that the Maryland Jesuits received permission from their Roman authorities to open the school.[7] Coincidently this was the date of the last graduation at Saint Mary's College. On 28 July, Oliver Jenkins placed the announcement in the Baltimore *American* "that St. Mary's was officially closed." On 3 September the Jesuits announced the opening of Loyola College (15 September) on Holliday Street.[8] Over half of those who entered Loyola College in 1852 were former students of Saint Mary's College, and the Jesuits followed the tradition established by the Sulpicians and by their own community at Georgetown by adopting a policy of open enrollment for students of all denominations.

Saint Mary's College had made a significant contribution to American higher education. Between 1829 and 1852, 1,628 students were enrolled; 134 received bachelor of arts degrees, 93 master of arts, 1 master of law, and 3 doctor of law degrees. Average enrollment hovered around 200 students, which was a significant figure as during the period between 1840 and 1851 forty-one Catholic colleges had been founded in the United States. Saint Mary's alumni included two governors of Maryland; several notables in medicine, law, and in Catholic and Protestant ministry; and members of such prominent Maryland families as the Carrolls, the Jenkinses, the Ellicotts, and the Knotts.[9]

II

While bishop of Philadelphia, Kenrick wrote four volumes of *Theologica Dogmatica* and translated the New Testament and a large part of the Old Testament; while in Baltimore he wrote three volumes of *Theologia Moralis*. Although intended as texts for seminarians, his works were seldom used in American seminaries. His broad theological vision was matched by his concern for the ecclesiastical life of the church in the United States, illustrated by his role in the seven provincial councils of

Baltimore and by his voluminous correspondence with leading members of the hierarchy in the United States, Ireland, and Rome. Shortly after he moved to Baltimore, the Vatican appointed Kenrick apostolic delegate to the first Plenary Council of Baltimore, which was convened on 9 May 1852. In attendance were the six archbishops and twenty-six bishops representing every state in the union. Eight bishops resided at Saint Mary's Seminary, and according to a custom originating in the First Provincial Council, the Sulpician superior (Lhomme), who was also one of the vicars-general of the archdiocese, was one of the theologians at the council.

The council issued twenty-five decrees, many of which were concerned with liturgical uniformity and with diocesan discipline, such as the establishment of a chancery office and a council of diocesan consultors composed of the clergy of the diocese. To evangelize the vast numbers of immigrants, the council fathers urged the erection of parish schools; to provide for clergy to meet the needs of the burgeoning Catholic population, they called for the establishment of a seminary in every diocese but acknowledged that one for every metropolitan province would be more realistic.[10]

The impact of immigration may be readily perceived in the following statistics gathered by Peter Guilday. From 1834 to 1844, the "personal and material force of the Church in the United States increased at the rate of about 100%; the number of dioceses, bishops, priests, churches, seminaries, colleges and female academies having about doubled during that period." From 1844-1854, the rate of increase was about the same except that the increase in churches and priests was almost 170 percent. In 1834, there were 316 priests, 299 churches, and 9 seminaries, whereas twenty years later the figures were 1,712 priests, 746 churches, and 34 seminaries. The vast majority of seminaries were attached to colleges or academies like Mount Saint Mary's in Emmitsburg and to episcopal households; there were only a handful of seminaries like Saint Mary's and Saint Charles'.[11]

At the time of the First Plenary Council of Baltimore there were 1,600,000 Catholics in the country, 100,000 of whom resided in the archdiocese of Baltimore. Only 100 priests served in the unofficial primatial see. There were 215 Sulpicians located in France, Canada, and the United States, with the Baltimore community totaling only 10 priests. Since no Sulpicians were in the American missions in 1852, the 10 represented seminary directors—3 at Saint Charles' and 7 at Saint Mary's. Of the 590 seminarians in the United States in January 1853, 62 were located at the Sulpician institutions.[12]

During the 1850s, seminarians at Saint Mary's were ordained for the following archdioceses and dioceses: Albany, Baltimore, Boston, Burlington, Buffalo, Covington, Detroit, Hamilton, Hartford, Mobile,

Montreal, Natchez, Newark, New York, Pittsburgh, Toronto, and Wheeling, with the majority from Boston, Baltimore, Buffalo, Hartford, and Wheeling.[13] For some curious reason Samuel Eccleston and Francis Kenrick both favored Mount Saint Mary's over the Sulpician seminary in Baltimore. Perhaps they viewed the rural setting at Emmitsburg as more suitable to clerical training than the urban location of Saint Mary's. Nevertheless, in 1853, Kenrick decided that before ordination his seminarians should spend some time at Saint Mary's. Kenrick was also supportive of Saint Charles' College; of the 81 students enrolled in 1853, about 75 were from Baltimore.[14]

Peter Richard Kenrick, archbishop of Saint Louis, wrote to his brother in Baltimore seeking advice on a community to staff his seminary. Francis replied that he should not rely upon the Sulpicians as they had refused to expand beyond Baltimore.[15] Perhaps F. P. Kenrick was aware of Archbishop John Hughes's unsuccessful plea that the Sulpicians staff his seminary, Saint John's at Fordham. Hughes commissioned Bishop David Bacon of Portland, Maine, to act as his representative with the Sulpicians at Montreal or at Paris, since Lhomme had no authority to negotiate such an enterprise. Hughes told Bacon, "You know what a blessing to this diocese and this Province . . . if the learned and pious Sulpicians would come to place themselves at the head of our theological teaching and ecclesiastical training. There is a great opening for the important and precious work to which God has evidently called them by a special vocation."[16] The New York archbishop was willing to offer the Sulpicians fifteen acres with a church and seminary building at a cost of $22,000, roughly 40 percent of the value of the property. Because there is no extant evidence of the Sulpicians' reply to Hughes, one presumes that neither the Montreal nor the Paris authorities could spare the personnel to staff the New York seminary. Ultimately Hughes purchased a bankrupt Methodist college in Troy, New York, where he established a provincial seminary, and sent Bishop John McCloskey to Louvain, the location of the only independent Catholic university outside of Rome. In late 1864, after the death of Hughes, three Belgian priests, including Henry Gabriels (later bishop of Ogdensburg), arrived to assume responsibility for the seminary.[17] Thirty-two years later, Saint Joseph's Seminary in Dunwoodie, the successor to the Troy institution, received its first students under the direction of the Sulpicians.

In the 1850s there was a strong resurgence of nativism and anti-Catholicism. Although the early years of the republic had been relatively free of anti-Catholic strife, from the beginning of the nineteenth century onward there were periodic outbursts of anti-Catholic hysteria, originating from traditional biases, popular evangelism, the institutional growth of the church (from 1789 to 1830 the church grew from about 30,000 to over 300,000), and widespread fear of immigrants. Religious intolerance ran both ways, as Catholics frequently responded virulently to nativism; moreover, Irish Catholic immigrants brought to the United States their own anti-British and anti-Protestant attitudes.[18]

The Sulpicians occasionally took part in religious disputes. DuBourg was compelled to defend Saint Mary's College against anti-Catholic protests in the first decade of the nineteenth century.[19] Deluol stood guard at the Carmelite convent in Baltimore when an impassioned crowd, incited by a leading Protestant minister, called for the release of the women "inmates" imprisoned behind the cloistered walls.[20] By the 1850s, nativism and anti-Catholicism achieved national notoriety in such putatively patriotic organizations as the Order of the Star-Spangled Banner (c. 1852) and the American Party (1854), whose members became known as the Know-nothings. Dedicated to the exclusion of Roman Catholics from political office, Know-nothing candidates had won victories in many state elections, including that of the governor of Maryland (1855). Former president Millard Fillmore was their presidential candidate in the election of 1856.[21]

Amid the rise of this national "no popery" movement, Archbishop Gaetano Bedini (supposedly on his way to Brazil as nuncio) toured the United States (1853–1854), ostensibly to make a personal visit on his way to his assignment. In fact, he had been instructed to resolve trustee problems, to explore the possibility of establishing diplomatic relations between Rome and the United States, and to report to Rome on the condition of the church in the United States. The Bedini mission exacerbated anti-Catholic tensions. For example, a former Italian priest who was a prominent lecturer on the anti-Catholic circuit accused Bedini of an antirevolutionary execution in northern Italy. In Cincinnati and Wheeling, mobs protested violently, and demonstrations took place in many other cities, including Baltimore, where Bedini was burned in effigy at several locations, one of which was outside of Saint Mary's Seminary on Paca Street.[22] The Sulpician superior, Francis Lhomme, recorded in his diary that on 16 January 1854, an anti-Catholic demonstration of about two hundred men "came down Pennsylvania Avenue on their way to Monument Square; fired pistols in front of the Visitation Convent. Their apparent object was to burn Msgr. Bedini in effigy; in reality to provoke Catholics to fight and so commit acts of violence chiefly on the Visitation Convent."[23] The only account of other anti-Catholic behavior toward the Sulpicians told of three "rowdies" who attacked seminarians and priests on their weekly promenade through the city; one priest was struck by a stone in the head, and another suffered facial injuries.[24]

Bedini's report to Rome contains a commentary on the state of the clergy, including the French Sulpicians in Baltimore. Although he praises them for their deservedly fine reputation, he notes that if anyone were to complain about the Sulpicians it would be about their excessive discipline and restraint, which was in opposition to the free American spirit. He also implies that this Sulpician rigidity was responsible for the high dropout rate of Saint Mary's. To provide a central seminary where students representing all immigrant groups and sections of the United States could experience common theological training and religious formation, Bedini proposed the establishment of an American college in Rome.[25]

In January of 1853, Martin John Spalding, then bishop of Louisville, negotiated with the cardinal archbishop of Malines for the establishment of an American college attached to the Catholic University of Louvain.[26] The Roman college was meant to train American students; the Louvain institution, on the other hand, was conceived as a missionary college with some American students in attendance. Given the strong focus of centralization characteristic of the papacy of Pius IX and of the Propaganda Fide under Cardinal Alessandro Barnabò, it is not surprising that the Roman venture took precedence over that of Louvain. However, the Roman project was not received unanimously by the hierarchy in the United States, and fund-raising problems delayed the establishment of the college until 1859. Meanwhile the American College in Louvain opened inconspicuously in 1857 with only three students.[27] Louis B. Binsse, consul general of the Papal States in New York and an enthusiastic advocate of the Roman college, explained to Cardinal Barnabò the views of the episcopal opponents of the project, who included Peter Richard Kenrick of Saint Louis and Anthony Blanc of New Orleans.

> There is an opinion among several eminent ecclesiastics that the education given at Rome does not impart a truly ecclesiastical spirit. It has been remarked that there is no particular excellence among those who have studied at Rome over those educated here, and that the result of the comparison, on the contrary, is that there is to be found a superiority in the students of the Sulpicians, whose system seems to give a truly ecclesiastical spirit well adapted and very necessary in the present circumstances in this country.[28]

Binsse's comment is in one sense contradictory to Bedini's, who was critical of the anti-American character of Sulpician rigidity; the Binsse opinion praised the Sulpician adaptability to the spirit animating American life. In another sense, however, the two commentaries are complementary; the Sulpician drive for excellence and for infusing an *esprit ecclésiastique* into their students was consciously derived from their dedication to discipline and restraint. Since the authorities in

Paris had rejected what they perceived as Deluol's overadaptability, the administration of Lhomme and Dubreul (1849–1878) focused instead on the traditional Sulpician preoccupation with the discipline of the rule and maintained a studied restraint from interaction with the world.

As the superior dedicated to the reassertion of the traditional interior ministry, Lhomme was confronted with problems subsequent to the closing of Saint Mary's College and with the burgeoning of Saint Charles' College. The old college building adjacent to the Saint Mary's Seminary was renovated to suit the needs of the seminary at a cost of $25,000, and on 25 July 1855, the "new" seminary wing was dedicated by Archbishop Kenrick.

The superior general, Louis de Courson, had been a director at the Sulpician seminary in Nantes. Because of his drive to improve the philosophy curriculum and to enlarge the course to span a two-year period according to the model at Saint-Sulpice, he separated the philosophers from the theologians and, with his personal fortune, he financed a philosophy building at Nantes. Apparently under de Courson's influence, Lhomme placed the philosophers in Saint Mary's old seminary building and housed the theologians in the renovated building. There was an attempt to provide separate institutional structures for the philosophers in 1857, but it ended in failure because of its administrative impracticality. With the opening of a new wing in 1878, and with the mandate of the Third Plenary Council of Baltimore (1884) that seminaries adopt a six-year program divided into two years philosophy and four years theology, the two divisions were finally separated, some sixty years after de Courson had established the division at Nantes. As a result of an 1859 visitation by Faillon and Guitter and in accord with the centralization of curriculum design, Lhomme introduced pastoral theology, liturgy, and an additional class in scripture into the curriculum, which until that time had been dominated by classes in dogmatic and moral theology. As early as 1856 he added church history to the program of studies. He also began the tradition of assigning the preparation of a sermon during the summer; the sermon was presented to the entire seminary community, at first, in the sacristy of the chapel and later at the noontime meal.[29]

With the demise of Saint Mary's College it was necessary to change the articles of incorporation to allow Saint Mary's Seminary authority to grant degrees according to the laws of the state of Maryland. After consulting with Chief Justice Roger Brooke Taney, who had been the Sulpicians' legal counsel long before he sat on the nation's highest court, the Maryland legislature passed a law transferring all the authority of the associated professors of Saint Mary's College to the faculty of Saint Mary's Seminary.[30]

Archbishop Bedini attended the commencement exercises at Saint

Jean-Jacques Olier (1608–1657), founder of the Society of Saint Sulpice in 1641. (Courtesy of the artist, Peter W. Gray, s.s.)

Jacques-André Emery, superior general of Saint-Sulpice (1782–1808). (Courtesy of Sulpician Archives Baltimore)

The Church of Saint-Sulpice, Paris. Detail from a lithograph of Benoist-Bayot. (Courtesy of Sulpician Archives Baltimore)

Saint Mary's College, Saint Mary's Chapel, Saint Mary's Seminary, Baltimore. (Courtesy of Sulpician Archives Baltimore)

RINES CARROLL, S.T.D. JOHN CARROLL, D.D.

John Carroll, first bishop (1789–1811) and first archbishop (1811–1815) of Baltimore. (Courtesy of Sulpician Archives Baltimore)

Ambrose Maréchal, ss., third archbishop of Baltimore (1817–1828). (Courtesy of Sulpician Archives Baltimore)

Samuel Eccleston, ss., fifth archbishop of Baltimore (1834–1851). (Courtesy of Sulpician Archives Baltimore)

Gabriel Richard (1767–1832), Sulpician missionary in Detroit, cofounder of the University of Michigan, Ann Arbor, and member of the U.S. Congress. (Courtesy of Sulpician Archives Baltimore)

James Hector Joubert (1777–1843), Sulpician founder of the Oblate Sisters of Providence, first community of black sisters in the United States. (Courtesy of Sulpician Archives Baltimore)

Mother Mary Elizabeth Lange (1784–1882), first superior of the Oblate Sisters of Providence. (Courtesy of the Oblate Sisters of Providence)

Saint Charles' College, Ellicott City, Maryland, founded in 1848 as a preparatory seminary in the archdiocese of Baltimore. (Courtesy of Sulpician Archives Baltimore)

Saint Charles' College, Catonsville, Maryland. Because of a fire at the Ellicott City site in 1911, the college moved to Catonsville where it remained until it closed in 1977. (Courtesy of Sulpician Archives Baltimore)

SUPERIORS OF BALTIMORE

François Nagot
(1791–1810)

Jean Marie Tessier
(1810–1829)

Louis-Regis Deluol
(1829–1849)

François Lhomme
(1850–1860)

Joseph-Paul Debruel
(1860–1878)

Alphonse Magnien
(1878–1902)

(Courtesy of Sulpician Archives Baltimore)

Third Plenary Council of Baltimore, Saint Mary's Seminary, 1884. (Courtesy of the Archives of the Archdiocese of Baltimore)

Cardinal James Gibbons, ninth archbishop of Baltimore (1878–1921). (Courtesy of Sulpician Archives Baltimore)

Charles' College in July 1853. The president of the college, Oliver L. Jenkins, recorded in his diary that a Boston student, M. Moran, presented an address in Latin to Bedini "to which the Nuncio [sic] responded by a beautiful reply."[31] (Three years later, James Gibbons, the future cardinal archbishop of Baltimore, was the featured student speaker at the commencement ceremonies.) The college's enrollment had increased from four students in 1848 to forty-five in 1853. By adding a third story to the original house, the college could accommodate 70 students in 1855. Five years later a new building was attached to the three-story addition, allowing the enrollment to grow to 115 students. That was the size of the student body when on 22 May 1860 Archbishop Kenrick presided at the laying of the cornerstone for the new chapel. Designed by a frequent visitor from Paris, Etienne Faillon, the chapel was modeled after Sainte-Chapelle in Paris and measured 110 feet in length, 30 in width, and 50 in height. Oliver Jenkins provided the major portion of the funding for the chapel from his personal fortune. Other prominent Baltimore families, including members of the Jenkins family, as well as clergymen of means, contributed to the fund. Because of the high cost of labor and materials during the Civil War, the chapel was not completed until the summer of 1866.[32]

Life at Saint Charles' was austere by almost any standard. Students and faculty frequently worked in the fields (the original farm of 253 acres was expanded to 552 acres by the 1890s), and meat was served but once a week. The students passed through the traditional *ratio studiorum* common in Jesuit colleges except the latter included a year of philosophy and more science than did Saint Charles'. Since many of the boys were from immigrant families, English composition, grammar, and literature were stressed. Jenkins taught the course in the history of English literature. Because most of the standard manuals in this subject ignored Catholic authors, Jenkins compiled notes to add balance to his own course. These notes were refined by Arsene Vuibert and posthumously published as *The Student's Handbook of British and American Literature* in 1876, a work that passed through eleven editions before it was superseded by other texts. Typical of the college curriculum of the day, public or private, popular fiction was not tolerated. Jenkins was a slight man of 105 pounds, but he was a stern administrator and disciplinarian, and the college earned the reputation of being almost monastic in character. Recreation periods were structured into the day at Saint Charles', and American games were played. Such games were not allowed at Saint Mary's Seminary, particularly under Joseph Paul Dubreul, the Sulpician who succeeded Lhomme as superior in 1860.[33]

In February 1850, shortly after Deluol's return to Paris, de Courson appointed Dubreul to Baltimore, where he became vice-president of

Saint Mary's College and professor of philosophy. In 1851 he moved to the seminary and was appointed treasurer. Later he was placed in charge of deacon formation and assigned to teach pastoral theology and canon law. As treasurer he reported regularly to the superior general. This correspondence reveals his rigid interpretation of the rule and his narrow notion of the *esprit ecclésiastique*. For example, he reports that theologians had petitioned the superior for permission to incorporate a "ball game" into their recreation. Dubreul views this request as a return to the "lax" Deluol administration. Writing in 1858, Dubreul notes that his major task during the previous eight years had been to "place the house . . . on the rigor of the rule of St. Sulpice, and that this rule was not considered to be contrary to the character, to the manner or to the prejudices of the country." He admits that the accidentals of the rule could be modified to suit the customs of the country but says that such modifications should not be made a priority. Viewed practically, ball games require "clothing, etc., in opposition to ecclesiastical manners and spirit." He even declares that such behavior "scandalizes the Protestants." To provide for more physical exercise, Dubreul says he would not be opposed to adding another promenade to the weekly excursion through the city, when in a column of two abreast the seminarians walked through the streets of Baltimore in full clerical garb, including black stovepipe hats.[34]

In another letter to Joseph Carrière, Dubreul states that "the great concern of this country is *opinion*" and that among those who were demonstrating disrespect for the rule "all are in favor of M. Deluol," including Oliver Jenkins. He lists several instances of student violations of the rule, such as smoking cigars and drinking liquor and beer, as evidence of a breakdown of authority at Saint Charles' College.[35] Since Lhomme's correspondence with Carrière does not include such alarming reports and since Jenkins was known for his effective administrative ability, Dubreul's views must have been extremely authoritarian. Even Henri-Joseph Icard (the superior general who later elaborated on the *esprit ecclésiastique* in his book *Traditions de Saint-Sulpice*) writes of Dubreul in the official obituary circular letter: "In the beginning, not yet understanding as he later did the American character, preoccupied moreover with the need for good order, there was some rigidity in his approach to things; it might have been better if authority made itself more attractive."[36]

Lhomme, who had been treasurer under Deluol, was considered to have been responsible for the restoration of the primary ministry of the Sulpicians in the United States by closing Saint Mary's College and by expanding Saint Mary's into a regional seminary. Whereas Dubreul represents rigidity, Lhomme conveys the image of restraint. Yet when it came to naming his successor, Lhomme chose Dubreul, though perhaps out of default. The two Americans, Jenkins and Elder, could not have been considered, as the former was vital to the progress of Saint Charles' College, and the latter never demonstrated the abilities of leadership. The five other French priests had also not manifested the qualities of a superior. With Dubreul, a decidedly strong-willed priest, the traditional rule and piety would at least be embodied in a dedicated superior. As Lhomme's physical condition weakened in the late 1850s, Dubreul was in constant contact with the superior general, and this relationship endeared him to Carrière, a strong traditionalist who, in 1848, had disapproved of Deluol's Americanizing leadership. On 18 December 1860, shortly after Lhomme died, Dubreul was appointed superior.

Lhomme was a quiet, reserved person who had gained the trust of Archbishop Kenrick and the religious and diocesan clergy. He was no doubt gratified that during his eleven-year tenure as superior 83 seminarians were ordained, while from 1791 to 1849 only 107 had been ordained. Although traditionalists in Paris, such as M. Faillon, viewed the rise in student enrollment as a result of the closing of Saint Mary's College and the restoration of the primary ministry, it was in fact due to the increase in immigration. Indeed, in proportion to the growth of the church in the 1850s, the increase in the number of ordinations was not significant. Nevertheless, the rise in enrollment was a challenge to the small Sulpician community, which averaged ten priests during this period.[37]

Less than four months after Dubreul became superior, hostilities at Fort Sumter marked the opening of the Civil War. Maryland's sympathies were with the Confederacy, but because of its proximity to the nation's capital, Lincoln placed the state under martial law. Archbishop Kenrick was a Unionist, but unlike John Hughes, who raised the Union flag above his cathedral, Kenrick refused to display his sentiments overtly. Since most of his suffragan bishops were Confederate sympathizers, Kenrick was in a very delicate position. However, he did ask Bishop Augustin Vérot, the Sulpician vicar apostolic of Saint Augustine, Florida, to suppress a pro-Confederacy, proslavery pamphlet.[38] In his manual of moral theology Kenrick states that since "all men are by the law of nature equal, no one is by nature master of another; yet by the law of nations not only the dominion of jurisdiction, but also the dominion of property is granted to man over man; and this the old law ratified."[39] Regarding American slavery, Kenrick opposed the slave trade (condemned by Pope Gregory XVI in 1839) and encouraged manumission, but he was opposed to the abolitionist movement, which he considered as engendering anarchy. Vérot went a step further and justified slavery as a permanent institution but only if the mutual responsibilities and duties of masters and slaves were codified. Vérot published his pamphlet privately, and it was soon translated into French for distribution in the archdiocese of New Orleans.

The Jesuits in Maryland and the Vincentians in Missouri owned slaves who worked on their estates. Because Sulpicians were not large landowners, they owned only a few slaves. There is one Sulpician document that records the purchase of a slave and one of manumission. For unknown reasons, by the 1830s the Baltimore community no longer held slaves. However, individual Sulpicians in Emmitsburg and Louisville owned slaves. As superior Deluol expressed his thoughts on American slavery in a letter to Charles Carroll's granddaughter:

> Born and educated in a country in which this state of things is utterly unknown may I say that my feelings are most violently opposed to...[slavery]. At the same time I have been taught that if we want to be right we must act from principle and not from feeling. Now we don't see that slavery is against either divine or ecclesiastical law. God himself sanctioned it in the messianic dispensation. We don't see that Jesus Christ has said anything about it. . . . The Church has never decreed that slavery, in itself, was illicit.[40]

Since the Sulpicians were the first community of priests to engage in special ministry to black Catholics (1796) and since they were closely identified with the foundation of the Oblate Sisters (1829), Sulpician history is intertwined with that of black Catholics in the United States.

The Catholic church, during the Civil War, did not experience a severe rupture along political and sectional lines. However, there were interdiocesan conflicts such as that between John Purcell in Cincinnati and Martin Spalding in Louisville, and there were excessively patriotic bishops in both North and South. In general, Catholic lay people held Confederate or Unionist views in accord with the general opinion of their Protestant neighbors. As a seminary in a border state, Saint Mary's reflected the conflicts of opinion found in Maryland. One student recalled his seminary experiences during the Civil War: "Some [seminarians] were Northerners, some were Southerners, and it required exercise of great self-control to restrain the partisan tendencies. There were heated arguments . . . comparison of the soldiers and their commanders, elation and depression accompanied by good natured bantering. . . ."[41]

Dubreul does not record such incidents in his diary, but he does note that on 4 July 1863 he raised the Union flag for the first time since the war began: "it had been insinuated by the military authorities that not to do it should be considered a sign of disloyalty."[42] Since the war prevented many seminarians from returning to their homes behind

Confederate lines, the Sulpicians allowed students from both Saint
Charles' and Saint Mary's to spend their summer vacations at Saint
Charles'.

Four days after the flag was raised on 4 July 1863, Francis P. Kenrick died. After the funeral Dubreul visited Archbishop Hughes, who,
Dubreul notes in his diary, "looks like a wreck, he cannot thrive long."
Dubreul writes that Hughes held no "ill feeling" against Carrière or
the Sulpicians for refusing to staff his seminary in Troy, New York.
Dubreul also had a long talk with Richard Whelan, bishop of Wheeling,
"about the names to be put on the list [i.e., *terna*] to be sent to Rome."[43]
Kenrick had left his own list of nominees, all of whom were Baltimore priests. His suffragan bishops rejected Kenrick's list and proposed
Spalding of Louisville and Richard Whelan, who himself proposed John
McCloskey of Albany, John Timon of Buffalo, and William Elder of
Natchez, with the last as his first choice to succeed Kenrick. With such
divisions among the American hierarchy, the influence of Cardinal Karl
von Reisach, Spalding's former professor at the Urban College and an
influential member of the Propaganda Fide, was crucial.[44] It was not
until 9 June 1864 that official word reached Spalding, but as early as
April the news of the impending appointment reached Baltimore, and
Dubreul immediately sent a congratulatory letter to Louisville. Spalding thanked the Sulpician superior but considered the congratulations
premature. He did refer to the Sulpician contribution to the church
in France and the United States and said, "[I am] well disposed [to
the Society] by education and by *spiritual inheritance*. Two ex-Sulpicians,
the Ven. Flaget and David were my spiritual fathers; and reverence
for their memory alone, without other weighty considerations, would
strongly incline me to your institute."[45]

Because of his ill health, Archbishop Spalding delayed his first visit
to Saint Mary's Seminary until seven weeks after the beginning of the
fall term. Dubreul notes the occasion in his diary entry of 24 October:

> He came alone a little before five o'clock. I had a long conversation
> with him in my room till 6¼ at least; he exposed some views in regard
> to the seminary and the rules. I exposed also mine on the same point
> and called his attention to the situation . . . of the seminary since
> 1850, viz; M. Deluol's departure and the suppression of the college.[46]

This frank exchange of views on the rule and the general condition of
the seminary may be viewed as a curtain raiser to a dramatic conflict
between Spalding and Dubreul, one that came to a head in early 1866.

In a 1 February 1866 letter to Michel Caval, the Sulpician superior general, Spalding clearly criticizes Dubreul. After prefacing his
remarks with sentiments of "great esteem and veneration for the Society," he tells Caval that despite Dubreul's "excellent" character, he

"lacks the *savoir-faire* necessary for dealing with students of differing nationalities." According to Spalding, Dubreul had not only failed "to adjust to the conditions and climate" of the United States but also interpreted the rule of the seminary as an almost sacred code, rather than as a practical and flexible guide for the direction of seminary life. Spalding writes:

> To work well and prominently in this vast country, your Society ought, it seems to me, to adapt itself to the circumstances and nationalities of those with whom it finds itself engaged. The Fathers, especially the Superiors, ought to remember that they are no longer in France; and in adhering to the admirable rules of the seminary quoad substantiam, they ought for the indifferent things to observe the rule of St. Paul and become omnia omnibus.

To substantiate his critique, Spalding cites the low number of American vocations to the society since Deluol left for France and refers to the many bishops and clergymen in accord with his own views.[47]

In a letter to Peter R. Kenrick, Spalding is less politic, referring to the Sulpicians as "old fogies."[48] The archbishop of Saint Louis, never one to withhold his honest opinion on ecclesiastical issues, responds, "[I am] sorry that you have occasion to find fault with the Sulpicians, a body which I have always regarded as the crowning glory of the Baltimore diocese."[49] Caval's response to Spalding, not extant, must have requested a more specific list of grievances than that contained in the February letter. On 7 March, Spalding wrote a "memorandum for the Seminary of St. Sulpice" with an introductory note indicating that if the "following ameliorations" were adopted "they would inspire more confidence in the Bishops and the Clergy and would promote the better training of the candidates." Although Spalding does not specifically call for the removal of Dubreul, as he had in his previous letter, the suggestion was clearly implied. His "ameliorations" include the appointment of a director whose native language is English to teach pastoral theology, elocution, and preaching; a strong effort to "obtain American vocations to the Society," to improve the quantity and quality of food, and to encourage "exercise and walks not too long but more frequent"; the abolition of fees for "small extras" such as surplice, candles, and so on; a raise in the standard of instruction to a higher level, including the appointment of "at least one professor who is au courant with modern systems of philosophy, geology, and spiritism and who would be able to teach the candidates how to meet and dispute these current errors"; and an attempt to find suitable candidates for orders as soon as possible within the seminary course "so as to save expense and trouble."[50] In response, Caval ably defends the traditions of Saint Sulpice and cites several bishops who extol the Sulpician dedication to the ecclesiastical life. He refers to Hughes's request for Sulpicians to staff his seminary. Nonetheless, Caval agrees to many of the ameliorations, though he implies that few Americans are suited to the Sulpician way of life and indicates that he will attempt to satisfy the request for curricular changes and for additional English-speaking professors.[51]

The next phase of the conflict centered on the financial relationship between the archdiocese and the seminary. This entailed a dispute over the interpretation of the traditional arrangement whereby all Baltimore students were enrolled gratis, while the archdiocese paid a gratuity at the end of each year. Dubreul requested that the archdiocese begin to pay the full tuition and fees for each of its seminarians. John Carroll had arranged for a subsidy and later provided the seminary with Bohemia Manor. From 1799 to 1852, seminarians taught at Saint Mary's College with their salary paid to the seminary for tuition, room, and board. Since the close of the college, the seminary received no compensation for the Baltimore seminarians (except for a small gift), while at the same time general enrollment and cost per student had increased substantially. To compound the situation, several dioceses had been sending their students exclusively to Saint Mary's and paying full fees, while Baltimore had not been entirely loyal to Saint Mary's. From Spalding's point of view, tradition weighed in favor of the archdiocese's privileged status.[52]

Dubreul attempted compromise by requesting only a half payment, but Spalding rejected this departure from the principle underlying the customary arrangement.[53] As a final solution, the entire proceeds of a special collection were provided for the seminary, and the superior had the authority to limit the number of students from the archdiocese in accord with the total of the proceeds. During this dispute, which took place over a two-year period, Spalding asked John McCaffrey, the priest-president of Mount Saint Mary's, how many Baltimore seminarians he could accommodate and what it would cost. He responded "that despite the fact that the seminary was full, at a few day's notice they could receive ten students at a fee of $200 for board, tuition, washing, ordinary mending, lights and fuel." McCaffrey asked Spalding to send him a priest professor but added, "Save me from a censorious Frenchman."[54] He concluded with characteristic deference: "Be assured that we are ready and anxious to do for you and for religion all that we can. If you are in an emergency calling for your promptest action, use us in any manner you think right and just. We will make shift for the time." Since Spalding requested the same information over a year later and received the same response, one can conclude that he had been ambivalent about both Saint Mary's and Mount Saint Mary's.[55]

The registration book for Saint Mary's includes an average of five students per year from Baltimore during the years of conflict (1866–1869). Ordination records from Mount Saint Mary's do not include a single ordination for Baltimore (1866–1872), while in the Baltimore archdiocesan archives the list includes one priest from the Mountain but lists eight ordinations for Baltimore from the Sulpician seminary (1866–1872). However, eight priests ordained for Baltimore during these years appeared in the archdiocesan records without any reference as to where they were trained; it is safe to say, however, that they were not from either Saint Mary's or the Mount, since during these years alumni from these institutions were listed.[56]

Since correspondence between Spalding and Jenkins did not include one remark on the need for reform, it is evident that the basis for the conflict was the clash between the views of the practical American archbishop and the traditionalist French Sulpician superior. One documented instance reveals this clash. In a letter from June of 1866, Spalding informs Dubreul that after consultation with his archdiocesan council, he disagrees with the superior's recommendation that a seminarian's ordination to the subdiaconate and the diaconate be postponed because of misbehavior:

> 1st—the fathers allege no serious charge or fault against him, *little more than might be explained by child-like simplicity and some levity*, 2nd—he has been for 11 years at St. Charles and the seminary and might be easily discouraged if put back now, 3rd—his family is good and pious and he himself has persevered through many trials, 4th—the want of priests in the archdiocese.[57]

In response Dubreul defers to the archbishop but tells him that the decision "will have a very injurious effect upon the discipline of the seminary." He explains that the student in question had "habitually manifested a disregard for the rules, a want of respect and deference to his superior's advices, a neglect of duty for which he has never shown himself truly repenting." Dubreul concludes this letter with expressions of "sentiments of veneration, filial affection, respect and obedience to the archbishop."[58] The student's name appears on one ordination list for 1866.

As mentioned earlier, the conflict over finances was resolved by a compromise; the proceeds from an archdiocesan collection, rather than direct payment per student, was the archbishop's subsidy for the seminary, while the superior was authorized to draw a limit as to the number of Baltimore students admitted to the seminary. By way of a response to the archbishop's plea for the need to staff the seminary with Sulpicians who could easily adapt to the customs of the United States, the superior general in 1869 assigned Alphonse Magnien to the theology faculty at Saint Mary's. Magnien's background, ecclesiology, and personal inclinations, which will be thoroughly explored in the following chapter, were well suited to the emerging American church. As for Dubreul, he was consistently a model of French decorum, and gradually his rigidity seems to have lessened.

Spalding died in 1872, and James Roosevelt Bayley (1814–1877), the nephew of Mother Elizabeth Seton and a convert from the Episcopal church (1842), succeeded him as eighth archbishop of Baltimore. Bayley had spent a year of seminary training at Saint-Sulpice, where his spiritual director was Arthur Le Hir, who later became, according to Ernest Renan and Alfred Loisy, the foremost Catholic scripture scholar in France. Bayley had been a theologian at the First Plenary Council of Baltimore in 1852; he became the first bishop of Newark in 1853. Upon his arrival in Baltimore, he indicated his loyalty to Saint Sulpice by choosing Dubreul as one of his vicars-general. Never in full health during his tenure as archbishop of Baltimore, in April of 1877 Bayley appointed Dubreul administrator of the archdiocese and sailed for Europe. In August he received the papal brief that James Gibbons, bishop of Richmond and an alumnus of Saint Charles' and Saint Mary's Seminary, had been appointed his coadjutor with right of succession.[59] Bayley died the following October. The following April Dubreul died and was succeeded by Alphonse Magnien. The new superior and the new archbishop formed a close association, one that marked the opening of a new era in the story of Saint Sulpice in America.

7

Americanism and Modernism: Alphonse Magnien and John Hogan

The Americanization of the Sulpicians was manifested in the leadership of Alphonse Magnien (1837–1902); in the scholarship of John Hogan (1829–1901); in the foundation of seminaries in Boston (1884), New York (1896), and San Francisco (1898); and in the rise of American-born Sulpicians (Charles Rex, Edward Dyer, and James Driscoll) to positions of responsibility. As superior in Baltimore; as personal secretary to Cardinal James Gibbons; as a confidant of John Ireland, John Keane, and Denis O'Connell; and as an intellectual in touch with the liberal currents in the French church, Alphonse Magnien was the keystone of the American edifice of Saint Sulpice. He was also deeply involved in the theological movement later known as Americanism.

John Hogan, who shared Magnien's Americanist vision, was primarily concerned with emerging trends in theology, in scripture studies, and in church history. Through the development of his own ideas and through his contacts with scholars and churchmen concerned with creating a new synthesis of contemporary methodology and traditional doctrine, Hogan was responsive to the European modernist vision. From the wings, Magnien and Hogan exerted a strong influence on the dramas of Americanism and modernism within the Society of Saint Sulpice in the United States. To Rex, Dyer, and Driscoll, these older Sulpicians symbolized the need for Americanization and modernization of seminary education, which all agreed could only occur with increased American vocations to the society and with increased autonomy.

II

Alphonse Magnien was born in the diocese of Mende in 1837. He attended the minor seminary in Mende, but at the request of Bishop Félix Dupanloup for seminarians to enter his diocese, which was then greatly in need of new priests, Magnien attended the Sulpician seminary in Orléans and received his theological training there. Although Magnien was attracted to the Sulpician life, Dupanloup required him to serve in the diocese before he would release him to the Sulpicians. Ordained in 1862, Magnien entered the society in the autumn of 1865; two years later he volunteered to serve at Saint Mary's Seminary in Baltimore. Well known for his missionary spirit, his rhetorical style, and his practical, analytical mind, Abbé Magnien became very popular among the seminarians and clergy in Baltimore and among the nascent progressive wing of the American hierarchy. In contrast to the two previous superiors at Baltimore, Lhomme and Dubreul, Magnien manifested an easy adaptability to the diverse needs of American seminarians. When he became superior in 1878, he represented a revival of the spirit of Louis Deluol, and in his reports to the superior general he stressed the need for Sulpicians who could readily absorb the customs, ideals, and language of the United States.[1]

Magnien's ecclesiastical vision was influenced by the evolution of liberal Catholicism in France, which was identified with the names of Montalembert and Dupanloup, and by developments within the Society of Saint Sulpice during the crucial decade of the 1860s, which culminated in the decree on papal infallibility at the First Vatican Council.[2] Later, Magnien would draw a parallel between the views of John Ireland in the 1890s and those of Montalembert and Dupanloup in the 1860s. French liberal Catholicism had evolved within a broad ecclesiological context. The evolution of the meaning of *ultramontanism* between 1830 and 1850 illustrates a profound shift in the ecclesiological significance of the term. In 1830, Lamennais, Montalembert, and Lacordaire viewed the papacy as the champion of human liberty. Just as

Pius VII had struggled against the Erastian Gallicanism of Napoleon, so in 1830 Pope Gregory XVI should, according to the liberal, struggle against the union of throne and altar during the reign of Charles X. When the revolution of 1830 swept away the reactionary regime and established a liberal constitutional monarchy, Lamennais's newspaper, *l'Avenir*, blended political liberalism with ultramontanism and urged the pope to lead a free church unfettered by any dependency on the state. But the papacy was tied to traditional ideals of the unity of church and state and to its dependency upon a reactionary regime in Austria, which was determined to fight all forms of liberalism. The pope ultimately condemned Lamennais.

The majority of French bishops were neither liberals nor ultramontanists but espoused the moderate episcopal Gallicanism associated with the ecclesiology of Jacques-André Emery and identified with Saint-Sulpice. During the 1840s a new ultramontanism, one that viewed all liberal ideas as deriving from the satanic forces of the French revolution, arose. Louis Veuillot, editor of the newspaper *Univers*, became spokesman for this new ultramontanism, which urged the papacy to restore the medieval order of Christendom. This theory gained a political following among many clergy who felt that the existing arrangement of the concordat legitimated episcopal tyranny. Both the theory and the politics of the new ultramontanes gained strength after the election of Pius IX in 1846. In the meantime, the old ultramontanes—identified with Montalembert and Lacordaire, who had embraced a liberal political agenda—viewed Veuillot's ideas as an extremist identification of the church with the papacy. The moderate Gallicanism of Saint-Sulpice, which had consistently extolled the ancient ideals of Bossuet on the spiritual supremacy of the pope, also consistently held to a conciliarist ecclesiology. Spokesmen for the new ultramontanism condemned the old ultramontanes as well as the moderate Gallicans for their apparently lukewarm loyalty to the authority of the pope.[2]

The following exchange of letters in September 1853 between Archbishop Marie-Dominique Sibour of Paris and Count Charles Montalembert illustrates the evolution of ultramontanism. Sibour wrote:

> When twenty-five years ago, you like myself, made fearless profession of 'Ultramontanism' . . . the Ultramontane school was the school of liberty. We defended against the pretensions and aggressions of the temporal power the independence of the spiritual; but we respected the constitution of the State and the constitution of the Church.... The Pope and the Emperor were not respectively the whole of the Church and the whole of the State. On the one hand, there were bishops and councils with a real authority: on the other, there were elements

both aristocratic and democratic which had their place and their right. Without doubt there are times when the Pope may raise himself above all rules . . . and when his power is as wide as the necessities of the Church—just as there are cases in which in civil societies (as we have recently seen) the political power may free itself from the laws and save the country in their despite. . . . The earlier Ultramontanes recognized this; but they did not turn the exception into the rule. The new Ultramontanes have rushed to extremes in both directions, and in reckless exaggeration of the principle of authority have argued *a outrance* against all liberties—those of the state and those of the Church alike.

Montalembert replies:

You are right a thousand times. When we Ultramontanes of former days defended the rights of the Holy See, of justice and liberty, against the Gallicanism of the lawyers and universities, the Ultramontane school was a school of liberty. The attempt is now made to turn it into a school of slavery—and with only too much success.[3]

The split between the old and new ultramontanes occurred over the education issue that emerged from the late 1840s to early 1850s. Dupanloup, who had risen from instructor in a small *petit séminaire* to the rectorship of Saint-Nicholas-du-Chardonnet, the most elite school in France, and ultimately to the episcopate of Orléans (1849), had advocated in 1846-1847 an agreement with the government of Louis Phillipe over the issue of freedom of Catholic schools from government supervision. Veuillot, on the other hand, condemned any accommodation with the liberal anticlerical government. During the republican interlude before Napoleon III became emperor, Dupanloup and Veuillot were at odds over the Falloux Law (1850), a very complicated measure that provided liberty to establish private secondary schools, based upon a compromise between liberal Catholics and Republican anticlericals. Dupanloup, who by this time controlled the newspaper *Ami de la religion*, defended his accommodationist position even though it had become a divisive issue among the French episcopacy. (It is ironic that one of the first Americanist battles, which also infuriated the traditionalists, was John Ireland's accommodationist educational arrangement between the church and public schools.) By 1860, Montalembert and Dupanloup had become identified as the leaders of liberal Catholicism, while Veuillot, supported by the conservative Bishop Louis François Pie of Poitiers, was the vociferous spokesman of ultramontanism. In August 1863, in a speech at the Catholic Congress of Malines, Montalembert proclaimed the ideal of a "free church in a free state," a principle that Pius IX condemned the following year in his Syllabus of Errors.[4]

Magnien was a student at Orléans when Dupanloup adroitly defended the Syllabus on the basis that it represented the thesis, namely, the principle of an ideal Christian society, whereas in the real world of nineteenth-century France, Catholics were allowed to be guided by the hypothesis, namely, recognition that people may work within the practical realm of existing social and political conditions. (The thesis-hypothesis principle had been evoked by the Belgian archbishop of Malines in the early 1830s when Pope Gregory XVI, who condemned Lamennais in his encyclical *Mirari Vos*, did not condemn Catholic support of the liberal Belgian constitution.) Pius IX did not repudiate Dupanloup's interpretation of the Syllabus, and meanwhile the bishop of Orleans was becoming the leader of the inopportunists at Vatican I, who were opposed not to the principle but to the untimeliness of the proclamation of papal infallibility.[5]

Gallican Catholicism ran counter to a strong ultramontane movement that included not only Veuillot's *Univers* but also the Jesuit journal *La Civiltâ Cattolica* and the proponents of a neoscholastic revival in the Roman colleges. This revival took hold among those who viewed rationalism and naturalism as leading to chaos. There was also a popular ground swell of devotion to Pius IX, who had suffered humiliation and exile in the revolution of 1848–1849 and who had been the butt of criticism by Italian radicals and nationalists. The older meaning of the term *ultramontanism* had been turned upside down by these developments, and the moderate Gallicanism of Saint-Sulpice, despite loyalty to the Holy See, had become suspect. Throughout the last half of the nineteenth century the Sulpicians were subjected to periodic waves of criticism from Catholic journalists, from the Roman Jesuits, and from curial officials.

As Yves Congar has noted, the history of ecclesiology is characterized by a tension between two poles, represented in the nineteenth century by the ultramontane and moderate Gallican understanding of papal authority as either executive or constitutional.[6] Saint-Sulpice became identified with the defense of the particular ecclesia, while the ultramontanism of the era of Pius IX defended the absolutism of the pope and, in the process, identified the papacy with the church. The polarized situation in the French church in the early 1850s prompted Pius IX to issue his encyclical *Inter multiplices* of March 1853, which included a severe criticism of Gallicanism.[7]

In late 1852, the theological texts of Louis Bailly, which had been used in Sulpician seminaries for nearly forty years, were placed on the Index of Forbidden Books because of their Gallican character. Adrien Dansette views this placement as harrassment of the Sulpicians because their twenty seminaries in France were identified with Gallicanism.[8] Louis Deluol records in his diary for 31 December 1852, that he, superior general Carrière, and two other confreres visited with Archbishop Sibour and "spoke of the recent condemnation of Bailly," which Veuillot had publicized in the *Univers*.[9] When Bailly was condemned, M. Vieusse revised the section on the four Gallican articles to make them more moderate in tone, and this became the basis for Artemon-Antoine Bonal's "Theology of Toulouse" (later adopted by the Paulists).[10]

In 1854, Carrière traveled to Rome, where he reaffirmed the society's loyalty to the pope, symbolized by the Sulpicians' immediate adoption of the Roman breviary and their rejection of Bailly. As Jean-Remy Palanque remarks, Carrière's visit to Rome was intended to demonstrate that Saint-Sulpice "was no longer Gallican"[11] Although the curé of the parish of Saint-Sulpice issued a strongly ultramontane catechism; the Sulpician theologian Henri Icard wrote a strongly propapal treatise on canon law (1859); and even Louis Veuillot affirmed Sulpician loyalty to his "cause," Rome's suspicions lingered throughout the century, and it is true that, although their leaders may have appeared to be somewhat favorable to the new ultramontanism, the vast majority of Sulpicians could not easily repudiate nearly 200 years of Gallican tradition.[12] Thus Arthur J. Captier, who became superior general of the society in 1894, wrote several letters to his brother during the period between 1862 and 1870 in which he extolled the Catholic liberalism of Montalembert and the moderate Gallicanism of Dupanloup and denied the vicious slanders of Veuillot.[13]

John Hogan and Alphonse Magnien were in accord with the views of their confreres. One of Magnien's close friends was the Sulpician philosopher Louis Branchereau, who had written a manual of philosophy popular in French seminaries during the mid-nineteenth century. He was compelled to submit a précis of his theory of religious knowledge to the Holy See. Such an action was deemed necessary because the affinities of Branchereau's work with ontologism was also under suspicion. He revised the book and resubmitted it to Rome in 1862, but in 1866 it was once again labeled dangerous.[14] The significance of Branchereau's thought in the Americanist context is that John Ireland was influenced by Branchereau, whose work he had encountered during his seminary days in France. Also, ontologism, with its stress upon intuition, was closely related to the Americanist emphasis upon the agency of the Holy Spirit in the church in the modern world. Neo-Thomism provided a conservative synthesis for the relation of the church to modern thought and developed, in part, as a reaction against ontologism.

In 1866, Etienne-Michel Faillon published a work on Olier's *The Interior Life of the Most Blessed Virgin*, based upon fragments of Olier's manuscript. Although the book received an imprimatur in Rome, two members of the Curia Romana criticized it severely on the grounds that Olier appeared to espouse quietism implicitly. The problem was later explained away by the work's fragmentary character, but Faillon was nevertheless forced to revise it.[15] His work on this book was interrupted by the discovery of a multivolume memoir written by Marie Rousseau, whose piety had been a source of inspiration to Olier. With this additional evidence of Olier's spirituality, Faillon prepared a new life of the founder with a view to presenting it as the basis for beatification. In 1866–1867 the bishops of Canada requested Pius IX to support the beatification process. At the same time, 230 priests of the diocese of Montreal wrote a similar letter, and on 20 October 1866, 40 archbishops and bishops in attendance at the Second Plenary Council of Baltimore also wrote in support of the beatification of Olier.[16] The cause was officially introduced, with Faillon as vice-postulator, in June of 1867. Faillon died in October of 1870, with most of the work completed.

The previous 18 July, at a solemn session of the First Vatican Council, the constitution *Pastor Aeternus* was adopted. Thus the ultramontane movement had culminated in the declaration of papal infallibility. But the Sulpicians were identified with Archbishop Georges Darboy of Paris and Bishop Dupanloup, who had publicly led the inopportunist bishops (those bishops who while not rejecting infallibility, did not consider the time opportune for its promulgation), and this identity further disrupted the cause for beatification of Olier.

At the Vatican council, the Sulpician Henri Icard was the theologian of Archbishop Victor-Félix Bernadou of Sens, a moderate inopportunist who ultimately veered toward the majority opinion. Dom Cuthbert Butler views Icard as a major voice for conciliation between the opposing forces at the council:

> He [Icard] was at the time Director or Superior of the Seminary of St. Sulpice in Paris, and had been during forty years professor there of theology and canon law. A number of the French bishops had received their training and had made their theological studies at St. Sulpice during these years, and they looked on Icard as their spiritual father and valued friend.[17]

Although Bernadou was an inopportunist, Icard himself had always taught a clear but moderate notion of papal infallibility. He will figure largely in the sequel, for his influence was great and extended to the American province.

Despite Icard's explicit ultramontanism, the Sulpicians were still viewed as being within the Gallican camp. For example, Cardinal Johann Franzelin, S.J., who guided the infallibility decree through the council and was a leading figure at the Propaganda Fide, interpreted the inopportunist attitude of some American bishops as deriving from the influence of the Gallican Sulpicians in Baltimore.[18] The church historian Roger Aubert supports Franzelin's interpretation; but rather than view this alleged Sulpician Gallican influence in the American hierarchy as an interpretation, he considers it an historical truism.[19]

The First Vatican Council marked the demise of Gallicanism. The triumph of ultramontanism entailed a temporary victory for a monarchist view of the church that was theologically grounded upon scholasticism and its implicit emphasis upon the medieval concept of Christendom. French Catholic liberalism had held to a conciliarist image of the church. Since the infallibility decree had implicitly declared this view untenable, French liberalism was without an ecclesiological base until Americanism supplied one.

In France, the persistent patterns of anti-Sulpician criticism were the charges that the society was promoting Gallicanism, rigorism (i.e., a veiled Jansenism), and ontologism. The church historian Justin Fèvre, who continued the forty-volume work of Joseph E. Darras, was the society's severest critic: "St. Sulpice had been for two centuries the citadel of French particularism."[20] In response to these attacks, Icard published a well-documented apologia in which he ably defends the Sulpicians' loyalty to the Holy See.[21] The following year, Fèvre defended his criticism of the society and mistakenly pointed out that Icard's Gallicanism was evident in his role as a *peritus* at the council, that the Sulpicians were associated with the liberalism of Lamennais, and that Olier's spirituality was suspect among the guardians of the Index.[22] Icard then published a second edition of his response, presenting facts that indisputably disassociated the Sulpicians from extreme Gallicanism and Olier from heterodoxy.[23] Although Fèvre was considered unreliable as an historian, his tract against the Sulpicians tended to give credibility to those ecclesiastics, particularly in Rome and among the Jesuits, who had never believed in Sulpician loyalty to the papacy.

III

Alphonse Magnien and John Hogan were in accord with the general drift of French Catholic liberalism. Hogan was close to the liberal wing of the French church, and Magnien was associated with Félix Dupanloup. Both extolled the principle of a free church in a free state, which had been proclaimed by Montalembert at the Malines Catholic Congress in 1863, and both believed in the practical value of religious and civil liberty, the acceptability of republican forms of government, the utility of scientific methodology to elucidate religious truths, and the certitude of the manifestation of the Holy Spirit in the general progress of modern society, with America as the paradigm of that progress. All of these factors were inherent in the Americanism of John Ireland and provided Magnien and Hogan, as well as the majority of French Catholic liberals, with the rudiments of a serviceable ecclesiology. Thus Americanism was popular in France and among many Sulpicians, not only because it filled the vacuum created by the demise of Gallicanism, but also because the two isms shared a common perspective based on the Holy Spirit's agency in particular national churches as well as in the universal church. Hence, the American church was viewed by both European and American liberals as providing the emerging model for the universal church's encounter with the modern world.

The Americanist network, which extended into France, Italy, and to a lesser extent Germany reverberated with an impassioned enthusiasm for a new age in the church's life, an age characterized by a fresh synthesis of religion and culture.[24] Americanism appears elitist because its proponents were conscious of the novelty of their prescient witness to the *Zeitgeist*. As they proceeded to mount a movement to promote liberal developments in the American church, they were forced to take the defensive by the traditionalists ever concerned about the dangerous tendencies of the modern world. Although the 1899 condemnation of Americanism resulted in the apparent defeat of the liberals, both Magnien and Hogan believed that in time their ideas would be generally accepted. With his liberal ecclesiological perspective Magnien saw John Ireland as another Lacordaire or Montalembert, a man before his time. Hogan, the liberal theologian and biblical exegete, also viewed Ireland as a representative of the new spirit in the church, while Magnien, though immersed in the Americanist movement, did not display any sympathy for the nascent biblical revisionism of the day, represented by Alfred Loisy. On the other hand, Hogan, a more serious scholar, was sympathetic to modern biblical criticism. In their struggles with conservatives, both drew upon their Sulpician heritage and their experience with liberal Catholicism in France.

Albert Houtin wrote that the Sulpicians in America, particularly Alphonse Magnien, were attached to the ideas of Lamennais, Dupanloup, Montalembert, and Lacordaire. Because of the close relationship between the Sulpicians and their alumni priests, Houtin viewed the society as a strong liberal force in the church of the United States.[25] By 1891, Magnien was deeply involved in the Americanist movement. He was supportive of the leadership of John Keane at the Catholic University of America and a proponent of Ireland's controversial Faribault-Stillwater school plan, whereby the parochial schools in these two Minnesota towns were rented to the local public school board, which in turn paid the salaries of the nuns and allowed religious instruction outside of regular classes. This controversy was another round in the fight between Michael Augustine Corrigan, archbishop of New York, and Ireland, with both extending the field of action to the Vatican and employing the weapons of the American and European press. The Jesuit Roman periodical *La Civiltà Cattolica*, through one of its editors, Salvatore Brandi, lashed out at Ireland and in the process implicated the Sulpicians. The controversy occurred during the 1891–1893 period when pro-Ireland forces, including Republicans of national stature, were urging the Vatican to elevate Ireland to the College of Cardinals.

On 17 March 1892, John Ireland wrote to Magnien a full report on his efforts to defend his school plan at the Vatican. He was pleased with Gibbons's letter to the pope on behalf of the plan and concluded that "the field seems now clear of difficulties—except for the *Civiltà*, which to my mind is particularly devilish. . . . The Jesuits evidently make the fight a matter of life and death." He told Magnien that he had heard that Archbishop Corrigan had brought the Jesuits in Rome into the school controversy. "They want him to be a Cardinal and thus have the leadership of the American Church transferred to New York." Apparently Ireland viewed Magnien's seminary life as a guarantee against the strife of ecclesiastical maneuverings. "In your holy seminary, you will believe me with difficulty when I tell you of the scheming that is going on to secure church dignities and church prerogatives. I charge most of our troubles on Archbishop Corrigan, whose ambition throws him into secret alliances with our enemies." Ireland closes this letter with the prescient remark "I may win this time a small victory, but the war, I fear, will continue."[26] Two weeks later Magnien wrote to Ireland, "You should not leave Rome until every difficulty has been solved and the path is clear." With what must have been irony, Magnien's closing line reads, *"Do not show this letter to Jesuits."* Magnien informs Ireland of a news story "which will give it out that the *Civiltà* got a rebuke from the Pope for attacking you and that the Pope has just received from Cardinal Gibbons an important study on the school question [in] which his Holiness is much interested." Magnien tells Ireland of Gibbons's fear that his letter "would fall into the hands of Miss Ella Edes [the confidante of Corrigan and bitterly anti-Sulpician] and the minutante at Propaganda Fide" who were allies of Archbishop Corrigan. Hence Gibbons directed Magnien to write to Ireland "to see that it should be kept out of his and anybody else's reach."[27]

With the Vatican's tacit approval of the school plan, Ireland's friends mounted a campaign for his elevation to the cardinalate. Magnien told Denis O'Connell that Gibbons and James G. Blaine, the U.S. secretary of state, had written letters to Cardinal Mariano Rampolla, Vatican secretary of state, favoring the promotion. After expressing his hope for the success of these two letters, Magnien shared with O'Connell his fears of Corrigan's elevation.

> The appointment of the other candidate would in the present circumstance be a true misfortune. It would give power and strength to the opponents of the University . . . and confer authority to those views and principles which in America and for America are fraught with mischievous consequences because they have no other effect than to make Americans consider the church as narrow minded and more or less inimical to the institutions of the country.

Magnien not only placed the Corrigan forces in an archconservative mold but also linked them with the machinations of Tammany Hall. "Think of the Tammany ring being glorified, and wire pulling becoming the policy of the church in the United States."[28]

At times Magnien's commitment to Ireland exceeded his loyalty to Gibbons, particularly on the issue of a red hat for the former. In a letter to O'Connell in Rome dated 3 August 1892, Ireland relates the following story.

> Dr. Magnien is stopping with me. We talk for hours at a time. It is amusing to hear him tell how he maneuvered to get the Cardinal [Gibbons] to write that famous letter in favor of my Cardinalate. After it was written and signed, the Cardinal refused to mail it for a week. At last he consented and Magnien rushed with it to the post office. Then a cablegram Magnien had to have torn up. . . . Gibbons is exactly the weak man we have been imagining but good at heart. . . . Magnien is a sterling man. But few like him.[29]

The Vatican's refusal to confer the red hat on Ireland and the apparent ascendancy of the Corrigan forces left Magnien with a sense of disillusionment. In March of 1895 he wrote to Ireland that he was "disconcerted."

> The enemy knows full well that they are strong in Rome, outside the Vatican, and the fact that the Holy Father, after promising to do so much to assert his policy, is doing so little, seems to imply that he himself is afraid of the men who oppose him, and then what can we expect?

Magnien informs Ireland of the latter's popularity in France. Although he refers to Ireland's enemies there, he is confident of the increasing number of friends:

> You stand before the public as representative of views which are sure to win and to rule, though you may not live long enough to see their triumph. Bishop Dupanloup and M. Montalembert fought to the end

and died apparently conquered; today their names are glorified and their policy rules the Church. So, I suppose, will it be in America. Let us have confidence in the future . . . in God's good time the fruit of your labors will be reaped by the American Church.[30]

From his letters to Ireland, it is obvious that Denis O'Connell was the manager of the archbishop's campaign to assert the Americanist cause in Rome. In July of 1897, O'Connell told Ireland that Archbishop Placide Chapelle would soon be transferred from Santa Fe to New Orleans. He then proposed that Magnien be appointed archbishop of Santa Fe. "If Dr. Magnien is going to die in Baltimore, it would be better to send him to Santa Fe, if you could get Hogan to replace him in Baltimore."[31] Apparently, O'Connell wanted a strong liberal to dominate the relatively indecisive cardinal archbishop of Baltimore. Less than a month later, O'Connell repeated the proposed strategy to Ireland. "With Chapelle at New Orleans, Maes in Cincinnati, and possibly Magnien at Santa Fe, you would hold the whole American Church [i.e., control a majority at the meetings of the archbishops]. But Magnien should not be sent to Mexico [sic] unless Hogan could take his place at Baltimore, 'Put only Americans in guard.'"[32] In a later letter O'Connell waxes hyperbolic. "If you put Magnien in Santa Fe you will rule the Church."[33] The only extant evidence of Magnien's own views on this proposal is a remark he made to O'Connell, "My place is here [in Baltimore]; not in Santa Fe where I would be like a fish out of water."[34]

By this time Walter Elliot's Life of Isaac Hecker had been translated into French by Félix Klein, an event that precipitated the Americanist crisis.[35] Magnien, who was in France for his health during the winter and spring of 1898, witnessed the bitter controversies, which included charges of heresy against Hecker and attacks on all those identified with Americanist views. While Magnien was in Paris, O'Connell wrote to Klein. "I hope you will make the acquaintance of Father Magnien of St. Sulpice now in Paris and President of St. Mary's Seminary, Baltimore. He is the head and heart of the whole movement in America."[36] Before leaving for France, Magnien had congratulated O'Connell on his recent address at the Fourth International Catholic Scientific Congress at Fribourg entitled "A New Idea in the Life of Father Hecker." O'Connell's "new idea" was that Hecker represented Catholic Americanism in both its ecclesiastical and its political forms. Political Americanism was manifested in Hecker's views on the harmony between the natural law and American principles embedded in the Declaration of Independence, the Constitution, and the Bill of Rights. Ecclesiastical Americanism, according to O'Connell, was manifested in Hecker's praise for the American tradition of separation of church and state. Since the Vatican had never accepted the theory of such separation, O'Connell justified it on practical grounds as suitable to a distinctly Protestant America. O'Connell proudly extolled the principle of religious freedom as fostering excellent "unhampered" relations between the American church and the Vatican. Indeed, he placed Hecker's Americanism within the plan of Providence.[37]

Magnien was so impressed with the address that he had it read to the seminarians at Saint Mary's and promised to see that it was published in the *Mirror*, the Catholic newspaper of the Baltimore archdiocese. Magnien was an admirer and friend of John Keane, who had been removed as rector of the Catholic University of America the previous year and was then stationed in Rome. However, Magnien told O'Connell, "Please . . . watch [your] tongue. I always fear that . . . [Keane] will commit himself to some extraordinary and very suspicious statement. Had he treated the subject of your paper he would have put his two feet in it."[38] O'Connell's speech precipitated an immediate attack by Bishop Charles Francis Turinaz that, according to Félix Klein, was the first of a long series of "diatribes against anyone associated with Americanism."[39] In December, Magnien wrote O'Connell: "A Jesuit Father even went so far as to speak against . . . [Father Hecker's life] in the pulpit of St. Sulpice and I am informed by reliable persons that the . . . [Jesuits] are doing their best to have the book placed on the index. I dropped a note to Archbishop Ireland on the subject." Nevertheless, Magnien remained hopeful. After reading reports of a speech delivered in Rome by Ferdinand Brunetière, editor of the liberal *Revue des deux mondes*, Magnien exclaimed, "All these things may open the eyes of many in Rome and convince them that the world is moving and that it is of no use to try to stop it."[40] No doubt, Magnien was encouraged by the popularity of Americanism in Europe, engendered by Klein's translation of Elliott's life of Hecker.

Thus, in March of 1898, while he was visiting friends in Milan, Magnien told O'Connell how impressed he was with the Parravicino family to whom O'Connell had introduced him. Magnien was particularly struck by the way they had united

> a truly Christian spirit with . . . very wise liberality of views and . . . I have gathered from their conversation that here in Milan and elsewhere in Italy there are lots of people who think as you and I do on many subjects, and that Americanism well understood has more partisans in Europe than are in America. Thanks be rendered to God for it. Let us be prudent and active and the future is ours.[41]

Magnien's optimistic, irenic views of the future of Americanism were not tempered by the publication of the most impassioned rejoinder to the Klein/Elliott life of Hecker—*Le Père Hecker: est-il un saint?* by Abbé Charles Maignen. Maignen's work charges that Hecker's writings are riddled with heretical subjectivist ideas of freedom and reflect a diabolical notion of the manifestations of divine providence in his own life and in the future of American society. Maignen also sees the Americanism of Keane and Ireland as a reflection of the liberalism condemned by Pius IX in the Syllabus. Magnien, who was in Paris in May of 1898 when the publication of Charles Maignen's book was announced, succeeded in convincing Cardinal François Richard to refuse it an imprimatur.[42] However, the book received an imprimatur in Rome in late May.

Nevertheless, two months later Alphonse Magnien expressed his optimism over the ultimate victory of the movement. He wrote to Klein, "Americanism (the real thing, not the caricature that they have created) cannot be killed. Its activity can be retarded and made slower; but it will persist and finally will conquer. You will have the glory and perhaps the happiness, I hope, of having contributed to its triumph."[43] But he was not so sanguine in his views of the immediate situation. He told Klein of Cardinal Rampolla's weak response to Cardinal Gibbons's protest at the Roman imprimatur for Charles Maignen's book. The Sulpician superior lamented the influence of the "three implacable enemies [in Rome] Mazzella, Satolli and Brandi, and they have the old Pope in their power."[44] According to Magnien, Rampolla's response included the remark that "the Pope will send to the Cardinal a Pontifical letter concerning Hecker's case." Magnien confided to O'Connell his confusion about the probable contents of the letter "as it could be a condemnation of Hecker, or, for the sake of peace, the Pope may say nothing on the matter."[45]

The worst fears were realized as *Testem Benevolentiae*, the papal letter condemning the error of Americanism (dated 22 January 1899), was sent to Gibbons on 31 January 1899. The pope based his letter on the fact that the French edition of Hecker had engendered serious controversy and had introduced erroneous opinions on the Christian way of life. The letter then elaborates on these alleged Americanist opinions, which include such errors as the stress upon the active virtues to the exclusion of the contemplative ones, the overestimation of the natural virtues, the assertion that individual liberty should be introduced into the church, and an exaggerated emphasis upon the role of the Holy Spirit in the life of the individual. Perhaps the most direct attack upon the overall liberal position is the pope's charge that Americanism was based upon the principle that the church should "shape her teachings . . . in accord with the spirit of the age . . . and make concessions to new opinions . . . changes not only in regard to matters of discipline but of doctrines in which is contained the 'deposit of faith.' "[46]

Of course Magnien, Ireland, and the others never advocated changes in doctrine, but they did strongly hold that the church should "shape her teachings to the spirit of the age." This reactionary tone of the letter, with its references to the "dangers of the age," stands in stark contrast to the Americanist embrace of the positive aspects of American culture.

Alphonse Magnien's response to the letter placed him squarely in the "phantom heresy" interpretation, as he viewed the encyclical as a caricature rather than an accurate summary of any current opinions. He told Ireland that those who consider the letter to have been "the result of intrigue by the monarchists of France and the Jesuits . . . [were] not far from the truth." He was surprised that O'Connell and Keane were so thoroughly deceived about the real state of the question: "Were they fooled or was there a change in the Pope's views?" Magnien was equally surprised at the "fierce tone" of the letter and the absence of "any soothing word for the Paulists." He expressed his pity for "poor Klein who had done so much for the American cause." However, the Sulpician superior never lost hope in the ultimate victory of Americanism. He suggested to Ireland that in his upcoming address on Joan of Arc to be presented in Orléans (the occasion was arranged by John Hogan) he "must . . . speak so that all Frenchmen, no matter what their political views are, will be pleased with your words. It will be a great success for Americanism rightly understood."[47]

There is a prophetic element in Ireland's visit to the diocese of Orléans, where Magnien's views on the spirit of the age had been nurtured by Félix Dupanloup. Magnien had drawn analogies between the bishop of Orléans and the archbishop of Saint Paul, Minnesota, considering both of them to be men whose successes would be known only after their death. Although the Sulpician was convinced that in the 1890s Dupanloup's views had been vindicated, in point of fact it was only at the Second Vatican Council that the church embraced Dupanloup's notion of collegiality and Ireland's posture toward the spirit of the age.

The Magnien-Ireland relationship weathered the stormy crisis of Americanism, and they remained close friends. Toward the end of 1902 when Magnien was nearing death, Ireland visited him. As Ireland wrote to O'Connell, "I cried when I saw him: 'Many battles you and I have fought,' I said to him, and he smiled."[48] After Magnien's death Ireland wrote,

> I shall think of him as my friend. I loved him and I believe he loved me. Our thought ran so much on the same lines; our affections reached out so much toward the same objects and the same purposes. . . . Father Magnien is gone, and around me there is a void never to be filled during this life of mine on earth.[49]

This Americanist portrait of Alphonse Magnien clearly reflects Gerald P. Fogarty's understanding of Americanism and its emphasis

on the *political* character of this reform movement. It also supports
Thomas E. Wangler's interpretation of Americanism as an international
reform movement.[50] Because John B. Hogan participated in both the
Americanist cause and the nascent Modernist movement, the story of
his role during the crisis of Americanism tends to give support to those
historical and theological interpretations that emphasize the common
general reform impulses shared by Americanists and Modernists.[51]

IV

John Hogan was born in County Clare, Ireland, in 1829. As a young
boy he was drawn to the priesthood, and at the urging of his uncle,
a priest of the diocese of Périgueux, he entered the preparatory seminary in Bordeaux at age fifteen. A brilliant student, Hogan enrolled
at Saint-Sulpice in 1849, joined the society in 1851, and was ordained
a year later at the age of twenty-three, whereupon he was immediately appointed to the chair of fundamental theology at Saint-Sulpice.
Of a decidedly liberal persuasion, Hogan gradually found himself in
sympathy with Lacordaire, Montalembert, and Dupanloup. Influenced
by the ontologism of the Sulpician philosopher Branchereau, Hogan
was disdainful of scholasticism and openly embraced the developmental theology of John Henry Newman, whom he visited on several occasions. Hogan, who became professor of moral theology in 1864, was
primarily a pedogogue rather than a scholar. Well known for his Socratic style of teaching, his flexible and open mind, and his breadth
of vision, he became identified as one of the leading liberal Catholic
thinkers.[52] As a master teacher, Hogan inspired his students to achieve
high levels of critical thinking. Several of his students, with whom he
developed lasting friendships, reflected the liberalism of their mentor:
Maurice d'Hulst (1841-1896) was rector of the Institut Catholique de
Paris; Exale Irénee Mignot (1842-1917) was the archbishop of Albi and
episcopal sympathizer with certain aspects of Modernism; Félix Klein
(1862-1953) was, as noted earlier, the French exponent of the ideas of
Isaac Hecker and John Ireland.[53]

Archbishop John J. Williams of Boston, whose spiritual director
was Henri Icard, had successfully sought the Sulpicians to staff his
seminary. John Hogan, who had become acquainted with Williams at
Saint-Sulpice, was appointed superior, and in the fall of 1884, Hogan
opened the doors to the first class at Saint John's Seminary in Brighton,
Massachusetts. Hogan was *au courant* with trends in American Catholic
intellectual life. His correspondence with the Paulist scripture scholar
Augustine F. Hewit illustrates a strong familiarity with the *Catholic
World* and a deep reverence for Isaac Hecker.[54] Shortly after his arrival
in the United States, Hogan notes in his diary that he was "of the same

mind on most things" as Alphonse Magnien and Cardinal Gibbons. He was enthralled by Bishop John J. Keane: "Never have I heard a man speak for a full hour with such grace, force and power."[55] As Archbishop Williams's theologian at the Third Plenary Council of Baltimore, Hogan was introduced to the major issues confronting the American church and to their major proponents.

Hogan was not as ardent an Americanizer as was Magnien. While the latter had matured as a seminary professor in the United States, Hogan's career had been nurtured in the austerity of Saint-Sulpice for over thirty years before he became superior of Saint John's. Hence, his piety and his style of administration were very much in accord with French Sulpician traditions. Fondly referred to as the "abbé" Hogan, he was certainly not a rigid man. Yet if one's knowledge of him were limited to contributions of those historians who focused only on his spirituality and administrative career, it would be easy, though incorrect, to conclude that Hogan was a strong conservative.

Thus, Donna Merwick has portrayed Hogan as Jansenist, as ever admonishing his students to fear the dangers of the modern world.[56] Merwick's research on Hogan was limited to his book *Daily Thoughts for Priests* (1899), a traditional and eclectic manual on the spirituality of the sacerdotal life.[57] She did not seem to know of Hogan's critical views on current theological and ecclesiastical tendencies. As Archbishop Mignot, the only major Modernist prelate, remarked, Hogan viewed "the progress of today as the tradition of tomorrow."[58]

Similarly, Patrick J. Ahern's study of the Catholic University of America under the rectorship of Keane provides merely a one-dimensional image of Hogan. As president of Divinity College from 1889 to 1894, Hogan did enforce a modified Sulpician seminary rule, and since residents of the college were priest-graduate students and priest-faculty members, he experienced many complaints about his rigidity.[59] Indeed, he had so alienated the faculty that, when he was appointed to the chair of apologetics in 1894, the appointment was rejected by the faculty senate.[60] While Merwick's Hogan is simply Jansenist, Ahern's Hogan is ambigious, but by selective quotations Ahern's final portrait is close to a caricature, one in stark contrast to that of Hogan's students. Archbishop Austin Dowling of Saint Paul recalled that Hogan "was by long odds the biggest [man] we had ever met or perhaps shall ever meet. . . . We rarely left him without feeling the ambition and obligation of looking up some further question. . . . He always held that 'a good deal could be said' for the worst side of any question."[61] Félix Klein referred to him as the "learned, pious, tactful, kindly Abbé Hogan."[62] In 1894 Hogan returned to Saint John's Seminary, but he remained close to Keane and several colleagues at the Catholic University in Washington.[63]

Hogan's correspondence reveals his strong endorsement of almost all aspects of the Americanist cause. He supported Ireland's school plan and hoped to see the archbishop of Saint Paul elevated to the College of Cardinals. He was enthusiastic in his admiration for the Paulist Fathers and was a confidant of Denis O'Connell.[64] During the crisis of Americanism he was supportive of the Paulists and Klein. Walter Elliot wrote to Klein that he had "a long talk with Father Hogan, the Sulpician . . . a man whom I esteem very highly indeed. He, to my surprise, said he knows you well, and then launched forth into such praises of you that I dare not shock your modesty by repeating them."[65] After *Testem Benevolentiae* Hogan wrote to George Deshon, the superior of the Paulists,

> I write to express my hope that you do not take much to heart the recent letter of Leo XIII. All I hear and read, and know convinces us that it finds no welcome in this country. The Paulists, their spirit and their work, stand before the Church and the general public of the United States stainless and bright. The strictures of the Pope have no application to them nor to their founder for those who knew him.[66]

(Hogan's correspondence substantiates Robert D. Cross's belief that the Paulists and the Sulpicians were the two most liberal religious communities of priests in the United States.)[67]

A few days later, Hogan's views of the encyclical appeared in the *Boston Globe*. After chronicling the controversy over the French edition of the Hecker biography, he remarks that the doctrines described in the encyclical are not held by either "enlightened Catholics in this country nor those who were so enthusiastic over the life of Father Hecker in France." The encyclical, according to Hogan, stems from "the sensitive orthodoxy of a certain number. . . . Thus, then, there seems to be no need of the letter, so far as America is concerned, and not much as regards France." Like Alphonse Magnien, John Hogan supported Klein's "phantom heresy" thesis. The pope's letter had relevance only as a warning against certain tendencies that, Hogan said, "must be watched and kept within bounds." As to Elliot's book on Hecker's life, he states that "if read in the proper spirit—that is to say without the desire to criticize or catch little details—[anyone] would see it in its true light. . . . I believe the book did little, if any, harm in France."[68]

Dispassionate analysis of the putative Americanist heresy provides an insight into Hogan's tactful yet straightforward rhetorical style. He did not enthusiastically elaborate on a proper interpretation of Heckerism and Americanism, but he certainly indicated his disapproval of Rome's overreaction to what were merely inconsequential excesses. Hogan did not share the encyclical's contempt for contemporary developments. On the contrary, his prodigious intellectual output during his time in America represents an attempt to struggle against the stultification of Catholic tradition engendered by those who wished to ignore the positive elements of modernity.[69] Albert Houtin, in his book *L'américanisme*, refers to Hogan as a liberal Catholic who was held in high regard by the American bishops and by the Paulists. Indeed, he was of such considerable influence that Houtin calls him the "doctor and theoretician of progressive Catholicism . . . [in the United States] which should be named religious Americanism."[70]

Hogan's religious vision was based upon his study of scripture. For many years he had approached scripture in light of the discoveries of modern archeological, historical, and literary research. The problem of reconciling inspiration and inerrancy with the factual evidence provided by this research became the major issue for scripture scholars and theologians.[71] Early in 1885 Hogan sent Augustine Hewit his notes on inspiration and wrote: "If the sacred writers could and did share in the scientific errors of their times, why not also in historical errors, so long as they remained foreign to the object for which their books were written? This, to my mind, is the great difficulty."[72]

In a later letter Hogan becomes more specific about this difficult historical problem, namely, the generally held belief by the New Testament writers that the second coming of Christ was imminent. He expresses his gratitude to Hewit for agreeing with him that this belief, indeed, is an error. He tells the Paulist scholar:

> I have seen many people startled at the mere suggestion of it. Most of our Catholic commentators, if not all, won't listen to it. They shut their eyes to the plain facts not to have to admit it. They resign themselves to the most distorted and unnatural interpretations to escape the conclusion. And to speak truly, I fear that it does detract somewhat from the fullness of the authority commonly conceded to Holy Writ to allow that what we must call a mistake was universally shared in by the apostles, believed to be taught by our Lord himself— made into an habitual means of exhortation, and finally given up on when belied by experience.[73]

Not only would Catholic scholars of that day have winced at Hogan's statement on the imminence of the kingdom; even most of the Protestant world of biblical scholarship was startled when Johannes Weiss published his first edition of *Jesus' Proclamation of the Kingdom of God* in 1892, a scholarly elaboration of the theme of Hogan's letter, dated seven years prior to that year.[74]

Hogan also tells Hewit of his intention to develop a theory of inspiration and inerrancy which would

> be at variance neither with orthodoxy nor with the facts. . . . Orthodoxy requires us to say there are *no errors* in the Bible. Facts tell us what manner and measure of departure from strict accuracy are actu-

ally to be met in the Bible. They give us, therefore, the sense in which we are to understand the word *error*. They certainly compel us to give it a very loose, vague sense far beyond what theologians commonly admit or imply.[75]

In 1893 Monsignor d'Hulst, Hogan's former student, published his famous article on the biblical question in which he divides Catholic scripture interpretation into three categories: rigid fundamentalist; moderate evolutionist, which affirms that all conflicts in interpretation will eventually be resolved; and the liberal position, which holds that inerrancy, like papal infallibility, should be very restricted. D'Hulst's article engendered a widespread protest that resulted in the virtually forced resignation of Alfred Loisy from the Institut Catholique de Paris, of which, one will recall, d'Hulst was rector. In November of 1893 Loisy published his own views on inspiration in which he expresses his notion of relative inerrancy, which was immediately interpreted as a doctrine of "relative errancy." The d'Hulst-Loisy controversy prompted Leo XIII's encyclical *Providentissimus Deus*, a reaffirmation of the traditional notions of inerrancy, namely, obvious errors were to be viewed within the context of the time and place and as secondary to the absolute inerrancy of the inspired word.[76]

Hogan corresponded with d'Hulst and Loisy during this crucial year. In a letter to Hogan, d'Hulst laments both his disagreement with Loisy and the regressive character of the pope's encyclical. He predicts that progressive literary and historical Catholic exegetes will be forced into duplicity and is disturbed at the prospect of the encyclical's effect upon the progress of the higher criticism.[77] In a previous letter d'Hulst confided to Hogan his opinion of the generally reactionary thrust of Leo's reign.[78] Hogan was very impressed with both d'Hulst's and Loisy's articles on the biblical question. Since Charles Rex (superior at Boston and a teacher of scripture) had hoped to have d'Hulst's article translated for American readers, Hogan suggests that Loisy's "would make an interesting sequel to d'Hulst." He considers Loisy's article on the inerrancy question to have been "the clearest and strongest I have seen yet."[79] Hogan congratulates Loisy, who responds with his gratitude for Hogan's "encouragement."[80] The French exegete was predictably annoyed at the encyclical, as was Hogan. The latter told Rex that the encyclical precluded any English translation of d'Hulst, as it "forbids any favor being shown the theories which . . . [d'Hulst] had exposed on the 'liberal side.'" Although he notes the encyclical's positive stress upon further scripture study among scholars and seminarians, he rightly anticipates that the encyclical would be "rather the beginning than the end of trouble." He sympathizes with those scholars who labored for years to develop a positive yet limited notion of inspiration, and he expects Protestant scholars of the progressive school to be "up in arms to disprove the Pope's doctrinal position," while he foresees many Catholics remaining silent or resorting to mental reservations to preserve their integrity. He expresses the hope that the pope's statement on the inerrancy of the Bible would not create a schismatic movement deeper and more abiding than the "old Catholic" reaction to the statement on papal infallibility.[81] A few weeks later Hogan told Rex that the faculty at the Catholic University of America "had sent an act of grateful acceptance to the Pope" for his encyclical on the Bible. However, he interprets this as a mere formality signifying only the faculty's loyalty to the papacy; "it is just as in Paris an act of general homage without internal assent."[82]

In an April 1898 letter to Loisy (one that was in response to a "long letter" no longer extant), Hogan remarks, "On certain points you and I are in perfect accord not only when you speak on the substantive divinity of religion, of the necessity of the Church, of the wisdom of individual conscience, etc., but also when you affirm the relativity of dogmatic formulation." Hogan refers to the impossibility of elucidating religious mysteries except by "analogous conceptions." However, he tells Loisy that the danger lies "in the very indefiniteness" of these analogous expressions. This will engender confusion, vague beliefs, and a disorganized religion: "Without neat conceptions and precise affirmations Christianity will survive . . . with little practical effect upon the mass of Christians." Like his theological mentor Cardinal Newman, Hogan says that "each of the doctrines [of the church] has a history, that is to say that they have been developed. . . . as germs of necessity become successfully in time doctrines, etc." Hogan tells Loisy that "it is clear that one cannot demonstrate [i.e., prove] the Church in Scripture . . . [but] the world is not ready for these facts—it is necessary to form a synthesis of the facts to make them acceptable."[83]

From this letter it appears that Hogan and Loisy were engaged in a nuanced discussion of ideas that were later published in Loisy's famous work L'evangile et l'église (1902), a polemic against Adolph Von Harnack, the Protestant scholar who advocated abstracting the "essence" of Christianity from its scriptural and cultural contexts. In contrast, Loisy held that the historical development of Christianity was embedded in the seeds of revelation, and he distinguished between the revealed truth and the acculturated expression, that is, doctrine, of the truth. It is impossible to understand the original revelation, but the human mind's interpretation of revelation by the Gospel writers may be understood through the methods of historical criticism. Alfred Loisy answered Harnack's "dehistoricalization" of the "essence" of the gospel by placing the fundamentals of Christianity within the historical development of Christianity, which originated "as a religious movement produced in the bosom of Judaism in order to perfect its principles and hopes." As the contemporary theologian J. Healy succinctly summarizes:

> Thus, contra Harnack, Christ, his mission and message, even primitive Christianity, cannot be wrenched from their intellectual and cultural milieu anymore than doctrinal and institutional developments can, in principle, be judged negatively. For this reason, then, Loisy believed that Catholicism must be seen as a legitimate development of the Gospel enculturated in the Greco-Roman world.[84]

Hogan died before the publication of Loisy's new apologetic in opposition to Harnack; but in his 1898 letter to Loisy, Hogan refers to Loisy's notion that the gospel must be viewed in terms of the fulfillment of Jewish apocalyptic literature rather than as biographies of Jesus. He tells Loisy that regarding "the explanation and transformation of the idea of God by the Jews and by the Christians I have nothing to say . . . it is a problem of research."[85] Hogan's radical openness, utterly free from the grip of a priori beliefs, was tempered by his reluctance to publicly articulate a new apologetic according to modern methodologies until a synthesis was fully developed by the scholars. While the theologians and exegetes were pursuing that end, Hogan urged seminaries to introduce their students to the defects of a priori reasoning so current among the neoscholastics; he also promoted the historical understanding of biblical criticism, an implicit attack upon the ahistorical neoscholastic synthesis.

In his book *Clerical Studies* (1898), Hogan tactfully avoids any direct disagreement with the encyclical on biblical inspiration, but he does remind his readers that the pope was not speaking ex cathedra, and therefore one should not approach the encyclical as an infallible statement.[86] However, he notes that since the pope's encyclical Catholic scripture studies had advanced remarkably, and he foresees the day when Catholic scholars will generally realize the fallacy of the Mosaic authorship of the Pentateuch.[87] (In 1905 the Biblical Commission still refused to countenance non-Mosaic authorship.) He views the tensions within the church in terms of a dialectic between exegetes and theologians: the latter tend to broaden the role of inspiration, while the scripture scholars tend to limit it. Hogan seems to imply that the theologians need to see the hand of God throughout scripture so that they might more easily incorporate scriptural proof texts into their systems, whereas theological assumptions tend to obscure the scientific vision of the scripture scholar.[88] In his chapter on dogmatic theology in *Clerical Studies*, Hogan explicitly tells theologians that they cannot treat the issues of modern scholarship by quoting traditional arguments, "nor can they settle them by *a priori* principles."[89] So thoroughly influenced was he by Newman's doctrine of development and by his own experiences with the conflict between scientific methodology and traditional theology that his book's motif is the necessity of forming a historical understanding of the faith and of the church.

Originally written as articles for the *American Ecclesiastical Revue*, *Clerical Studies* was very well received in the United States. *The Catholic World*, for example, considered the book to be replete with "erudition, practical common sense . . . [and] cultured learning."[90] Hogan did not expect the book to receive such a warm reception in Europe, and he informed Denis O'Connell that the French edition was "sure to be attacked." Ever tactful and always aware of the enemy's potential strategy, Hogan told O'Connell, "I am trying to proceed in such a way as to prevent what could be harmful."[91]

The Roman authorities took an inordinate amount of time to process the request for an imprimatur for *Clerical Studies* during 1900–1901. In the summer of 1901 Hogan was called to France by his superior general, Father Jules Lebas. Lebas had just been elected to office in a reaction against the progressive leadership of his predecessor, Arthur Captier.[92] Lebas's views on the higher criticism were directly opposed to Hogan's literary and historical methodology. After several months of anxious waiting, *Clerical Studies* received an imprimatur in September 1901. Unfortunately, Hogan died on 30 September of that year.

In his necrological letter to the members of the society, Lebas never mentions *Clerical Studies* nor any of Hogan's many articles. When he comments on Hogan's Socratic style of teaching, Lebas does not focus on the many distinguished students who were inspired by Hogan but instead implies that Hogan was a woolly thinker: "Some of his students quite often wished for more precise solutions, more rigid rules, more positive answers, and fewer questions. . . ; he might have made his teaching more generally useful by spending more time on theses and giving less to the objections which his mind enjoyed dealing with."[93] Lebas's conservatism prevented an appreciation of Hogan's scholarly and intellectual contributions. Conversely, Alfred Loisy was grateful for Hogan's work, particularly *Clerical Studies*. Indeed, the leading French Modernist closely identified his own work with that of Hogan. In late 1901 Loisy wrote to Baron Von Hügel, "Rome condemns in me that which she approves in Hogan."[94]

Shortly after Hogan died, Loisy wrote a lengthy review of the French edition of *Clerical Studies*. He refers to Hogan's "discreet, yet profound" qualities. Characteristically, Loisy focuses on Hogan's liberal interpretation of Leo XIII's encyclical on Thomist thought, *Aeterni Patris* (1879), and on Hogan's literary and historical approaches to scripture. After lengthy quotations from both of these sections of *Clerical Studies*, Loisy points out two interesting discrepancies between the American and French editions. In the French publication Hogan does not include the introductory commentary on *Aeterni Patris* that appears in the American edition. In the American introduction he stresses the importance of independent thought derived from experience over and above well-developed rules "when they are the outcome of *a priori* theories or principles." Loisy also notes that the French edition does not recommend that seminarians read the journal in which Loisy's review of Hogan's work appears. In the English edition, Hogan says that the *Revue d'histoire et de litérature religieuses* contains "articles of the greatest value."[95] Since Loisy's orthodoxy was under such suspicion in 1900, Hogan's endorsement of Loisy's journal would have precluded an imprimatur for the French edition of *Clerical Studies*.[96]

Hogan was never identified as a Modernist. Unlike Loisy, he was not a polemicist. He was consistently respectful of authority, affirmative in outlook, and irenic in tone. His opposition to the a priori reasoning so embedded in neoscholasticism, his antipathy to ultramontanism, his endorsement of much of the Modernist enterprise, his liberal political views, and his support of the Americanist cause make him a singular participant in the progressive movements in modern church history. John Hogan, who died before Modernism entered its radical doctrinal phase, would not have identified with the movement after 1903 when Loisy attacked the traditional basis of the sacraments.[97]

Alphonse Magnien was an impassioned Americanist, but he was also *au courant* with modern trends in scholarship. For example, in 1898, he wrote to Denis O'Connell asking him to introduce a young Sulpician candidate, John Fenlon, who was in Rome to study oriental languages, to such liberal scholars as Von Hugel, Louis Duchesne, and Giovanni Gennocchi.[98] Like Magnien and Hogan, most Americanists and nascent Modernists felt a strong intellectual kinship. However, John Hogan represents that point on the intellectual spectrum where Americanism and Modernism intersect. Neither ism was promoted by a coherent movement with well-developed strategies. Both were infused with a heightened historical consciousness, a critical attitude toward traditional apologetics, and a determined spirit to articulate the faith in modern terms. Hence both Modernism and Americanism shared a general perspective on the pressing demands of the era, and both fostered a climate of intellectual liberty. Of course, there were wide variants among personalities within each movement as well as broad divergences of opinions. But both movements heralded a new age in the church: Americanists focused on the evolution of social and political reality from a pastoral and ecclesiastical point of view, while Modernists focused on the role of personal experience and on the scriptural roots of faith from scientific, historical, and theological perspectives.

Perhaps the most inclusive term to describe both the Americanist and Modernist is *tranformationist*. Hogan told Loisy that modern scholarly methodologies would lead to a transformation of the church, one that would entail an alteration of perspectives from a static view of doctrine to an historical view of the development of dogma. Félix Klein refers to Isaac Hecker as embodying a transformationist spirit: "Humanity transforms itself and demands a new apostolate. The apostle has come. In Father Hecker it has found the ideal priest for the new future of the Church."[99] Both Modernists and Americanists were consciously engaged in a broad and diverse movement to develop a new apologetic for the new age, which was grounded upon republican liberty. The Americanist ecclesiology that extolled a free church in a free society and emphasized the role of the Holy Spirit in the evolution of American culture, vis-à-vis the institutional structure of the universal church, appealed to the Modernist; only within the free atmosphere that gave rise to that ecclesiology could modern scholarship have a transformationist impact upon the church and, more importantly, could the church have a transformationist impact upon the modern world. Many of the ideas of the Americanists, and to a lesser degree of the Modernists, were vindicated several decades later by the Second Vatican Council.

8

Americanization

In accord with their ecclesiological vision, Alphonse Magnien and John Hogan initiated what might be defined as an Americanization process in the two Sulpician seminaries where they presided as superiors. The positive tone of their leadership was in marked contrast to that of their predecessors, Lhomme and Dubreul. Although Magnien and Hogan were imbued with the French traditions of Saint-Sulpice and though they never deviated from those traditions, they were very sensitive to the need for adapting seminary life to the American character of their students. In the process they raised expectations for reform among such young American Sulpicians as Charles Rex and Edward Dyer. When these men were placed in positions of authority at the seminaries in Boston (Rex, 1889–1894) and in New York (Dyer, 1896–1902), they established what may be appropriately termed "new model" institutions. The influence of Magnien and Hogan was evident in their reforms; however, as exceptionally talented priests who were ordained in the latter part of the nineteenth century, Rex and Dyer also reflected an intellectual movement in the church aimed at reconciling traditional belief with modern methodologies.

Sulpician Americanization involved moderate adjustments in the traditions of Saint-Sulpice to accommodate the needs of American seminarians. The desperate need for native vocations led to a movement for an American Solitude (i.e., novitiate) and for greater self-government among the Sulpicians in the United States. Americanization also entailed the opening of the seminary to contemporary intellectual and social trends. Ultimately, the Americanization process was frustrated for the same reasons that caused Americanism and Modernism to have little contemporary impact on the church; neither Saint-Sulpice nor the Vatican was ready to acknowledge the positive character of American and modern culture.

II

Soon after his appointment as superior of Saint Mary's in 1878, Magnien imposed his Americanist imprint on the seminary. At the annual retreat for the diocesan priests in September 1878, he announced that the customary silence would not be observed during daily recreation; this action elicited some criticism from the Jesuit retreat master.[1] On the occasion of the renewal of priestly promises on the feast of the Presentation of the Blessed Virgin Mary (21 November 1878), Magnien hired a French chef for the dinner. He noted in his diary for that day:

> Heretofore there had been complaints on the part of the Rev. clergy that they were not on that day and similar occasions properly treated in the Seminary. . . . These complaints were certainly well grounded and as such a manner of acting was ascribed to stinginess and want of proper regard for the guests, it was urgent both for the good name of the Seminary and the regard due to the Archbishop and the Rev. clergy to do away with a tradition which nothing could justify and [which] was in opposition to the Spirit of the Society of St. Sulpice.

After a meeting of the seminary faculty it was decided "that the dinner to be served on the feast day should be warm, abundant and choice without however savouring in the least of luxury and worldliness."[2]

Sulpician hospitality was abundant during the Third Plenary Council of Baltimore in November 1884. The private sessions were held in the prayer hall at Saint Mary's Seminary. In attendance were 14 archbishops, 62 bishops, 6 abbots, 34 superiors of religious congregations, 11 seminary rectors, and 81 theologians, including both Alphonse Magnien and John Hogan.[3] Since many prelates and priests dined at the seminary, Magnien hired a French chef and two waiters for the occasion. The theologian's refectory was for the exclusive use of the guests; the entire student body had their meals in the philosophers' refectory.[4] Magnien later commented that before this historic meeting several bishops had held unfavorable views of Saint Mary's as too rigid and austere for Americans. The superior worked to dispel such notions and in the process made many friends for Saint Sulpice. His hospitality was anything but austere, and apparently it had positive impact upon enrollment; in 1880 there were 115 students at Saint Mary's, and in 1886 the figure was 220.[5]

John Hogan was Archbishop William's theologian at the council. In his diary Hogan highlights the informal discussions during the council. He mentions John Ireland's criticism of seminary training in Montreal:

> What he objects to in Montreal is the lack of literary training . . . what is needed is men *who know the period, the condition* of peoples' minds—the prevailing errors and the way to combat them and then good speakers—men . . . of refinement of thoughts and feelings—*gentlemen* that no man of education need be ashamed to acknowledge as pastor.

Hogan notes that Ireland stressed the need to emphasize scripture and church history in the seminary curriculum. He also writes that the bishop of Saint Paul failed "to see the good of Leo XIII's letter on Philosophy [*Aeterni Patris*]," which required Thomistic philosophy in the seminaries.[6]

Hogan also records John Keane's thoughts on Catholic youth within the context of American seminarians. "*Bishop Keane of Richmond* thinks that what is most needed among the youth of Northern states is *refinement*. It had been said that the youth from the Western States were rough but reliable, those from the South refined and reliable, those from the North rough and not reliable." Keane told the newly appointed superior of the Boston seminary, "Nowhere is culture more spoken of than in Boston, nowhere more appreciated, yet it is strangely wanting in the clergy—they have brains, they have heart but they are coarse. They are rough in their tastes—the animal portion of their being is too prominent."[7] Hogan reports that one Jesuit remarked that the Sulpicians "keep their students . . . at a dead level. . . . He said [that] the Baltimore priests are good men, but not one of them has a good name as a preacher."[8] The next day Hogan visited the Jesuit seminary at Woodstock, and in his diary he expresses nothing but praise for the quality of the curriculum and the general spirit of excellence that prevailed.[9] Since Hogan held such high standards and since the Jesuits and the Sulpicians had never been allies in ecclesiastical or in educational affairs, such praise bespeaks credibility.

The Third Plenary Council of Baltimore had a significant influence upon American seminaries as the council fathers adopted a new structure for ecclesiastical training: six years of college followed by two years of philosophy and four years of theology. Referred to as the six-six plan, this new program was assigned to a bishops' committee, which was to devise a detailed curriculum. On the printed copy in the Sulpician archives is the handwritten note "Magnien's Plan."[10] There is little extant evidence of Magnien's involvement in the development of this Concursus, but Saint Charles' and Saint Mary's were the models for the six-six plan, and as one of the major leaders in U.S. seminary education, Magnien was consulted. However, the six-six structure was not implemented in most diocesan seminaries until many years after the Third Plenary Council. Alphonse Magnien considered it very important for Saint Mary's to be a model for the nation because of its significant role in the development of the reform and because of its history, so linked with the nation's first see. Hence, at the 1886 visitation of representatives of Superior General Henri Icard, there was considerable discussion on the ways in which the six-six reform required specific adaptation.[11]

In the early 1880s Saint Mary's separated the philosophers from the theologians. Saint Charles' minor seminary had, from its origins, a six-year program. The two-year course at Saint Mary's for the philosophers included science, scripture, church history, and philosophy. The six-six reform entailed adding a year to the theology program, particularly extending for an additional semester the two major courses in dogmatic and moral theology and limiting as final preparation for ordination the second semester of the fourth year to pastoral courses. The added year also necessitated a change in the time for calling seminarians to tonsure and the various orders. Since Saint Mary's was authorized by the state of Maryland to award university degrees, and was a pontifical university as well, the fourth year of theology allowed the seminary to consider more applicants for advanced degrees.

During the 1886 visitation, Magnien made several references to the need for Sulpician adaptation to American customs. When it was announced that the superior general requested that the Sulpicians in Canada and the United States share a common retreat in Montreal, Magnien, with the unanimous support of his confreres at Saint Mary's, strongly objected. Tempering his objection with reference to the consistently "warm reception" provided them by the Canadian Sulpicians, Magnien stated that the Sulpicians in Baltimore were not in "complete agreement with them concerning the spirit in which the Seminaries in America should be run." In response to the visitors' request for clarification, he elaborated on the difference between the Canadian practice and American preferences regarding the spirit suitable to Saint Mary's Seminary:

> it would be a wrong method to follow with the young men of the United States if predominance were given to severity in discipline [as was the case in Canada.] A certain element of fear must be present: the seminarians [in the United States] must realize that there are certain limits beyond which they may not go without being punished: their mentality accepts a reasonable firmness, even when it affects them . . . . But once these basic principles are established, there must

not be too much repression towards these young men. They have a taste for freedom and are used to it: appealing to their reason, their conscience and their heart is the means to teach them gradually how to use that freedom responsibly and to be able to give up some of it in matters required by our Rules. . . . Kindness towards them is quite fruitful, and they are sensitive to what we may do to please them. Finally, treating them with a broad mind and trust, we have the great advantage of seeing them open up to us, and thus letting us know them as they really are. On the contrary a supervision filled with anxiety and suspicion would put them on their guard: they might make efforts to circumvent it, and they would succeed. Once their hearts are closed to us, we might lose any salutary influence we might have over them.[12]

In other meetings the Saint Mary's community advocated what appears today as very minimal changes in the rule, such as allowing an additional fifteen minutes before retiring for the night because "Americans rarely go to bed before 10:00 P.M." and permitting seminarians to smoke only in private and off the seminary grounds during the afternoon excursion into town and on vacations. To make major changes in the rule would have been considered almost sacrilegious, but changes in the ways in which the rule was administered for American Catholic youth, who cherished their independence and freedom, were crucial to the success of the society in the United States. For example, to enforce an absolute ban on smoking would have entailed adopting "a manner of inquisition which might ruin filial trust and freedom which is essential to maintain between seminarians and directors."[13]

Icard responded to Magnien's request for additional Sulpicians who were committed to learning English and to adapting to the openness of seminarians in the United States by assigning Adolph Tanquerey to Baltimore. Born in the village of Blainville in 1854, Tanquerey attended the Sulpician seminary in Coutances. As an aspirant to the society he was sent to Rome for graduate work at the Minerva, where he studied Thomistic theology, and at the Apollinare, where he studied canon law. He was ordained a priest in 1878 at Saint John Lateran and entered the Solitude later that year. Prior to his assignment to Baltimore, he was at Rodez. During his time in the United States (1887–1902), Tanquerey completed his three-volume manual of dogmatic theology and two of the three volumes of his moral theology; both works became standard texts in American and European seminaries and were in use up to the time of the Second Vatican Council. Written in clear and lucid Latin, Tanquerey's manuals were considered progressive at the turn of the century. Like all manuals they are apologetic in character, but his advanced polemics stress the scriptural and historical bases for the defense of the traditional faith. He does not view apologetics as a distinct branch of theology but rather as an integral part of the theological enterprise.[14] Tanquerey's two last works, *Introduction to Ascetic and Mystic Theology* and *The Spiritual Life*, also became popular in American seminaries. With an encyclopedic grasp of the history of spirituality, Tanquerey demonstrates that the source of his world view was not neo-Thomism but a more eclectic spiritual vision. He relished his experience in the United States and was very supportive of Magnien's Americanist views on the church in the new republic. After he returned to France in 1902, he frequently extolled the American seminaries as models for Europe.

Magnien emphasized the value of accommodating to the American character and of developing an ambience of freedom and trust. The superior general however, was not sympathetic to Magnien's implicit attack upon traditional standards. Icard had been jailed by anticlerical radicals during the period of the Paris Commune (1870) and had defended Saint-Sulpice against those who accused the society of Gallicanism and liberalism.[15] Indeed, the conflict between Magnien's moral optimism and the puritanism endemic within the seminary tradition represents a perennial struggle among groups responsible for religious formation. Although Magnien enunciated his principles in distinguishing the Baltimore Sulpicians from their Canadian confreres, he was implying that the Canadian Sulpicians (the majority of whom were born in France) represented an Old World tradition with an emphasis upon fear, mistrust, and the need for severe discipline.

From 1886 until the 1894 election of Arthur Captier as superior general there were rumors that Icard planned to place the Baltimore and Boston seminaries under the authority of the superior in Montreal (since 1881, Frederick Louis Colin). Magnien and Colin held contradictory views not only on the ethos of the seminary but on general ecclesiastical affairs as well. While he was head of Rome's Canadian College in 1896, Colin virtually expelled Bishop John Keane from his guest room at the College because of Keane's controversial views. The Sulpician Procure in Rome (residence of the society's representative to the Holy See), adjacent to the Canadian College, welcomed Keane, a gesture that revealed the cordiality between the bishop and the society as well as the traditionalist character of the Canadian superior.[16]

Upon the election of Captier, Magnien immediately wrote a report on the Sulpicians in the United States. He told the new superior general that Saint Mary's housed 260 seminarians from more than 30 dioceses. He underlined the national character of the Baltimore seminary in contrast to Saint John's in Brighton, which was a regional seminary limited to students from New England. He pointed out that the spirit of the seminarians was good and that the piety and zeal were satisfactory. "They are very open with us. . . . They are happy to return [to St. Mary's] and they have greatly contributed to dissipate the prejudices

which existed against us and toward the authority of St. Sulpice."
Magnien said that he had personally experienced the impact of the
spirit of Saint Mary's throughout the United States, and, by way of a
parenthesis, he remarked that through his own many tours as a retreat
master and those of John Hogan, Charles Rex, and Edward Dyer, the
Sulpicians themselves had contributed to the general good will of the
bishops and priests toward Saint Sulpice.[17]

Despite these signs of progress, Magnien reported to Captier that
several specific problems desperately demanded attention. For example,
only ten Sulpicians and one auxiliary professor were in charge of the
260 students. Because of expansion of the curriculum it was necessary
to augment the faculty for courses in church history, scripture, canon
law, liturgy, and homiletics. The ardent Americanist superior told the
superior general that those Sulpicians appointed to Saint Mary's faculty
must be

> men of value. As I have said, this seminary represents St. Sulpice in
> the United States. It is truly a center. Numerous bishops and priests
> visit here. . . . The seminarians express very liberally their views of
> their professors . . . [and] toward the end of this year . . . there was a
> rather poor spirit. Certain ideas circulated in the ecclesiastical public
> and fortified the prejudices which existed in America as well as in
> France [viz] that St. Sulpice provides a good ecclesiastical education
> but that the studies there are weak.

Magnien noted that the spirit of criticism was in accord "with the
spirit of the country" and that some of his confreres failed to adapt
themselves to the American students and saw no need "to assert a
personal influence and to give authority by their character and their
direction." Instead they approached them with "a priori" views as if they
were dealing within a French milieu where the Sulpician traditions and
customs were more easily accepted. "It's necessary to live with them
[i.e., the American seminarians] . . . to speak their language, to get a
clear idea of their nature, and their national and personal character in
order to wisely direct their conduct and their formation. . . . Between
the Spirit of St. Sulpice and the American character well understood
there is no conflict; but it is easy to imagine that there is a conflict"
and to live according to one's prejudices.[18]

Magnien concluded his report with his views on the rumor that
Paris was "indirectly" and "obliquely" putting the Sulpicians in Baltimore and Boston under the authority of the superior in Montreal.

> This union and this dependency . . . would have a disastrous effect.
> It would be the ruin of St. Sulpice's influence in the United States.
> Our Americans accept direction from Paris but direction from Canada
> would strike them as odious. Americans and Canadians share a ge-

ographical position but their ideas and appreciations of persons and things are opposite of each other . . . . St. Sulpice is well established in both countries but our works are absolutely independent from each other, and . . . in the United States we want no other authority than Paris.

Magnien hoped Captier would visit the United States and judge for himself. "Having been away from France for such a long time, [Captier was in Rome from 1874-1894] it is necessary for you to understand that the depth of a substance is not necessarily attached to a particular form."[19] Captier did make a visitation in 1896, and in general he supported Magnien's Americanization efforts.

With the concurrence of the faculty at Saint Mary's, Magnien introduced enlightened measures that opened the seminary to the modern world. A student reading room contained newspapers, weekly periodicals, and literary reviews "more or less on the light side and more recreative than instructive." Another reading room

> is a library where the students can find . . . some serious reviews treating [various] questions, especially theological and social. Some of these reviews are Catholic; others Protestant or of no particular religious character. The Fathers thought that these reviews, read only by the more serious students, gave them greater interest in theological studies. They can also give them useful insights into the intellectual state of the world; they would prepare them to help people they would meet . . . in their ministry. . . .[20]

Saint Mary's had also encouraged its best students, as well as faculty members so inclined, to attend classes at Johns Hopkins University in order to give "the young men a closer look at the life of intense labor of this or that professor," to introduce them to the "scientific progress" in academic life of the university, and to engender in them "a serious taste for study which is quite rare, until now, in the clergy of America. It could also produce in the professors feelings of esteem and benevolence towards the Seminary and the Catholic clergy."[21] Saint Mary's students and faculty were primarily interested in courses in mathematics, biology, and "Oriental philosophy" (i.e., biblical languages). Magnien explained the difficulties entailed in this practice:

> The university is lacking in any religious character and therefore offers no guarantee as to the methodology of the courses; . . . the practice creates a delicate situation for the Seminary, in regards to Catholic University; . . . the young men taking the courses at John's Hopkins are, by that very fact, put outside ordinary Seminary life, at least partially so, and that could easily lead to some relaxation on other points.[22]

Because of these disadvantages, Captier, during his 1896 visitation, prohibited students from attending classes at Johns Hopkins unless mandated by their bishops. However, he did allow faculty, including Sulpicians, to study at the university. Captier agreed with the rationale of the reading rooms and "remarked that one must know the mentality of the country." However, he urged the faculty to achieve a "just medium" in the choice of reviews and to direct students by means of "critical analysis" to the explicit and "hidden sophistry found in works which are contrary to our sound doctrines."[23] Hence, Captier was a moderate liberal on the issue of adapting the seminaries to modern intellectual trends and allowing a measure of intellectual liberty, attitudes that placed him in the tradition of Lacordaire, Montalembert, and Dupanloup. Captier was also critical of the course of studies at the Propaganda Fide in Rome. He remarked to the Josephite superior general John R. Slattery that it was "a special course of studies for dullards, covering but two years with the catechism of the Council of Trent as a text-book."[24]

Slattery had formed a close relationship with the Sulpicians. The Society of Saint Joseph of the Sacred Heart developed out of the Mill Hill Fathers, founded by Herbert Vaughan (while he was bishop of Salford, in Manchester, England). The Josephites were dedicated to the evangelization and ministry to the black community in the United States. Officially separated in 1893 from Mill Hill, which pursued its apostolate in other areas of the world, the Josephites continued the original mission and accepted black candidates for their society. Even prior to the separation from Mill Hill, Slattery had founded Saint Joseph's Seminary (on property abutting that of the Baltimore seminary) for candidates for the Josephites.[25] From 1888 to 1930 these students lived in Saint Joseph's but attended classes at Saint Mary's Seminary. The Josephite superior general was drawn to the Sulpicians because the Third Plenary Council of Baltimore had established a Catholic mission office for blacks and Indians and had designated that a Sulpician should be the executive secretary of that commission. (From 1884 to 1976 a Sulpician occupied that post.) Slattery was also personally impressed with the Sulpicians; his spiritual director was Paulin Dissez, the vice-rector of Saint Mary's.[26] In addition, for a brief period he sent Josephite candidates to the Sulpician Solitude at Issy, which he considered as the equivalent to a Josephite novitiate.[27]

The arrangement between Saint Joseph's and Saint Mary's led to a form of integration when Charles Uncles, the first black Josephite seminarian, enrolled at the Sulpician institution. He was followed by John Dorsey and Joseph Plantevigne. For their prephilosophy studies Dorsey and Plantevigne attended Archbishop Ireland's Saint Thomas College in Saint Paul, Minnesota, the only diocesan seminary that would accept blacks.[28] (It was not until the 1950s that the Sulpicians accepted a black student at Saint Charles' College.) Ireland was even more advanced than the Josephites, who refused to accept blacks after Slattery withdrew from the society in 1903. Slattery was an impassioned Americanist and a good friend of John Ireland, who referred to the Josephite mission as a "crusade." He wrote to Slattery, "I will give you as far as you may wish my personal cooperation. Thank God I am a Christian and a Republican."[29]

Disillusioned by the segregation entrenched in the church and (as a self-styled Modernist) convinced that the Vatican was myopic in its suppression of advanced scriptural exegesis, Slattery left the church in 1903.[30] He later recalled that Magnien was a strong liberal, but he stated that the Sulpician superior was too lenient with students. Slattery related an incident when he expelled two students from Saint Joseph's because they had left the seminary without permission and noted that for the same violation students were not expelled from Saint Mary's.[31] Although Slattery wrote his autobiographical reflection some twenty years after he left the church, his recollections of life in the Baltimore church and of his relations with the Sulpicians did not reveal bitterness nor the vindictive condescension characteristic of many apostates. Slattery was a significant figure in the Americanist network, but because his involvement was relatively brief, he did not exert as much influence as either Magnien or Hogan.

III

John Hogan, superior of Saint John's Seminary at Brighton (1884–1889), appears to have acquiesced in Magnien's leadership on the need for Paris to understand the unique and positive character of the American seminarians. Hogan's class notes reveal an encyclopedic grasp of philosophy, theology, church history, and exegesis, and, as noted earlier, he was an inspirational teacher well known for his Socratic effectiveness in the classroom. Both he and Magnien were deeply committed to the implementation of the curriculum reforms of the Third Plenary Council of Baltimore. The council fathers decreed that Hebrew and Greek, along with courses in church history, scripture, and homiletics, should be mandatory. During the 1886 visitation to Saint John's, Hogan noted that in light of the emphasis upon scripture in Protestant theological education it was necessary to "strengthen as much as possible . . . [scripture] studies in the seminary."[32] He introduced at Saint John's a series of scripture courses for the entire six years, with the philosophers concentrating on the Old Testament and the theologians focusing on the New. Francis Gigot, a Sulpician scripture scholar, who later became nationally recognized for his introduction to the Old Testament, was a strong asset at Saint John's.

Courses in homiletics were augmented by the requirement to prepare homilies during the summer vacation. Two classes a week in church history were required for the six years because in America there was frequent and serious discussion on the pressing need for an appreciation of the church's past. Hogan was particularly sensitive to the general ignorance of church architecture among the American clergy. Hence, he presented a weekly conference on the topic in order to enlarge the vision of seminarians who were destined to work closely with architects in constructing new parish churches for the burgeoning Catholic population.[33] Hogan's views on theological education, which first appeared in the *American Ecclesiastical Review* and later in his book *Clerical Studies*, would be considered modern even by today's standards. Influenced by John Henry Newman's notion of development, Hogan revealed a singular appreciation for the intellectual and cultural interrelationships within the unfolding of Christian tradition.

Hogan, like Magnien, injected an optimistic tone into the seminary. Just as the Socratic method in the classroom was based upon belief in the student's natural inclination to truth, so his style of discipline was founded on trust in the drive toward honesty among his seminarians. An American Sulpician comments on Hogan's leadership as superior of Saint John's:

> Father H. has a number of strong and 'thick-set' notions of his own and which he almost always manages to carry out, still he has shown a great regard for the Fathers, consults freely and does not disguise his views. . . . [He displays] excessive easiness in giving permission to go out into the city and even to go home for a night. . . . But . . . I do not think that much evil advantage has been taken of this leniency; while on the other hand, things really seem to be going very well, in several respects. Regularity at the exercises; very little sleeping over; . . . and less disorder in corridors; none at all in the classes; very good conduct in the refectory; and very docile and respectful manner toward the Fathers . . . besides his rather broad and loose notions of discipline and administration he has . . . very *revolutionary* ideas about systems or ways of teaching. . . .[34]

Charles Rex, Hogan's successor as superior of Saint John's, was also liberal in his methods. Rex was only thirty-three years old when he became superior of Saint John's, the first native American to head a Sulpician major seminary. He was the eldest child in a Quaker family of Baltimore. Sometime after his mother had converted to Catholicism, he entered the church and soon found himself drawn to the priesthood.

In 1878, after six years at Saint Charles' and two at Saint Mary's, Rex went to Paris to complete his theology and his Solitude. Edward Dyer and Richard Wakeman were his classmates during these years. Of the three, Rex was the most gifted and easily adapted to the culture of Saint Sulpice. From the Solitude at Issy, Rex wrote to Magnien of "the great ability the American Church can derive from the spirit that M. Olier bequeathed to his disciples. . . . I mean that spirit of complete self-abnegation . . . [that is] particularly needed in our country which is so impatient of any yoke . . . and is so devoted at the same time to material ends."[35] After two years of graduate study in Rome, Rex joined the faculty of Saint Charles' College; a year later he was appointed to Saint John's. During his tenure as superior, Rex initiated several reforms. With the aid of Hogan and the support of the faculty, he vigorously pursued an arrangement with the Catholic University of America to confer bachelor degrees in philosophy and theology at Saint John's. Although he was unsuccessful in gaining such authorization, several seminarians were allowed to attend the university during their fourth year of theology in order to secure a theology degree. Rex also introduced student argumentations on various topics with the intention of stimulating the intellectual life of the seminary as well as awarding recognition to students who excelled in their studies. He also separated the philosophers from the theologians, placing the former in a so-called junior house.

Rex himself taught courses in the New Testament and was more or less under the guidance of Hogan. On one occasion Hogan advised Rex not to get too immersed in the textual difficulties in his course on Saint Paul.

> You see I am as great an utilitarian as ever, believing in gathering from the apostle what brings light and edification, and touching lightly on the obscure parts . . . ; could you not at least confine yourself to giving what you take to be the sense of the words of the apostle, leaving those who care for more to hunt it up in the commentaries you may point out to them?[36]

Symbolic of the entire seminary's indebtedness to Hogan was a statue of the founder-superior that was commissioned almost immediately after Hogan left for the university in Washington. In accord with Hogan's generally liberal intellectual posture, Rex encouraged students to be thoroughly conversant with intellectual and social trends of the day. Hence the seminary reading room was well stocked with scholarly reviews and newspapers to which the students had easy access. As mentioned in the previous chapter, Hogan advised Rex to circulate among the Saint John's community a translation of d'Hulst and Loisy's articles on biblical inspiration. Correspondence between Dyer and Rex on the need to modernize pedagogical methodology to replace the rote memorization of philosophical and theological manuals illustrates Americanization in the U.S. Sulpician seminaries of the 1890s.

Charles Rex was extremely concerned with the health of the students. Several notations in the faculty minutebook attest to the young superior's attention to the need for extra holidays for rest and relaxation at the end of the semester. Because he considered the traditional weekly promenade through the city with priest chaperons as "humiliating" for the students "as if they were incapable of proper conduct on their own," he terminated the practice and substituted small, unchaperoned group outings. After the Sulpicians left Saint John's in 1911, the grand promenade was reintroduced, and as late as the 1950s seminarians in full clerical dress, including biretta and cape, walked in columns of twos throughout the area adjacent to the seminary. Rex also introduced physical education into the curriculum. A special lay instructor was hired, and the students were allowed to do exercises and games in mufti rather than in the hitherto prescribed cassocks. In March of 1894, when M. Colin, the Canadian superior, visited Saint John's, he found the American departures from the canons of French tradition shocking.

Richard Wakeham's letter to Edward Dyer provides us with a liberal American's view of Colin's reaction. He compared Colin's expression to "the let-out sharpness à la Dubreul." Wakeham described the visitor's encounter with physical education:

> There was the whole community [of philosophers] in shirt-sleeves. Some with red belts on and some with purple; some with black and some with brown. As the old man gazed in silence upon the scene he was "a study"—and was doubtless *studying*. Finally he *pried his mouth open*, with this safe and uncompromising proposition: "Oh well, after all, there is nothing here against the natural law!" Once the lockjaw was overcome, he managed to express his approval of the thing, and to say that he would not be opposed to the introduction of something of the kind *au collège!* . . . Charlie [Rex] was pretty well pleased with the experiment and thought he had better make a bold dash and show the old man the *worst thing* in the house—the *Reading Room*. Of course many questions were asked. The magazines had a pretty hard time to pass muster; while the poor newspapers "hung fire" altogether. "But you do not let them read the newspapers?" asked Père Colin. To which Charlie replied, "Oh well just as you say. . . . After all it is not against the natural law." And so they had it out. The old man did not say "Amen" to the whole business, but he tried very hard to show that he had "large ideas."

Wakeham reflected the general fear among the Sulpicians in the United States that "old Père Colin [was attempting] to effect some kind of union of all the houses on this side of the water, with the primatial dignity at Montreal."[37] To defend against such an offensive foray by Colin, Wakeham agreed that Rex should accompany Magnien on his visit to Paris for the general assembly of July 1894. As mentioned earlier, Rex, rather than Magnien, was elected to the general council; later he was appointed superior of Saint Joseph's Seminary in New York, which had been scheduled to open in the fall of 1895 but was not ready to accept students until September 1896. Rex's rise to positions of responsibility far beyond that of any other U.S.-born Sulpician was testimony to his deep loyalty to Saint Sulpice and to his diplomatic skills, both of which, despite his liberal reforms at Saint John's, elicited trust and confidence in Paris. The rise of Rex was in accord with the character of the Captier administration, which appears as a moderately progressive interlude between the traditionalist administration of Icard and the reactionary regime of Lebas.

IV

There was a Sulpician personnel crisis in the United States during the late 1890s. The Sulpicians had agreed to staff Saint Joseph's Seminary for the archdiocese of New York, which opened in the fall of 1896. Two years later they opened Saint Patrick's Seminary at Menlo Park in the archdiocese of San Francisco. Just as the New York commitment originated with a request of Bishop Hughes, so the commitment to San Francisco originated with a request from Archbishop Joseph S. Alemany, O.P. In 1888, Archbishop Patrick Riordan of San Francisco renewed his predecessor's request for Sulpician seminary personnel, and, to exert pressure upon Henri Icard, he sought support from the Propaganda Fide. Although New York would take precedence over San Francisco, Icard's commitment to Riordan was strong enough to warrant the archbishop's planning the construction of a seminary on a large tract of donated property in Menlo Park some thirty-two miles south of the see city and just a mile from the future location of Stanford University. In 1896, Captier visited San Francisco and renewed Icard's commitment. Magnien, who had known Riordan as a friend of John Ireland and as a strong ally of the Catholic University of America, visited the archdiocese in 1898; the following autumn Saint Patrick's, staffed by four Sulpicians, opened its doors to its first class. It began as a minor seminary, and during its first years it experienced several problems that will be treated later.[38] For now it should be noted that the westward expansion of the Sulpicians, though in accord with the tone of Manifest Destiny so characteristic of the Americanists, represented a severe challenge to the small community of priests. Between 1884 and 1898 the society had assumed responsibility for seminaries in Boston, New York, and San Francisco, and the administration of Divinity College at the university in Washington. Never had the need for native-born vocations been more acute. Notwithstanding the westward expansion and Magnien's Americanizing reforms, vocations had not increased notably. There was a growing realization that candidates would only be attracted to the society if it had a strong degree of autonomy, including a novitiate in the United States.

V

Charles Rex and Edward Dyer, who had been together in the Solitude in Paris and during graduate studies in Rome, carried on a lively correspondence on the need for reform within Saint Sulpice in the United States. Only letters from Dyer to Rex are extant, but they reveal the general drift of their ideas. In 1892 Dyer tells Rex that the Sulpicians in Baltimore are apprehensive of Icard's views of the work in the United States: "The old gentleman, I think, has got it pretty well into his mind that there is little of the *esprit surnaturel* in the American ecclesiastic." Dyer defends his fellow priests in the United States: "When we go down to the substance of the Christian and sacerdotal spirit it seems to me they have as much of it as any body of men I have yet met."[39] Shortly after Icard's death (19 November 1893), and before the election of Captier, Dyer asks Rex if during his visit with Magnien in the summer of 1893 he had said "anything to him about the novitiate question."[40] After the election of Captier, Dyer urges Rex to accompany Hogan and Magnien on their summer visit to Paris for a meeting of the general assembly. "I think the interests of our work here demand that you should have a hand in . . . the direction of Father Captier's administration. . . . Father H. [Hogan] has but little sympathy for our young men and Father M. [Magnien] is not the out and out American he is sometimes taken for." Some five weeks later Dyer reports, "For the first time Magnien did not repel the idea of some sort of provincial organization for the United States."[41] By July of 1894, when Rex, Hogan, and Dyer were in Paris, Dyer has refined his ideas

> on Americanizing our work. . . . I believe there will be little or no difficulty about their [i.e., the authorities in Paris] leaving this work pretty substantially to Americans as soon as Americans are numerous enough to show themselves fully competent. A council for this country would certainly do much to help things along, to

increase the number of vocations, I believe, by putting our work in
all its parts more and more in touch with the needs of the times and
of the country.[42]

Dyer based his hope on the fact that Magnien and Hogan had
indicated their support for the Americanization of the work. Magnien's
1894 report to Captier, noted earlier, was presented personally during
this July 1894 visit to Paris. Magnien wrote to Dyer that he had "said
some very plain and good things to Captier," but he was suspicious
of Colin's influence upon the superior general and the general council.
Magnien told Dyer that Colin "is pretty well known as a man of strong
imagination asserting things without much hesitation. . . . I have said
plainly to Fr. Captier that if they judge America and Americans by
the views of Fr. Colin . . . they will put their foot in it and greatly
damage our work."[43] Magnien was unsure of the effectiveness of his
own views on Captier and the council, but he found support among
"many intelligent confreres . . . [who] consider the Canadians, Fr.
Colin included, as warrior-minded and as men who cannot be of much
help for the transformation the need of which is felt very keenly in
France, whilst they *comptent beaucoup sur nous americains*. . . ."[44] Apparently
Magnien's friends were a minority at the July assembly meeting, for
when it came time to elect a member of the general council, Charles
Rex, rather than Magnien, was the choice. There is no evidence,
however, that Magnien was disappointed. Dyer was very pleased with
the results and wrote to Rex, "We had all wished that an American
should be represented . . . but had naturally thought of Father Magnien. . . . Indeed, taking all in all, I believe your influence would likely be
stronger than his."[45]

In the spring of 1896, when he made a visitation to the United
States, Captier announced the recent establishment of the Ecole
Saint-Jean, a house of studies for Sulpician candidates on the Rue de
Vaugirard, directly across from the Institut Catholique.[46] Magnien immediately responded that such a school in the United States had been
a longstanding concern "in forming the [Sulpician] personnel for the
seminaries in America."[47] After Captier returned to Paris and after
Sulpician seminaries had been established in New York and San Francisco, he announced plans to open a house of studies attached to the
Catholic University of America. However, it was intended to accommodate not only American Sulpician candidates but also French Sulpicians
who would require a transition year to adapt to the needs of American
seminarians and to improve their English-language skills.

Magnien had promoted the venture as a house of studies and as
a novitiate, an American Solitude. Captier's ideas on the house are
contained in an 1899 circular letter for the seminaries in the United

States. To open a Solitude outside of France is considered "a radical innovation" that would entail "many risks" and would not provide "guarantees for the Sulpician formation." Captier then launches into a eulogy on the traditions of Saint Sulpice and the need for one novitiate where all aspirants to the society would "be unified in principle and conduct," while conversely more than one novitiate would engender a diverse spirit and perhaps divisiveness within the society. Since the seminaries in the United States relied upon the services of many non-Sulpician teachers, referred to as auxiliary faculty, it is extremely important to "solidly implant the spirit of the Society" in one centralized novitiate.[48]

In a commentary attached to the circular letter, Magnien defends his proposal to establish a U.S. Solitude. He quotes from his 1894 report on the need to dispel anti-Sulpician prejudices and to adapt to the openness and independence of American students. A house of studies attached to the university in Washington would contribute substantively to fulfilling these needs. However, he considers that a novitiate would evolve from the house of studies "with all that a novitiate is supposed to impart."[49] The Baltimore superior expresses his regard for Captier's emphasis upon the value of unity for the society, but he notes that "unity of spirit is not dependent exclusively on the unity of the novitiate. . . . [The spirit] should exist and exists in fact, with the plurality of novitiates." He refers to the many religious communities, including those of French origin, that established novitiates in America. He specifically mentions the Little Sisters of the Poor who, by order of the Holy See, had opened a novitiate in Brooklyn. "It does not seem that these diverse novitiates have introduced a different spirit in the diverse orders. . . . A French Jesuit is no more nor no less a Jesuit than a German or an Italian Jesuit." In response to Captier's outline of the spiritual "exercises" for the house of studies, which was merely a replica of that for all Sulpician seminaries, Magnien respectfully takes issue only with the implication that the superior general was advocating Sulpician uniformity rather than "unity of spirit . . . the general tone of the memoir seems to suppose that an American [must] give up his Americanness in order to become a true Sulpician. The comparisons are odious, but I believe that our American confreres as well as the others [i.e., French] have the spirit of their vocations."[50]

Captier envisaged the house as including those priests who wished to become auxiliaries so that they may be introduced "to the life, the spirit, and the method of St. Sulpice." Magnien disagreed on the ground that such priests would have been introduced to the Sulpician way of life during their seminary years. Subjecting them to the discipline designed for an aspirant to the society would create tension between the two categories of students. Magnien agreed with Captier that

French Sulpicians assigned to serve in the U.S. seminaries should benefit from a year at the house, but he also encouraged the superior general to assign some French confreres destined for assignments in France, as they would broaden their experience and improve their understanding of the diversity of cultures.[51] That Magnien could say that Sulpicians, as Sulpicians, would grow intellectually and spiritually as a result of this experience in the United States is a measure of the depth of his Americanist commitment.

During this controversy over the establishment of an American novitiate, John Fenlon, a young Sulpician aspirant, was in Rome studying theology with a view to studying scripture at the Ecole Biblique in Jerusalem. In November of 1899, Fenlon wrote Dyer his views on the distinctions between the French and American religious character, as well as his hope for an American novitiate. He told of one French priest who said the "Anglo-Saxons worship comfort and have no high idea of spirituality." Fenlon then commented,

> our comfortable way of life [is blended] with a philosophy of common sense religion, which . . . [the French] have not done, as far as I can see. And, therefore, the dominating influence must be French, they believe. Well there does not seem to be much hope for the Church among French people or Latin people, nor German Catholics; and if the future is not with us Anglo-Saxons . . . it is hard to see where it is. The secular clergy is the strong power among us and the Sulpicians ought to be the strong power among the secular clergy. And I therefore agree in your opinion that nothing ought to give more hope for the future of the Church in America than the establishment of a Sulpician novitiate there.[52]

There is some evidence that Fenlon, Magnien, and Dyer's views on the need for an American novitiate were not supported unanimously among the Sulpicians in the United States, but these views were certainly supported by the vast majority.

In September 1901, Saint Austin's College, analagous to the Ecole Saint-Jean, opened with James Driscoll as superior. This house of studies, located near the grounds of the Catholic University of America, had a distinctly American character, but it did not gain the status of a Sulpician Solitude until 1911. Arthur Captier was close to Keane, Ireland, and Denis O'Connell and sympathetic to the Americanists, but he was only moderately supportive of the Sulpician Americanization process. In July of 1901 he requested that his assembly of twelve assistants appoint a vice superior general, with right of succession, to assist him in the administration of the society. Although his health had declined, Captier's motives are difficult to discern. According to a memoir written by a Canadian Sulpician with strong anti-Colin views, Captier wished to appoint Alphonse Magnien as vice superior general for American affairs. The memoir also states that Magnien and Hogan were in Paris to promote the measure among the members of the assembly but that Colin mustered a majority in opposition to the proposal, and Captier, in order to save face, resigned.[53] The documents in Paris do not verify this rendition of events but instead refer to Captier's resignation as originating in his inability to administer the society without a vice superior general.[54] Because the election of Jules Joseph Lebas represented a distinctive swing to the right, it is evident that the assembly considered Magnien's Americanist views as dangerously liberal. Hence, Edward Dyer, rather than the Baltimore superior, was elected as one of the twelve assistants to the superior general.

When Magnien was ill during the last year and half of his life, Tanquerey, as vice-superior, frequently assumed the role of superior. When it became evident that Magnien would be incapable of administering Saint Mary's in the fall of 1902, Lebas appointed Tanquerey to replace him, but because Magnien wanted Dyer, and because the French Sulpicians in the United States felt Tanquerey was a poor administrator, Lebas rescinded the appointment, and Dyer became superior of Saint Mary's. The following year he was appointed the first vicar-general for the United States, which was a quasi-provincial office with authority to administer the American houses according to policies and directives originating in Paris.[55]

In 1903 the Sulpicians in the United States were a definite minority in the society. There were only 46 members (13 of whom were born in the United States): 14 at Saint Mary's, 13 at Saint Charles', 4 at Boston, 6 in New York, 5 at San Francisco, 2 at Saint Austin's, and 2 at Divinity College of the university. There were 73 Sulpicians in Canada, the majority of whom were born in France. However, 35 were assigned to parishes, 35 were on the faculties of the minor and major seminary in Montreal, and 3 were at the Canadian College in Rome. Of the 291 Sulpicians in France, the vast majority staffed the twenty-five seminaries, but the society was responsible for administering the seminary residences attached to the Catholic institutes in Paris and Toulouse, analogous to graduate seminaries. There were 16 Sulpicians at the parish of Saint-Sulpice and 2 at the Procure in Rome. The society was still one of the church's smallest community of priests in 1903, with a total of only 410 members. The enormous influence of the Sulpicians was far in excess of membership; the superiors of Saint Sulpice in Paris, Montreal, and Baltimore had achieved national ecclesiastical stature.[56]

Alphonse Magnien was indeed a national figure in the Americanist movement, which, one will recall, was based upon a moderate Gallican ecclesiology with an emphasis upon the Holy Spirit's manifestation in the new forms of culture apparent in the evolution of American society. Just as Magnien extolled the virtues of cultural pluralism within the church, so he strongly urged the society to decentralize its authority structure by allowing for an American Solitude. He emphasized the need not only to accommodate Sulpician tradition to the needs of seminarians but also to allow the American Sulpicians to contribute to the renovation of the traditions of the French community. Magnien's ecclesiastical Americanism and his drive to Americanize the Sulpicians were expressed in his high regard for intellectual trends in the United States and in his insistence on freedom and self-determination for Saint Sulpice.

9

The New York Crisis

In 1891 Archbishop Michael A. Corrigan decided to transfer his provincial seminary from Troy to a recently purchased site on Valentine Hill in the Dunwoodie area of Yonkers, just two miles from the northern limits of the city of New York. The transfer to the immediate environs of New York was motivated by the need for a seminary more accessible to his clergy and more directly under archdiocesan control. Although he had been in communication with Henri Icard, Corrigan negotiated the final arrangements with Captier during 1894. In late 1894 Charles Rex was appointed the first superior of Dunwoodie, and from then on Rex and Corrigan were in close correspondence on the general direction and specific policies of the new seminary named Saint Joseph's.[1]

Magnien and Hogan, the two most notable Sulpicians in the United States, were diametrically opposed to Corrigan on the character of the Catholic University of America, on public schools, on the Americanization of German immigrants, and, indeed, on all the issues that distinguished the Americanists from their opponents. Hence, the Sulpician association with Corrigan's seminary was replete with irony. Of course, Magnien and Hogan limited their advocacy of Americanism to the medium of correspondence and refrained from public statements, but Magnien was closely identified with Gibbons and Ireland and Hogan with Keane. Although Rex was sympathetic to the Americanist positions, he was neither an activist nor publicly identified with the controversy; Rex's Americanizing reforms at Brighton were departures from Sulpician tradition, but they were not in themselves rooted in any ideological relation to Americanism. Indeed, the most forceful anti-Americanist bishop, Bernard J. McQuaid, fashioned his seminary at Rochester according to a strong American model. The seminary at Dunwoodie, with its gymnasium, large recreation rooms, and chemistry and physics laboratories, was certainly in accord with Rex's ideas. There was no doubt that the young liberal Sulpician enjoyed the trust of the conservative archbishop.

Corrigan had been a director of the seminary at Seton Hall in New Jersey and had later become president of the entire college.[2] Upon becoming archbishop of New York, Corrigan confronted the liberal faction of his clergy, a faction headed by Edward McGlynn. McGlynn was active in Henry George's campaign for mayor, was a participant in radical Irish politics, and because of these activities was a controversial figure in the archdiocese, in national ecclesiastical offices, and in the Curia Romana. McGlynn, along with Richard Burtsell, Sylvester Malone, and others, had been members of the Accademia, a clerical study and discussion club whose agenda would be considered radical even today: optional clerical celibacy, antiauricular confession, propublic education, a Catholic social gospel, reform of parish structures, and prointegration on racial issues.[3] Concerned with the liberal proclivities of the intellectuals among his own clergy, Corrigan confided to Rex that "for forty years the Bishops of this Diocese have been worried with the *liberal* views of some of the clergy. . . . I need not rehearse my own trials and sorrows from the same cause." By this time he had received word that Rex might not be able to fulfill the role of superior and was quite anxious that Captier appoint a conservative to fill the position: "I could not tolerate the liberalism accredited to his Eminence of Baltimore, which even Cardinal Satolli and the Holy Father had to reject in the recent letter on the Parliament of Religions (at the Chicago Columbian Exposition)—not to speak of other questions." Corrigan told Rex that "the vast majority of our clergy are opposed to liberalism: and I fear that existing prejudices already entertained by them against the Sulpitians [*sic*] (even though unfounded) would be very much strengthened" by an appointment of a liberal Sulpician as superior.[4] A week later Rex assured Corrigan that, if it were necessary, someone else would be "chosen [superior], it will be a man who will consider it his duty to endeavor to co-operate heartily with you in your views and your work." He then informed Corrigan of the principles of authority within Sulpician tradition:

> Whilst St. Sulpice allows to her individual members the widest possible range of thought consistent with the rules of prudence and orthodoxy, it is at the same time an invariable tradition with her to stand loyally by the Bishops in whose dioceses she is called to serve . . . it has been

a grave preoccupation with the Superior of St. Sulpice to send to the Bishops as heads of their seminaries men who would be agreeable to them and who when at work would feel themselves bound to consult and be guided by the views of the Chief Pastor of the diocese.[5]

Rex was then in a tuberculosis sanitarium in Colorado Springs but was optimistic about fulfilling his appointment at Dunwoodie.

With this principled assurance from Rex, Corrigan went to his board of consultors to discuss the contract with the Society of Saint Sulpice. Among the consultors, Auxiliary Bishop John Farley was strongly opposed to the proposed Sulpician presence at Saint Joseph's Seminary. His position was that because there were diocesan priests who could staff the seminary the Sulpicians were unnecessary, that they would appear as outsiders to the New York clergy as well as to the many lay people who had contributed funds for the construction of the seminary, and that the Sulpicians would tend to control the institution to the detriment of the freedom of archdiocesan authorities.[6] Corrigan responded that the diocesan clergy generally lacked the discipline and piety to form priests. Secular priests also tended toward factional strife, which would lead to "divided rule."

Perhaps influenced by his mentor, Archbishop James R. Bayley, who had attended Saint Sulpice, Corrigan told his consultors, "There is no question but that if we have the Sulpicians we will have better priests. . . . Seculars will not give their recreation time with their students. . . . [The Sulpicians dedicate] their lives individually. . . . [They] will not be thinking . . . about . . . large parishes. . . . We [secular priests] do not enjoy a reputation for piety."[7] In order to protect the archdiocese's interest, and perhaps to satisfy Farley and others who were opposed to the Sulpicians, Corrigan placed a clause in the contract stipulating that the seminary was not given "in perpetuity" to the Sulpicians and that either party might terminate the arrangement upon a year's notification. Corrigan also inserted a clause that some of the faculty positions should be open to priests of the archdiocese.[8] By the time of the consummation of the contract in which the society was to send six Sulpicians to Dunwoodie, Rex's health took a turn for the worse, and Edward Dyer was appointed superior. Rex's response to the appointment of his close friend was predictably positive. He wrote a glowing letter of introduction to Corrigan:

I have known Dr. Dyer from boyhood, and I am confident that you will find him, as I have always known him, a man of unusual mental acumen, of most self-sacrificing energy, of great force of character, and of rare priestly virtue. The remarkable success that he has had with the young men of his charge at Baltimore is a pledge of what may be expected of him at New York.[9]

Dyer's first task was to complete the recruitment of the faculty. Rex had recruited James Driscoll, a Sulpician born in Vermont; Driscoll had entered the society in Montreal, where he was teaching when Rex was forming the core Sulpician faculty. In 1891 John Keane had attempted to appoint Driscoll to his faculties of scripture and Oriental languages, but the Grand Séminaire in Montreal refused to allow him to leave, particularly since he had returned from studies in Europe only in 1889. At Dunwoodie, Driscoll deferred to Joseph Bruneau as the scripture professor and instead taught dogmatic theology. He was the most popular teacher among the students, and after Dyer became vicar-general in 1902, Driscoll was appointed superior of Dunwoodie. In 1904 he was the prime mover behind the foundation of the *New York Review*, the most important Modernist periodical in the English language (the full story of which will conclude this chapter). The two other Sulpicians at Dunwoodie were Richard Wakeham, treasurer, and Victor Marre, professor of moral theology and canon law. Three members of the faculty at Saint Joseph's Seminary at Troy joined Dunwoodie's staff: Rémy Lafort taught scripture to the philosophers, William J. Livingston taught church history, James Fitzsimmons taught philosophy. William Temple, a diocesan priest who had taught at Saint Mary's, Baltimore, and who was "familiar with . . . [the Sulpician] methods and highly esteems them" was appointed to teach philosophy.[10] However, Dyer rejected another diocesan priest because of a report from Paris that the priest was unsympathetic to the Sulpician way of life. A Dunwoodie seminarian, James Cassidy, was a part-time teacher of physical science. Although the Sulpicians were in the minority, they filled the administrative posts and were the core faculty of the theology department.[11]

At the solemn blessing of Saint Joseph's (16 July 1896), Archbishop Corrigan welcomed the Sulpicians:

> Thus far they are known to the majority of us only by reputation—a reputation for earnest and sustained devotion to their work which was voiced so impressively on his deathbed by the illustrious Fénelon, when he declared: "I know nothing in the Church of God more venerable or more apostolic than the Society of St. Sulpice."[12]

With 850,000 Catholics in New York, 500,000 in Brooklyn, and over 250,000 in Newark, Saint Joseph's was at the center of American Catholic life.

At the first faculty meeting limited to Sulpicians (there were generally two such restricted meetings per academic year), discussion centered on the "question of place to be occupied by the directors." Although some favored the directors dining at the superior's table, "the principle of effacing as much as practicable the distinction between directors and students, and of considering all as members of one family prevailed." The directors were assigned to students' tables "with nothing special being served to them."[13] Such a measure, though in practice in the provincial Sulpician seminaries, was a departure from the traditional lines of separating faculty from the students in both Paris and Baltimore and was a symbol of the Americanizing policies of Edward Dyer. (As late as 1970 the faculty at all Sulpician seminaries dined at a separate table.) Another democratic reform introduced by Dyer was the establishment of a clerical proprieties committee, which Dyer mentions in his house diary as sort of a student council for self-government.[14] Dyer was very pleased with the general climate of discipline of the seminary; he refers to the "self-sacrificing gentlemen." Like Magnien, Hogan, and Rex, Dyer instilled a positive moral tone based upon the principle of self-discipline, rather than on the severity of authority from above. He told the students that the "easy way in which permission is given and can only go on . . . [is by evidencing] a strong sense of duty on your part. If inclination is not spontaneously brought under control for the full performance of duty, then inclination must be contradicted [by] . . . strictness about permissions."[15]

Dyer's pedagogical methodology was quite advanced. In 1899, at a national meeting of seminary directors at Overbrook (a meeting that was in embryo the seminary department of the National Catholic Education Association), he presented a paper on the problems of teaching students of varying backgrounds and abilities. He urged seminary teachers to refrain from falling into the habit of addressing only the brightest. Instead he advocated allowing the brightest students to instruct the class on different occasions and to prepare advanced papers for a series of special seminars. While the latter were employed in their research, the teacher would then have a relatively homogeneous class of average students to whom he would present a thorough explanation of the material with an abundance of concrete examples to support the general ideas of the course.[16] Problems resulting from the intellectual and cultural heterogeneity of seminary classes had been common from 1791 to the present. Dyer's solution entailed a considerable amount of work for the professor; however, it not only reveals his own sense of duty but also illustrates his liberation from the manuals and the methodology of rote memorization. Like the other American Sulpicians, Dyer was aware of advanced trends in higher education and was committed to pedagogical and curricular adjustments that would allow students to achieve their highest potential. Hence, under Dyer, Saint Joseph's explored ways by which its best students might attend Columbia or New York University.[17]

Dyer's relations with his fellow Sulpicians at Dunwoodie were at times troublesome. His old classmate, Richard Wakeham, proved to be incompetent during his first year as treasurer. During the

1897–1898 academic year there occurred a fiscal crisis characterized by a large deficit and compounded by general ignorance about its origin. Ultimately, the budget was balanced by a reduction in the kitchen and housekeeping staffs.[18] That same year Dyer was told by Joseph Bruneau, in a rather oblique way, that he had written a book on scripture, *Harmony of the Gospels*, which had been read by Driscoll and had received an imprimatur from Archbishop Corrigan. Dyer was disturbed by the *post-factum* way in which he was informed of the book, particularly since the book identified Bruneau as a professor of scripture at Dunwoodie Seminary. Ironically, Bruneau was such an unpopular scripture teacher that Dyer was compelled to assign him to teach dogma and replace him with Driscoll. According to Dyer, Bruneau merely consulted with Driscoll by way of reading him notes for the book; Driscoll "did not think there was anything in point of doctrine to be objected to . . . [but] that he had never considered himself as acting as a Sulpician examiner." Since Bruneau "has given himself no particular pains about learning English," Dyer was apprehensive about the book's reception. He remarked that Bruneau was driven to publish "almost without control." Bruneau's scripture classes were controversial as he appears to have introduced his students to the "higher criticism." Dyer heard more stories of Bruneau's classes, and one influential pastor caustically asked, "What kind of heretic do they have teaching Scripture at the seminary?"[19] Dyer's fears were unfounded, however, as *Harmony of the Gospels* was well received by Catholic reviewers. Bruneau had published a series of bibliographical articles on scripture for the *Ecclesiastical Review* that, though they revealed a progressive bias, had been applauded by the editor, Herman J. Heuser. Heuser's praise pleased Dyer because the "known conservatism of this Ecclesiastical organ will help not a little to silence the ignorant criticism that may be made by some of the priests of this diocese." Hence the superior of Dunwoodie was satisfied with Bruneau's contribution and was very grateful for his hard work in the library, where he cataloged twenty-one thousand books in one year.[20]

Bruneau had been ordained in 1889 and studied scripture under Paulin Martin and Alfred Loisy at the Institut Catholique de Paris, just before Henri Icard prohibited all his seminarians and aspirants to the society from attending Loisy's lectures. Assigned to Baltimore in 1894, Bruneau studied under Paul Haupt, the Spence Professor of Semitic Languages at Johns Hopkins University. One of Bruneau's articles in the *American Ecclesiastical Review* was a bibliographical review of recent scholarly literature on the Gospel of John, with particular emphasis upon Loisy's exegesis published in 1897–1898 in the *Revue d'histoire et de littérature Religieuses*. He was impressed with Loisy's stress upon historical criticism and the theological development of the John's gospel. Although Bruneau was not teaching scripture in 1899, this essay reveals his thorough familiarity with the significant contemporary research.[21] Unlike Hogan, Bruneau did not possess a strongly analytical mind. Instead he was more eclectic and almost encyclopedic in his embrace of various new trends in scripture scholarship. Hence, he dedicated his *Harmony of the Gospels* to his four former professors of scripture, whom he seems to have consciously listed from conservative to liberal: L.C. Fillion, S.S.; Fulcran Vigouroux, S.S.; Paul Martin; and Alfred Loisy.[22]

Dyer was particularly proud of Francis Patrick Duffy (1871–1932), a member of Dunwoodie's first ordination class (1897), who had been ordained the previous September to allow him to pursue graduate work at the Catholic University of America. Poor health prevented Duffy's completion of his studies, but after a year's convalescence at Saint Gabriel's Church in New Rochelle (when Farley was pastor) he was appointed to the Dunwoodie faculty. From September of 1898 to June of 1912, Duffy taught a variety of courses ranging from the physical sciences to theology. He achieved fame in World War I as the chaplain of the sixty-ninth Regiment and was memorialized in a statue overlooking New York City's Times Square; later, actor Pat O'Brien played Duffy in the movie *The Fighting Sixty-ninth.*[23]

Francis Duffy also wrote for the *American Ecclesiastical Review.* One of his articles, published in late 1907 and entitled "Does Theology Serve Religion?" was a lengthy analysis of the defects of scholastic theology in elucidating religious truths to contemporary believers. After an elaborate treatment of the subjective character of religious belief and the shallow basis of much of what passed for theological thought, Duffy embarks on a discourse on the relationship between literature and religious belief. In the process he cites several poets and novelists, but the only theologians he refers to favorably are Cardinal Newman and George Tyrrell. On the arid mathematical logic of the manualists' methodology, Duffy quotes Tyrrell: "For such persons, religion has the same kind of interest as the multiplication table, and no more. There is nothing mysterious, or beautiful, or awful about it; nothing to feed the mind or to subdue it with inexhaustible wonder." In short, like the Modernists, Duffy was groping for a new apologetic "based upon the facts of psychology, which our logical training seems to dispose us to overlook."[24]

It is, of course, ironic that at Archbishop Corrigan's seminary, Dyer was fostering relations with Columbia and New York universities, Bruneau was lauding the higher criticism of Loisy, and Duffy was writing a Modernist critique of scholastic methodology. It is also important to note that these developments at Dunwoodie occurred while Edward Dyer was superior. There is a tendency to view the origins of Dunwoodie's critical intellectual life with the appointment of James

F. Driscoll as superior in September 1902 and with the foundation of the *New York Review* in 1905. According to Dyer's correspondence with Captier and others, Dyer relied upon Driscoll for advice on all issues regarding the direction of the seminary and of the Sulpicians in the United States. In one letter Dyer notes that Corrigan had appointed Driscoll and himself "synodal examiners," in which position they passed on the credentials of all clerics who wished to enter the archdiocese.[25]

James Driscoll (1859–1922) was born in Vermont, entered the Sulpician seminary in Montreal and completed his theological studies at Saint-Sulpice and his Solitude at Issy. An apocryphal account holds that Driscoll attended Loisy's classes at the Institut Catholique; actually Driscoll never met the French exegete, as is clear from their correspondence in 1903.[26] At Rome, Driscoll studied Semitic languages and biblical literature with Ignazio Guide and Henri Hyvernat (1859—1941). When Driscoll returned to teach at the Montreal seminary in 1889, Hyvernat was settling down to a long teaching career at the Catholic University in Washington, D.C. Driscoll corresponded with his former professor on a variety of topics, particularly on Driscoll's interest in Middle Eastern languages. Hyvernat himself was a master of Babylonian and ancient Egyptian; later, he wrote a multivolume study of Coptic culture.

In 1893 Hyvernat confided to Driscoll his hope of founding a biblical review, perhaps influenced by Père Marie Joseph Lagrange, O.P., who had founded his *Revue biblique* the previous year at the Ecole Biblique in Jerusalem. Driscoll responded pessimistically. Although he saw the need for a scripture journal, he warned Hyvernat that "given the animus of a certain very *orthodox* and professedly anti-liberal religious society [i.e., the Jesuits] towards the University, I feel that the new publication would meet with a very determined opposition, not to say a passionate one." Driscoll presumed that the review would publish authors representative of "modern Bublical criticism," whose views would appear "alarming to certain ultraorthodox defenders of Christian doctrine, who under the cover of great names and exaggerated principles would all along the lines, from Beyrouth to Woodstock, open fire on the new publication." Driscoll reminded Hyvernat that the Jesuits had attacked his colleague Professor Thomas Bouquillon when he dared to defend the state's right to engage in the education of the young.[27] Ironically, twelve years later Driscoll and others founded the *New York Review*, with apparently no inordinate fear of a Jesuit assault upon its orthodoxy.

After five years at Dunwoodie, Driscoll was appointed the first superior of Saint Austin's College, the Sulpician house of studies near the Catholic University of America. Captier made the assignment shortly before he was compelled to resign over the issue of a vice superior general and coadjutor. Since Captier and Magnien had arranged for the opening of Saint Austin's, Lebas, who succeeded Captier, imposed his own stamp of authority upon the college. Driscoll explained to Dyer that Lebas intended to place the college directly under Paris because "he probably fears that under the supervision of Fr. M. [i.e., Magnien] it might become too American."[28] Driscoll was determined to maintain a distinctively American character at Saint Austin's. Indeed, he chose the name Austin, rather than Augustine, because Austin "is the true anglo-saxon form of the name."[29] Francis Gigot (1859–1920), the other Sulpician at Saint Austin's, was a scholar who had completed graduate work at the Institut Catholique de Paris in 1883 and taught at Brighton from 1885 to 1899. He was on the faculty of Saint Mary's (1889–1904) while he lived at Saint Austin's. Driscoll was quite pleased to have Gigot as a colleague. "Happily, Fr. Gigot is very practical," he told Dyer, "and his attitude as regards America is *all right*. Had I been left to choose a companion among the available confreres I could not have done better or found one more congenial."[30] Driscoll and Gigot were the spiritual directors of the five students who lived at Saint Austin's and attended classes at the university. Together Driscoll and Gigot represented the most advanced thought on scripture studies at the university. Edward Arbez, who became the foremost Sulpician scripture scholar of his generation and a founder of the Catholic Biblical Society, came under their influence while at the university. In 1901, Gigot published a two-volume introduction to the Old Testament that became the standard text in seminaries throughout the English-speaking world.

Meanwhile, the distinctively rightward drift of Lebas's administration was alienating Driscoll. On 8 September 1901, shortly after his election, Lebas issued a circular letter in which he quoted his pledge to Leo XIII that the society would adhere to both *Aeterni Patris* (on the place of Thomism in the seminaries) and the encyclical on biblical inspiration, *Providentissimus Deus*. He also underscored the significance of the pledge in a special commission of studies for all Sulpician seminaries that emphasized the vital importance of traditional theological manuals and warned against historical methodology in scripture and a developmental approach to dogma. In regard to the Sulpician houses in the United States, Lebas said that "it is necessary that they work in a perfect dependency on the superior of St. Sulpice [i.e., the superior general]."[31]

As mentioned earlier, Edward Dyer was elected as one of the twelve assistants on Lebas's council in 1901. Driscoll seems to have interpreted Dyer's election optimistically on the assumption that Dyer would represent the American cause. Indeed, in his letters to Dyer, Driscoll is candid in his criticism of Lebas's conservative policies. In February

1902, Driscoll reports to Dyer that Lebas had informed Magnien (then in the last months of his life) of the rules regarding censorship and told him to send Gigot's last two books to Paris for examination. These were actually the two parts of Gigot's *Introduction to the Old Testament*. Part I had been published under a provision, approved by Captier, that allowed Magnien to pass on Sulpician publications. Part II was printed and circulated (but not commercially published) with Driscoll's permission as superior of Saint Austin's. Fearful of support for Loisy, Lebas introduced a rigid censorship policy. Driscoll wrote to Dyer, "evidently someone—perhaps Fr. Colin—had denounced Fr. Gigot at headquarters and they are after him." Driscoll indicates that although Gigot's work had already been approved by one of the scripture professors at Saint-Sulpice, Lebas might submit the works to Fulcran Vigouroux or Fillion, both very conservative scholars. "In the light of the Letter on Studies [i.e., the report of the special commission on Studies]," he tells Dyer, "it is not unlikely that having been denounced there is a determination on the part of the 'reactionaries' to suppress him with his methods and views." Driscoll informs Dyer that Gigot was "already casting about to see where he can find a place when asked to resign as a member of the Society, for this is what he expects, and I must say it looks that way to me. Rather than withdraw his books he will sever his connection with the Company." Driscoll continues:

> I do not know how far the war will be carried on, but it is coming round in my direction and I begin to see ugly possibilities for myself. Already last summer I was denounced in France—probably by Fr. Colin—as holding unsound, heretical doctrines concerning scrip . . . so any campaign that should culminate in the withdrawal of Fr. Gigot would probably involve me as well. . . . I am not very aggressive or revolutionary . . . in my presentation or defense of the new views, but my convictions in the matter are very definite, and it would be impossible for me to teach the old rubbish. . . .

He concludes this long letter to Dyer with a plea for close communication and for concerted action: "If this campaign against all progress be carried over here, it will be impossible for me to encourage any intelligent American to join us."[32]

Two months later Driscoll wrote again to Dyer regarding the Gigot affair. Portions of a circular letter from Lebas appeared to Gigot and Driscoll as directed against them. Driscoll writes, "In this new document the reactionary principles are reiterated and emphasized in such a way as to leave no doubt as to their being rigidly enforced. . . !" Driscoll viewed Lebas "as the kind of man . . . brooking no opposition . . . no remonstrance on our part would have any [positive] effect whatever. . . ." Instead, Gigot considered resigning from the society before there was a crisis and without making any remonstrance: "If we do protest we will merely compromise our own reputation and confirm the anti-American prejudices, whereas if there be nothing said the storm will blow over in due time."[33]

During this period Gigot visited Dyer at Dunwoodie to seek his advice on the matter of publishing part 2 of his work on the Old Testament. Later, Dyer explained his views on the Gigot affair: "I told him, without hesitation or obscurity, that I thought it would be wrong to allow his book to come out,—that it would only be looked upon as an act of defiance to authority,—that I felt sure Father Magnien would not give the approbation necessary to secure the *imprimatur* of Cardinal Gibbons."[34] Ultimately Gigot decided to wait until there was a change in administration before seeking permission to publish part 2. In 1903, Lebas passed unfavorably upon part 1, and since by this time he was vicar-general of the Sulpicians in the United States, Dyer protested to the superior general that the criticism was not against Gigot's own ideas but those of others cited in part 1. Dyer also explained that despite the traditional character of the American hierarchy, Gigot's book had been well received throughout the church in the United States.[35] Such protest did not elicit a positive response, and throughout this period Gigot frequently considered leaving the society.

Driscoll became involved in promoting Gigot's work not only within the society but also within the larger intellectual community. At the end of May 1902, Driscoll wrote to Albert Houtin, originally a priest of the diocese of Angers, who had lived at the parish of Saint-Sulpice. Houtin was living in Paris and had become a popularizer of the Modernist movement. His book *La question biblique chez les catholiques de France au XIX siècle* had just been published and was placed on the Index in 1903. After introducing his own academic background, Driscoll writes:

> This letter is to introduce you to the last book of M. Gigot, his Special Introduction to the Study of the Old Testament, a work which though moderate and scientific, has been considered extreme, which is a comment on the state of biblical studies, so singularly fastened to the 'Manual' (divine classic!!!!) of M. Vigeroux [sic] that the French reviewers ignored Gigot.

Driscoll also writes that he wishes to translate *La question biblique* into English. He suggests that Houtin consult Félix Klein or Frédéric Monier, the Sulpician confessor of Alfred Loisy. However, he asks Houtin "not to mention my name publicly because at this moment St. Sulpice suffers a crisis of orthodoxy; nervous and reactionary, this condition at times resembles constipation and at other times diarrhea."[36]

Houtin's response to this letter is not extant, but some six months later Driscoll again wrote to Houtin. This time Driscoll says that his duties as superior of Dunwoodie do not allow him to translate *La question biblique.*[37] Nevertheless, after withdrawing his offer to translate Houtin's work, Driscoll wrote to Loisy and asked permission to translate *L'evangile et l'église.* Driscoll said that he would translate it anonymously "because of the book's condemnation." (Ironically, Letourneau, the Sulpician pastor of Saint-Sulpice, composed much of the formal act of condemnation for the archbishop of Paris, Cardinal Louis Richard. This treatise formed the basis of the papal condemnation of Modernism, *Lamentabili,* dated 3 July 1907.) Although Driscoll was probably unaware of Letourneau's condemnation, he did want Loisy to know "that there are some priests, indeed Sulpicians (!) who greatly appreciate your work."[38]

Upon Edward Dyer's assignment as vicar-general of the U.S. Sulpicians, James Driscoll was appointed to the presidency of Saint Joseph's Seminary at Dunwoodie. Had he not been discreet in his correspondence with Houtin and Loisy, and had he not maintained the confidence of Dyer, Driscoll never would have been appointed to this prestigious office. Under Driscoll, Dunwoodie flourished as the most avant-garde seminary in the United States. However, because of Dyer's support of the scholarly pursuits of Bruneau and Duffy, because of his modern pedagogical style, and because of his dedication to promote a climate of student self-esteem and of moral autonomy, his contributions represent a continuum upon which Driscoll built his own reputation. For example, Driscoll has been praised for arranging for Dunwoodie students to be admitted to graduate study at Columbia University on a tuition-free basis, but the official trustee minutes that record the affiliation were dated 3 February 1902, when Dyer was still rector of Saint Joseph's.[39] Nonetheless, it was not until September 1902, when Driscoll was rector, that the first students attended Columbia. Driscoll was far more knowledgeable than Dyer of intellectual trends in Europe and the United States. As a member of the Oriental Club of New York, composed of scholars and patrons of Near Eastern languages and culture, Driscoll's background was totally ecumenical. Among the club's members was Charles A. Briggs (1841-1913), whose advocacy of the higher criticism was investigated between 1891 and 1893 in a series of heresy trials conducted by the Presbyterian church. Although acquitted twice by his presbytery, Briggs was suspended as a minister. He entered the Anglican church in 1898 and was ordained a priest the following year; when Driscoll met him, he was on the faculty of Union Theological Seminary. In 1903, Briggs was a guest lecturer at Dunwoodie, and Driscoll occasionally attended Briggs's lectures at Union. Driscoll was particularly gratified to see Gigot appointed to Dunwoodie in 1903 and continued to be concerned about the society's censorship policy regarding Gigot's work.

In 1904 Gabriel Oussani was appointed professor of Oriental history and biblical archeology at Dunwoodie. Born in Baghdad, Oussani studied Arabic, Syriac, and Turkish at the patriarchal seminary in Mosul, Mesopotamia; was ordained at the Urban College in Rome; and was a lecturer in Semitic languages at Johns Hopkins University. With Driscoll, Gigot, and Oussani, Saint Joseph's Seminary possessed the foremost faculty of biblical scholars in Catholic higher education in the United States. In his work on the intellectual history of the American clergy, Michael Gannon considers the entire faculty at Dunwoodie to have been "intellectually the most distinguished body of priests in New York, possibly in any diocese of the United States."[40]

John F. Brady (1871–1940), who was in the third ordination class at Saint Joseph's in 1898 and then studied philosophy at the Catholic University of America for a year, was appointed to the faculty at Dunwoodie in 1899. He was the founder and editor of the *Homiletic Monthly and Catechist*, predecessor to the *Homiletic and Pastoral Review*, a journal dedicated to providing parish clergy with sermon outlines and information on current trends in catechesis. Although it was not edited by a Sulpician, the *Homiletic Monthly* was published in the name of the seminary,[41] and hence it required Sulpician approval. Dyer gave such approval when he was superior at Saint Joseph's. In 1902, Richard Wakeham, the Sulpician treasurer at Dunwoodie, received permission from James Driscoll to submit a series of sermon outlines in the journal; after they were published, Brady wished to distribute them in book form. Under Captier, a superior held such authority, but according to the constitution establishing the vicariate general of the United States, the superior general alone had the authority to approve reviews published by Sulpician seminaries. Hence, as vicar-general, Dyer sought to regularize all that had been done and asked Lebas for his official approbation for the *Review*, even though its contents were "not of a delicate or dangerous nature." In October 1903, Lebas approved the *Review* but cautioned against too close an association of the journal with the society. Since Driscoll was a member of the vicar-general's council one assumes that he agreed with Dyer's policy of strict observance of the rule governing publications.[42]

In the fall of 1904, Auguste Berrué, a relatively liberal French Sulpician, made an official visitation to all the Sulpician seminaries in Canada and the United States. Accompanied by M. de Foville, Berrué found little to criticize at Saint Joseph's. On the contrary, he remarked that "the piety of the seminarians is particularly remarkable," characterized by regular devotions to the Sacred Heart and to the Way of the Cross. He also stated that the "regularity of the community is good in substance" and that the "rule of silence . . . is remarkably observed during study hours." He noted that there was some anti-Sulpician sentiment among the diocesan clergy but that the alumni of Saint Joseph's were a countervailing force. From the minutes of this visitation, one can not discern that Saint Joseph's was the most avant-guarde seminary in the United States.[43]

The academic year 1904–1905 was eventful in both France and the United States. In November of 1904, Lebas died; two months later the assembly elected Pierre Garriguet as superior general. Garriguet seems to have been a less doctrinaire conservative and more of a pragmatist than his predecessor. Garriguet experienced the severe effects of the anticlericalist legislation of Premier Emile Combs, which culminated in the separation of church and state in France and the seizure of many buildings of the seminary. Although two Sulpician seminaries remained open by the stubborn will of two prelates, many Sulpicians were compelled to return to their dioceses, where they were placed in diocesan seminaries as local priests. Then, in 1906, Sulpician seminaries began to reopen. Separation led ultimately to a religious revival, characterized by the rise of parish, diocesan, and national religious associations; more churches were built during the first ten years of separation than during the 100 years after the 1801 concordat. Vocations, however, experienced a severe drop during this same period; in some dioceses, seminary enrollments fell by 75 percent. The radical anticlericals fed the anger of the extreme right within the church, which was manifested in the growth of the supernationalistic Action française.[44] The political right perceived a grand Modernist conspiracy of Jews, Freemasons, radical democrats, and socialists. While representatives of the religious right often shared this perception, they also saw a Modernist conspiracy among intellectuals and scholars who supported the Americanist "heresy"—the new historical methodologies and the new apologetics. Garriguet attempted to steer a moderate course. Unsympathetic with the political, social, and religious right, he was also opposed to the new methodologies, particularly to the higher criticism. Still pursuing the beatification of Olier, the Society of Saint-Sulpice stressed its loyalty to Pius X. Immediately after his return from Paris, where he participated in the election of Garriguet, Dyer received word from Driscoll of the creation of the *New York Review*, a bimonthly journal of religion and culture that aimed to publish such scholars as George Tyrrell, Baron Frederick von Hügel, Wilfred Ward, George Fonsegrive (editor of the French liberal newspaper *La Quinzaine*), and Archbishop Eudoxe-Irenée Mignot. These names were bound to antagonize the archconservative defenders of orthodoxy, particularly Merry del Val, the cardinal secretary of state.[45]

In his 11 January 1905 letter to Dyer, Driscoll explains that Duffy and Brady had conceived the idea of the *Review*, that it would be published at Saint Joseph's Seminary, that he and Duffy would be the editors, and that Archbishop Farley had expressed his hearty and enthusiastic approval. . . . It was just what he [i.e., Farley] wanted. He expressed his deep, long-standing regret at the backwardness of Catholic writers in matters of modern scientific interest, and gave as his opinion that it was due in great measure to the exaggerated restrictive policy of the ecclesiastical authorities, who, through their unreasonably stringent methods of censorship [Index, etc.] only succeed in stifling all initiative on the part of the ablest and best disposed Catholic scholars.

Driscoll considered the archbishop's approval the final authorization to publish the *Review*. Hence he tells Dyer,

We do not ask you to assume responsibility of a positive and formal approval. All we desire and expect is to be let alone. If the project succeeds, then you may endorse it; should it fail, then you may claim your right to say "I told you so," and leave the responsibility with us and the archbishop who has the project so much at heart.[46]

In a response to Driscoll's letter, Dyer indicates his surprise at the announcement of the *Review*. Although he notes that "there could be no question of the desireableness [sic] of the proposed periodical," Dyer wishes to dissociate it from the seminary. He suggests that the archbishop publish it from Cathedral College, the minor seminary of the archdiocese of New York. He also cautions Driscoll that Farley may drop the periodical as soon as "a whisper of disapprobation is wafted from Rome."[47] Driscoll's disregard of Dyer's authority as vicar-general and of proper procedures regarding formal approval for the journal caused Dyer much concern. He was apprehensive about Garriguet's response to Driscoll's initiative. In his response to Dyer, Driscoll defends his original plan with characteristic clarity and determination. After dismissing Dyer's argument of separating the *Review* from the seminary as not "very cogent," he presents his position on Garriguet's authority.

As regards Father Garriguet and the others in Paris, there seems to be no reason why they should be embarrassed or preoccupied about the matter unless they needlessly chose to do so. It need not give them anymore trouble than the Homiletic. They have at present enough to engross their attention without taking cognizance of such details over here. I may as well add that in the present condition of things the Archbishop is not disposed to allow much interference in this or any other matter on the part of the Sulpician authorities. He sees that things are practically broken up as regards the Congregation in France. There is no organization on this side, and consequently there is nothing to depend on. While here he called in Mr. Ryan [a student at Dunwoodie] and told him that he would not allow him to join us. From a conversation which I had with him, it was plain to me that he would like to get the seminary into the hands of the clergy of the diocese—not because he is dissatisfied with the manner in which it has been conducted, but because he is convinced, and has been so from the beginning (as he frankly admitted) that it was a great mistake to give the seminary over to any body of men other than the diocesan clergy. He has, he says, more men to choose a faculty from, than all of our Society put together, even if all of the latter were available subjects. There was a time when the needs of the country justified a dependence on foreign congregations, but that time was past, especially in the Eastern dioceses, none of which ought to be better able to suffice for its own needs than New York. His plan would be to select the brightest of the young men (such as Ryan and Mitty, there would always be enough) and send them to the University and abroad, giving them an opportunity to become thoroughly competent—and this, in fact, he is going to do. In the present circumstances, it is what I would do if I were in his place. He has not yet digested the idea of having two inspectors [the 1904 visitors] come over from Paris to investigate things in his Seminary, and it would surely not be prudent on the part of any Sulpician authorities to interfere with this *Review*, unless they wish to precipitate a rupture, which to my mind is bound to come sooner or later.[48]

Dyer was apparently stunned by the news of Farley's attitude. He wrote a brief note to Driscoll asking him to seek a letter from Farley in which the archbishop would state that the *Review* had, "from its inception, full episcopal approval and that the editors are to be responsible to the archbishop of New York."[49] After a minor conflict with Driscoll on the propriety of requesting a letter from the archbishop, Dyer, rather than Driscoll, succeeded in the request, and in March, Farley wrote a brief note authorizing the *Review*.[50]

Shortly after he received Driscoll's letter on the threat of Dunwoodie's separation from Saint-Sulpice, Dyer heard from Richard Wakeham, vice-president of Saint Joseph's Seminary. Gigot had returned from a visit to Baltimore the night before Wakeham wrote his letter. Gigot reported that Dyer had asked him directly, "Is it true that you are all unanimous in favor of breaking away from Paris?" "I said yes," said Gigot, "excepting, of course, Bruneau; I don't know about him." "And Father Wakeham?" Dyer asked. "Yes," I said. Wakeham then discussed the general dissatisfaction at Dunwoodie but did not make any reference to the *Review*. He said that Dyer, who visited New York on his way home from Paris in January of 1905, limited his report on events in France to the anticlerical crisis and to the fact that the superior general had hoped to maintain the Solitude at Issy. Wakeham told Dyer, "Everybody thought you should have done something about autonomy, and that whether you had done it or not, or had succeeded or failed, we had a right to know something about it. . . . From all that you said we could not know whether there was really anything left that could be considered a stable organization or not." Wakeham also told Dyer that the situation of the Sulpicians in the United States was absurd: "left to go on with our work without knowing where we are, and *for all we know,* merely tacked on 'to an airy nothing.' " Wakeham pledged his loyalty to the spirit of Saint Sulpice and to the traditional authority in Paris; however, he was "at the same time, most *absolutely in favor of a real practical autonomy.*" He then listed the conditions of self-determination for Sulpicians in the United States.

> Freedom to have our own novitiate, accept our own members; regulate our own financial matters . . . and lastly, the responsibility of censorship, etc., for our writings, etc. I would believe in leaving the *ratification of local superiors* to the superior-general; in giving him a report of our work, and in receiving a visit of inspection from him or his delegate from time to time. . . . Without . . . [such autonomy] I do not believe there is anything ahead but for us to simply *die out.* . . . On the other hand, I firmly believe that if the autonomy I speak of be promptly obtained, things would soon change for the better. If we had it, I believe the present sentiments of our archbishop could easily be changed.

According to Wakeham, Farley did not understand the Sulpicians. The archbishop considered them members of a "religious order, scheming to perpetuate itself and living on its own conceits."[51]

In his response to Wakeham, Dyer reaffirms his surprise at the tone and content of the remarks of Driscoll, Gigot, and Wakeham on the conditions at Dunwoodie. Dyer tells his old classmate that none of the Sulpicians from the other seminaries in the United States had expressed impatience with the development toward autonomy. Nor had anyone on the council of the vicariate-general in the United States, which included Driscoll, ever indicated such impatience. In his defense Dyer commits himself to a gradualist policy of autonomy: "our present duty is to take advantage of all occasions that offer to make . . . [reform] grow" and develop.[52] Since neither Wakeham nor Dyer places the autonomy issue within the context of the Dunwoodie *Review,* the threat to separate from Saint Sulpice, though not unrelated to the prospective periodical, formed a backdrop to all subsequent relations between Dyer and the Sulpicians at Saint Joseph's Seminary.

Garriguet reported to his council the contents of a letter from Dyer on the situation at Dunwoodie regarding the *Review,* the attitude of Archbishop Farley, and the probability of the separation of Saint Joseph's from the society if the superior general did not approve the periodical. In a letter to Dyer, Garriguet expresses his views, supported by the council, on the Dunwoodie affair. After indicating his disappointment that Driscoll did not consult with him before embarking on the publication of a periodical, Garriguet says that the

Sulpicians should not be too conspicuous in the *Review*, that they should submit their articles to the society for censorship, that no financial burden should be placed upon the society, and that the review should be published under the imprimatur of the archbishop of New York.[53] Since the *Catholic World*, the *American Ecclesiastical Review*, the *American Catholic Quarterly Review*, and the *Dublin Review* were published without an imprimatur, this last stipulation was viewed as burdensome.

Although there is no extant correspondence revealing Driscoll's response to Garriguet, Dyer later recalled that in personal discussions Driscoll did not appear to oppose the superior general's stipulations and, indeed, assured Dyer that relations between Saint Joseph's Seminary and the society were not insecure.[54] There was some tension caused by the persistent delay in the final approval of Gigot's second volume, his *Special Introduction to the Old Testament*, but it did not manifest itself in any further discussion about breaking away from the society. After Richard Wakeham's 5 February 1905 letter to Dyer, which illustrates the general frustration with the lack of progress toward autonomy, there were no further warnings of impending rupture. Hence, when the first issue of the *New York Review* appeared in June 1905, relations between Dunwoodie and Dyer were relatively peaceful.

Under its subtitle, *A Journal of Ancient Faith and Modern Thought*, the *New York Review* surpassed all other United States Catholic periodicals in its commitment to the new apologetics and in providing its readers with the finest representation of European and American Catholic scholarship. Several of the articles published in 1905 illustrate the quality of the new journal: "Consensus Fidelium," by George Tyrrell; "The Spirit of Newman's Apologetics," by Wilfrid Ward; "Catholicity and Free Thought," by George Fansegrive; "Tyrrell as an Apologist," by Henri Bremond; and "Judaism, Was It a Church?" by Pierre Batiffol.[55] The Sulpicians who contributed to the first volume were Joseph Bruneau, James Driscoll, Francis E. Gigot, and Wendell S. Reilly. However, as if to protect the society from association with the *Review*, these Sulpicians were not identified as such by an S.S. following their names or by reference to their membership in the society in the biographical notes on authors. Paulist contributors such as Joseph McSorley and William L. Sullivan, who later left the church as a self-proclaimed Modernist, were identified clearly, as were such other members of religious communities as Vincent McNabb, O.P., Romain Butin, S.M., and Charles D. Plater, S.J.

The *New York Review* refrained from direct polemics, but from the selection of its topics and authors it clearly promoted historical criticism of scripture and the new apologetics rooted in religious experience and in a developmental notion of dogma; all in all, it presupposed a spirit of free inquiry among Catholic intellectuals. Although it did not contain an attack upon the Thomist synthesis, the entire journal was based upon the need to form a new synthesis between faith and modern culture; this new synthesis implicitly ran contrary to the neo-Thomist condemnation of the dangerous trends in rationalistic methodologies, subjectivist opinions, and Protestant pluralism.

Dyer and Garriguet were apparently inhibited from responding to the publication of the *New York Review* by fear that any attempt at censorship would precipitate a crisis and by the fact that the *Review* was published with the imprimatur of Archbishop Farley. In retrospect, this restraint on the part of the American vicar-general and the French superior general was superfluous because the crisis, from the point of view of Dunwoodie, had reached such a level of intensity that it was merely a matter of time before the denouement. In a letter dated 9 January 1906, two days before the first anniversary of Driscoll's letter announcing the conception of the *Review*, the president of Dunwoodie and four other Sulpicians on the faculty—Richard K. Wakeham, Francis E. Gigot, John R. Mahoney, and Timothy P. Holland—announce their decision to leave the society. They explicitly state that they are not going to enter "into a lengthy discussion of the motives that have prompted this action or the occasion that has precipitated it." Hence, there is no mention of any reference to Gigot's work or to the *Review*. Their case was simply that there was no future for the Sulpicians in the United States and that they had "accepted the offer of the Most Reverend Archbishop and his council to continue the seminary work as priests of the Archdiocese of New York."[56]

With an almost clinical tone and a studied sense of understatement, the five Sulpicians present the core of their argument:

> In the present condition of things, the prospect of recruiting desirable subjects in America for Sulpician work on the old lines is practically nil. We are convinced that in the near future, through lack of subjects or from other causes, we would be obliged to sever our relations with the seminary of New York: and we were equally convinced that by taking advantage of the present disposition of the Archbishop, we could lessen the evil that would have resulted from our withdrawal for the interests of both religion in the diocese and the work of St. Sulpice in this country. For by remaining in a body we shall be able to continue the work on the same lines as heretofore, such being the explicit desire of the Archbishop. . . . At the same time, we sincerely hope to maintain more intimate and cordial relations between Dunwoodie and Baltimore than could have been hoped for under a complete change of regime. We believe, too, that our action in the matter will do less

harm to the work of the remaining confreres than would have been caused by our withdrawal later on. For by remaining in the conditions on which we are accepted we obtain a very practical endorsement of the work that has been done, notwithstanding the Archbishop's well known objection to having his seminary under any other control than his own. We beg, therefore, to affirm that we have followed our judgment in the sole desire of doing what we consider the best for the interests above stated, for we have ample reasons to believe that nothing better was to be hoped for after all that has transpired since the suppression of the Society in France. We regret that circumstances entirely unforeseen have caused us to act with what may seem to be unbecoming haste. We hope, however, that fuller knowledge of the circumstances, which will come in due time, will serve to explain and justify our action.[57]

Dyer was shocked by this announcement. On 9 December, just four weeks before the climactic letter was written, Driscoll had attended a regular meeting of the council of the vicariate-general in which he appeared in complete accord with the majority on the traditional policy of sending American candidates to Paris for their Solitude. Indeed, from Dyer's recollection of his own visit to Dunwoodie six months prior to the break, "all apprehension that any step of a serious character would be taken by the Fathers of the New York Seminary vanished from my mind as entirely as if it had never been there."[58]

Upon receiving the news, Dyer immediately wrote to Farley and Driscoll. He reminds the archbishop of the contract between Saint Sulpice and the archdiocese of New York, which stipulated a year's notice for the withdrawal of either party from the agreement.

Would we not have to look for some crime committed in the conduct of your seminary by St. Sulpice to merit the requital of a summary dismissal, with the privation of five of her subjects? . . . I cannot understand how the infliction of so grave an injury upon our Society could be reconciled with the high appreciation of the manner in which St. Sulpice has conducted your seminary that I have so often heard from Your Grace.[59]

In his letter to Driscoll, Dyer lists five observations. He questions Driscoll's right to "hand over" the seminary to the archbishop. He points out that the precipitous departure of the five Sulpicians from the society "would appear as a practical endorsement of all that has been done against us in France." He tells Driscoll that each of the five defectors occupies a more "honored position" as a Sulpician than he would have attained on his own. Since there had been neither prior consultation nor any warning of their action, the five, Dyer concludes, are guilty of "treason." Lastly, the vicar-general doubts that such an action could be perpetrated by "right thinking men."[60] The following weekend Dyer visited with Farley at his home; later the archbishop, Dyer, and the five Sulpicians met at the seminary, during which time the archbishop withdrew on two occasions to allow the Sulpicians to discuss the matter in privacy. Dyer's notes on these meetings and other private talks with individuals occupy many pages of a privately published explanation of the Dunwoodie affair. Several conclusions may be drawn from all of this. The five Sulpicians would not have considered leaving had they not been assured that Farley would accept them. Although originally the archbishop had stated to Dyer that the Sulpicians might remain in charge of the seminary if they were able to staff it and that he merely accepted the de facto control of the seminary with the resignation of all but Joseph Bruneau, he later admitted that his willingness to incardinate the five men precipitated their resignations. Farley also acknowledged that he eventually intended to assume full responsibility for staffing the seminary and to restrict the Sulpicians to spiritual direction similar to the arrangement between Saint Sulpice and the Catholic University of America, whereby the Sulpicians administered Divinity College, the resident hall for priest graduate students and some priest faculty members.[61]

Gigot indicated that despite his recognition that Dyer had adequately represented his case for publishing, the society's censorship policy prevented his returning to the status of a Sulpician. Once again Gigot expressed his disillusionment with the future of Saint Sulpice in the United States, views that were reflected by Holland and Mahoney, each of whom had been in the society for only a few years.[62] Driscoll's remarks were purely perfunctory, as if any serious comments were a waste of time. He seems to have had a deep abhorrence of any direct confrontation with authority. Dyer later concluded that Gigot and Driscoll had been alienated for years, that they seized the opportunity of the crisis in Paris, and that after they had gained the support of Farley, they were able to remain at Dunwoodie while at the same time withdrawing from Saint Sulpice. Dyer was so embittered that he referred to the five as rats fleeing a sinking ship.[63]

Sometime later in 1906, Driscoll published a pamphlet at the Dunwoodie Press entitled *A Statement of the Facts and Circumstances that Led to the Withdrawal of the Dunwoodie Seminary from the Society of St. Sulpice*, which is identical to a typed copy of the rationale for the Prefect of the Propaganda Fide in Rome.[64] Prefaced by a brief history of Saint Sulpice in the United States, which concludes with a misconceived description of the legal dissolution of the society in France in 1904–1905, the *statement* then enters into a summary of "local conditions," (i.e., Archbishop Farley's views on the need for full archdiocesan control of the seminary).[65] In the part titled "Discouraging Future," Driscoll highlights the personnel crisis in the United States, the prospect of Saint Sulpice withdrawing from Dunwoodie and the archbishop assuming control, and concludes with the decision of the five priests to side with the archbishop and thereby maintain the "rule, spirit, and discipline" upon which the seminary was founded.[66] In the section "Was the Action of the Professors Legitimate?" Driscoll presents several examples substantiating his belief that the Sulpicians are diocesan priests; he writes, "they are not religious and they have the right to leave whenever they wish to do so."[67]

The pamphlet concludes with "Reply to Charges to the Accusation that the Five Professors" handed over "the seminary to the archbishop." Driscoll asserts that because Saint Joseph's was under the ultimate authority of the archdiocese, and because the five "were thoroughly convinced that the end of [Sulpician] control was inevitably not far distant . . ." they merely did nothing but "hand over . . . their *own personal services* to the archbishop. . . ." Driscoll also denies as false the charge that they had "forced the situation" by citing the cause for the break as deriving from actual conditions rather than from a situation contrived to force the hand of the archbishop. Driscoll explains the apparent violation of the contract with the assertion that the Society of Saint Sulpice had never abided by the stipulation to furnish at least eight Sulpician members of the faculty. According to Driscoll, had the professors waited for a year before withdrawing from the society, "no other Sulpicians would have been put in their places." The pamphlet concludes:

> This statement which has been made honestly and without any attempt at special pleading represents the circumstance and motives which actuated the Professors of Dunwoodie in withdrawing from the Society of St. Sulpice. They believed that they were acting in their own legitimate rights; and were not violating the rights of others, or inflicting any injury upon them. They simply elected to remain where they believed their labors would be most fruitful.[68]

In his response to this pamphlet, Dyer notes a few factual errors regarding the crisis in France, refers to the "unsophisticated naiveté" regarding the contractual affairs, cites the lack of commitment to "natural justice, not to speak of honor or devotion to a cause," and concludes that the five professors left because they were more loyal to Dunwoodie than to the Society of Saint Sulpice.[69] On 8 January 1906, Saint Joseph's Seminary was in the hands of Saint Sulpice; on January 9, it was in the hands of priests accountable only to the archdiocesan authority.

Since the Sulpician administrations in Baltimore, Boston, and San Francisco were not motivated to respond so radically to the critical conditions Driscoll describes in this pamphlet, it is apparent that the Dunwoodie affair represented a unique set of conditions. It not only allowed Farley to seize the opportunity to gain complete control of the seminary; it also allowed the five professors to delegitimate the authority of Saint Sulpice, thus providing an opportunity for Farley to justify his action. Gigot had personally suffered at the hands of Sulpician censors in Paris; Driscoll and Wakeham, whose views appear to have motivated Holland and Mahoney, seem to have been experiencing emotions derived from the frustration of rising expectations. With Dyer as one of the twelve assistants to the superior general and as the vicar-general of the U.S. Sulpicians, the five must have anticipated that he would exploit the opportunity of the crisis in France to demand greater autonomy from Paris, which would have entailed an American novitiate and a liberalized censorship policy. Wakeham and Driscoll were very close to Dyer; the three had shared their own vision of Saint Sulpice in the United States. When Dyer returned from Paris in 1905 without optimistic news of further liberalizing developments, they were left without hope. Had the hoped-for Americanization developments actually occurred, Gigot would have been free to pursue his research and writing, Driscoll's *Review* would have been free from Garriguet's meddling policies, Wakeham would have been satisfied with a condition of American self-control, and all would have felt encouraged that their views would be represented in the direction of the community in the United States. Edward Dyer had contributed to those rising expectations. His administration of Dunwoodie (1896–1902) was characterized by enlightened reforms; as early as 1894 he had favored greater independence from Paris and the establishment of a novitiate in the United States. On matters of censorship he had strongly represented Gigot's case to the authorities in Paris, and it was he who had convinced Garriguet to tolerate publication of the *New York Review*. By temperament, however, Dyer was cautious, ever sensitive to the need for steering a moderate course when dealing with the authorities in Paris, who jealously guarded the centralized character of Saint-Sulpice and who were influenced by their biases against American Catholicism. With the resignation of Captier, the Americanist ideals of Magnien and the Modernist ideals of Hogan were viewed with suspicion, if not fear. Dyer and Driscoll both represented the ideals of the leaders of the older generation, but whereas Dyer inherited their deep loyalty to Saint Sulpice, Driscoll's Sulpician loyalty gave way to his dedication to ideals embodied in the seminary at Dunwoodie, which included, above all, publishing the *New York Review*.

Driscoll consistently denied that the *Review* had entered into his decision to leave Saint Sulpice, while Dyer intimated that it must have been a factor. Writing to the editor of the Catholic *Transcript*, the official newspaper of the diocese of Hartford, Driscoll said that "the action recently taken by certain Sulpician professors . . . was not the outcome of any controversy concerning their orthodoxy or that of the *Review*, but . . . [as a result of] a concurrence of circumstances . . . they felt that they could render greater service to the cause of clerical education in the archdiocese of New York" as priests of the archdiocese of New York rather than as Sulpicians. In this same letter Driscoll responds to another misunderstanding included in an editorial in the *Transcript* that referred to the *Review*'s identity with "a new liberal Catholicism." He said such a term was "absurd" and denied that the journal could in any way be associated with a movement to promote a

> new Catholicism. . . . The purpose [of the *Review*] is not to abandon the old in favor of the new, but rather to interpret with becoming care and reverence the old truths in the light of the new science. The task, as it appears to us, is not one involving doctrinal change, but restatement and readjustments—in other words, the preservation and not the rupture of continuity.[70]

About eighteen months after this letter (3 July 1907) the Vatican's Holy Office issued the decree *Lamentabili*, which lists sixty-five propositions said to be in opposition to orthodoxy. On 8 September 1907, Pius X issued the encyclical *Pascendi Dominici Gregis*, a condemnation of much of the theological and scriptural enterprise associated with Tyrrell and Loisy, and in 1908 both of them were excommunicated. In the May–June 1908 issue of the *New York Review*, the editors announced that despite the continued need for a journal of modern apologetics, the lack of financial support prevented further publication of the journal. Although Farley had defended the *Review* against the criticism of Archbishop Diomede Falconio, the apostolic delegate to the United States, an abundance of evidence suggests that the journal was suppressed by Farley because Roman authorities had branded many of its authors with the hot iron of heterodoxy.

Driscoll's journal was indeed Modernist in the sense that it was committed to a reinterpretation of the faith according to principles of the higher criticism, of developmental theology, and of democratic freedom in society and in the world of ideas. Such an agenda entailed a new synthesis that collided with the dominant neoscholasticism and with the ultramontane ecclesiology so closely identified with the Rome of Pius X. Six months after the demise of the *Review*, Farley replaced Driscoll with John P. Chidwick, who had no academic qualifications. There is no extant correspondence on Driscoll's reaction to his assignments as pastor of a parish in Manhattan and later in New Rochelle (1922), but after leaving Dunwoodie he never published again. Francis Gigot, who published an article on scripture in the *Review*'s final issue, remained on the faculty until his death in 1920. In the post-Modernist climate Gigot officially accepted the decree of the pontifical biblical commission that supported the Mosaic authorship of the Pentateuch. Such acceptance was, of course, contrary to his own research and writing. Timothy Holland became a pastor in Ogdensburg, New York, in 1908; John Mahoney taught at Dunwoodie until he became a pastor in 1916; Richard Wakeham remained on the faculty until his death in 1914.[71]

In the 18 September 1909 meeting of the Sulpician superior general's council, it was noted that the *Review* had been suppressed, that the personnel had been dispersed, and that several of its articles had been delated to the Holy See.[72] By this time the society had returned to normal conditions in France, but between 1906 and 1909 only two Americans had successfully passed through the Solitude at Issy. As will be fully explained in the next chapter, Dyer's policies of cautious moderation were vindicated, as in 1911 a Solitude was established in the United States. Driscoll's rationale for leaving the society was not vindicated, however; Dunwoodie gradually became transformed from a modern American seminary to a traditional Roman institution with no lingering aura of the Sulpician spirit. The Dunwoodie affair of January 1906 was a tragedy for Saint Sulpice in the United States. Had it remained in Sulpician hands, there is no doubt that, like the society's other American seminaries, Saint Joseph's would have preserved the spirit of Saint Sulpice, which was a countervailing force to the omnibus Romanization of seminary life. Because the *New York Review* was the creation of Driscoll and Duffy and because it was fostered by Farley, it was connected only remotely with Saint Sulpice in the United States and would probably have been suppressed much earlier than June of 1908 had the Sulpicians still been in control. However, the *Review* was a Dunwoodie creation as well, and the modern character of Saint Joseph's Seminary developed under the leadership of James Driscoll but occurred during the administration of Edward Dyer.

10

Progress in San Francisco, Disaster in Boston

Intrinsic to the tradition of Saint Sulpice is the principle of deference to the local ordinary as the final source of authority in the governance of Sulpician seminaries. Occasionally, irreconcilable conflicts between a bishop and the Sulpician faculty have occurred. On one occasion during the life of Jean-Jacques Olier, the Sulpicians were forced out of a seminary. As noted in the last chapter, the conflict between the Sulpicians and Archbishop Farley did not entail a clash of views on basic ideas of theological education but was simply a dispute over management. Farley wanted to staff the seminary with his own diocesan priests. Had Dunwoodie been run by the Vincentians rather than the Sulpicians, Farley would probably have pursued the same course of action.

The present chapter deals with the seminaries in San Francisco and Boston. The story of the Sulpician seminary in San Francisco, like that in Baltimore, centers on a strong sense of mutual loyalty between the archbishop and the Sulpician faculty. Archbishop Riordan and the Sulpicians also shared an Americanist vision of the role of the church in the United States. But while the Sulpicians were thriving in the West, they experienced another major setback in the East. The conflict between Archbishop William Henry O'Connell and the Sulpicians was nothing less than a clash of ecclesiology. Whereas in the Dunwoodie affair, Driscoll's liberal Americanist and quasi-Modernist leadership sided with the archbishop against what was perceived as the reactionary Society of Saint Sulpice, the Brighton debacle entailed an anti-Americanist archbishop who perceived the Sulpicians as harboring Gallican and Modernist sympathies. Hence, the first ten years of Edward Dyer's tenure as vicar-general of the Sulpicians in the United States involved a continual challenge to develop a workable relationship between the society and the local ordinaries.

Patrick Riordan's first contact with the Sulpicians was in the summer of 1860 when, after withdrawing from the North American College in Rome for reasons of health, he sought entrance into Saint Sulpice. Henri Icard, the superior, felt that the frail youth could not withstand the rigorous life of Saint Sulpice and rejected the young Chicago seminarian, encouraging him to attend the Colonial Seminary in Paris staffed by the Holy Spirit Fathers.[1] The following year Riordan entered the American College in Louvain, where he was influenced by the liberal cardinal archbishop of Malines, Engelbert Sterckx. At Louvain Riordan also became friendly with John Lancaster Spalding, a seminarian of the diocese of Louisville and subsequently bishop of Peoria and a major intellectual force in the American church. Later, befriended by James Gibbons, John Ireland, and John Keane, Riordan held strong Americanist views, though he never assumed a major role in the conflict.

In 1883, Riordan was named coadjutor archbishop of San Francisco. He succeeded Joseph S. Alemany, O.P., in 1884 and, as mentioned in the previous chapter, almost immediately sought the Sulpicians to staff his projected seminary, which finally opened in 1898. Riordan's strong attachment to the Sulpicians was in marked contrast to the attitude of his own clergy, the vast majority of whom were trained at All Hallows College, Dublin, and at Saint Patrick's College at Carlow. Alemany had established Saint Thomas Aquinas Seminary, which was staffed by diocesan priests and later by Marist Fathers. Located thirty-six miles from San Francisco and with virtually no parochial school system from which to draw vocations, the seminary never had more than five students. Riordan's clergy considered his new institution at Menlo Park too costly and viewed the Sulpicians as too rigorous for the putatively undisciplined northern California youth. However, Riordan's chancellor, George Montgomery,[2] an alumnus of Saint Charles' and Saint Mary's seminaries in Baltimore, was very supportive of the new seminary.

Saint Patrick's Seminary, perhaps so named to mollify Irish apprehensions, suffered several problems during its first years. Its high dropout rate, because of a lack of any screening process, was exacerbated by problems among the original Sulpicians. Richard Wakeham, the treasurer who had been responsible for laying the groundwork for the opening of the seminary, was unable and perhaps even unwilling to get along with the rector, Jean-Baptiste Arsène Vuibert. As a result, Vuibert made Adriene-Antoine Serieys responsible for internal affairs and left Wakeham in charge of external affairs, particularly the management of the property.[3]

Born in Virginia of Protestant parents, Wakeham was, as noted earlier, unsympathetic to the French style of leadership. He tolerated Vuibert, but Serieys, who never achieved a command of English, struck him as utterly incompetent, and the tension between the two became a source of instability within the small Sulpician community. Riordan complained to Magnien that the seminary suffered because there is "no business head" to the institution.[4] Wakeham was transferred to Dunwoodie, but Vuibert's generally inept leadership still caused tensions among the Sulpicians. According to John Doran, a young Sulpician from San Francisco assigned to Saint Patrick's in 1901, Vuibert was indiscreet, lacked dignity, had a "violent temper," and made "his own will the sole principle of authority. . . . His partiality is remarked in the fact that he never resents a public insult from a Frenchman; woe to the American who opens his mouth."[5]

Edward Dyer visited San Francisco in January 1904, and after consultation with the faculty and with Riordan he decided that a new superior should be appointed, particularly since the academic year of 1904–1905 would mark the start of theology studies. The following summer, Henri Amans Ayrinhac was appointed superior.[6] Born in Saint-Gregoire in Aveyron, France, in March 1867, Ayrinhac was an alumnus of the Sulpician seminary at Rodez. After studying theology at the Minerva and canon law at the Apollinaire in Rome, he entered the Solitude at Issy. Upon completion of the Solitude, he was assigned to Saint Mary's, where he taught theology. When Tanquerey returned to Paris, Ayrinhac became the major professor in moral theology and was appointed head of the philosophy department of the seminary. Although only thirty-seven years old when he became superior of Saint Patrick's, he already had an excellent reputation as a strong, impartial leader and as a solid canonist.

Edward Arbez, another young French Sulpician, was also appointed to Saint Patrick's in the summer of 1904. Born in Paris in 1881, Arbez was among the first group at Saint Austin's College under the direction of Driscoll and Gigot. After two years of theology and Oriental languages at the Catholic University of America, he returned to France for his Solitude and ordination. Saint Patrick's was his first assignment, but because John Doran was teaching scripture there,

Arbez first taught theology. However, in 1906 he was assigned to teach scripture to the college students, and later he became one of the foremost Catholic scripture scholars in the United States.[7] In 1912 he requested permission to study scripture at the Ecole Biblique in Jerusalem, but Superior General Garriguet refused permission on the grounds that Arbez would "not offer sufficient guarantees on the point of view of doctrine and regularity."[8] In later life Arbez became chairman of the editorial board for the revision of the Douay-Rheims Bible, oversaw an entirely new translation of the Old Testament, and was one of the founders and the first president of the Catholic Biblical Association. These appointments were made while he was a professor at the Catholic University of America, where he taught scripture from 1928 to 1951. The appointments of Ayrinhac and Arbez to San Francisco were important not only to the opening of the theologate but also to the stability of the Sulpician community.

The San Francisco earthquake of 18 April 1906 resulted in the destruction of about two-thirds of Saint Patrick's Seminary. Fortunately, no member of the community was injured. While Saint Patrick's was under reconstruction, the fifteen seminarians and members of the faculty lived in an adjacent mansion rented by the archdiocese.[9] It was nearly a year before seminary life in Menlo Park returned to normal. Archbishop Riordan so cherished his seminary that he had an episcopal residence built on the grounds, financed by an old friend from Chicago, Michael Cudahy.[10]

In national affairs Patrick Riordan was aligned with the progressive prelates of the American church. Although he was not very supportive of Archbishop Ireland's school plan, he was sensitive to the need of the church to accommodate itself to the dynamic trends in American culture. Riordan was a thorough Americanist, standing, as it were, midway between the intellectual Americanism of John Lancaster Spalding and the political, activist Americanism of John Ireland.[11] Patrick Riordan became very active in the opposition to the rise of William O'Connell, an ardent anti-Americanist whose anti-Sulpician animus at times appeared almost pathological.[12]

Riordan, who was a close friend of William Stang, bishop of Fall River, Massachusetts, entered into the controversy surrounding the appointment of a coadjutor for Archbishop Williams in 1904. The suffragan bishops had placed Matthew Harkins, bishop of Providence, Rhode Island, at the top of their list of candidates on two different ternae. William O'Connell, then bishop of Portland, Maine, wrote to his good friend Merry del Val, totally discrediting not only Harkins but also his fellow suffragan bishops for their Americanism and their lukewarm loyalty to the Holy See.[13] For nearly two years the Vatican refused to make a decision on the appointment, but during this time O'Connell received support from one bishop in the province and several pastors in Boston, all of whom praised him for his fierce defense of Rome against what one pro-O'Connell priest said was a conspiracy dedicated to "Jansenistic Americanism."[14]

In January of 1906, when Rome announced the appointment of William O'Connell as coadjutor to Williams, it sent a wave of shock among the leadership of the American church. Since O'Connell's name had not appeared on the *ternae* sent to Rome, several indignant bishops considered petitioning the Vatican to respect the traditional process of selecting bishops. However, when Williams, who had expressed to Rome that his own candidate was Harkins, accepted O'Connell's appointment as "the expression of God's will," the anti-O'Connell movement waned.[15] Riordan had cautioned against a formal complaint, but privately he expressed his frustration at the success of the O'Connell-Merry del Val alliance. The archbishop of San Francisco referred to the appointment as "a national scandal" and said, "I do not see any use in holding any meetings and sending money across the Atlantic when no attention is paid to the proceedings of the Bishops and Archbishops." Riordan was particularly disturbed by the appointment because during a visit to Rome he had been assured that O'Connell was not among the candidates under consideration. Hence, Riordan said that the appointment was "the most disastrous thing that has happened to religion in a century."[16] Riordan also knew that O'Connell's appointment did not augur well for the Sulpicians' presence in Boston. During the summer previous to O'Connell's appointment, Daniel E. Maher, the superior of Saint John's Seminary in Brighton, wrote to Edward Dyer that "in a document forwarded to Rome by the O'Connell party the incompetent management of this seminary by the Sulpicians was cited as proof of the Archbishop's negligence in not looking after the important affairs of his diocese."[17]

William O'Connell's first experience with the Sulpicians was as a student at Saint Charles' College in 1876–1879. In his autobiography he mentions the kindly Father John B. Menu but avoids any mention of the society other than a reference to its French character and general ignorance of Thomistic philosophy. After two and a half years at Saint Charles' he transferred to Boston College to complete his pretheology course.[18] He attended the North American College in Rome and later became its rector. He left that post to become bishop of Portland, Maine. Because the records of Saint Charles' College were destroyed in a fire (1911) there is no extant account of O'Connell's years at the college. According to his own recollection his poor health prevented his return to Saint Charles'. His biographer, John E. Sexton, wrote that because of a death in his family O'Connell considered it appropriate to remain in Boston. One Sulpician on the faculty of Saint Charles' during O'Connell's time there later recalled that O'Connell and several of his friends became the butt of jokes among the students because they preferred poetry to playing games. Since O'Connell felt that the Sulpicians did not properly prosecute the "offenders," he indicated his displeasure and ultimately did not return to Saint Charles' because he felt betrayed and unwelcome there.[19] Regardless of the origin of O'Connell's anti-Sulpician animus, it was not long after his arrival as coadjutor to Archbishop Williams that life at Saint John's Seminary was affected.

Francis P. Havey, the Sulpician rector of Saint John's, an alumnus of the Boston seminary, was appropriately deferential to O'Connell. Havey hosted a reception for O'Connell at the seminary, and when the coadjutor expressed a wish to present a series of conferences, Havey, with the approval of Williams, assented to the proposal. He later remarked that O'Connell's first conference was "a good one"; Havey "suggested that the seminarians might take notes with a view to having the talks in print."[20] During the early period of these conferences, O'Connell took Havey into his confidence. The latter wrote that the coadjutor

> said that a load of anxiety had been pressing on his breast because of what had come to him from this side and that of the real conditions of affairs in the Archdiocese. Then he asked me if there were not things to be remedied in the seminary. I told him the seminary was a good and sound one. . . . I felt, I confess, that the coadjutor might be expecting that Rome would, if the need were urgent, give him the administration of the archdiocese immediately.[21]

O'Connell assumed full authority upon the death of Williams on 30 August 1907. Over the next three years, he gradually transformed Saint John's Seminary from a traditional Sulpician institution to one designed according to the Roman model. In the process, he not only denigrated the Sulpician way of life but also went to extreme measures to undermine the authority of the superior. The archbishop directly interfered in the administration of the seminary by making the treasurer accountable to him alone, by excusing the auxiliary faculty from attending the daily spiritual exercises, by directly appointing faculty members without consultation with the superior, and by reserving the right to expel not only students of the archdiocese but also those of other dioceses. Three other measures were particularly damaging to Sulpician morale: he removed Havey from the board that passed on ordinands; he demanded that Dyer remove Pierre Chapon, Jules Baisnée, and Joseph Bruneau from the faculty; and he questioned the traditional style of Sulpician spiritual direction. Lastly, O'Connell removed the ceremony of renewal of priestly vows from the seminary to the cathedral—a severe blow, as it was the foremost feast day in the Sulpician calendar as well as the unofficial alumni day.[22] The removal of Havey from the board of examiners was, according to Dyer, an unprecedented action in the history of American seminary education. Havey remarked that O'Connell had Chapon removed because he was a retired priest and therefore was "not earning his salt. . . . His Grace objected to his Seminary being used by Sulpicians for a boarding house." According to Havey, O'Connell personally disliked Baisnée, "a young cub," and Bruneau was "a man who by his theological views might involve His Grace in trouble at Rome."[23]

With the departure of Bruneau in 1909, "rumors began to fly among the student body that the Sulpicians would soon be leaving."[24] Edward Dyer was worried that a second seminary would be taken away from the American Sulpicians within a matter of a few years. He was therefore in frequent communication with Superior General Garriguet and with the Sulpician procurator-general Marie-François-Xavier Hertzog in Rome.[25] The latter wrote to Dyer in March of 1909 that Bruneau had been denounced in Rome, apparently by O'Connell, for his association with the *New York Review*. Hertzog reported that during an audience with Pius X, he had told the pope that the reason that he had not been at recent audiences was that he had been attempting "to control an accusation made against one of our confreres to guarantee his orthodoxy." Hertzog warned Dyer that because of the "great importance attached here on the certitude of doctrine . . . all our professors should . . . in their teaching, be very exact."[26] Some two months later Hertzog told Dyer that "the situation of Msgr. O'Connell in Rome is certainly good because of his generosity." He urged his confreres in Boston to be as patient as possible. "It appears to me," he wrote, "that the tactic of the Archbishop toward us is to force us to leave so that he can say that we left of our own free will."[27] Six months after the report on Bruneau, Hertzog wrote to Dyer of a conversation with Merry del Val in which Hertzog assured the cardinal secretary of state of Bruneau's orthodoxy. Hertzog wrote, "All is therefore alright for the moment, but it is important that dear M. Bruneau be very prudent in his teaching and in his statements."[28]

During the period in which his association with the *New York Review* was haunting his reputation in Rome, Bruneau's French translation of H. N. Oxenham's 1865 work, *The Catholic Doctrine of the Atonement*, was widely reviewed in Catholic periodicals. Then, in February 1910, *La Civiltà Cattolica* attacked Oxenham's notions of redemption and also Bruneau's endorsement of the work in the introduction. In a series of letters Hertzog kept Garriguet informed of the Vatican's reaction to the *Civiltà*'s condemnation. At one point Hertzog reports that

Bruneau's translation was to be placed on the Index. A brief notice of *Civiltà*'s review of the book was published in the *Pilot* of Boston, which reads in part:

> The *Civiltà Cattolica* reviews a book recently translated by the Rev. Joseph Bruneau, a Sulpician professor of theology. The Roman periodical dissects the book learnedly and points out that it is without any value whatever to the Catholic student, and moreover that it is full of pernicious ideas.
>
> The book bears besides the name of the translator the title of "professor of theology at Brighton Seminary." To set at rest all inquiries, it is due the Seminary to say that there is no such professor at our diocesan seminary at present.[29]

O'Connell was delighted with the condemnation of Bruneau, as it justified his previous removal from the seminary. O'Connell wrote to Merry del Val shortly after the translation's publication:

> "The *Civiltà Cattolica* has done a noble duty exposing Bruneau. That is a wound which will smart in certain quarters. But, thank God, it is not the Church and true doctrine which will feel the smart. A few more masks pulled down and we shall know just where we stand, here as well as in Europe. Of all things, God save us from the hypocrisy of these pharisees."

In that same letter O'Connell reports that he is "pleased with Fr. Nilan's succession in Hartford. He is at least not a Sulpician. Anything which breaks that blighting tyranny in this Province is a thing to be gratified to God for."[30]

Even before O'Connell wrote this letter, Merry del Val wrote to Diomede Falconio, the apostolic delegate to the United States, informing him that the Oxenham book and Bruneau's introduction were "severely criticized and declared full of errors" by *La Civiltà Cattolica*, "which considers it a dangerous work for young students and especially for those in the ecclesiastical career." He also told Falconio that the *Osservatore Romano* "approves this just and severe criticism of the book and its translation, warning young students against such writing." Merry del Val instructed Falconio to inform Cardinal Gibbons of these charges "knowing that Fr. Bruneau is teaching in your seminary and consequently expecting your Eminence will see about the manner of his teaching and writing."[31]

In response to a request by Gibbons to comment on the value of Oxenham's *The Catholic Doctrine of the Atonement*, Bruneau wrote a five-page letter to the cardinal archbishop of Baltimore documenting the orthodoxy of this work by the British theologian. After noting that his publication had received the imprimatur of the archbishop of Paris, Bruneau cites Oxenham's contributions to the American *Catholic Encyclopedia* and the *Directorium Sacerdotale*. Bruneau also quotes a review of the book that appeared in the *Tablet*, published in London, which refers to the work as "Oxenham's masterpiece." Rather than harm seminarians, Bruneau says, Oxenham's book should "prove a fruitful source of inspiration" because it contains "such a breath of fervour, piety, poetry and eloquence, prompted by the great mystery of our salvation. . . ."[32] Bruneau cites several favorable reviews of his publication, such as the one found in the "decidedly thomistic *Revue augustinienne* and in journals published by the French Dominicans (*Revue des sciences philosophiques et théologiques*) and the French Benedictines (*Revue bénédictine*). Although Bruneau does not directly defend himself against the criticism of *Civiltà* or *Osservatore Romano*, he intimates that the basis of their criticism may have been a narrow neoscholasticism. He states that a feature of Oxenham's thought, "which of course displeased some,—is the fact that he warmly advocates the Franciscan theory about the final motive of the Incarnation, emphatically proclaiming himself,—perhaps to a fault,—a fervent disciple of Duns Scotus, St. Francis de Sales and Fr. Faber." Bruneau closes his letter to Gibbons by affirming:

> If there is in my translation anything which Christ, through His Vicar, should condemn, I would wish it blotted out ere it was written. For I believe all that Holy Mother Church teaches and believes.
>
> I hope these explanations will enable Your Eminence to see perfectly through the facts and my actual and unchanged dispositions. I hereby submit myself unreservedly to the judgment of the Holy Father, and am very sorry if there was anything which did not please Him perfectly in my endeavor.[33]

On 15 March 1910, just one week after Falconio's letter on the Oxenham controversy, Gibbons wrote to Merry del Val a brief letter with a copy of Bruneau's five-page explanation of the value of his translation. Gibbons says that he had never read Oxenham, nor had he known of Bruneau's translation "as it was written and published whilst Father Bruneau was teaching in the Boston seminary." Of course, Gibbons's response to the *Civiltà* article and his evaluation of the contribution of the Sulpicians were diametrically opposed to the views of William O'Connell. Gibbons wrote, "This incident is very painful to myself and to the Sulpician Fathers, who since they came to Baltimore (where is situated their Mother House for this country) at the end of the 18th century, they have always been conspicuous for piety, orthodoxy, and devotion to the Holy See." Gibbons assured Merry del Val "that so long as Father Bruneau remains in my seminary, he shall write and teach nothing but what is in strict accordance with sound Catholic doctrine."[34] Perhaps this show of support for Bruneau put the case to rest, for this is the last reference to the controversy except within those documents that refer to it in the past tense. Indeed, the

Bruneau affair appears almost as a form of anti-Sulpician harassment or, at best, as an outburst of paranoia by the extremist defenders of orthodoxy. Since there was no doubt of Oxenham's orthodoxy, perhaps Bruneau's association with the *New York Review*, rather than his translation, was the source of the severe criticism from the two Roman periodicals.

O'Connell followed his anti-Bruneau denunciations with an attack on the very heart of the Sulpician system: he threatened to appoint a spiritual director and remove the Sulpicians from their traditional role dating from the time of Olier. At an extraordinary meeting of Dyer's council on 19 May 1910, the discussion centered on ways to counter O'Connell's intention to remove the Sulpicians from all spiritual direction.[35] The archbishop seems to have been undaunted by Dyer's assertion that as recently as 1903 Rome had approved the Sulpician system of uniting the roles of confessor and spiritual director. Besides another appeal to the Vatican for a confirmation of the system, the council decided to highlight the significance of the society's contribution to the church at the International Eucharistic Congress at Montreal the following September. Bishop Harkins, who was the president of the American Alumni Association of Saint-Sulpice in Paris, had scheduled a reunion meeting during the congress. Dyer's council proposed that Garriguet, Hertzog, and Vincent Vannutelli, the cardinal protector of the society, attend this reunion not only as an international show of support but also as a sign of the society's loyalty to the papacy and of its stature in Rome: "this reunion may prevent the Archbishop of Boston from touching a point so important to our Sulpician life."[36]

Dyer, who was advised by his doctor to take an immediate vacation, decided to visit Rome to seek written approbation for the Sulpician system of spiritual direction as well as to personally invite Cardinal Vannutelli and others to the reunion in Montreal. In anticipation of Dyer's visit, Hertzog wrote to Garriguet that it was necessary to proceed "with great prudence. We should not engage in a struggle against the Archbishop of Boston, whose position here is too strong, particularly with the Secretary of State." Hertzog pointed out that the Bruneau affair was still a negative factor in the atmosphere of Rome and that an alumnus of Saint-Sulpice in Paris had been refused a doctorate in scripture on doctrinal grounds.[37]

Dyer arrived in Rome in the second week of June. During his ten-day visit he met with Vannutelli and other members of the Curia Romana sympathetic to Saint Sulpice. On 18 June, Dyer and Hertzog "had a very good audience with Pope Pius X. M. Dyer . . . with great conviction, informed him of our work in America." Dyer also spoke to the pope about Joseph Bruneau's fine work at the seminary and, by implication, testified to his loyalty to Rome, to which Pius

X responded with words of "great benevolence."[38] Dyer also visited with Merry del Val but did not mention Bruneau "because of the close relations between the Secretary of State and the Archbishop of Boston."[39] Dyer left Rome without a letter of approbation for the Sulpician system, probably because to secure such a letter would have required an elaboration of O'Connell's threat to the system; this would have brought the struggle with the archbishop to the surface in Rome, and O'Connell was by far more influential in Rome than were the Sulpicians.

In mid-September, some three months after Dyer's visit to Rome, Garriguet, Hertzog, and Vannutelli attended the Sulpician alumni reception at the Eucharistic Congress in Montreal. Among the many priests and bishops who attended, it is very probable that four of the seven suffragan bishops of Boston, each of whom were alumni of Sulpician seminaries, were also present. No doubt O'Connell was not in attendance, but he and Garriguet did have a brief meeting during which the archbishop invited the superior general to visit him in Boston. Garriguet met with O'Connell on 29 September 1910. After a brief private session, Havey and Hertzog joined the superior general, while Michael J. Splaine, chancellor of the archdiocese, and James P. O'Connell, the archbishop's nephew and secretary, also participated. From O'Connell's point of view, the purpose of the meeting was to release the archdiocese from its contract with the society, which stipulated that the Sulpicians would have control of the seminary "in perpetuity."[40] The superior general wanted the meeting in order to receive the archbishop's commitment that he would not interfere with the Sulpician traditional methods of religious formation of seminarians. The notes of both the Sulpicians and the archbishop state that Garriguet was willing to nullify the contract as it stood. At the archbishop's suggestion, Garriguet agreed that, if either party wished to see the society removed from the seminary, a two- or three-year notice should be given to the other party. Garriguet's notes contain a reference to O'Connell's promise to respect the customs of Saint Sulpice, but there is no reference to Sulpician customs in O'Connell's notes.[41]

Two other points in the meeting were not recorded by the superior general. O'Connell

> brought up for consideration . . . the fact that a book published and destined for the friends of the Sulpicians criticizing the action of Bishops very clearly, had been widely disseminated among the clergy of the United States to the scandal of all and with the evident purpose of forming coteries and cliques against the bishops, especially with regard to their governing of seminaries.

O'Connell referred to Garriguet's expression of "regret that this fact existed. . . ; they both seemed to know very little about the book. . . ."[42]

According to Havey's recollections, this book was the explanatory letter written by Dyer after the Dunwoodie affair.[43] Intended only for Sulpicians, this "open letter" of over one hundred pages was critical of Driscoll's collusion with Farley, but in tone and content it could hardly be construed as lacking in respect for the hierarchy. O'Connell's reference to "coteries and cliques" and, indeed, the very inclusion of this publication within the discussion between himself and Garriguet appear to have been a warning that the Sulpicians should not publish an anti-O'Connell pamphlet when and if they ever left Brighton. The other point mentioned only in O'Connell's notes was that Havey spoke out of turn by commenting on the contract after it had been declared null and void: "whereupon the archbishop called Father Havey's attention to the fact that the matter had been settled and that his remarks were entirely out of order."[44] In what seems to have been a fit of pique, O'Connell informed Garriguet of a remark Havey had made "that the Roman system [of seminary governance] was worth nothing. Whereupon the archbishop told Fr. Garriguet that he could not tolerate a man of those sentiments in the Brighton seminary, much less at the head of the Institution, and that he wished the removal of Father Havey."[45]

The Havey dismissal never became an issue, because twenty-two days after the meeting O'Connell wrote to the superior general informing him that the Sulpicians were to leave Saint John's Seminary at the close of the academic year 1910–1911. "I am convinced" he wrote, "that to delay this any longer would only complicate the situation and enlarge the difficulty." Without specifying any complaints against the Sulpicians at Brighton, he merely stated his wish that the archdiocese assume full control of the seminary. He asked Garriguet to "communicate [his] order to the Sulpicians at Brighton and inform them that they are to obey without needlessly spreading the knowledge of this fact in a manner which would prejudice the good order existing in the seminary and in the diocese."[46]

O'Connell's letter, addressed to Saint-Sulpice in Paris, did not reach Garriguet, who was touring the States, until he arrived in Baltimore several weeks later. In his response, the superior general assured the archbishop that the Sulpicians would leave Brighton at the appointed time "without any recrimination . . . but not without very deep regret." Since the Sulpicians had "served the clergy of the diocese for twenty-five years," the letter, according to Garriguet, came as a "sad surprise," particularly since O'Connell had promised that he would give a two- or three-year advance notice before the Sulpicians would be required to leave the seminary. After implying that O'Connell had violated the verbal agreement of 29 September, Garriguet writes that he was confident that the society has been conformed to God's will in "their good services to the Church and that his confreres are worthy of being employed in other fields of work which God's Providence will provide for them."[47]

Upon the death of Archbishop Williams in August 1907, O'Connell had embarked upon a policy of rigid centralization of ecclesiastical life in Boston. Even if he had not harbored anti-Sulpician sentiments, it is likely that he would have eventually assumed control of the seminary. The Sulpician system ran contrary to the views of seminary training he gained from his experience as a student and as rector of the North American College in Rome. However, the way in which he harassed Havey, Bruneau, and others and the shabby manner by which he expelled Sulpicians from the seminary illustrate the depth of his anti-Sulpician obsession. He not only viewed their system as contrary to Rome; he also viewed them as the enemy in the war between Christendom and modernity. As late as 1933, O'Connell told Cardinal Cajetan Bisletti, prefect of the Sacred Congregation of Seminaries and Universities, that many bishops in the United States were convinced that "the Sulpicians still continue to teach doctrines tainted with Modernism." He recalled to Bisletti

> that in both New York and Boston they had to be sent away, because they were interfering with the Bishops' administration of the diocese, forming cliques and factions instead of maintaining unity of faith in the bond of love . . . many bishops all over the country have disapproved of the French Propaganda, both in civic and in spiritual matters.[48]

When the Sulpicians withdrew from Boston in June of 1911, they left behind loyal alumni numbering 498 priests. Because O'Connell feared the lingering influence of the Sulpicians, he told his new seminary faculty that he did not wish to see them intermingling with the other diocesan clergy; rather, they should live in seclusion at Brighton. Shortly after the opening of the newly staffed seminary, O'Connell received word that he had been appointed to the College of Cardinals. Clearly his standing in Rome was never higher than during those years in which his close friend Merry del Val dominated the Vatican. However, with the election in September 1914 of Benedict XV, who was opposed by a group headed by the cardinal secretary of state, O'Connell's friend no longer commanded influence. John Ireland's reaction to the election of Benedict XV represents the views of the American liberals: "What marvelous changes in Rome . . . Della Chiesa [i.e., Benedict XV] and Ferrata! [i.e., Dominico Ferrata, the architect of Leo XIII's policy of *ralliement* toward the French Republic, who was cardinal secretary of state from August 1914 until his death the following October]. I am overjoyed. Both have been long my friends. . . . I feel that the reign of William [O'Connell] is cut short, and for good."[49] Ireland penned these sentiments in a letter to Louis Walsh, bishop of Portland, a loyal alumnus of Brighton who had also served as an auxiliary faculty member at Brighton under both Rex and Hogan.

Cardinal Gibbons, who had informed Ireland of Pope Benedict's fond recollections of the archbishop of Saint Paul, was also unsympathetic to O'Connell's position. Indeed, Gibbons wept upon hearing of O'Connell's elevation to the College of Cardinals.[50] In a speech at Boston College (12 March 1912), the archbishop of Boston extolled the virtues of his Jesuit training vis-à-vis his previous seminary experience at Saint Charles' College. Although O'Connell named neither the college nor the Sulpicians, it was apparent to all who knew his background that when he said, "I had earlier experiences which were more puritanical and Jansenistic than Catholic," he was referring to the French Sulpician influence in Baltimore.[51] Shortly after this address, Gibbons gave the commencement address at Saint Charles' College as a response to O'Connell's attack upon the Sulpicians. After expressing gratitude to "the Fathers of St. Sulpice for having trained my heart to virtue and religion," he consciously answered O'Connell's charges:

> What Bishop Carroll was to the hierarchy of the United States, the Sulpician Fathers have been to the clergy; he was the model of the American episcopate; they have been the model of the clergy. They have been with us now nearly a century and a quarter, and during all that time they have upheld the honor and dignity of the priesthood. No stain has ever sullied their bright eschutcheon. No breath of calumny has ever tarnished the mirror of their fair name. . . . I have never in the course of my whole life met a Sulpician who was not worthy of his high calling.[52]

The period from 1906 to 1911 was riddled with disasters for the Sulpicians. In 1906 they lost Dunwoodie, and their seminary in San Francisco was severely damaged by the earthquake. In June 1911 they left Brighton, and on 16 March of that year a fire completely destroyed Saint Charles' College. The origin of the fire was never discovered. It started in the cellar under the chapel about 1:00 P.M., and by dusk the conflagration had razed every building on the campus except for a section of the sisters' convent. Three weeks later, over two hundred students and eighteen faculty members moved to Cloud Cap, a farm and country retreat located in Catonsville, which since 1885 had been owned by Saint Mary's Seminary. By 1911 two major buildings and several "shacks" were located on the property. A new Saint Charles' College was constructed on the site of Cloud Cap; a dormitory wing opened in 1913, followed by a powerhouse and an administrative wing. The chapel was entirely funded by the Jenkins family in honor of Father Oliver Jenkins, first president of Saint Charles' and the major

Saint John's Seminary, Brighton, of the archdiocese of Boston; founded in 1884. The Sulpicians withdrew in 1911. (Courtesy of Sulpician Archives Baltimore)

John B. Hogan (1829–1901), first president of Saint John's Seminary and author of Clerical Studies *(1901), a classic in progressive theological education. (Courtesy of Sulpician Archives Baltimore)*

Saint Joseph's Seminary, Dunwoodie, of the archdiocese of New York; founded in 1896. The Sulpicians withdrew in 1906. (Courtesy of Sulpician Archives Baltimore)

James Driscoll (1859–1922), second president of Saint Joseph's Seminary and editor of The New York Review. *(Courtesy of U.S. Catholic Historical Society)*

U.S. PROVINCIALS

Edward R. Dyer
(1922–1925)

John F. Fenlon
(1925–1943)

John J. Lardner
(1943–1948)

Lloyd P. McDonald
(1948–1967)

Paul P. Purta
(1967–1977)

Edward J. Frazer
(1977–1985)

(Courtesy of Sulpician Archives Baltimore)

Saint Patrick's Seminary, Menlo Park, of the archdiocese of San Francisco; founded in 1898. (Courtesy of Sulpician Archives Baltimore)

Saint Joseph's College, Mountain View, minor seminary for the archdiocese of San Francisco; founded in 1924. (Courtesy of Sulpician Archives Baltimore)

Saint Mary's Seminary and University, Baltimore, a national seminary in the archdiocese of Baltimore; founded in 1791. Theologate moved to Roland Park in 1929. (Courtesy of Sulpician Archives Baltimore)

Theological College of the Catholic University of America, Washington, D.C. Founded in 1919 as the Sulpician Seminary, it became the Theological College in 1940 when the university assumed responsibility for all theology courses as well as for the Basselin Foundation, the philosophy department for scholarship students. (Courtesy of Sulpician Archives Baltimore)

Saint Edward's Seminary, Kenmore, in the archdiocese of Seattle; founded in 1931 as a minor and major seminary. The minor seminary closed in 1976. (Courtesy of Sulpician Archives Baltimore)

Saint Thomas's Seminary, Kenmore, in the archdiocese of Seattle; founded in 1958 as the successor of the major seminary department of Saint Edward's Seminary. Closed in 1977. (Courtesy of Sulpician Archives Baltimore)

Saint John's Provincial Seminary, Plymouth, located in the archdiocese of Michigan; founded in 1949. The Sulpicians withdrew in 1971. (Courtesy of Sulpician Archives Baltimore)

Members of the Sulpician General Council of 1983. Front row, from left: Bishop Rodrigo Arrango, Constant Bouchard, Emilius Goulet, and Fernand Paradis; second row, from left: Gilles Chaillot and William J. Lee; third row, from left: Raymond Deville, Yves Le Chapelier, and Edward J. Frazer; fourth row: Robert B. Eno. (Courtesy of Sulpician Archives Baltimore)

Robert F. Leavitt, Sulpician president-rector of Saint Mary's Seminary and University; Archbishop William D. Borders of Baltimore; and Gerald L. Brown, provincial of the U.S. Sulpician Province; October 1986. (Courtesy of Suzie Fitzhugh)

contributor to the original chapel at the old college. This was the first major commission of the architectural firm of Murphy and Olmstead, two architects who had founded the Department of Architecture at the Catholic University of America. Solemnly dedicated in June of 1915, the chapel, designed in the manner of the Italian Renaissance, became an architectural and ecclesiastical landmark.[53]

Saint Charles' College, which enrolled students from over twenty dioceses, was, like Saint Mary's, a national seminary, one of only a few six-year minor seminaries with its entire enrollment boarding at the college. Saint Charles' maintained high academic standards and was known for its loyal alumni. It was also the first minor seminary to be accredited by a nonecclesiastical agency. The rise of a new Saint Charles' College was no small achievement, but it offered little compensation for the loss of Dunwoodie and Brighton. Although Dyer had failed to win the loyalty of Farley and O'Connell, the devoted sentiment of hundreds of Sulpician alumni, including several bishops, must have been a source of consolation. Five of O'Connell's suffragan bishops—those of Hartford, Portland, Fall River, Burlington, and Providence—sent their seminarians to Baltimore. With widespread support among the hierarchy, Dyer was determined to restore the prestige of Saint Sulpice in America. However, it was through the intervention of Cardinal Gibbons, the most significant member of the Sulpician alumni, that this prestige was fully restored with the establishment of a Sulpician seminary in Washington, D.C.

PART THREE

From Romanization to the Second Vatican Council (1911–1967)

The dominant emphasis on *Romanitá* in the American church from the time of Pius X to that of Pius XII has its parallel in the history of the Sulpicians. Although it is true that, first, many immigrant groups became Americanized during this period, second, the church in the United States organized its own national conference (National Catholic Welfare Conference, hereafter NCWC) in the nation's capital, and, third, many Catholic organizations reflected the American drive to modernize their structures, it is also true that the leading members of the hierarchy were trained and dominated by Rome, there was an acceleration of centralized ecclesiastical authority in the Vatican, and the revision of the Code of Canon Law (1917) imposed a strong regulatory system upon the entire church. Hence, while the church in the United States experienced quantitative expansion, because of the dominance of the Vatican and because of a defensive attitude toward religious pluralism and the growth of secularism, it maintained a cultural separatism, giving rise to a condition often referred to as the "ghetto church." During the post–World War II period, devotional life flourished, Catholic culture thrived, and educational institutions in diocesan and national bureaucracies, as well as vocations to the priesthood and religious life, grew rapidly. More seminaries were founded between 1945 and 1967 than in the entire pre-1945 era. However, as more Catholics entered colleges and universities; achieved eminence in commerce, industry, and politics; and moved to the sprawling suburbs, the ghetto walls gradually broke down. This movement was nearly imperceptible to the participants, but from our vantage point it appears synonymous with the development of a reconciliation between religion and culture and the transition to the Second Vatican Council.

As this period opens, morale among the Sulpicians, who had just been expelled from New York and Boston, was at a very low point. However, the foundation of an American Solitude, the Sulpician counterpart of a novitiate, increased the number of vocations, and by 1920 the native-born Americans had achieved a majority in the society. The following year—130 years after the opening of Saint Mary's Seminary—the United States became a separate province. Although Romanization affected the curriculum of Sulpician seminaries, the Sulpicians preserved their traditional practices of individual spiritual direction and collegial governance, which set them apart from Roman-styled seminaries. In addition, several leading Sulpicians had been educated in the pre-Modernist period, thus maintaining some continuity between the two eras. Unable to publish freely, they nevertheless composed class notes in accord with the new apologetics and advanced scripture studies. Sulpicians such as Joseph Bruneau, Edward Arbez, and Wendell Stephen Reilly constituted a countervailing force to the widespread Romanization of seminary life.[1] The first two provincials, Edward Dyer and John Fenlon, were deeply influenced by the Americanist vision of Alphonse Magnien and hence were close to those second-generation Americanist bishops and priests who were active in the formation and development of the NCWC. Also reflective of the growth of the church, five Sulpician seminaries were founded, and more than one hundred priests joined the U.S. province during the period 1911–1967.

11

Edward Dyer and the Restoration of Stability

Unlike Alphonse Magnien or John Hogan, Edward Dyer was not imbued with a scholarly or intellectual spirit. As rector of Dunwoodie from its origin to 1902, however, he developed what one may call a new-model seminary, which was characterized by a relatively open attitude toward student life, by a concentrated stress on the introduction of current intellectual trends, and by the freedom of students to matriculate at secular schools. Dyer's writings and correspondence conspiciously lack any references to an ecclesiological or a theological world view, but he was close to Magnien and Hogan and earned the trust of Gibbons, Ireland, Keane, Denis O'Connell, Riordan, and other Americanists. As superior, Dyer was a traditionalist attached to the ideals of religious formation; his larger ecclesiastical vision was moderately progressive, while his intellectual views seem to have been subordinate to his religious outlook. Yet he continually expressed the need for high academic standards in order to improve the quality of the American priesthood.

Dyer never evidenced any strong attachment to the church in Europe. Although he spent the last two years of theology and his Solitude in France and studied at the Minerva in Rome, he did not correspond with anyone in Europe except those in positions of authority, namely, Lebas, Garriguet, and Hertzog. With a strong practical sense and broad academic vision, he was a dedicated administrator. Besides heading Dunwoodie and later Saint Mary's, he administered the national office of the Society for the Propagation of the Faith and the funds for what was then known as the Negro and Indian missions. Well known for his strong character, Dyer marshaled all his forces to establish a seminary adjacent to the Catholic University of America, to which he had a particular loyalty as the intellectual center of the American church.[2]

Dyer had been active in the movement that led to the formation of the Catholic Education Association (CEA; later NCEA), which was begun in 1898 as the Educational Conference of Seminary Faculties. He presented a paper at its second meeting, held at Saint Charles' Seminary, Overbrook, and he hosted a later meeting at Dunwoodie.[3] With the birth of the CEA in 1904, Bishop Denis O'Connell, rector of the university in Washington, was elected president, and Dyer became the organization's first vice-president. O'Connell, an alumnus of Saint Charles' College and of Saint Mary's Seminary, was very close to the Sulpicians.[4] Shortly after Dyer became vicar-general of the Sulpicians in the United States, O'Connell, who had embarked on a plan to add an undergraduate division to the university, approached Dyer about establishing a Sulpician undergraduate school in theology. As mentioned earlier, Saint Austin's, the Sulpician house of studies, opened in 1901, when Thomas J. Conaty was rector of the university. O'Connell's proposal to Dyer was supported by the Paulist and Marist communities, who wished to have their scholastics enrolled in such a school, thereby allowing their teacher-priests to devote full time to their regular apostolates.[5]

Despite the fact that Cardinal Gibbons endorsed O'Connell's proposal in 1905 and Garriguet offered no strong opposition to it, the Baltimore Sulpicians did not support the proposal to establish a seminary at the university. Dyer, however, was not one to be easily put off. Prompted by the availability of land adjacent to the university, he commissioned four Sulpicians to devise a twenty-year plan (1906–1926) for a possible transfer of the entire Saint Mary's community to Washington, D.C. If the community sold all its Baltimore property, as well as the Saint Austin's property, its assets, combined with annuities and deposits of an alumni chapel fund, would amount to about $400,000. The academic and social advantages of becoming the official undergraduate seminary for the university were offset by such disadvantages as the potential threat that the university environment would diminish the discipline and piety of the seminary and that the seminary faculty would tend to become too involved in academic life at the expense of their Sulpician calling. Moreover, the risks entailed in abandoning over a hundred years of tradition in Baltimore and giving up the university and pontifical status of Saint Mary's appeared to be greater than the prestige attached to the Washington location, even if the latter were to become an independent diocese.[6]

When Thomas J. Shahan became rector in 1909, he wrote to Dyer that he hoped "to sustain the closest relations between the University and St. Mary's" and referred to the mutual interests between the two institutions. While student enrollment at the university was only 225 in September 1909, that at Saint Mary's was over 250, which was more than the seminary could easily accommodate. Dyer arranged with Shahan to have Saint Mary's more gifted fourth-year students enrolled at the university. In May 1910, he selected six students to be sent to the university the following fall semester. According to Father Louis Arand, a Sulpician who was later president of Divinity College and on the theology faculty of the university, these fourth-year students were ordained at the end of their third year, thereby qualifying them to begin graduate study the subsequent semester.[7]

Despite the absence of a consensus on the prospect of a Sulpician seminary at the university, on 10 February 1910 Dyer, in the name of the Associated Professors of Saint Mary's Seminary—as the Sulpicians' corporation was then entitled—successfully negotiated the purchase of property, adjacent to the Paulists' College and opposite the main gate of the university, from the Oblates of Mary Immaculate. Although the Oblates later challenged the legality of the purchase, leading to nearly five years of litigation, the Sulpicians now had a foothold in the area.[8]

In the fall of 1915, Shahan publicly announced that "the time is approaching when it will be possible to open a theological seminary at Catholic University."[9] Over the next two years Dyer and Shahan engaged in a series of discussions on the role of the Sulpicians in the university's projected major seminary with Cardinal Gibbons, chancellor of the university, and with Superior General Garriguet. Shahan's original plan envisioned the Sulpicians as responsible for the internal discipline and spiritual direction of the students while the university theology faculty would be responsible for the academic affairs. Dyer, representing the vast majority of his confreres, viewed such a plan as contrary to the Sulpician way, which was based upon a total sharing between the directors and students in the academic and spiritual life of the seminary. By late 1916, Shahan, Dyer, Gibbons, and Garriguet were in agreement that the seminary adjacent to the university would be entirely under the auspices of the Sulpicians.[10]

In February 1915, before the Sulpicians received approval for the new seminary, Dyer explained his vision of this institution at a meeting of the Saint Mary's faculty.[11] Rather than establish another Saint Mary's, he saw the need for an institution limited to advanced studies in theology. He said that he agreed with those who pointed to the contributions of the Catholic University of Louvain, the first—and for many years the only—Catholic institution of higher education in Europe. It was there that "leaders in ecclesiastical, civil, professional, and commercial life were trained . . . [and] studied the underlying social, economic, and political principles . . . in the light of the philosophy approved by the Church and of divinely revealed truth." Dyer also noted that the apologetics developed at the five Catholic institutes in France had been of such a character as "to compel recognition from the intellectual world outside the Church." He referred to a recent biography of Maurice d'Hulst, first rector of the Institut Catholique de Paris, that indicated that the French Sulpicians were generally "unsympathetic" to these new Catholic institutes. Dyer proudly referred to faculty members, such as John Fenlon, who had simultaneously attended classes at Johns Hopkins and taught courses at the seminary. What was needed, however, was a "special course for bright students who would have the opportunity for higher studies. This was one of the dreams of Father Magnien."[12] As a professor of dogma, Dyer had introduced an ad hoc seminar for his exceptional students that met one evening a week for the presentation of students' research papers.[13] Dyer's plan was to limit the new seminary to fourth-year students who had the ability and the inclination to pursue advanced studies.

In the fall of 1917 the plan became a reality. Forty students were enrolled at the ad hoc Saint Mary's annex in Washington, D.C. Housed in Caldwell Hall, they attended classes at the Paulist Mission House under the direction of three Sulpicians and one Paulist professor. Some members of the faculty of Saint Mary's became alarmed that as the Washington institution gained a reputation as a theologate for the elite, Saint Mary's would be considered a seminary for mediocre students. In response, Dyer wrote a long defense entitled "Reasons for the Plan We Follow at the Washington Seminary." According to Dyer, the homogeneous grouping stimulates the gifted, allows them to pursue independent study, prevents them from being bored, and prepares them for graduate school. He envisioned that within ten years

> a large number of students from all parts of the country will wish to avail themselves of the courses there. Our old seminary at St. Mary's will, in the meantime, stand on the same footing as any other seminary in the country, receiving young men from all grades who can be properly fitted for the priestly office. We expect always to have some of the best here who for one reason or the other could hardly take up the work the Washington Seminary would demand.[14]

From 1917 to 1924 the Sulpician Seminary in Washington was an extension of Saint Mary's. At first, only fourth-year students were en-

rolled, then a smattering of third- and second-year students transferred to Washington until it became a full theologate in 1919. That
year, the seminary building opened, and Francis Havey, the former superior of the Boston seminary, was appointed rector. The new buildings were designed by the architectural firm of Maginnis and Walsh
of Boston. In 1924 the seminary attained its independence from Saint
Mary's when the university decided to house the Basselin Foundation
students at the seminary.[15]

Theodore B. Basselin, a wealthy lumberman from northern New
York, bequeathed most of his estate to the university so that it would
inaugurate a program of studies for training seminarians in homiletics. Although Basselin died on 14 April 1914, Shahan and his board
of trustees deferred a decision on how to implement the will until financial conditions at the university became more stable. In the spring
of 1922, Shahan proposed that Basselin College should not be separate from but connected to the Sulpicians, who would represent the
university in the religious formation of the students. After receiving
approval from Dyer and Garriguet, Shahan presented his proposal to
a special committee on Basselin College. In November it was decided
that the Sulpicians were to be responsible for housing the students,
appointing a president and vice-president, and directing the spiritual
life of the college. Basselin's curriculum included a three-year course
in philosophy, and the college's Sulpician officers would also be its philosophy professors; for other subjects in the curriculum, however, the
Basselin students would attend the university. Courses in sacred eloquence (i.e., homiletics) were not assigned to the Sulpicians, though
frequently the courses were taught by a member of the society. On 1
October 1923, Basselin College opened with an enrollment of twelve
students. After suffering the losses of Dunwoodie and Brighton, Edward Dyer could claim a significant victory with the establishment of
the seminary in the nation's capital.[16]

II

In 1904 Pius X announced plans to issue a new code of canon law. On
Pentecost Sunday 1917, Benedict XV published the new code by the
constitution *Providentissima Mater Ecclesia*. In early 1916, Garriguet had
visited Rome and was warmly received by Pope Benedict. The latter had
just appointed François X. Hertzog, the Sulpician procurator-general
in Rome, as a counselor of the Sacred Congregation of Seminaries
and Universities, an appointment that was perceived as symbolic of
the pope's high regard for Saint-Sulpice. Some time after his visit to

Rome, Garriguet was given a draft of the new code so that the society might begin to adapt its constitution to the new reforms. At a subsequent meeting of the Sulpician general assembly, a commission was appointed to revise the society's rule. This resulted in the constitution of 1916, which, after consultation with members of the Congregation for Religious and with a specialist on canon law, went through further revision. It finally received the Holy See's official approval 27 November 1921.[17]

The constitution of 1921 preserved several essential traditions of Saint Sulpice, namely, the diocesan character of the work with the bishop as head of the seminary, the collegial direction of the houses by an assembly of directors, and the Sulpician's dual role as director and confessor. Certain governance features that reflected aristocratic traditions were abolished, including the superior general and his council's right of appointment of the twelve assistants who voted for the superior general and consultors among themselves. This arrangement was replaced by a more democratic system in which members who had served for six years (later changed to five years) were eligible to vote for delegates to a general chapter (one delegate for every twenty-five members in the province), the major legislative body. The superior general was elected for life by the general chapter, which met every seven years. By this constitution, the society was divided into three provinces. The superior general was ex officio the provincial of the French province. The Canadian province received special consideration because of its articles of incorporation according to a royal charter of the British government of 1840, which prescribed the election of a provincial every five years by an appointed council. Each of the U.S. delegates to the general chapter, which met every seven years, submitted a list of three names from which the superior general and his council appointed the provincial superior of the U.S. province and the members of the provincial council. The provincial council in turn appointed, with the approval of the superior general, local superiors, but contrary to the guidelines of the new code of canon law these superiors had no fixed terms of office. Rome approved this exception on the basis of Sulpician tradition, by which the relationship between the bishop and the local superior of his seminary would be best served by either maintaining the superior in office as long as he and the bishop were on good terms or immediately replacing him if the relationship became untenable.[18]

The 1921 constitution was accepted on a ten-year trial basis. In 1931 Rome introduced slight changes, such as the length of the solitude from an academic year to the full canonical year. By this time Jean Verdier was superior general and also cardinal archbishop of Paris. He accepted this change but decided that the solitaires should receive a two-month vacation each year, thereby maintaining tradition on a de facto basis. Another change in conformity with the spirit of canon law allowed seminarians to choose a confessor other than the director assigned to them.[19]

The first general chapter in the history of the Society of Saint Sulpice was held in the summer of 1922. Of the roughly four hundred Sulpicians in the society, there were fewer than fifty members in the U.S. province, which meant that it qualified for only one delegate at the general chapter. (One delegate was appointed for each group of twenty-five members.) Dyer, who had been appointed provincial, was an ex officio member of the chapter. Henri Ayrinhac, the French-born superior of Menlo Park, was the elected delegate. Hence, the two superiors of the major Sulpician seminaries in the United States attended the meetings held from 12 to 18 July.

This first meeting was almost entirely dedicated to implementing the new constitution, to informing the members on the status of the society, and to demonstrating the vitality of Sulpician tradition within new forms of governance. Frequent references were made to the society's obedience to the decrees of the Holy See, particularly those on seminaries. The commission on studies strongly endorsed "superior preparation" for young Sulpicians in Catholic universities, with a preference for those in Rome. It also encouraged all qualified Sulpicians to publish articles and books on topics related to philosophical and theological studies "but strongly adhering to Roman directives on the scholastic tradition and the Thomist doctrine." Although these two resolutions represent a traditionally uncharacteristic emphasis upon scholarship, this portion of the Sulpician way of life was secondary to the commitment to religious formation.[20]

The chapter unanimously approved a central office for theological studies that would disseminate directives on curriculum, particularly the study of scripture. The standard scripture work in use in Sulpician seminaries was the *Manuel biblique* written by Louis Bacuez and Fulcran Vigouroux, which had been through many editions and had been translated into several languages. Before he died, Vigouroux requested that the work be updated; accordingly, Garriguet assigned Augustin F. Brassac and Joseph Ducher, two scripture scholars at the seminary at Issy, to work on a revised edition of the *Manuel*. On the occasion of his audience with Benedict XV (spring 1921) for the approbation of the 1921 constitution, Garriguet discovered that the revised edition had been criticized in Rome. In February the superior general met with Cardinal Merry del Val, the secretary of the Holy Office, who assured him that though the new edition was very advanced, there was little concern that it would be condemned. Hence, it caused consternation when on 22 December 1923, the Holy Office announced that the twelfth through the fifteenth edition of the *Manuel biblique*, under the authorship of Vigouroux, Brassac, and Ducher, had been placed on the Index of Forbidden Books.[21] Immediately, the two living Sulpician authors sent a letter of submission to the Holy Office, which was not published until 12 March 1924. The reason for the condemnation related to the book's notion of inspiration, that is, it departed from the Catholic fundamentalism of the Biblical Commission, of which Vigouroux, ironically, was a charter member. Henri Cheramy, a director at the Sulpician Procure, informed Ducher that "theologians of all schools" were critical of the thesis on inspiration. He also reported that Pope Pius XI was aware of the condemnation and that even those bishops who were not in agreement with the decision would not speak out against it out of fear of the *intégristes*, the ultraconservative faction that identified any compromise with modern methodology as capitulation to the forces out to destroy the church.[22] Cardinal O'Connell received advance notice of the Brassac condemnation from Cardinal De Lai, who implied that both might take delight in the placing of a Sulpician work on the Index.[23]

The members of the faculty at Saint Mary's Seminary who used the Sulpician *Manuel biblique* in scripture classes asked (4 February 1924) if it "would . . . not be expedient for us to make the announcement," even though the seminary was not under obligation to inform the students of the condemnation.[24] Although no subsequent remarks appear in the official minutes, it is probable that the Sulpicians at Saint Mary's did inform their students on the condemnation of their confreres' work rather than have them receive the news without some explanation. Archbishop Michael J. Curley, former bishop of Saint Augustine, Florida, who succeeded Gibbons in 1921, was aware of the condemnation of the *Manuel*. He met with Dyer who presented Curley with the interpretation of Wendell S. Reilly (a Sulpician scripture professor at Saint Mary's) of the Holy Office's charges, "which had made an excellent impression" on the archbishop. Anthony Viéban, then the superior of the American Solitude at Saint Charles' College and secretary of the provincial council, informed Garriguet that Curley "believed that the condemnation of the *Manuel biblique* would not stir up any serious opposition to his project of having our house in Washington recognized as the seminary of the University."[25]

III

When Edward Dyer returned from Paris in the fall of 1922, he presented to the faculty at Saint Mary's a decision of the general chapter relating to the then-tense relations between Saint Mary's and the

Sulpician Seminary in Washington. The latter was to offer a complete course in theology, while the former was to be maintained as a standard ordinary seminary (*au niveau d'un ordinaire séminaire*). The Washington seminary was envisioned as a theologate for students of exceptional ability destined by their bishops to pursue advanced studies after ordination. The principal sources of recruitment were Basselin College, the lay students at the university, and the various colleges and seminaries throughout the country. Until the Washington seminary achieved independent status, Saint Mary's would continue to send fourth-year students and those from the second year of philosophy in order to make up a student body of about eighty students.[26]

The following September (1923) the faculty at Saint Mary's decided to send students from each of the theology classes rather than exclusively from the fourth year. Resentment of the "brain drain" was still apparent; some members of the faculty suggested sending money rather than students.[27] Three days after this faculty meeting, Jean Verdier, Garriguet's representative, made his official visitation to Saint Mary's. The polarization on the question of depleting Saint Mary's of intelligent students was strongly manifested. After a period of heated discussion Verdier suggested a compromise that was supported by a faculty vote: that the better students be divided equally between the Baltimore and Washington seminaries and that a special course of studies for the most intelligent students be introduced at Saint Mary's. The Washington seminary was to engage in direct recruitment as soon as possible and to "broaden its contacts with the University" in support of Archbishop Curley's desire to see the Sulpician institution recognized as the university seminary. The latter issue was not resolved during Edward Dyer's lifetime, though, as noted earlier, in 1924 the Sulpician seminary in Washington became autonomous, no longer dependent on students from Saint Mary's.[28]

Verdier's official visitation to Saint Charles' College focused on the particular problems associated with life in a minor seminary. He noted that the society's rule was intended for "theological seminaries [and] is not adapted in all its details to preparatory seminaries." With the prospect of establishing an independent minor seminary in the archdiocese of San Francisco (Saint Joseph's College opened in September 1924 in Mountain View, California, some twelve miles from Menlo Park), and with the possible foundation of other Sulpician preparatory seminaries, Verdier projected that in the near future there could be about fifty Sulpicians who would not be attached to theological seminaries. The major problems of life in the minor seminary were associated with the need to harmonize the spiritual traditions of Saint Sulpice with the stronger demands upon the time of the individual priests. Verdier pointed to the danger entailed in teaching classes in secular subjects as distinct from the sacred sciences in a theologate.

These Sulpicians "may unconsciously feel that they get less support to maintain and develop their spiritual life than if they were in the parochial ministry." Hence they may feel a "taedium vitae Sulpitianae" and even be tempted to leave the society. Saint Charles's faculty voted to accept Verdier's recommendation to improve the spiritual life of the community through the establishment of a period of common meditation and of a monthly conference on an aspect of the Sulpician life or rule.[29] Although Verdier's projections were not entirely accurate, in 1933, ten years after his visitation, twenty-nine of the seventy-five Sulpicians in the United States were teaching in minor seminaries. During his visitation to both Saint Mary's and Saint Charles', Verdier spoke on intellectual trends in the American church. In his visit to Saint Charles' he noted that in his journey throughout the country he heard the following remarks:

1. That there is in this country a strong tendency to form an intellectual elite and that with our facilities for work we shall soon have an aristocracy of learning as well as one of wealth.
2. That American priests while they are good and faithful workers, are not as a body interested in intellectual pursuits. Hence, there is a danger of their being left behind as they were in France and with sad results.[30]

The faculty agreed with these remarks and informed Verdier of the trends among teaching orders of sisters who were sending their younger members to universities for graduate work and to summer schools. "It must be admitted," they said, "that the priests have not kept pace with this progress." After committing themselves to pursue advanced studies, the Sulpician faculty at Saint Charles' agreed to "do something special—[for the brighter students] . . . so as to prepare them as far as we can to become intellectual leaders, to be able to speak and even to write as well-informed and thoroughly trained men."[31] However, because Saint Charles' 1923 enrollment was 333 students representing 37 dioceses located in 21 states and because there was little room for curricular experimentation, the faculty relied upon its traditional prize certificates and extracurricular activities to encourage the better students.[32] In 1923 Saint Mary's Seminary had an enrollment of 318 (226 theologians and 92 philosophers) from 51 dioceses. For over a century it had possessed the authority to grant undergraduate and graduate degrees and the pontifical degrees of licentiate in sacred theology and doctorate in sacred theology. Its extracurricular activities included the Saint Camillus Association, by which Saint Mary's offered students the opportunity for pastoral ministry outside the seminary in hospital, prison, and catechetical works. Saint Camillus originated in 1894 when a group of students received permission to make pastoral visitations and received formal status in 1898. By 1923, 160 students were enrolled in the association.[33] Since 1914 the seminary had encouraged its students to spend some of their summer vacation at Camp Saint Mary in Long Lake, New York. Although a stay was not mandatory, the camp was a nod to the Roman tradition of a summer villa for seminarians.

Despite the apprehension that the Sulpician seminary in Washington would decrease the student body at Saint Mary's, the Baltimore seminary actually experienced an increase in enrollment during this period. Motivated to relieve overcrowding in what was fast becoming an antiquated complex of buildings, Dyer and Curley agreed to plan for the construction of a new seminary. In April of 1923, Curley embarked on a major fund campaign to raise one million dollars for the new Saint Mary's. In a 4 April letter to each of the pastors of the archdiocese, the archbishop informed them that they must complete their quotas within three years. He also sent them a letter addressed to the Catholic laity of the archdiocese in which he speaks of the plan to provide "for our young men preparing for the holy priesthood . . . a modern, fireproof building and larger grounds for recreation. . . . I wish to see St. Mary's Seminary second to none in this country, maintaining the prestige she has so long enjoyed and merited; . . . a beautiful but not extravagant seminary, where we hope to see the same Sulpician spirit continue as in the old."[34] Although Dyer never lived to see the result of this campaign, he was thoroughly involved with the plan and development of the new theologate.

For many years Edward Dyer suffered from ill health. He later recalled that he "had a weak heart . . . due to the strain of the first years . . . [as superior] at Saint Mary's."[35] As early as 1909, when he was fifty-four, his doctor had recommended a visit to Europe for a rest. In the summer of 1925 Dyer visited Germany, where he was treated by a specialist in cardiology. Although he felt the visit had effected an improvement, his health failed during October, and he died on 3 November 1925. In the official obituary of Edward Dyer, Superior General Garriguet wrote: "Those who knew him best . . . could from time to time run up against what they would call deviousness, egocentricity, stubbornness, but all acknowledged his good will and the efficiency of the administration. He was not violent nor capricious but he was headstrong." After a detailed biographical portrait, Garriguet remarks that toward the end of his life Dyer's "goodness, which had always been respected for its sincerity, became more relaxed and appealing."[36]

One may recall that Dyer was an ardent Americanizer in the tradition of Deluol and Magnien but without their savoir-faire and their French flair for theoretical rhetoric. Like Charles Rex, his fellow Marylander, Dyer was primarily an administrator who was committed to upgrading the academic life of the seminary. Unlike Rex, however, he did not possess strong scholarly interests. His major achievements were associated with modern developments as rector of Saint Joseph's, Dunwoodie; with the establishment of the seminary adjacent to the Catholic University of America; and with the society's transition to stability after the severe crises at Dunwoodie and Boston.

12

Conflict and Expansion in the American Church: John Fenlon

John Francis Fenlon, the eighth superior of Saint Mary's Seminary and the second provincial of the Sulpicians in the United States (1925–1944), possessed the social poise of Louis R. Deluol, the broad ecclesiastical vision of Alphonse Magnien, and the sense of practicality of Edward Dyer. Born in Chicago in 1873, he entered philosophy at Saint Mary's in 1891. His spiritual director was Dyer, and in his theology years Magnien was his mentor. He also came under the influence of Joseph Bruneau, who had established a short-lived Saint Jerome Society dedicated to "the elucidation of the more important controverted passages of Holy Scripture." Fenlon was a gifted student of Oriental languages, and while at Saint Mary's he had attended Professor Paul Haupt's Semitic-language course at The Johns Hopkins University.[1] Although drawn to the academic life, Fenlon did not pursue graduate work immediately after ordination; rather he served as curate at the Chicago cathedral. After two years in parish ministry (1896–1898) he explored the possibility of joining the Society of Saint Sulpice. Apparently the decision to return to Baltimore was prompted by Bishop Thomas Conaty, the rector of the Catholic University of America, who offered Fenlon the chair in sacred scripture at the university. After consulting with Magnien and Dyer, Fenlon decided to pursue academic life as a Sulpician rather than as a priest-scholar at the university.[2]

Alphonse Magnien sent the young Sulpician candidate to Rome, where he studied theology at the Minerva and Oriental languages at the Sapienza. As noted in a previous chapter, Magnien wrote to Denis O'Connell asking him to introduce Fenlon to all the "right people," namely, Giovanni Genocchi, Baron Frederick von Hügel, and Louis Duchesne.[3] Fenlon hoped to pursue Scripture studies at the Ecole Biblique in Jerusalem, but because Captier was sensitive to the Roman biases against Père Lagrange's new school, Fenlon was instructed to enter the Solitude after he received the S.T.D. degree in 1900.[4] Although he was thoroughly American and somewhat alienated by the French stress upon an emotionally zealous piety, the young Chicago Sulpician was deeply committed to his vocation as a spiritual director; throughout his nearly twenty years as provincial he strongly urged his confreres to identify with this particular charism of Saint Sulpice.

John Fenlon taught scripture and Hebrew at Dunwoodie (1901-1904) under the presidencies of both Dyer and Driscoll. He then became superior of Saint Austin's College (1904-1911), and from 1911 to 1924 he was president of Divinity College at the university. During these twenty years in Washington, Fenlon established a network of friends and colleagues among the faculty and the religious communities attached to the university. He was active in the Seminary Department of the NCEA; he served as its secretary from 1904-1909 and president from 1916-1919.[5] He was particularly close to the Paulists, and over the years he wrote several articles for the *Catholic World*.[6] During his student days in Rome, Fenlon had expressed admiration for the Americanists in the hierarchy, particularly John Ireland and John J. Keane and he later became a close friend of Cardinal Gibbons.

Perhaps his closest friend in the hierarchy was Peter Muldoon, first bishop of Rockford, Illinois, who was an alumnus of Saint Mary's and a confidant of both Magnien and Dyer. Muldoon had been rector of the cathedral parish in Chicago during the two-year period when Fenlon was stationed there. The two worked closely together on the National Catholic War Council, an organization of the bishops that was formed in 1917 to coordinate the Catholic volunteer organizations, such as the Knights of Columbus and Chaplain's Aid Association, and to represent American Catholic interests in the tasks of mobilization. The Knights of Columbus, then the only national organization of Catholics capable of mounting a campaign to support the war effort, organized its hut program to provide for recreation centers and for Catholic chaplains under the banner Everyone Welcome, Everything Free.[7] John J. Burke, C.S.P., editor of the *Catholic World*, was the major figure in promoting the formation of the Catholic War Council, which was approved by the fourteen archbishops at the November 1917 meeting of the trustees of the Catholic University of America. Burke was appointed president of the council, and an administrative committee of bishops included Peter Muldoon of Rockford; William Russell of Charleston; Patrick Hayes, auxiliary of New York; and Joseph Schrembs of Toledo. John Fenlon, then president of Divinity College, was named secretary of the War Council. Dyer told Bishop Russell that Fenlon had successfully proposed to Gibbons that he appoint a small administrative committee. Dyer said that Fenlon "would be the best [secretary] . . . you could get for such work. . . . I would be only too glad to have Father Fenlon take it up, though such work might occasion developments that would not be helpful to him in his seminary duties."[8]

Besides answering the pressing need for a coordinated Catholic effort in tandem with that of Protestant and Jewish welfare agencies, the Catholic War Council, as viewed by Burke, Muldoon, Fenlon, and others, represented a new phase in the public life of the Catholic church in the United States. These leaders were, in a sense, second-generation Americanists who not only recognized the hand of Providence in the evolution of Catholicism in American culture but also perceived the need for national structures through which American Catholics could have an impact upon the formation of public policy. Hence, shortly after the armistice was signed in November 1918, the leadership of the National Catholic War Council proposed the formation of a permanent organization to represent Catholic interests. Numerous factors coalesced in establishing such an organization representative of episcopal leadership: the National War Council was charged with the administration of peacetime welfare programs for veterans. The council had successfully demonstrated the effectiveness of national Catholic action; the need for direction and support of local Catholic education, press, and welfare agencies; the need to monitor legislation in light of Catholic ideals and interests; the general trend toward special interest lobbying in Congress; and the perennial need to defend the church against anti-Catholicism and nativism.[9]

Burke and Muldoon were in the forefront of the movement to create a permanent organization, but Dyer and Fenlon were also active behind the scenes, particularly in convincing Cardinal Gibbons to lend his support. At the celebration of the golden jubilee of Gibbons's episcopate (20 February 1919), Archbishop Bonaventura Cerretti, Pope Benedict's representative, proposed that the American bishops develop a program for peace in the fields of education and social justice.[10] Gibbons, in frequent consultation with Dyer, took the lead in promoting what became in 1919 the National Catholic Welfare Council (NCWC), composed of an administrative committee of seven prelates who would oversee five permanent departments—social action, education, press, the laity, and foreign missions. Benedict XV had approved the proposal for the NCWC the spring prior to the meeting of 24 September, when almost 100 prelates agreed to the precise constitution of the council. John Fenlon was appointed secretary and John Burke the executive secretary (later changed to general secretary).

Three of the seven bishops on the administrative committee—Muldoon, Russell, and Austin Dowling (Saint Paul)—were Sulpician alumni. Of the rest, Schrembs (Cleveland) had attended the Canadian Sulpician seminary in Montreal; Edward Hanna, the chairman, was very close to the Sulpicians in his archdiocese of San Francisco; and only Dennis Dougherty of Philadelphia and J. Regis Canevin of Pittsburgh were outside the Sulpician orbit. At the September meeting, Sebastian Messmer of Milwaukee, William H. O'Connell, and Charles McDonnell of Brooklyn expressed opposition to the NCWC as a potential threat to the autonomy of individual bishops. By 1922 the anti-NCWC forces had gained momentum. Cardinal Gibbons died in March 1921, and Benedict XV died on 22 January 1922. Shortly after the election of Pius XI, Cardinal Gaetano DeLai, secretary of the consistorial congregation, presented Dennis Dougherty with a decree that ordered the immediate dissolution of the NCWC on the basis that it was implicitly contrary to canon law.[11] Dated 25 February 1922, this decree, which Pius XI had approved as merely unfinished business of his predecessor, was rightly viewed by several American bishops as the product of the efforts of O'Connell, Dougherty, del Val, and DeLai. As a result of a 6 April meeting, the administrative committee sent a cable to the pope stating that "legal and business operations make it imperative to continue the work" that had originated with the approval of Benedict XV.[12] Two days later, Cardinal Pietro Gasparri, the secretary of state, responded by cable to the effect that the decree would not be promulgated in *Acta* and that "fuller information will shortly be given by apostolic delegate."[13] This cable allowed the committee time to develop its strategy. Bishop Schrembs was sent to Rome to represent the interests of the NCWC; Fenlon, Muldoon, and Burke were assigned the task of composing a *relatio*, which was a formal defense of the NCWC and a petition to quash the condemnatory decree. Since Fenlon composed several copies of the *relatio* prior to his visit with Burke in New York, it appears that he was its primary author. For example, a handwritten copy of the introduction is identical to the final draft. Fenlon wrote that the decree came "suddenly like a lightning bolt from a sunny sky . . . [and] filled us with astonishment and grief. Upon the whole hierarchy of our country it seems to put the stigma of suspicious loyalty and of incompetence; and it suppresses our most cherished organization upon which we had founded the greatest hopes for the defense and prosperity of religion in our Country."[14] The *relatio* presents a detailed account of the internal structure of the NCWC and the need for the national promotion of Catholic principles of social justice and for the defense of Catholic interests in such areas as education, the press, and marriage and the family. Dated 25 April 1922, the *relatio*, which received the support of 90 percent of the hierarchy in the United States, was effective in having the decree remanded, and by July 1922 the NCWC was in effect restored with the instruction that the title *council*, which invoked a sense of binding authority, be changed to *committee* or to another name indicating its advisory character.

Fenlon had been in consultation with Filippo Bernardini, an adviser to the apostolic delegate and a professor of canon law at the Catholic University of America, and with a nephew of Cardinal Secretary of State Pietro Gasparri. Bernardini informed him that Cardinals O'Connell and Dougherty were responsible for the condemnatory decree.[15] When Fenlon's *relatio* was circulating in Rome, O'Connell wrote to DeLai that the tactic of polling the bishops for support of the NCWC was a "plebiscite" that illustrated that "today we are in full 'Democracy, Presbyterianism, and Congregationalism. . . . It is incredible that Rome does not see the danger in conceding today in order to concede *much more tomorrow*."[16] A year after the restoration of the NCWC status, with the term *conference* now substituted for *council*, the seven bishops of the administrative committee were reelected at the 1923 meeting of the bishops of the United States. O'Connell viewed this reelection as the result of a Sulpician conspiracy. He wrote to Dougherty,

> The usual bombast on the part of Dowling, Walsh [bishop of Portland, Maine], and Muldoon flooded the reports and interminable orations. The first two were professors (or at least that was the title) with the Sulpicians here, and were made by the Sulpicians. Muldoon has always been a great favorite with them and has always been slated for higher honors, which however did not materialize. [Actually Muldoon had been appointed coadjutor to the bishop of Los Angeles but declined.] . . . It is unquestionably the continuation in a condensed form of Sulpicianism *contra mundum* but especially *contra nos*. Generally the little clique work in secret and in the dark. But Fenelon [sic] is beginning to give the trick away.

O'Connell then told Dougherty that during the last meeting of the bishops, Fenlon told O'Connell's chancellor,

> You can make Rome do whatever you want if you get a *crowd* behind you. This from an officer of the NCWC and from the *Spiritual* Director of the University. The centre of all things, say what they will, is St. Sulpice and the purpose is obvious—to keep the power in their own hands by demolishing us and our prestige. We are obviously intruders and must be kept in our place—by the crowd.

O'Connell urged Dougherty to join with him in a united action against the Sulpicians, "for with St. Sulpice we can see only an enemy not merely personal but in principle. . . . We know them and they will never change. Fenelon [sic] was clearly voicing them, not originating them."[17]

The archbishop of Boston had hoped to succeed James Gibbons as the unofficial primate of the United States but had neither the following at home nor the support in Rome. His friends DeLai and del Val were uninfluential in the pontificate of Pius XI, while O'Connell himself had suffered a gross humiliation as a result of the scandalous behavior of his priest nephew, who had been secretly married for years while acting as his uncle's secretary and who had fled the archdiocese with funds from its bank accounts. From 1914 to 1921 Bishop Walsh of Portland, Maine, led a movement to have O'Connell removed from the see of Boston because of this and other scandals.

Bishop Walsh personally presented his case against O'Connell in May 1921. Walsh reported to a fellow bishop on this meeting:

> The Holy Father was very positive and proposed himself the means; namely for the Bishops to refuse absolutely to attend any more meetings where Bill [i.e., O'Connell] was to preside, whether in the Province or at Washington and the affair would be clenched without any canonical process and with very sure success . . . he asked me to let him think over the best method of carrying out his purpose to take him out of Boston and to come up for another audience the following week.[18]

According to his report of the second audience, Walsh said that Benedict XV was convinced that

> the whole affair was a case of wholesale lying on the part of the big man [i.e., O'Connell], then I went into the story of how O'Connell had deceived Rome from the beginning, how he was caught by me in the financial crackdown in Portland, how the old archbishop [i.e., Williams] had quickly sized up the man and finally that our . . . Province of Boston was now in danger of ruin from the words and deeds and maladministration of the present metropolitan . . . the cordial reception and official response of the Holy Father made me feel that our case was won.[19]

Walsh presented to Benedict XV an affidavit that told of the clandestine marriages of the Reverend James O'Connell and of the Reverend David Toomey, editor of the *Pilot* of Boston, both of whom lived in the archiepiscopal residence. In a letter to O'Connell, Walsh and the four other suffragan bishops of Boston stated that O'Connell was "primarily responsible for all those scandals . . . we do not consider . . . [him] a worthy or fitting ecclesiastic to be even a nominal leader among or for the bishops of the country and we have so stated to the proper authorities."[20]

John Tracy Ellis has written that when Benedict XV confronted O'Connell with the scandal of his nephew, "the cardinal denied it, whereupon the pontiff reached into his desk and took out a copy of the marriage license from Crown Point, Indiana, handed it to O'Connell, and the latter dropped to his knees and begged for mercy."[21] Although Benedict thought of removing O'Connell from Boston, he obviously let him off with a reprimand and/or an admonishment. O'Connell's friends in the Curia, DeLai and del Val, must have been instrumental in defending him in Rome. It was in deference to O'Connell that these two prelates steered the anti-NCWC decree through the Vatican to gain Pius XI's approval. Although the NCWC forces finally gained the upper hand in this struggle, O'Connell always appeared undaunted by Walsh's very substantial and factual case against him. As late as 1924, Walsh wrote directly to Pius XI seeking O'Connell's removal from Boston "as the only effective remedy to a sad, serious, and dangerous disease which has existed for twenty years in the Diocese of Boston and the Province of New England."[22] Since Walsh and the other bishops of New England had been close to the Sulpicians and provided Saint Mary's Seminary with an average of nearly one-half of its student enrollment, O'Connell's detestation of the Sulpicians, though it predated his appointment as coadjutor archbishop of Boston, was certainly not entirely without foundation. However, there is no evidence of a wholesale anti-O'Connell conspiracy among the hierarchy. While the cardinal's personality and episcopal style alienated many bishops, the conflict between O'Connell and the Sulpicians was rooted in conflicting ecclesiologies: ultramontanism versus moderate transplanted Gallicanism, that is, Americanism.

II

Upon his appointment as provincial in 1925, John Fenlon left the NCWC, but he remained close to the organization, to John Burke, and to the Paulists. Fenlon later wrote of Burke's patriotism in a eulogy in the *Voice*, the publication of the students at Saint Mary's. According to Fenlon, Burke held to "Americanism . . . [which] was nurtured and intensified by his Paulist inheritance." He praised Burke's "clear vision, great organizing and great executive power" as executive secretary of the National War Council and the NCWC.[23]

For many years the Paulists had sent several young aspirants to their congregation to Saint Charles' College, where they formed a sort of satellite community. In 1926 Joseph McSorley, C.S.P., superior general of the Paulists, and John Fenlon arranged to have the Paulists establish their own residence for minor seminarians who attended classes at Saint Charles'. The following year the Paulist Juniorate opened near the Sulpician minor seminary in Catonsville, Maryland. This arrangement was analogous to that formed with the Josephites and Magnien at Saint Mary's. In 1950 the Paulist Juniorate became Saint Peter's College, and only high-school students attended Saint Charles', an arrangement that lasted until 1966. This Sulpician-Paulist association originated in the friendship of Deluol and Isaac Hecker and was maintained by Hogan, Magnien, Dyer, and Fenlon. It was an association based upon an affinity of views on ecclesiology, apologetics, and missiology.[24]

In September 1925, James A. Walsh and Archbishop Hanna of San Francisco agreed on a site for a Maryknoll preparatory seminary adjoining the Sulpician minor seminary at Mountain View, where the foreign mission students were to attend classes. The origin of the Maryknoll-Sulpician association originated at Saint John's Seminary, Brighton, where James A. Walsh, one of the founders of Maryknoll, came under the influence of John Hogan. The latter, a classmate of Theophane Venard, frequently expressed his devotion to the saintly missionary martyr in the Far East. In 1903, Walsh became director of the Society for the Propagation of the Faith in Boston. The next year he met Thomas F. Price, who had been breaking new ground in rural mission work in North Carolina and who became a cofounder of Maryknoll.[25] Price was a Sulpician alumnus of Saint Charles' College and Saint Mary's Seminary and was close to Edward Dyer. By 1907, Walsh was working with Joseph Bruneau on *Field Afar*, the first mission magazine published by Walsh prior to the foundation of the Maryknoll Society in 1911. Because of his pioneer work for the first American foreign-mission society, Bruneau has been venerated by Maryknoll as one of the crucial figures in the formation of the original community.[26] The Maryknoll constitution and seminary were influenced by the Sulpicians, while the Sulpicians, Paulists, and Maryknoll implicitly shared a common Americanist vision of the church in the United States.

Fenlon, who had been a member of the provincial council from its inception in 1922, took part in the development of plans to build a new Saint Mary's Seminary. The building committee's first report (May 1923) called for the selection of the local architectural firm of Parker, Thomas and Rice, but Fenlon, supported by Francis Havey and Edward Dyer, was in favor of commissioning the Boston-based firm of Maginnis and Walsh, which was then in the process of completing the new Sulpician Seminary in Washington, D.C. Fenlon preferred a Catholic architectural firm with a national reputation to a local non-Catholic firm, not only because the former offered greater experience in Catholic architecture, but also because the Catholics of the archdiocese who were asked to contribute one million dollars for the new seminary would "be better pleased to see us choose a Catholic architect even if he be an outsider than a non-Catholic local architect."[27] Some members of the committee pointed out that both Saint Charles' College and Loyola College were built by non-Catholic architects, but Fenlon's views prevailed, and in the spring of 1925 the Sulpicians purchased about eighty acres in Roland Park, an affluent and then predominantly Protestant, suburb.[28] Several Sulpicians expressed concern that the new seminary should not only express the dignity of the priestly vocation but also be a stately building in keeping with its location in Roland Park.

The people of the archdiocese of Baltimore generously responded to the appeal for funds; in the spring of 1928 they had $1,125,000 on hand, but the final cost exceeded the original figure of $1,000,000 by $300,000. When the seminary opened in September 1929, it was only two-thirds completed. Hence, it could accommodate only 236 students, meaning that the first-year theologians and the philosophers (a total of 270 students) remained at the Paca Street seminary under Joseph Bruneau, the new superior. It was not until September 1933 that the first-year theologians were housed in the new seminary, making the enrollment there 305 students. By that time the economic conditions of the Great Depression and the continual rise in vocations precluded closing the old seminary; in 1933, 160 students were enrolled at Paca Street, which remained the philosophy school of Saint Mary's until 1969.

The dedication ceremonies of the new Saint Mary's Seminary on 5 November 1929 drew thousands of spectators and such dignitaries as the apostolic delegate, Archbishop Pietro Fumasoni-Biondi; fifty other archbishops and bishops; and hundreds of priests. The civic dignitaries included Governor Albert Ritchie of Maryland; William F. Broening, mayor of Baltimore; Supreme Court Justice Pierce Butler; and Paul Claudel, the French ambassador. Traditionally, seminary dedications are very festive occasions; apart from a cathedral, no other building in a diocese is considered more significant. In the entire history of seminary dedications, however, that of Saint Mary's appears to have been unparallelled because it was an occasion not only to dedicate a new seminary but also to recognize Saint Mary's as the mother seminary of the church in the United States. Several speakers referred to the Sulpician journey from One-mile Tavern to Roland Park as if it reflected the evolution of the Catholic church from the era of John Carroll to that of Michael Curley. Such an outpouring of sentiment symbolized the triumphalist character of the church in 1929. The traditional hedge separating the seminary from the world was evident in the relative isolation of the seminary property from the Roland Park community. But through the Camillus Society seminarians visited hospitals, asylums, and missions and also provided catechetical instructions to the Catholic boys attending the Gilman School, a highly regarded preparatory school named after the first president of Johns Hopkins University and located across the street from the new seminary.[29]

During the celebration, John Fenlon successfully recommended to the alumni association at its 1929 meeting that Edward F. Hoban, bishop of Rockford, Illinois, be elected president of the alumni association. The move to the Midwest was a departure from tradition, as the two previous presidents had been bishops Harkins and Hickey, both of Providence, Rhode Island. Present for the meeting were two rectors from other seminaries: Joseph M. Corrigan of Saint Charles Borromeo Seminary in Philadelphia and Charles L. Souvay, president of Kenrick Seminary in Saint Louis. Souvay, an alumnus of Saint Sulpice who was later elected superior general of the Vincentians, expressed the filial friendship between Jean-Jacques Olier and Vincent dePaul as a living reality in the common concerns of their respective communities in the United States. John Fenlon told his fellow alumni of the rise in enrollments, of the need to raise funds, and of "a blessing from God greater than any other he has given us . . . [and that is] at the present time we have . . . about fifty men of great promise . . . aspiring to the work of St. Sulpice."[30] Although most of the Sulpician aspirants were still in seminary training, the American province was then experiencing a considerable growth in vocations. Seven priests were doing their Solitude in 1929–1930. Between 1928 and 1938 the number of Sulpicians in the United States rose from 82 to 110. Such growth allowed John Fenlon to seriously consider responding favorably to requests to establish Sulpician seminaries in other dioceses.

The longest-standing invitation to found a new seminary originated in 1910 when Henri Garriguet, accompanied by Edward Dyer, visited Alexander Christie, archbishop of Oregon City. Christie was an alumnus of the Grand Séminaire in Montreal and had served in the archdiocese of Saint Paul. One of several bishops to have come under the influence of John Ireland, Christie exhibited a special loyalty to the Sulpicians. In August 1917 he and his seven suffragan bishops of the province of Oregon City formally stated in a letter to Dyer their "belief that the time has come for the establishment of a Provincial Seminary [and that] they are pleased to learn that the Sulpician Fathers have agreed to take charge of the Seminary."[31] Apparently Garriguet left the impression that the society would indeed assume responsibility for the seminary in the Northwest, as the Sulpicians from Saint John's in Brighton would be free in 1911. However, in 1917 Dyer had to postpone the implementation of Garriguet's commitment because, as he told Christie, "there have been some very important developments in our work. You doubtless heard of our undertaking to establish a branch of St. Mary's Seminary near the Catholic University. This we look upon as a matter of such great importance for us and it will for a time tax to the limit our resources in men and money."[32] Archbishop Christie died in April 1925 without receiving positive word on his prospective Sulpician seminary. Later, one of his suffragans remarked that the archbishop's plans for a seminary never had been taken seriously.[33] Christie had purchased land, but he had no other resources to support the project.

When Verdier visited the Northwest in 1922 he stopped in Seattle and spoke with Bishop Edward O'Dea about a seminary in his diocese. In the spring of 1927, John Fenlon visited the two Sulpician houses in the archdiocese of San Francisco, after which he went to Seattle to discuss with O'Dea the prospect of a Sulpician seminary located in his diocese rather than in the archdiocese of Portland. O'Dea's original plan envisioned just a minor seminary, but Fenlon told him that the Sulpicians would take charge of the seminary only if it included philosophy and theology. Upon his return to Baltimore, Fenlon explained the situation to his provincial council:

> The Bishop has secured a piece of property of 300 acres in the suburbs and he is ready to build a preparatory seminary as soon as we can supply the men. He would let some priests of the diocese help us for a time and would gladly give us any of his subjects who would desire to join our Society. Moreover, he is ready to give us part of the property for a seminary of Theology which would be our own and to help us to build that Seminary.[34]

The council agreed to accept the offer because "Seattle is becoming more and more the metropolis of the Northwest" and because it was such "a great opportunity and [there was] a great need." Since the major seminary would be owned by the Sulpicians, it promised to provide "the same security of tenure as we have in Baltimore." With the loss of Dunwoodie and Brighton as a haunting memory, Fenlon pressed for assurances that ownership would entail "security of tenure."[35] The apostolic delegate, Archbishop Pietro Fumasoni-Biondi, who had been urging O'Dea to establish a seminary, consulted with Fenlon on the Sulpicians' staffing both the preparatory and the major seminaries. The Sulpician Provincial informed the apostolic delegate that O'Dea had stated that the major seminary would be owned by the society. Francis Havey noted that "Father Fenlon expressed anxiety for the permanent tenure of the Sulpicians in the projected college, as we have had experience of the favor and disfavor of Prelates."[36] As a result of this meeting Fumasoni-Biondi influenced the Congregation of Seminaries and Universities to include a safeguard for Sulpician tenure in the Seattle seminary. On 1 June the apostolic delegate wrote to Fenlon that the cardinals of the congregation

> approve the giving of the direction of the Provincial Seminary to the Sulpician Fathers who merit so well of the Church in the United States, by reason of the sound work they have done in building up the American clergy. . . . In order to allay any fears on your part as the Provincial of the Sulpician Fathers, that sometime in the future the direction of the seminary may be taken away from the . . . Sulpician Fathers, Their Eminences, conscious always that they cannot bind the successors of the present Bishops of the Province, have concluded that the direction of the Provincial seminary . . . be put in the hands of the Sulpician Fathers, and after they have accepted this change, it shall not be taken away from them at some future date, without the explicit permission of the Holy See.[37]

Fenlon responded by informing Fumasoni-Biondi that this "judgment . . . has given great consolation to the Sulpician Fathers." He was now assured that the bishops of the province "would never desire to exclude the Fathers from the Administration of the seminary unless they merit the exclusion through their own fault."[38]

When he visited O'Dea in the summer of 1929, Fenlon discovered that a lack of funds prevented construction of the preparatory seminary. The bishop had purchased 365 acres adjacent to scenic Lake Washington, had $100,000 in a seminary fund, and had been promised another $100,000 from the estate of a wealthy Catholic family. Fenlon suggested that "the best way to secure . . . the permanent tenure by the Sulpicians, would be to have the Sulpicians build and own the seminary."[39] O'Dea agreed, and by a contract of 31 July 1930 the Corporation of the Catholic Bishops of Seattle conveyed to the Sulpician Seminary of the Northwest the deed to the property. In return the Sulpician community agreed to construct "out of its own funds" a building for a minor seminary. By a 1931 addendum to this contract, O'Dea agreed to give $200,000 for the construction; the total cost of the building amounted to $600,000.[40]

Thomas Mulligan was appointed first president of the seminary, and from July of 1930 he lived at the bishop's residence during the planning and construction. On 19 September 1931, fifty-one high-school seminarians were received by a faculty of five Sulpicians and one auxiliary priest. Situated on a hill overlooking Lake Washington, Saint Edward's Seminary—named after Bishop O'Dea's patron saint, Edward the Confessor—was, like the first seminary at Saint Charles' College, entirely isolated from the secular world. On 13 October 1931, Cardinal Dennis Dougherty (Cardinal O'Connell's friend and an "enemy" of

Sulpicians) solemnly dedicated the seminary with eleven other prelates, many priests and religious, and 1,500 lay people in attendance.[41]

Saint Edward's opened with three high-school classes; by 1934 it was a full six-year minor seminary. Before the seminary opened, Thomas Mulligan organized the curriculum to satisfy requirements for affiliation with the Catholic University of America and for accreditation with the Department of Education of the State of Washington. Fenlon was in favor of accreditation but "not as excited about it," as was Mulligan. The latter viewed accreditation as important "for the standing of the students," and he advocated education courses as a requirement for all Sulpicians.[42] Since accreditation requirements included a faculty with teaching certificates, many of the priests at Saint Edward's were obliged to attend classes at the University of Washington. Fenlon supported such study, telling Mulligan: "Intellectual stagnation in colleges and seminaries is a much worse evil than is commonly recognized."[43] By the end of the first year Fenlon had achieved both goals: Saint Edward's was the first high-school seminary to be accredited by a state agency. The drive for accreditation, which represented an opening toward the recognition of nonecclesiastical authority, was later motivated by the practical need to provide students, most of whom did not become priests, with diplomas recognized by colleges and universities.

The economic distress brought on by the Great Depression meant that many families and dioceses could not afford to pay tuition, thereby slowing the growth of student enrollment. In 1934, only three boys registered for the first year of high school. The unused space led to the decision in the spring of 1935 to open the major seminary a year later with two philosophy classes and the first year of theology. In the spring of 1939 the first ordination class of twelve students was elevated to the priesthood.[44]

Edward O'Dea died in December of 1932 with the consolation of seeing his dream of a seminary finally fulfilled. He had been a loyal friend of the Sulpicians, but many of his clergy feared that the parishes would be assessed funds for development of the seminary. Neither O'Dea nor his successor Gerald Shaughnessy, S.M., (1933–1950) initiated a diocesan fund-raising campaign, as Archbishop Curley had for Saint Mary's in Roland Park. Although Saint Edward's was referred to as a provincial seminary, it was under the canonical supervision of the ordinary of Seattle. Shaughnessy, who had been involved in seminary education prior to being appointed to the staff of the apostolic delegation, was supportive of Mulligan's professionalization of the seminary. After the bishop was informed that the president of Saint Edward's was applying for accreditation of the four-year college by the Northwest Association of Secondary and Higher Schools, he wrote to Mulligan that he was "very happy" with the prospect of Saint Edward's receiving such a mark of recognition.[45] In time for the June 1937 graduation, the seminary received accreditation, which allowed those students who passed second-year philosophy to receive the bachelor of arts degree. By this time enrollment was increasing, and in 1939 it reached a new high with sixty-three students in philosophy and theology and fifty-seven in the high school and junior college.

Relations between Bishop Shaughnessy and the Sulpicians became strained during the late 1930s over the seminary's general character. The bishop questioned the provincial status of the seminary as well as the Sulpician ownership of the institution. These conflicts originated with a Sulpician request that the diocese sponsor a fund drive that had been promised by O'Dea. After nearly two years of discussion, Shaughnessy was finally convinced of the Sulpician interpretation of the historical documents compiled by Fenlon. Shaughnessy had questioned the degree of Sulpician financial commitment to the seminary only to discover that it had cost the community nearly $350,000. The bishop agreed to pay 50 percent of the seminary indebtedness without requiring diocesan ownership. His only formal request was the establishment of a summer school in canon law in order to prepare his priests for chancery and curial procedures. Fenlon assigned James H. Brennan, Sulpician specialist in canon law, to teach this course, which terminated after three summers.[46] (In 1986 Brennan was still teaching a course in canon law at Mount Saint Mary's Seminary during his quasi retirement.) Although Shaughnessy and the Sulpicians resolved the conflict over the seminary, the bishop was never really close to the society during his long tenure (1933–1950).

III

The Sulpician Seminary in Washington, D.C., experienced considerable growth during its first decade, but from its origin there were signs of conflict between the university and seminary. Less than a month after Fenlon became provincial, he was notified by Archbishop Curley of plans of the theology faculty for the establishment of a seminary course at the university. Curley, ex officio chancellor of the university, held to the "conviction that our Seminary should be the Seminary of the University." The archbishop proposed a compromise: in exchange for Sulpician control of the university seminary, some university professors would be appointed to the faculty. Bishop Shahan, the rector of the university, "is known to favor control of the teaching by the university . . . [with but] a few important chairs . . . left to the Sulpicians."[47]

The university's plan to open its own seminary was motivated by the need to provide students for its theology faculty and, of course, to augment its general enrollment. From its origin, the Sulpician seminary struck many professors as an intolerable anomaly.

Fenlon brought the issue to the provincial council. There was unanimity on the principle of the Sulpician institution becoming the university seminary and on the appointments of some university professors for courses in apologetics, church history, canon law, and some courses in fourth-year theology, but "under no consideration [could we] surrender control of the discipline of Spiritual Training; neither could we give complete control of the teaching to the University. The Sulpicians would not have proper standing or influence in the Seminary if they were only to have spiritual direction and a few minor courses." The council was divided on a compromise proposal to allow the university full control over the curriculum and the authority to appoint one-half the faculty. Francis Havey and Anthony Viéban supported such a compromise because without an agreement "our seminary will never become the Seminary of the University." In that event, the Sulpician institution could not compete with the course of study at the university seminary, which would offer licentiate and doctoral degrees. Havey and Viéban reported to the provincial council that there was "a feeling at the University that in the past the interests of St. Mary's Seminary have blocked the progress of the University. This feeling will be intensified if now we oppose the organization of a University Seminary."

John Fenlon and Michael Dinneen supported the archbishop's plan of cooperation with the university, but they wanted to maintain "full control" because "we have a very good faculty" and because "our seminary has been built by our alumni" who would oppose surrendering control to the university. It appears that without a consensus on the cooperation between the Sulpician seminary and the university, Archbishop Curley, a friend of the Sulpicians, protected the seminary character. When the university seminary opened in 1927, it was limited to only seminarians from small religious communities located in the environs of the university, while the Sulpician institution continued to train diocesan seminarians.[49]

The existence of two independent adjacent seminaries was dependent upon the political protection of Curley and others. This protection began to crumble in the mid-1930s when Joseph Moran Corrigan was appointed rector of the university from his previous position as rector of the archdiocesan seminary of Philadelphia. Archbishop John T. McNicholas, O.P., of Cincinnati had been appointed chairman of the Pontifical Commission of the University in 1934 and appears to have been the major force behind Corrigan's appointment. McNicholas was alienated by Bishop James Hugh Ryan, rector from 1928–1935, who fostered scholarly research and redesigned the graduate and under-graduate schools along modern university lines. Such innovations seem to have offended the traditionalist sensibilities of McNicholas, whose commission was mandated by Rome "to revise the program of sacred studies, to draw up or complete the programs where necessary and to look for the faithful observance" of a newly drafted university consti-tution and of the policies of the Holy See.[50]

Both McNicholas and Corrigan were convinced that the Sulpician Seminary must give way to the university, but rather than take the is-sue to the chancellor, Archbishop Curley, they decided to go through Cardinal Cajetan Bisleti, prefect of the Congregation of Seminaries and Universities. In the winter of 1937, Corrigan went to Rome, where he won the support of Bisleti for the establishment of a full diocesan sem-inary at the university.[51] Archbishop Amleto Cicognani, the apostolic delegate, was also supportive of the Corrigan plan but advocated ap-pointing some Sulpicians to the faculty and consulting with Curley. McNicholas explained to Cicognani that he and his committee were reluctant that he should meet with Fenlon or with Curley.

> We felt that if I saw him [i.e., Fenlon] he would go immediately to Archbishop Curley, who might strengthen him in his opposition. Both Father Fenlon and the Chancellor might think that our committee is urging the Holy See to put a plan through which could not well be undertaken at this time by the American Hierarchy with the cooperation of the Sulpicians.[52]

McNicholas suggested that Bisleti, through a visit by Corrigan, no-tify Cardinal Verdier, the superior general of the Sulpicians, of the Holy See's desire for cooperation between the Sulpicians and the university.[53] It would be the first step toward clearing away the oppo-sition. McNicholas was also concerned about the potential opposition from "the very many bishops of the United States [who] are friendly to the Sulpicians. Many of them have been trained in their seminaries and think them the best qualified to give spiritual formation to sem-inarians." He then interjected his own views on the character of the American Sulpician:

> It is recognized that the self-sacrificing and hidden, the learned and spiritual Sulpician of the French School is passing from the scene, not to return. Not withstanding this, a great many American bishops think that the American Sulpicians, even though they are not the equal of the French Sulpicians for learning and attractive spirituality, are the best qualified to impress seminarians and give them a spiritual formation.[54]

To gain the support of these bishops, McNicholas favored a plan whereby the Sulpicians would control the discipline and spiritual direction and teach a few courses in the university's School of Theology, which would have complete control of the curriculum and academic life of the seminary. In short, Shahan's proposal to Dyer became the plan of McNicholas, Cicognani, Corrigan, and Bisleti.[55]

Corrigan told Bisleti that he was opposed to approaching Verdier directly: "I know that such an act on my part would be construed in America by the Sulpicians and their many powerful friends in the Episcopate as an unfriendly act." Corrigan wrote to McNicholas that some days later Bisleti informed him that

> the seminary problem at the University was too important to be settled without the Holy Father's knowledge. So I went to the Pope and explained the situation. His Holiness not only confirmed the fact that there must be a seminary, and only one, at the University, but told me to write at once to Cardinal Verdier and say that the Holy Father authorized me to tell him that the Sulpician seminary was to be placed at the disposition of the University at once.[56]

This collusion among Corrigan, McNicholas, and Bisleti remained veiled in secrecy. Fenlon was well aware of Corrigan's designs on the Sulpician Seminary, but he was not aware of the strong role played by McNicholas. One should be cautious, however, in assigning too much weight to the influence of either Corrigan or McNicholas, as both may be viewed as instruments in the general trend of centralized seminary reform initiated by Pius XI in his 1931 decree *Deus Scientiarum Dominus*. This decree modified the standards for pontifical degrees, and in conformity with these new regulations, Saint Mary's pontifical seminary had to prepare a new constitution, which Fenlon brought to Rome.

Moses Elias Kiley, an alumnus of Saint Mary's and then bishop of Trenton, told Fenlon that "the Pope never would have approved the action depriving us of the right to teach in our own seminary if he understood the situation and if Cardinal Verdier had protested against it." Fenlon communicated that observation to Pierre Boisard, the vice superior general, and added,

> the more I think of that act the more outrageous it seems to me. In Cardinal Bisletti's [sic] letter to Cardinal Verdier, he wrote as if all the religious houses around the seminary would be obliged to send their students to the [University's] Faculty of Theology. Of course, the decree has been applied only to the Sulpician seminary. It was never the intention of applying it to other houses such as the Dominicans, Franciscans, etc. They feel that the Sulpicians thoroughly agree with Rome on this point.[57]

Events forced Fenlon to comply with the will of Rome, but he wished to maintain Sulpicians in the chairs of theology and Sulpician control of Basselin College, the three-year philosophy course taught at the Sulpician seminary. In both instances the university was victorious, though two Sulpicians, Edward Arbez and Louis Arand, received university appointments in theology, and Jules Baisnée was appointed to the philosophy faculty.[58] The university absorbed one theology class each year beginning in the fall of 1937, so it was not until 1940 that the old Sulpician Seminary was limited to being simply a house of formation, ironically called Theological College.[59]

Fenlon was disturbed by the events of 1937-1938, and his condition was compounded by an attack of angina. During Pierre Boisard's official visitation of the Sulpician seminary in Washington in 1938, the frustration of the Sulpician community surfaced over the question of the tenure of the institution. If the university were allowed to purchase the building, then the Sulpician presence in Washington would be very precarious. At one point in the discussion, Louis Arand said, "The University at present has no mind to give us a guarantee of tenure. I think we have taken too much 'sitting down'; we just bow and say: 'Go ahead'; a fight would do us good. Otherwise we shall have nothing left."[60] Boisard agreed that a contract stipulating the conditions of tenure should resolve the issue but stated that the decision resided in the U.S. province rather than in the general council in Paris. Later he told the community that there were several university seminaries in which the Sulpicians provided the spiritual formation and the universities the theological training.

Between faculty meetings, Boisard visited Cicognani and was told that the apostolic delegate would support a contract protecting the tenure of the Sulpician college at the university. He advised Boisard to ask Verdier to inform Rome on the contracts in force in France as a model for the Catholic University and Theological College. Anthony Viéban, the rector of Theological College, pointed out that in France the universities supplied the buildings and paid salaries to the Sulpicians. He then stated that

> the best arrangement *per se* would be to have the University buy the place and pay the money to the Sulpicians. What we turn over to the university is far greater than the money they would pay us; for we are giving them not only the grounds and the stones of the building but a body of students picked with care through twenty years and the reputation this seminary has made for itself.[61]

The university, however, could not afford the $700,000 for the building. In June of 1940, a contract between the Sulpicians and the university was approved in Rome. It guaranteed tenure for Theological

College and Sulpician spiritual direction of both the theology students and the Basselin philosophy students.

During Boisard's visitation with the Washington community, a portion of the discussion centered on the students' summer catechetical and social-work program that involved, on a volunteer basis, the third and fourth-year theology students but attracted nearly fifty students from various other seminaries in the Washington area. The significant point in the discussion was that such a program was considered far more important than the Roman practice of the summer villa for seminarians. Viéban suggested that a report of the Sulpician-sponsored summer work be circulated in Rome; "such a report might offset possible legislation in respect to the establishment of a villa system." He said that such a system "takes all life from the students; they become institutionalized." Louis Arand stated that

> the villa system is a hothouse system. No one knows de facto if a student is capable of doing priestly work. Whereas our students come to have first-hand knowledge of conditions among which a priest must work; they get to know the life of the people, their life amid poverty; they come to be sympathetic. They face actual problems.

Boisard concluded that "the Roman authorities are not properly informed about this phase of our Sulpician system."[62]

John Fenlon was convinced that Rome was biased against the Sulpicians. He told Bishop James E. Cassidy of Fall River, Massachusetts, that "such a profound change [at the Sulpician Seminary in Washington, D.C.] would never have taken place so easily if the seminary had been in the hands of a strong religious order. An event like this is good for the soul. It makes us realize how little we amount to in a political way in the church."[63] In a 1939 evaluation of the relations between the Sulpicians and Pius XI, Fenlon wrote to a Sulpician confrere in Rome that the pope had "certainly done us a great honor in making Father Verdier Archbishop and Cardinal. The Brassac business [i.e., condemnation of the *Manuel biblique*] and our Washington seminary, on the other hand, were hard blows." He told him that the theological faculty at Washington "follows the Roman model and, of course, has lowered the requirements for the doctorate." Fenlon expressed his disappointment with McNicholas's apostolic visitation commission appointed by Rome, which was "in control of the University . . . ; the Chancellor, Monseignour [sic] Curley, is now merely an ornament."[64] The American provincial harbored his own biases against Roman education, which perhaps originated in his experience as a graduate student. He didn't see much progress over the years. In 1939 he wrote:

> I do not think there is any comparison between the theological training which is given at Louvain and that which is given in Rome. Certainly

> our [Sulpician] students in Louvain have been much more satisfied
> and feel they have been doing real university work, whereas our
> recent students in Rome, in theology, felt that the whole regime was
> unprofitable and not conducted with good sense.[65]

On another occasion Fenlon expressed his deep regret that "the Sulpicians in the United States have little standing as scholars. Very few
have published any work; they ought to study more and take up the
work of writing for publication."[66]

Never in the history of the society in the United States was such
loyalty displayed toward the Sulpicians than in the sesquicentennial
celebration of the foundation of Saint Mary's Seminary in November of
1941, which was also the tricentennial of the society itself (1641-1941).
The three-day celebration, from 10-12 November, was arranged to
precede the annual meeting of the hierarchy at Catholic University in
Washington. With over 103 prelates in attendance, it was the largest
gathering of American bishops in the history of the church. Only one
major figure was absent, Cardinal William O'Connell, who for obvious
reasons sent his regrets. (In 1928 he had had the Sulpicians who were
buried at the Brighton seminary disinterred.) The principal public event
marking the two anniversaries was held at the Fifth Regiment Armory
in downtown Baltimore; over 10,000 people joined the celebration at
which Archbishop Curley presided. Formal letters from Pope Pius XII
and from the American hierarchy preceded the sermon preached by
John J. Mitty, archbishop of San Francisco and an alumnus of the
Sulpician seminary at Dunwoodie. Mitty declared:

> In very truth, the Sulpicians have lived the hidden life; they are
> unknown to the faithful at large; they are known only to the students
> and their Bishops. There have been scholars and saints among them
> but little has been written of them and their work, for their sole
> ambition has been to train priestly priests by the example of their
> own priestly lives. . . . The Church in America pays tribute to St.
> Mary's . . . as the Mother Seminary of the many schools of Christ
> throughout the land that are giving Christs to the Church in the
> United States.[67]

Other sermons and speeches resounded with praise for the Sulpician
contribution to American Catholic culture.

Throughout the sesquicentennial the one note of sorrow was that
France had been defeated by the Nazis. Cardinal Verdier died in 1940,
and without the possibility of a general chapter, Pierre Boisard assumed the title of acting superior general. Less than four weeks after
the sesquicentennial, the United States entered World War II. During the Great Depression and the war, the American province grew
considerably, but the bishops could not afford to open new seminar-

ies. In 1938, immediately prior to the appointment of Francis Spellman as archbishop of New York, Fenlon had been led to believe that perhaps the new bishop would ask the Sulpicians to return to Dunwoodie. A short time later Cicognani approached Fenlon on the possibility of the Sulpicians returning to Mount Saint Mary's Seminary in Emmitsburg. The rector had died, and the apostolic delegate, apparently not impressed by the seminary during his official visitation, wished to see Sulpicians assume the offices of rector and spiritual director and fill one or two of the teaching positions. Curley was in agreement with Cicognani, but because of Fenlon's and the provincial council's reluctance to enter an institution in which the faculty and alumni were so opposed to outsiders, the plan never materialized.[68]

The economic condition of the American province was never very prosperous. There was a sizable indebtedness at Saint Mary's in Roland Park. The old Paca Street buildings required continual repairs; Theological College needed an additional wing; the new Saint Charles' was still in debt; and the Seattle seminary was a continual drain upon the province's assets, particularly because of Bishop Shaughnessy's reluctance to support or subsidize the cost of new buildings or to help liquidate the debt. Although the exact value of the province's assets is difficult to determine, income from property accumulated over a period of 150 years was considerable, enough to provide a sense of security but not a sense of wealth.[69] Authorized to transact the major business of the province was the corporation known as the Associated Sulpicians of the United States, composed of the provincial as president, the provincial council, and the superiors of each of the seminaries. In 1936 Fenlon was required by an act of the general chapter to relinquish the title of superior of Saint Mary's, but he was elected president of the seminary by his council.[70]

John Fenlon was, as noted earlier, a second-generation Americanist who reflected a Gallican skepticism toward Roman regulations and a practical zeal characteristic of Sulpicians in general. During his administration, Francis Havey, Anthony Viéban, Michael Dinneen, and Eugene Harrigan (superior at Saint Charles') were members of the provincial council and were dominant figures in the province. Fenlon was not a forceful speaker, but he was a recognized savant and spoke with authority on a wide variety of topics. He promoted graduate study among the younger Sulpicians and was a paternalistic provincial. His correspondence with such friends as Joseph McSorley reveals a personal warmth and a clever wit. He was a traditionalist on the spiritual exercises and a strong authority figure in the province.

Francis Havey was a veteran American Sulpician (he reached eighty years of age in 1944) and was very influential as a spiritual leader. He was the head of the first two American Solitudes (1911–1912 and 1913-1914). A strong-willed and rigid man, he appealed to those priests who admired structure and the values of authority and order. Anthony Viéban, who was head of the American Solitude from 1921 to 1933 and superior at the Sulpician Seminary from 1933 to his death in 1944, was a compassionate man with a strong appeal to those priests who valued cosmopolitanism and a spirit of independence and to those who needed to be spiritually nurtured with gentleness. During the period 1943-1945, Fenlon, Havey, and Viéban died; it was the passing of a generation, one that had been trained in the pre-Pascendi period, had served under Magnien, had felt the influence of Hogan, and had experienced the loss of Dunwoodie and Brighton. They also witnessed the rise of Sulpician seminaries in San Francisco and Seattle, and most importantly they witnessed the creation of the American province and the growth of American vocations. By 1944, there were 123 Sulpicians in the United States; 114 of them were natives and 56 of them were under forty years of age. This was the generation that would experience the profound cultural and ecclesiastical changes associated with the Second Vatican Council.

13

Transition to Vatican II

In the United States, the Second Vatican Council marks the last hours of the "ghetto church." By the time of its demise the Catholic ghetto had become quite modernized and professionalized; its attempts to set up relatively independent components entailed meeting the increasingly rising standards established by accrediting agencies and professional societies. Catholic schools, hospitals, newspapers, and magazines were modernized, and the clergy and religious involved in the modernization of these institutions became professionalized. Hence, there was a large group of Catholics trained in the 1950s and ready to respond to the call for adaptation, reform, and renewal in the 1960s. Since there were several signs of change during the immediate pre–Vatican II period it is appropriate to label the era from 1945 to 1965 (a period practically corresponding to the combined provincial terms of John Lardner and Lloyd McDonald, 1943–1967) as "the making of the modern church," with *modern* signifying an acceptance of the principle of open-endedness, symbolized by such theological and ecclesiological terms as *the development of dogma, the pilgrim people of God,* and the *pursuit of the Kingdom,* each of which conveys movement, process, and evolution.[1]

This period in American social history witnessed vast population shifts from the rural areas to the cities and from the cities to surburbia. These moves deeply affected the religious life of Catholics, as many were separated from their urban ethnic neighborhoods with their structured piety and devotionalism. Economic affluence and veterans' benefits encouraged many young Catholics to enter college, thereby compounding the movement away from ethnic communities. There was considerable institutional growth in the Catholic church in the United States between the end of World War II and the termination of the Second Vatican Council: in 1945 there were 14,302 parishes and 38,451 diocesan and religious priests; in 1967 there were 17,942 parishes and 59,892 priests. Although Catholic educational institutions from the primary to the university levels experienced continual growth, diocesan seminaries had a comparatively higher rate of growth: in 1945 there were 53 diocesan seminaries with 7,433 students; in 1967 there were 123 seminaries with 15,859 students. Just as the National Catholic Educational Association became more modern during this period, so did its seminary section, which was headed by Sulpicians for several years, become modernized.

The Catholic Biblical Association (CBA) was founded in 1936, and the Sulpician scripture scholar Edward P. Arbez was elected its first president. In 1946 the Catholic Theological Society in America (CTSA) was founded. Through the *Catholic Biblical Quarterly, Theological Studies* (sponsored by the Jesuits), and *Worship* (published by the monks of Saint John's Abbey), new intellectual trends in the life of the American church gained momentum.[2] By the mid-1950s John Courtney Murray, S.J., Gustav Weigel, S.J., Godfrey Dieckmann, O.S.B., and others were promoting religious pluralism, ecumenism, liturgical renewal, and racial integration.[3] Several small but effective lay movements advocated changes in the church; these movements included the Catholic Evidence Guild with its street preachers, the Catholic Worker movement with its houses of hospitality, the Catholic Interracial Society, as well as the Grail, the Young Christian Students, and the Christian Workers. As the traditional ghetto walls of the church crumbled, the hedge separating the sacred seminary from the secular world also withered away in a matter of a few years.

Several Sulpicians participated in these nascent reform movements prior to Vatican II. Eugene Walsh of Baltimore, who published his dissertation on the French school of spirituality, was active in the Catholic Evidence League and the liturgical movement; some of his students, such as Joseph Gallagher, editor of Baltimore's *Catholic Review*, and Joseph Connolly, head of the Baltimore archdiocesan commission on the liturgy, became priest-activists in the 1950s and 1960s. In 1986 Walsh was still active in parish liturgical renewal. Another Sulpician, Frank Norris, who was also influenced by Walsh, was introducing his students to Karl Rahner and others prior to the Second Vatican Council. Peter Chirico, on the faculty of the Seattle seminary in the early 1960s, was teaching the new ecclesiology before the council. Chirico and Norris were also involved in ecumenism. Joseph Collins, who had been prominent in the foundation of the Confraternity of

Christian Doctrine in the 1930s, was on the faculty at the Catholic University of America, where he was a leader at the National Center for Religious Education (1942–1968). John Cronin, a prominent labor priest in Baltimore and an assistant to John A. Ryan in the Social Action Department of the NCWC, was instrumental in the development of the bishops' pastoral on the evils of racism and later became a speech writer on social issues for Vice-President Richard Nixon. Cronin's influence was felt within the society as well; William J. Lee held a Ph.D. in economics and was a Sulpician leader during the reform period. The most prominent Sulpician scholar was Raymond Brown, whose work in scripture spans the period from the 1950s to the present. He occupies the Auburn Chair in Scripture at Union Theological Seminary in New York, and his many scholarly articles and books have earned him worldwide recognition as the most significant Catholic biblical exegete. James Laubacher, rector of Saint Mary's (1945–1967), did his dissertation on George Tyrrell and was conversant with the new theology of the 1940s; he and Edward Hogan, theology professor at Saint Mary's, met monthly with John Courtney Murray and other theologians in the Baltimore-Washington area during the pre–Vatican II period of ferment. Each of these Sulpicians represents, in his unique way, the voice of advanced thought in particular areas of American ecclesiastical life during the period immediately prior to the Second Vatican Council.

The vast majority of the American Sulpicians reflected the generally traditional posture of the Catholic community. Although the structure was modern, the spirit of the American church was quite traditional; the seminaries reflected that spirit, and the leaders of the Society of Saint Sulpice, particularly the two provincials during this period, John Lardner (1943–1948) and Lloyd McDonald (1948–1967), perceived their roles as primarily preservationist. Although McDonald was provincial during the Second Vatican Council, he was pushed by the forces of reform, which were far stronger than his power to maintain the traditional forms of seminary life.

II

The growth of the Sulpicians reflected the general trends in ecclesiastical life. From 1945 to 1967 worldwide membership of the Society of Saint Sulpice went from 537 to 653; in the United States it rose from 126 members in 1945 to 159 in 1967. In World War II ten Sulpicians served as chaplains in the U.S. Armed Forces, while many French Sulpicians were conscripted; during the Nazi occupation of France the seminary in Issy was in the hands of the Germans. Because of a 1943 ruling of the Selective Service Commission by which those classified 4-D (deferred as a student of ministry) could lose their deferment status during the summer months between terms, the U.S. seminaries went on an accelerated schedule of three semesters a year with only brief vacations between semesters. This measure prevented the drafting of seminarians, and it was a small sacrifice considering the general wartime constrictions of normal life in the United States.

John Fenlon died in July of 1943, and because the Nazi occupation in France precluded a Paris appointment of a successor, Archbishop Curley convoked a meeting of the provincial council for the election of a new provincial. The members elected John Lardner as interim provincial, and in 1945 the authorities in Paris confirmed the election.

Lardner, a native of Baltimore, was fifty years old in 1943. An alumnus of Saint Mary's, he was ordained in 1920, received a licentiate in theology from the Catholic University of America in 1921, and did his year of Solitude in 1921-1922. After some teaching, he went to Rome, where he earned his doctorate in theology at the Angelicum. His first post as rector was at Saint Patrick's in Menlo Park, where he succeeded Henri Ayrinhac, the revered French Sulpician from Rodez, who died in 1930. Lardner returned to Baltimore in 1934 and two years later became rector of Saint Mary's Seminary at Roland Park. Neither an inspiring speaker nor an astute administrator, Lardner was nevertheless highly respected as a priests' priest and was particularly regarded for his clergy conferences. Because he was plagued with high blood pressure and a heart condition, he was strained by the demands of the office.

During Lardner's administration the American province embarked on its first missionary endeavor, the foundation of a minor seminary in Oahu in the Territory of the Hawaiian Islands. Bishop James J. Sweeney of the diocese of Honolulu, an alumnus of Saint Patrick's Seminary, sent his seminarians to Saint Joseph's College in Mountain View and to Saint Patrick's for theology. The diocese of Honolulu, a suffragan to the archdiocese of San Francisco, had been entrusted to the Sacred Hearts Fathers in 1826. Sweeney, appointed bishop in 1941, was the first secular priest elevated to the position. During his visits to Saint Patrick's Seminary, he frequently spoke of his hope to found a Sulpician seminary in his diocese. His major concern was to develop a native diocesan clergy. In 1944 there were only five secular priests in the diocese, while there were sixty-five priests of the Sacred Hearts of Jesus and Mary, ten Maryknoll priests, and three from the Society of Mary. Between 1826, when a prefecture-apostolic was erected for the Hawaiian Islands (then called the Sandwich Islands), and 1944 there had never been a native vocation to the diocesan priesthood.

At the provincial council meeting of 5 November 1944, John Lardner informed the members of a letter he had received from Sweeney in which the bishop formally invited the Sulpicians to staff a preparatory seminary "as soon as conditions permit." The provincial noted that Archbishop Mitty "urges us to accept." The archbishop of San Francisco had been reluctant ever to allow his seminarians and priests to join the Society of Saint Sulpice, but Lardner concluded that since Mitty urged the province to expand into the diocese of Honolulu, "it is hoped that Archbishop Mitty will be willing to allow us to draw on the archdiocese for candidates for the Society."[4]

In March of 1946, Sweeney asked for two Sulpicians to staff a high-school seminary in his diocese. Sixteen students were supplementing their high-school studies with classes in Latin, Greek, chant, and liturgy at a "seminary" staffed by local priests. The provincial council decided to send two men.[5] The following September, John Linn and Richard Cullinan opened the high-school seminary in an old mansion on twenty-two acres of property (purchased by Sweeney the previous June), located about ten miles from Honolulu. Linn, who entered the society in 1929, had left the post as vice-rector and Latin professor at Saint Mary's philosophy seminary on Paca Street. Cullinan, who entered the society in 1943, had been teaching physics and chemistry and directing the athletic program at Saint Joseph's College in Mountain View, California.

Nearly 1,000 people attended an open house on 15 September. The converted two-story L-shaped mansion was situated on the side of a mountain range from which one could see the Pacific Ocean at a distance of four miles. The seminary, named Saint Stephen's, opened with thirteen seminarians at various stages of educational development. The mission character of the diocese was strongly manifested in Saint Stephen's. These young boys, so immersed in a tightly knit Polynesian communal society with a strong tie to extended families, did not easily adapt to the somewhat rigorous Sulpician system within a boarding school. Although Linn and Cullinan were sensitive to the common complaints of homesickness and adapted the schedule to provide some variety, Saint Stephen's remained a traditionally rigid Sulpician seminary.[6]

Since the seminary was located in a rainy climate, the priests also found it difficult to adjust. At first both the Sulpicians and the students appear to have experienced varying degrees of culture shock. To teach Latin to students who had little formal training in the rudiments of English grammar was a major effort.[7] One extreme case of culture shock involved several experiences with a young seminarian who heard the voice of Saint Margaret Mary. He manifested visible crosses of blood on his arms and was tormented by convulsions and swelling of his throat. Both Linn and Cullinan reported witnessing these events as well as other unusual signs. Although this situation was obviously not typical, it struck the two Sulpicians as one of several severe challenges endemic to Saint Stephen's.[8] Enrollment increased very gradually. There were only twenty students in 1952 when John Ward became superior. However, in 1955 Saint Stephen's added a two-year junior college and thus became a full minor seminary. In 1964 the seminary reached its peak enrollment with seventy students. Although it had educated hundreds of students in classical studies and had introduced them to Sulpician spirituality, Saint Stephen's never achieved Sweeney's goal to provide a native clergy; between 1946 and 1970 only eleven alumni were ordained. In 1970 seven of the thirty-one diocesan priests had been educated at Saint Stephen's. The diocese's mission status was still evident in 1970 as there were 131 priests of religious orders living in the diocese of Honolulu. Hence, in the fall of 1970 Saint Stephen's became a formation community limited to post-high-school seminarians who did their course work at Chaminade College, run by the Brothers of Mary.[9] Analagous to the role of Sulpicians at Theological College, the few Sulpicians at Saint Stephen's provided spiritual direction and religious exercises to the seminarians of the diocese of Honolulu.

While Bishop Sweeney was laying the foundation for his Sulpician preparatory seminary in Honolulu, Archbishop Edward Mooney (made a cardinal in 1946) was soliciting the Sulpicians to staff a major seminary for the province of Detroit. An alumnus of Saint Charles' College and of the philosophy section of Saint Mary's Seminary, Mooney was ordained for the diocese of Cleveland, where he served as principal of the Cathedral Latin School from 1916 to 1922. After a year as a pastor he was appointed spiritual director of the North American College in Rome, where he had studied theology prior to ordination. From 1926 to 1933, he served in the Vatican diplomatic corps, as apostolic delegate to India (named titular archbishop of Irenopolis) from 1926 to 1931, and as apostolic delegate to Japan during the following two years. After serving as the ordinary of the diocese of Rochester for four years, Mooney was named the first archbishop of Detroit in April of 1937.[10] In 1919 his predecessor, Michael J. Gallagher, had founded Sacred Heart Seminary, which offered an eight-year course of high school and college. (There was also a preparatory seminary in Grand Rapids founded in 1909.) As the chairman of the administrative board of the NCWC, (1936–1939, 1941–1945), Mooney became reacquainted with the Sulpicians while in Washington, D.C. After several informal discussions, Archbishop Mooney formally asked the Sulpicians to take charge of the provincial seminary in June 1945. Because Sacred Heart Seminary included two years of philosophy, the new seminary would be a four-year theologate. On 12 June 1945, the Sulpician provincial council accepted the offer "to prepare men to staff the seminary."[11] Since it would be a few years before the seminary would be ready to open, there was time to develop a Sulpician faculty. In 1947 twelve Sulpicians were in graduate school; two of them were later assigned to the first faculty of the Detroit seminary. Because this was the first Sulpician seminary limited to theologians, each of the faculty members was expected to have either an S.T.D. or a Ph.D; because Mooney wished to see the seminary affiliated with the university in Washington, his own preference was for the pontifical S.T.D.[12]

Almost immediately after the provincial council agreed to take charge of the seminary in Detroit, John Lardner was hospitalized for a heart condition. In a 19 July 1945 letter to Mooney he tells the archbishop that he is "eternally grateful to you for the opportunity you are giving us." Lardner was still sensitive to the loss of Dunwoodie and Brighton; he informs Mooney that the prospect of a Sulpician seminary in a major metropolitan province "compensates adequately . . . for losses we sustained as far as prestige goes in this country in past years."[13]

The development of a contract between the Sulpicians and the five ordinaries of the Detroit province covered a period of over two years. Although there were no conflicts in the negotiations, it was not until the fall of 1947 that Lardner and Mooney, the bishops of the province, and the Congregation of Seminaries and Universities had reached an agreement on the final terms of the contract, which stipulated that the Sulpicians would have the responsibility "to conduct the Seminary under the authority of the Bishops, in accordance with the constitution, rules and usages of the Society [of Saint Sulpice]." The bishops owned the seminary and possessed the "advice and consent" authority on the rule for the seminary and on the appointment of the rector. Additions to the faculty had to be approved by the bishops, and they could call for the removal of any faculty member. The Sulpicians had the right to expel any seminarian without prior consultation with the bishops. The contract was to be in effect for six years, but if an irresolvable conflict occurred, the bishops and the Sulpicians were to submit the case to the Congregation of Seminaries and Universities.[14]

As mentioned in the previous chapter, John Fenlon was adamant in his pursuit of ownership of Saint Edward's Seminary in Seattle because he identified ownership with a guarantee of tenure. Lardner explained to Mooney the history of Sulpician attitude toward tenure:

> As I mentioned to you, I think, in conversation, the traditional view of the Sulpicians in France is that if the Ordinary at any time prefers that the Sulpicians leave his Seminary, they should do so, a year's notice being given. As your Eminence knows very well, the older Sulpicians

[in the United States] who have nearly all died out, made a strong point of tenure after their loss of the Seminaries of Brighton and New York. We of this generation feel that there is an element in such a view which may effect Saint Sulpice adversely since it is likely to frighten off Bishops who would otherwise be pleased to engage us."[15]

Lardner suffered a fatal heart attack on 5 October 1948 while visiting the Seattle seminary. He had been scheduled to travel from the Northwest to Detroit to attend the laying of the cornerstone of Saint John's Seminary in Plymouth, Michigan.[16] In Lardner's funeral eulogy, Bishop John M. McNamara, auxiliary of the newly established archdiocese of Washington, D.C., captures the personality of the third provincial of the Sulpicians in the United States: "Father Lardner was possessed of a fine mind and splendid judgement, but he showed no disposition to assert himself unduly or emphasize his authority. In truth he gave evidence of a certain shyness which had its roots in humility." McNamara refers to Lardner as "the priest of gentleness," a title that would not be appropriate to either of his predecessors, the practical and stubborn Edward Dyer and the urbane, forceful John Fenlon.[17]

The newly appointed provincial, Lloyd P. McDonald, graduated from Columbia (now Loras) College in 1917 prior to entering Saint Mary's Seminary. After ordination he taught at Saint Charles' College and then attended the Catholic University of America, where he received a Ph.D. in education in 1927. He was superior of the philosophy seminary on Paca Street (1933-1944), superior of the Solitude (1941-1943), and rector of Theological College (1944-1948). As provincial from 1948 to 1967, McDonald witnessed profound changes both within the Society of Saint Sulpice and within the life of the church.

A month prior to his death, Lardner had appointed Lyman Fenn as rector of Saint John's Seminary, which was scheduled to open in September 1949. George E. Ott was appointed treasurer and lived and taught at Sacred Heart Seminary in Detroit during the academic year 1948-1949 so that he could oversee the construction of the new Plymouth house just ten miles from Detroit. Located on 186 acres, the new seminary was designed according to a modified Renaissance style of architecture characteristic of Assisi and the central Italy district of Umbria. Six wings jutted from a rectangular central core of buildings where the chapel was located. However, because of the high costs of construction, it was decided to defer building of the chapel, gymnasium, auditorium, and two resident wings. Originally planned to house 226 students, Saint John's would accommodate 162 when it opened in September 1949.[18] At that time there were over 400 students enrolled at Sacred Heart Seminary, staffed by diocesan priests. Located at Orchard Lake, likewise in the archdiocese, was Saints Cyril and Methodius, a full minor and major national seminary that trained priests for the Polish community in the United States. In 1949, 36 students were enrolled at Orchard Lake seminary.

Saint John's opened with an enrollment of 75 students in three years of theology. Because the students came from nine different seminaries, the major task for the faculty was to mold them into a unified body and give them strong Sulpician imprint.[19] The fact that there were over 200 Sulpician alumni in the province of Detroit meant that the faculty was well respected in the area. In his visitation report of 1950, McDonald comments that "the Cardinal and the Bishops seem well pleased with the administration of the Seminary by the Sulpicians. The Cardinal expressed himself as being delighted. . . ."[20] Lyman Fenn was a very strong rector who possessed the confidence of McDonald and the bishops.

McDonald had been a member of the provincial council during Lardner's period as provincial superior. McDonald was therefore knowledgeable of the plans, personnel, and problems that confronted Saint Sulpice. As early as 1930 Bishop John A. Floersh of Louisville had asked the Sulpicians to return to the diocese and staff a new minor seminary.[21] In the spring of 1948, Floersh, who was made archbishop in 1937, renewed his seminary plans, but Lardner and his provincial council, concerned with the personnel problems of staffing a minor seminary and dubious about whether the province should limit itself to major seminaries, deferred the decision until a later date.[22]

In November 1948, McDonald reported to his council on a meeting he had with Floersh, "The archbishop very definitely wants the Sulpicians to take his proposed Minor Seminary. He proposed that he would give all the help in men we needed."[23] The following March, the provincial council voted three to one in favor of accepting the Louisville seminary, but without unanimity McDonald once again postponed a final decision. The negative voice, not identified in the minutes, expressed doubt that the "Sulpicians knew how to run a minor seminary" and concluded that the young Sulpicians tended toward teaching in major seminaries.[24] On 5 April 1949, however, the council definitely decided to accept Floersh's offer; there was no discussion and no dissenting vote recorded in the minutes.[25]

Joseph White was appointed rector of the Louisville seminary, which was scheduled to open in 1952. In the interim, White was encouraged to pursue a Ph.D. in education at the University of Louisville. Floersh, who had been a seminarian in Rome for the entire twelve-year course and had founded Bellarmine College in Louisville, urged White to attend the Catholic University of America, as he had prohibited his priests from attending the University of Louisville. To sanction White's enrollment there "would be taken by the Catholics of Louisville as an implicit approval of the University by me for the faithful at large."[26] Hence, McDonald sent White to Washington (though ultimately he obtained his doctorate at Saint Louis University). Except for minor changes, the contract for the Detroit seminary was the model adopted for the Louisville seminary.[27]

As mentioned in a previous chapter, Flaget and David had founded Saint Thomas's Seminary on a flatboat on their journey down the Ohio River to the see of Bardstown. After several years in a log cabin, the seminary moved to land adjacent to the cathedral in the town of Bardstown. Bishop William George McCloskey moved the seminary to Louisville in 1870; it was closed in 1888 and reopened in 1902 only to close again upon the death of McCloskey in 1909. When the Sulpicians returned to the archdiocese in 1952, they began with just one class in the six-year minor seminary with rooms for 250 students.[28] In 1958 when it achieved its maturity as a full minor seminary there were 192 students enrolled; in 1961, on the eve of the Second Vatican Council, 235 seminarians were taught by eight Sulpicians supplemented by a few priests from the archdiocese of Louisville. The building was elaborate, but the recreational facilities were especially poor. In a sense Saint Thomas's Seminary maintained a pioneer character, as it was on the periphery of the province. It was the only Sulpician minor seminary except for Saint Stephen's in Hawaii, which was not directly connected to a Sulpician major seminary in the same diocese. From the point of view of financial support the seminary seems to have been low among the priorities of the archdiocese of Louisville. Among the Sulpicians stationed there, however, a strong loyalty and dedication to Saint Thomas's prevailed.

The Sulpicians were invited to take charge of several other seminaries during the period from 1945 to 1960: Fall River, Massachusetts, and Columbus, Ohio, and seminaries as distant as the Philippine Islands and the Union of South Africa. The French province had established a mission seminary in the Saigon diocese in the 1930s, and the Canadian province had founded mission seminaries in Japan and Colombia during the 1930s and 1940s. In the 1960s the U.S. province engaged in missionary efforts in Africa and Latin America. Lawrence Bender, an American Sulpician, served in four Latin American seminaries (as well as in Samoa). His most recent assignment was in Panama (1978 to 1985).

The U.S. province experienced continuous growth during the 1950s but not in proportion to the growth of the church in the nation. Personnel shortages and overcrowded seminaries were common problems during this period. Archbishop Thomas A. Connolly of Seattle (1950–1975) relieved the overcrowded conditions at Saint Edward's when he built a new major seminary that opened in 1958. The financial conditions at both Saint Edward's and Saint Thomas's were a constant drain upon the province's resources. Hence, John Fenlon's insistence on ownership of the Seattle seminary had proved to be counterproductive. Both Lardner and McDonald had hoped that the archbishop (Seattle was made an archdiocese in 1951) would assume ownership, but instead Connolly merely helped pay off the annual deficit.

Saint Charles' College in Catonsville was also overcrowded, with 420 students enrolled in 1959. To relieve such conditions a new college building with its own chapel was erected in 1962, providing individual rooms for the students. The Paca Street philosophy seminary, with its very old buildings, demanded continual capital improvements, and overcrowding at Theological College was relieved by the erection of a new wing. Relations between the Sulpicians and the archdiocese of Baltimore during Michael Curley's episcopate had been very good, symbolized by the one-million-dollar fund drive for the construction of the Roland Park seminary. Since Saint Mary's is a national seminary owned not by the archdiocese but by the Sulpicians, this was a particularly generous move. Curley's successor, Francis Patrick Keough (1948–1960), was an alumnus of Saint-Sulpice in Paris. Keough was cordially supportive of his seminary, but he released few Baltimore priests to the society: in the decade between 1949 and 1959 only 3 men entered Saint Sulpice from the archdiocese of Baltimore. Archbishop Mitty, determined to develop his diocesan clergy, was also very reluctant to release men to join the Sulpicians. Only 6 seminarians from the archdiocese of San Francisco entered the society from 1931 to 1959. Seattle, always short of diocesan clergy, released 4 men from 1931 to 1959. In 1959, 130 Sulpicians were staffing twelve seminaries with a total enrollment of 2,600 students. Hence, the province was dependent on non-Sulpician priests and laymen to provide their students with theological education.[29]

Lloyd McDonald had been the superior of the Solitude for two years (1941–1943), during which time he was also superior of Saint Mary's philosophy seminary on Paca Street. Although his dual role was not common, it does signify the inherently ambiguous character of the American Sulpician Solitude. One may recall the 1898 conflict between Magnien and Captier on the issue of establishing an American Solitude; the superior general was adamant about the need for all Sulpician candidates to immerse themselves in the priestly piety of the French school, and Magnien was equally adamant about the need to adapt French spirituality to the American character. In retrospect both seem to have been correct; the establishment of an American Solitude did tend to remove American Sulpicians from specifically French forms of piety and to let them be free to absorb outlooks and attitudes more consonant with "American" spirituality.

Even John Carroll had considered the Sulpician spirituality too severe. John Fenlon was ambivalent about his experiences in the Solitude at Issy; he deeply admired the French zeal with its flare for the contemplative life, but because he considered Americans to be practical and businesslike he had little confidence in their ability to grasp the inherent value of a Solitude based on contemplation and isolation. Hence, when the American Solitude was established in a house adjacent to Saint Charles', each of the solitaires taught a class to earn his bed and board and to gain teaching experience. Although the Solitude was structured on the seminary model—with periods of prayer, silence, and classroom instruction on the rule, on spiritual direction, and on priestly piety and social poise—the rationale for teaching was indeed very businesslike and practical. When the provincial council discussed a proposal to abolish the custom of assigning solitaires to teach, there was a great deal of concern on how they would occupy their time—as if the life of prayer and general study would not be sufficient.[30]

American practicality affected the ways in which Sulpician spirituality was incorporated into the U.S. province. This American Sulpician spirituality was clearly manifested in one Sulpician's persistent Americanist slip. For years he introduced his students to Olier's form of mental prayer, but rather than saying "Jesus before your eyes [adoration], in your heart [love], and in your hands [cooperation]," he reversed the order, thereby unconsciously implying that the path to adoration and love of God begins in the practical realm. Several Sulpicians who passed through the traditional American Solitude, where Tronson's late seventeenth-century *Particular Examens* were required reading, could not identify themselves with its formula for contemplative character. There was a strong consensus among the many Sulpicians I interviewed that the reason they entered the society was to be a spiritual director rather than a professor or teacher. Few considered the Solitude a very positive experience. Such ambivalence reflects the general confusion of a society of diocesan priests that has its roots in both diocesan and religious life.

In 1941, because of personnel considerations, the Solitude moved from the Saint Charles's location to that of old Saint Mary's Seminary. Since over two hundred students were occupying the Paca Street seminary, the Solitude was later moved to the Dohme estate (now Roland Park Country School for Girls), adjacent to Saint Mary's in Roland Park. In the mid-1960s while the seminary was fostering individual responsibility within a relatively flexible schedule, the Sulpician Solitude also loosened its routine with longer periods of recreation, but it was nevertheless highly structured according to the practical zeal so characteristic of the Sulpician charism.

Lloyd McDonald was a traditionalist who stressed the communal identity of the society. In a 1959 letter to all the priests of the province, McDonald reminds them of the first article in the society's constitution of that time, which states that the primary object of the society is "personal sanctification" while the secondary object is to prepare men for the priesthood. Although many would interpret the above by the statement that one achieves personal sanctification through preparing men for the priesthood, McDonald's interpretation was that personal sanctification entailed a separate cultivation of the spiritual life. His letter focuses on violations of the spirit of obedience and poverty that he had observed during his canonical visitations to the houses during his second term as provincial (1954–1959). McDonald found the origins of these violations in "a growing spirit of independence concerning the duties and functions entrusted to us in the Seminary. . . . This spirit of independence [is] . . . expressed by 'I don't think it is necessary.' " He listed six abuses:

1. In failure to get permission for trips.
2. In failure to get permission for outside work.
3. In publishing without permission.
4. In failure to follow all that is required by Articles 43–49 [which deal with attendance at all the spiritual exercises of the seminary community].
5. In lack of care about [regular] direction of penitents.
6. In the failure to observe the confidence and secrecy of Council matters [i.e., faculty meetings].[31]

The spirit of independence was, according to McDonald, manifested in the general trend away from the

> spirit of Christ toward poverty, deprivation, [and] detachment. . . . Our young students come to us today with much good will in their hearts; but they are products of the age of cars, movies, phones, radio, television, air-conditioned homes—the age of pleasure and comfort. You know how many cannot take the Seminary and leave. Only one thing can hold them—the vision of the real Christ of the Cross and the Resurrection. We have a glorious calling and a sacred duty to set before them the full example of Christ—like living in poverty and detachment.

McDonald concludes by stating that the "work of St. Sulpice is sound and good" and that "among us we have saints." Nevertheless, the tendencies toward a spirit of independence and worldliness were factors that obviously disturbed McDonald's vision of the ideal Sulpician.[32] Clearly the province was moving toward a principle of freedom and individual responsibility and away from uniformity and authoritarianism. That the spirit of independence was taking hold in the American province on the eve of the Second Vatican Council is an instance of the breakdown of traditions in the modernization of the seminary and the professionalization of the clergy.

Such modernization was exemplified in liturgical practices. Dialogue masses were introduced at various times during the late 1950s. Although a few Sulpicians—such as Eugene Walsh, William Morris, William O'Shea, and Frank Norris—were involved in the liturgical movement, the Sulpician seminaries were not in the forefront of liturgical developments. It was not until the Sacred Congregation of Rites issued instructions on the liturgy that some seminaries felt free to make changes, while others did not even follow the spirit or letter of these instructions. For example, John Sullivan, rector of Saint Thomas's Seminary in Seattle, indicated in 1956 that he felt little need for a dialogue Mass since the seminarians followed the liturgy in their missals. However, he did allow the dialogue Mass on a trial basis twice a week. The faculty at Saint John's Seminary, Detroit, which had approved a weekly dialogue Mass as early as 1954, adopted a solemn Mass for the daily community liturgy in 1958.[33]

The Sulpicians were in the vanguard of the professionalization of seminary education, a process that entailed acquiring accreditation by secular agencies and certification of the faculty. Of the ninety-four seminaries in the United States in 1959, only eleven were accredited. As mentioned previously, Thomas C. Mulligan, rector of Saint Edward's Seminary, successfully pursued accreditation with the Western Association of Schools and Colleges for both the secondary and college levels in the mid-1930s. When he became rector of Saint Patrick's in Menlo Park in 1944, he followed the same pattern for the college courses of studies. Saint Charles' received accreditation with the Middle States Association of Colleges and Secondary Schools in the 1930s, and the combined college course at Saint Charles' and Saint Mary's philosophy seminary on Paca Street was accredited by that agency in 1951. Thus nearly one-half of those seminaries accredited by 1959 were run by the Sulpicians.

Cornelius Cuyler and J. Cyril Dukehart were national leaders in the movement for the professionalization of high-school and college seminaries. Cuyler, who was dean of studies at Saint Charles's for many years, was active in the annual Minor Seminary Conference sponsored by the Catholic University of America. Dukehart, who was influenced in the accreditation tradition of Mulligan in Seattle, was appointed president of Saint Charles' College but was unable to introduce academic reforms. Perhaps his abrasive style of administration, rather than his policies, was at the source of the conflict between him and the faculty. He left Saint Charles' in 1958 to become head of the seminary section of the National Catholic Educational Association. In 1959 he wrote that seminaries suffered "an isolation from and an insulation against the main stream of current educational thought, method and administration."[34] With outside agencies making on-site evaluations of accredited seminaries, the professionalization process appears to some as an assault upon the traditional separatism of the seminary.

As mentioned earlier in this chapter, the foundation of the Jesuit publication *Theological Studies* (1940) and the establishment of the Catholic Theological Society in 1949 gradually fostered a moderately critical spirit toward the manualization of theological education. In his encyclical *Divino Afflante Spiritu* (1943), Pius XII encourages a revival of scripture studies, which had a positive impact upon the intellectual life of the seminaries. Theologians such as Henri de Lubac, Jean Daniélou, and Yves Congar were influential among Sulpician professors. In the pages of *The Voice*, a publication of Saint Mary's Seminary, one clearly perceives the force of new ideas in theological education. For example, in the December 1956 issue, two young Sulpicians, Frank B. Norris and Raymond E. Brown, wrote articles discussing the recent trends in Christology and scripture studies. Norris, with a blend of biblical exegesis and Christology, examines the meaning of "the Lord Incarnate." Brown's article, "Priest and King," was an analysis of the Qumran community's concept of the Messiah as revealed in the Dead Sea Scrolls and the traditions of messianism.[35]

The tercentenary of the death of Jean-Jacques Olier was celebrated in 1957. In March of that year, *The Voice* published several articles on Olier and the society, one of which was Eugene Walsh's study of the French school of spirituality with particular emphasis upon the relationship between Olier and Bérulle's spirituality; the article develops the "original charism" of the founder some ten years before the term became popular during the Second Vatican Council.[36] The next issue (April 1957) features a lengthy examination of the contribution of Rudolf Bultmann, which is actually a summary of a public lecture on Bultmann delivered by David M. Stanley, S.J. For Catholic seminarians to be introduced to the ideas of this German existentialist theologian in 1957 was quite unusual.[37] In February of 1958, a noted biblical scholar, Roderick A.F. MacKenzie, S.J., then professor of the Jesuit seminary in the University of Toronto, was the featured speaker during Catholic Bible Week at Saint Mary's. (John L. McKenzie, S.J., was a lecturer during 1959.) William F. Albright, professor of Semitics at The Johns Hopkins University, was in attendance, and one of his former students, Raymond E. Brown, spoke on the pre-Christian concept of mystery. Brown, who received his Ph.D. in Semitic languages from Johns Hopkins in 1958, was a recent recipient of a research fellowship at the American School of Oriental Research in Jerusalem.[38]

The Sulpicians had always been considered as learned, but their mark upon the intellectual life of the church had been limited to writings related to religious formation or to theological and philosophical treatises useful for seminaries. Only in scripture studies have Sulpicians contributed works of pure scholarship. LeHir, Vigouroux, Fillion, Gigot, Brassac, and Brown represent a continuum of over 125 years of Sulpician scholars who have achieved international recognition. (Later, Addison Wright and John Kselman continued this legacy.)

The list of lecturers at Saint Mary's during 1958-1959 included such progressive thinkers and activists as John Courtney Murray, George Higgins, and Gustav Weigel. The *Voice* published reports on these lecturers, and its book-review section included works by many of the leading European progressives. Of course, many Sulpicians were very traditional, and several *Voice* articles were reflective of the traditional ambience of seminary life of the 1950s, but the opponents of advanced theology, ecclesiology, and exegesis, such as Joseph Fenton, Francis Connell, and John Steinmueller, were not represented among its articles or among its books under review. It was a period of general calm in church and society; the civil rights movement, campus unrest, the putative sexual revolution, and the development of rising expectations of reform and renewal in the Catholic community were trends beyond the horizons of the late 1950s. In retrospect, the progressive movement of this period represented by the Sulpician publication, *The Voice*, may be viewed as the prologue to the dramatic changes that occurred during the 1960s.

The introduction of new ideas by way of guest lecturers and articles in *The Voice* was matched by changes in the content and methodology of courses taught by some Sulpician theologians. By the spring of 1956, James Laubacher, representing the aforementioned trend, suggested a provincewide meeting of Sulpician theologians to discuss problems with the traditional curriculum and the need for a new synthesis of theological explanation and for an updated apologetic. Laubacher, a member of the provincial council, was a very traditionalist rector who presided at his daily spiritual conferences at Saint Mary's with a strong sense of authority and with a deep reverence for the rule. Hence, his promotion of fundamental academic changes in the theological curriculum carried great credibility. His doctoral dissertation at the Catholic University of Louvain (1939) was on the development of doctrine in the work of George Tyrrell. To choose a Modernist for his principal subject of study was quite rare in the post-*Pascendi* academic world.[39] Laubacher treated Tyrrell with respect and was distinctively objective in his analysis without any of the banalities so characteristic of a manualist's approach to "heterodox" deviants.

In his proposal for the conference, Laubacher stresses the need for the dogma course to rely no longer upon Tanquerey's apologetical approach, which "reflects the mentality of the period of the Council of Trent." Instead, he asks "should not the aim of our Dogma course be to present Dogma as a living body of truth having a unity and a vital purpose rather than a series of defined truths. . . ?" He suggests the "doctrine of the Mystical Body . . . as the central theme of all Theology . . . [thereby linking] all the Tracts . . . as aspects or constitutive elements of this theme."[40]

He also wished to change the method of class presentation from the "stereotyped order of *status quaestionis* (i.e., scripture, tradition, reason) to an expository method. To include more scriptural exegesis, Laubacher proposes "to introduce each tract [e.g., *De Ecclesia, De Verbo Incarnato*] by tracing the *development of doctrine* from revelation through the history of the Church and thus show how the Church came to represent understanding of the doctrine. Then in the theological explanation more scripture could be introduced." The theological explanation had to be presented "*ad mentem Sancti Thomae* [but] might not there be more adaptation of St. Thomas to the 20th century and would it not be the mind of St. Thomas to emphasize . . . the interrelation between the doctrines [thus] bringing out the practical application to Christian living." To incorporate these changes into a text, rather than provide supplemental material, was preferable to Laubacher. He proposed an extensive revision of Tanquerey by enlarging sections with emphasis on the theme of the Mystical Body and the development of doctrine and contracting those sections which deal defensively with theological controversies. He also wished to separate apologetics from the course on fundamental theology, thereby allowing the latter to center on the doctrine of the Mystical Body. To remove canon law and moral theology from the tract on the sacraments would allow the students to focus "on the unity and beauty of the doctrine on the Sacraments."[41] Laubacher's proposal, no doubt influenced by other theologians at Saint Mary's, followed the tradition of John Hogan's 1901 publication, *Clerical Studies*, and clearly presaged many trends characteristic of the era of Vatican II, particularly the stress upon the organic unity within the development of doctrine.

The meeting of Sulpician theologians was not held until June of 1957. Without evidence of the discussions one may surmise from an examination of subsequent meetings of the theological faculties that Laubacher's proposals had little impact upon the curriculum. An additional hour of scripture was added to the weekly schedule; sacramental theology was freed from the juridical influences of canon law and moral theology. Perhaps Laubaucher's notions on the development of doctrine, on a thematic approach to the logical exposition of theology, and on a positive nondefensive apologetics were incorporated into lectures on an ad hoc basis. Strained by the burden of being rector of

Saint Mary's for fourteen years, Laubacher resigned his office in 1957 and became the superior of the Solitude. The implementation of portions of his new theological agenda was achieved only after the entire demanualization of the theology courses and after the introduction of the new ecclesiology and of the transcendental Thomism of Karl Rahner into the seminary curriculum during the second half of the 1960s.

The Second Vatican Council convened on 11 October 1962. During the second and third sessions (1963-1964), James Laubacher was present as the *peritus* for Lawrence Shehan, the recently installed archbishop of Baltimore. An alumnus of Saint Charles' and of Saint Mary's (two years of philosophy and one year of theology), Shehan mentions in his memoirs the many Sulpicians who guided him through his seminary years.[42] He recalls his debt of gratitude to the former rector of Saint Mary's: "The theologian I knew best and in whom I had the greatest confidence was Father James Laubacher, S.S. . . . While I was Auxiliary at Baltimore . . . he was kind enough to serve as my confessor and spiritual director."[43] Laubacher assisted Shehan with his notable work on the Commission on Ecumenism and on Religious Liberty.

John P. McCormick, since 1949 rector of Theological College, was the *peritus* for Archbishop O'Boyle, who since his installation as the first ordinary of the archdiocese of Washington, D.C. had gravitated to the Sulpician house associated with Catholic University. With a Ph.D. in classics and a background in seminary administration and in liturgy, McCormick's expertise was particularly valuable when O'Boyle was elected to the commission on seminary education. As chairman of the administrative board of the NCWC and ordinary of the nation's capital, O'Boyle was regarded by several European prelates as the voice of the American hierarchy. McCormick wrote to McDonald, "I am emphasizing the necessity of preventing a return to the pre-*Divino Afflante Spiritu* repression of Catholic scriptural exegesis."[44]

John R. Sullivan, rector of Saint Thomas's Seminary in Seattle, was the *peritus* for Archbishop Thomas Connolly during the first session of the council. The rector and archbishop had forged a very friendly and informal relationship. Sullivan did his graduate work at Louvain with Laubacher and, like Laubacher, was on the provincial council during this period. Sullivan reported to McDonald that Raymond Brown and other scripture scholars made a positive impact upon the bishops for "a sane approach" to the discussion on Revelation. He noted that "Leo Maher [of Santa Rosa, California] invited him [Brown] to a dinner of about ten bishops (including Archbishop McGucken [of San Francisco]) and they all told me how well-balanced and well-informed he is."[45] The French, Canadian, and U.S. Sulpicians in Rome for the council arranged for a special ceremony on the Feast of the Presentation, a day traditional in Sulpician seminaries for alumni and students to renew their clerical promises. Superior General Girard asked Sullivan and McCormick to draw up invitations to the U.S. prelates. The celebration was held at Saint Mary of the Angels, the titular church of Cardinal Paul E. Leger, the Canadian Sulpician archbishop of Montreal. In attendance were over 150 archbishops and bishops. The occasion included 35 prelates from the United States.[46]

During the council several Sulpicians published articles related to its decrees. Since 1962, Frank B. Norris, who was the most advanced Sulpician on the faculty of Menlo Park, was publishing a regular column in the *Monitor* of San Francisco. According to John Sullivan, Bishop Maher and Archbishop McGucken "were worried about Norris . . . and the bad influence he is having on seminaries."[47] When Paul Purta became rector of Saint Patrick's in August of 1964, he reported to McDonald that Norris "has had a self-initiated interview with the archbishop [that] . . . seems to have served both to great advantage. Because I informed him [i.e., Norris] that I intend to give him much work during the coming year, Frank has begun to cut down outside activity. . . . He submitted his final column [in the *Monitor*] this past week."[48] The next year Frank Norris and Eugene Walsh had essays published in *Apostolic Renewal in the Seminary in the Light of the Vatican Council II*. In his article "The 'De Ecclesia' Tract in the Seminary," Norris elaborates the contemporary relevance of Gustav Weigel's remark that "all theology was in some way ecclesiology. . . ." Norris wrote, "The truth of Weigel's observation has come to me at every turn. The creation, elevation, and fall of man; the Incarnation; the Redemption; grace: none of these tracts can possibly be understood correctly apart from the ecclesial context in which it is situated."[49] In his essay, Eugene A. Walsh explains the dependent relationship between liturgy and the apostolate, revealing his adherence to the most recent reforms and to his old attachments to the thought of Virgil Michel, O.S.B., on relationships between liturgy and social action.[50]

During the four years of the council, the Sulpician institutions, particularly the major seminaries, experienced several changes in the rule governing the liturgical, academic, and social character of the daily schedule. Special Bible vigils and communal recitation of portions of the divine office replaced traditional devotional exercises. Tronson's *Particular Examens* were unknown to those who entered a Sulpician seminary after the mid-1960s. As participants in a society experiencing the impulses of social reform, seminarians entered into the various social movements of the day. The life of the seminary tended toward individual responsibility rather than the dicta of traditional authority. However, in 1965, when the conciliar decree on priestly formation was published, these changes, particularly in the social life of the seminarian, were sporadic tendencies even in progressive dioceses.[51]

Change was more likely to occur in Sulpician seminaries in which a majority of the faculty decided questions of policy rather than in the Roman-style seminary in which all final authority was invested in the rector. There were, of course, instances of faculty polarization that affected the student body. Lloyd McDonald, a strong traditionalist, attempted to steer a moderate course. As he mentioned to the faculty of Saint John's Seminary (Plymouth, Michigan) in April 1965; "There is also the problem of the old and the new, in things intellectual, student attitudes, etc. We should not be afraid of the new things, but not throw away the old either. Try to find where the true middle ground is."[52]

Student-faculty relations tended to suffer during this period; the Sulpician seminaries gradually adopted the measure of establishing a faculty-student committee to facilitate communication and prevent polarization. For example, in May of 1965, a constitution of the Faculty-Student Conference on Seminary Life for Saint John's was approved. The purpose of the conference, a permanent body of the seminary governance structure, was to "make studies and offer recommendations to the faculty . . . in all matters of community interest. This purpose is to be carried out in the spirit of the Second Vatican Council, particularly according to the intention of the Church expressed in the Constitution *De Ecclesia*."[53] The establishment of this conference placed Saint John's in the forefront of seminary reform in 1965. It is also a tribute to the flexibility of Edward Hogan, rector of the Detroit seminary after 1959. The leadership of John Dearden, appointed archbishop of Detroit upon the death of Mooney in 1958 (and made a cardinal in 1969), must have injected high expectations for reform and renewal in the archdiocese and the seminary. A theologian and former rector of Saint Mary's Seminary in Cleveland, Dearden was aligned with the progressives at the council. As early as September 1963, Dearden, according to the minutes of the faculty meeting at Saint John's, indicated "that the seminaries must be opened up—that we can do too much scheduling—there should be more freedom for study on their own."[54]

In 1966, at the celebration of the 175th anniversary of the foundation of Saint Mary's Seminary in Baltimore, Archbishop Gabriel Garrone, head of the Vatican's Congregation of Seminaries and Universities, was the guest of honor. Garrone's talks and an article by Monsignor John Tracy Ellis appeared in a special anniversary issue of *The Voice*. Each addressed the general impact of the Second Vatican Council on seminary life with references to the conciliar decrees, particularly the "Decree on Priestly Formation." Garrone elaborated on the creative tension between the need for seminaries to adapt to the modern world and the need to develop a "deep interior life" in order that adaptation may be balanced. He also spoke of scripture as the unifying principle in curriculum reform and emphasized the importance of placing reform within the guidelines established by seminary authorities, national episcopal conferences, and by his own congregation in Rome.[55]

John Tracy Ellis's article stresses the need for intellectual excellence and a "genuine love of learning" within the seminary. He views the movement of the seminary away from isolation to affiliation with Catholic universities as a positive means to further academic growth and the intellectual life. Few historians could match Ellis's understanding of the story of seminary education in the United States. An alumnus of Theological College, he was influenced by Anthony Viéban and Louis Arand, the Sulpician president of Divinity College. Hence he had experienced directly the impact of the Sulpicians on seminary education. With great insight Ellis chose John Hogan as the paramount figure of the past who would be at home in the postconciliar seminary. According to Ellis, Hogan would have been "cheered by the conciliar directive that excessive multiplying of subjects and classes is to be avoided."[56]

In 1967, the Synod of Bishops met in Rome; successor of the NCWC, the National Conference of Catholic Bishops (NCCB), directed its committee on pastoral research "to conduct an extensive study of the life and ministry of the American Priest."[57] The NCCB was also sponsoring research on priestly formation. In the spring of 1967, Lloyd McDonald resigned because of a serious illness, and the following June, Paul Purta became the first elected provincial of the Sulpicians in the United States.[58] At the 1966 general chapter it had been decided that each province should hold its own chapter. McDonald's resignation was a catalyst in the formation of the first U.S. chapter, which, because of its representative character, was entitled a senate.

After attending Saint Mary's Seminary, Purta was ordained for the diocese of Scranton in 1952. Subsequent to his three-year service at the minor seminary at Mountain View, California, he entered the Solitude, from which he went to Rome to study canon law at the Lateran University. Purta then joined the faculty at Saint Thomas's in Seattle, and after four years he was transferred to Saint Mary's in Roland Park (1963). The following year Purta was appointed rector of Saint Patrick's Seminary, where he presided until his election as provincial. He was the first Sulpician born in the twentieth century to hold the post. Although there was still a sense of optimism in the church and the society in 1967, it was not long before disillusionment set in, before the priesthood and the religious life suffered an "identity crisis," before the idealism of the 1960s expired and the cynicism of the 1970s became dominant, and before respect for all institutional authority became almost an achronism. In this condition it was difficult for Saint Sulpice or any seminary community to be a positive influence on the ecclesiastical life in the United States.

Epilogue

Change and Consolidation (1967–1986)

The provincialate of Paul Purta opened in 1967 during a period of optimistic belief in the inherent value of renewal, reform, and experimentation. Although a slight decline in seminary enrollment was evident in 1967 and the traditional boarding high-school seminary was rapidly disappearing, there was a broad consensus within the province and the church in the United States on the positive character of liberal change. By the end of 1968 the mood in church and society had experienced a profound shift. Daniel and Philip Berrigan had led an assault on draft records in Catonsville, Maryland, marking a move toward radicalism among Catholic war resisters; the assasination of Martin Luther King, Jr., resulted in riots in many American cities; and the idealism of Eugene McCarthy's challenge to Lyndon Johnson was dashed by the assassination of Robert Kennedy and culminated in the cynicism and violence of the Democratic National Convention in Chicago. The expectation that Pope Paul VI would confirm the liberal report of the Vatican commission on birth control was frustrated by the 1968 publication of *Humane Vitae*. Gradually an antireform reaction gained momentum, symbolized by the publication in 1971 of James Hitchcock's

The Decline and Fall of Radical Catholicism, which catalogs the rhetoric and behavior of the extreme left and in the process tends to discredit moderate progressive reform. Indeed, Hitchcock concludes that the liberals in the church were demonstrating a loss of faith.[1]

The growing pessimism was exacerbated by the increasing numbers of persons leaving the religious orders and the priesthood; their departure weakened the voice of reform and strengthened the conservative reaction. Within this context of increasing polarization in the church, the Sulpicians in the United States were situated on the moderate left, but from the conservative point of view they were perceived as extremists. Frequently the Sulpician drive for renewal and reform was used as a scapegoat by those who sought a facile explanation for the crisis in the seminary and who did not appreciate the cultural factors influencing declining enrollments and the exodus from the priesthood. Because polemicists in both camps tended to caricature their opponents, it is difficult to attain a nuanced appreciation of positions on a wide spectrum of issues. One must distinguish various shades of opinion as well as divergencies of positions on specific issues. For example, during this period several Sulpicians were traditionalists on authority questions but progressive on moral issues such as birth control, social justice, and peace. Of course, there were Sulpicians located on both extremes of the spectrum, but rarely did they achieve a significant following within the society.

The ten-year provincialate of Paul Purta opened with the support of a broad consensus within the society. Purta was the first "modern" Sulpician provincial: he valued dialogue and easily coped with dissent and conflict, he had a command of the current ecclesiology and applied it to practical governance situations within the seminary and the province, and he articulated the role of Saint Sulpice in the United States in a language abundant with scriptural, theological, and ecclesiological imagery. One definition of *modern* is open-endedness or constant change; Purta's provincialate is characterized by his attempt to provide a structure through which change might be channeled with the maximum of confidence and consensus. As the first elected provincial, Purta was a leader in developing governance structures that were in accord with the principles of subsidiarity and collegiality. Prior to his administration provincial appointments were made with little or no consultation with those individuals who were transferred or elevated to positions of authority. The conciliar reform fostered the breakdown of the traditional authoritarian character of the provincial, and Purta embodied the new spirit of stewardship. Several committees were established to deal with a variety of issues. The most significant one was the research and planning committee (1972), which directed the establishment adjacent to Saint Charles' College of Saint Charles' Villa for retired Sulpicians, engendered a thorough rationalization of budgetary and investment procedures, and planned the first provincewide renewal conference in 1974.[2]

As noted in the previous chapter, the Sulpician institutions, like most seminaries, were subject to the cultural forces affecting higher education. The Sulpicians of the late 1960s and 1970s directly experienced racial turbulence and student unrest. In 1967 students at Saint Charles' College mounted a strike to protest the lack of progressive changes in discipline. Saint Mary's Seminary on Paca Street was located in the vortex of a neighborhood where turbulent riots followed the assassination of Martin Luther King, Jr. Under the leadership of William J. Lee, the Sulpician rector, students and faculty responded to their black and white neighbors who had been victimized by the conflagration. When Richard Nixon ordered the invasion of Cambodia in 1970, the faculty at Saint Patrick's Seminary, acting on the students' recommendations, suspended classes for several days in protest against the escalation of the war in Southeast Asia. The general anti-institutionalism of the times permeated the seminary structure as well as the life style of Sulpician faculties. For example, Saint Patrick's Seminary formed small, personalist-based groups that dealt with prayer life, academic issues, and disciplinary questions. The general sense of individual freedom and responsibility on college campuses was manifested in such measures as permission to work outside the seminary, liberal rules on entertaining guests, and freedom to spend weekends away from the seminary.

As rector of Saint Patrick's Seminary (1964–1967), Purta responded positively to the ecumenical developments that established the Graduate Theological Union (G.T.U.) at Berkeley, California.[3] There was some hope of a gradual move toward an affiliation between the G.T.U. and Saint Patrick's, but Archbishop Joseph T. McGucken opposed the idea, and in 1970 the Sacred Congregation of Seminaries and Universities officially prohibited an affiliation.[4] When the Solitude moved to Berkeley in 1977, it formed a loose affiliation with the G.T.U. The Sulpician solitaires attended the Institute of Spirituality and Worship at the Jesuit School of Theology. By this time the traditional emphasis on mental prayer and the spiritual exercises in the Solitude was replaced by a stress upon spirituality, scripture, and a specialized preparation for life in the contemporary seminary, with particular focus on the relationships between counseling and spiritual direction.

As noted in the previous chapter, the Sulpician seminaries had set the pace in seeking accreditation by such secular agencies as the Western States and Middle States associations; they were also in the vanguard of the movement for accreditation by the American Association of Theological Schools, which until 1967 had limited its evaluations to

Protestant divinity schools and seminaries. The most significant ecumenical thrust of the society in the United States, however, was the establishment of the Ecumenical Institute of Theology at Saint Mary's Seminary in 1968. The idea for this pioneer institution germinated in 1967 in exploratory conversations among Bishop Harry Lee Doll of the episcopal diocese of Maryland; Father C. Stephen Mann, an Episcopal priest and a graduate student at Johns Hopkins; and Professor William F. Albright of Johns Hopkins. William F. Hill, a Sulpician at Saint Mary's, entered the discussions, and soon it became evident that as the oldest chartered university in Maryland Saint Mary's would be the most suitable location for an ecumenical graduate school of theology. John F. Dede, the Sulpician rector at Saint Mary's, was responsive to the idea. Early in 1968 Cardinal Lawrence Shehan, who had been active in ecumenism, approved the institute, which by this time had been endorsed by Jewish, Orthodox, and Protestant leaders. On 3 May 1968, Doll and Shehan appeared on television to announce the opening of the institute the following September. With Mann as the first dean, the institute opened with an enrollment of seventy students, most of whom were in pursuit of graduate degrees in theology or religious education. In 1985, James Brashler, a scripture scholar with experience in continuing education at the Claremont School of Religion, Claremont, California, became dean. Although there had been plans to establish an ecumenical seminary at Saint Mary's in the late 1960s, both Shehan and Rome had opposed the project. However, the Ecumenical Institute of Theology represents a significant development in Sulpician institutional life in the United States.[5]

Several other positive developments occurred during Purta's provincialate. Many Sulpicians were influential in the preparation of the bishops' document on priestly formation. Eugene Van Antwerp was head of the seminary division of the NCEA, and Purta served on the NCCB's Committee on the Spirituality of the American Priesthood. During the 1970s he led many clergy retreats and workshops related to contemporary ministry. He eagerly supported the missionary thrust of Saint Sulpice and encouraged volunteers to serve in interprovincial seminaries in the Congo, Argentina, Bolivia, Guatemala, and Panama.

In the late 1960s and early 1970s there was a trend to close the high-school seminaries and consolidate the two-year college program of the minor with the two years of philosophy. The phasing out of the high school at Saint Charles', combined with the prohibitively high cost of renovating the old Paca Street seminary, led to the philosophy college moving to Catonsville to form Saint Mary's Seminary College in 1969.[6] The following year low enrollment and high costs led to the closing of Saint Thomas's Seminary in the archdiocese of Louisville.[7] Although this last development was a difficult experience for the Sulpicians involved, it represented the termination of only a nineteen-year commitment. To leave Paca Street, where the Sulpicians had lived since 1791, engendered a severe sense of loss for many Sulpicians, particularly for those who wished to maintain an urban pastoral witness in the Baltimore community. The Sulpicians still maintain a house and the old chapel, which is a national trust. In 1985, under Joseph Bonadio, the Paca Street house became a small center of spirituality for the archdiocese, and liturgies at the chapel are now open to the neighboring community.

Purta urged the provincial council to appoint Eugene Walsh as rector at Theological College in 1968. In the postconciliar age Walsh's liberal theological and liturgical ideas were legitimated, and his open-mindedness was manifested in suggestions for reform. Working with students and faculty Walsh proposed a new governance system that would give students a majority vote and authorize the House Council to veto some decisions made by the provincial council. The council did not accept Walsh's proposed constitution, however, because it violated Sulpician constitutions and Roman and American documents on priestly formation.[8] Under Walsh's leadership Theological College introduced an advisory system, separate from spiritual direction, that became a model for many seminaries throughout the country. The adviser was responsible for working with his advisee on matters related to the student's academic and personal life. He or she was in a sense a pastoral and vocation counselor rather than a spiritual director.

The most difficult problem confronting Theological College was financial. Because the Theology Department at the university did not consider the pastoral program within its purview, the Sulpicians filled the vacuum. In 1969 Walsh appointed two supervisors of Clinical Pastoral Education (CPE) to develop a program that would include a blend of classroom lecture and discussion with supervised field experience. This program was considered a model for seminaries in the United States. (Thomas Reese also developed a similar program at Saint Mary's.) The cost of the program and the rising costs of Theological College resulted in long but ultimately successful negotiations with the university for financial support and permission to raise student fees for room and board.[9]

As provincial in the postconciliar church, Purta's major responsibility was to maintain the Sulpician way of life within the context of renewal and reform. From 1968 to 1977 Purta confronted a series of crises, each of which entailed problems between a Sulpician seminary and the local ordinary. During a period in which there is a broad consensus within the church, relations among students, faculty, administration, and bishops proceed smoothly. In the post-conciliar church, however, there was no consensus, and relationships, particularly between the bishop and the seminary, were characterized by periodic conflict and polarization. Although an episcopal consensus was behind the bishops' Program of Priestly Formation (1970), conflicts arose as to how the guidelines of that document were to be implemented. The Sulpician system of religious formation also became problematic during this period because the society's constitution holds that the faculty possesses policy-making authority. A strong rector who is able to broker a consensus within the faculty and who is able to articulate that consensus to the bishop and represent the latter's views to the faculty, with particular emphasis on the Sulpicians' traditional deference to episcopal authority, can bring about harmony. However, some students and faculty members may feel driven to take a stand on a particularly controversial issue, which action may be viewed by a bishop as dissident behavior, resulting in a crisis of authority. Since there were frequent periods of tension and polarization within the Sulpician community, Purta was confronted with internal as well as external crises. At each of the Sulpician theologates a crisis occurred, and in each situation the Sulpician system appeared to be cumbersome in the reaching of the neat resolution of the conflict.

On 25 July 1968, Pope Paul VI issued his encyclical *Humanae Vitae*. Five days later, Charles E. Curran, a priest of the diocese of Rochester and an instructor in moral theology at the Catholic University of America, and nine other professors of theology at the university, held a press conference in which they issued a 600-word "Statement of Dissent" to *Humanae Vitae* endorsed by seventy-two Catholic theologians throughout the country. Curran and others elaborated on the ecclesiological and natural law bases for the dissent, which according to Lawrence Shehan was a scandal; "never in recorded history . . . has a solemn proclamation of a Pope been perceived by any group of Catholic people with so much disrespect and contempt."[10]

Five Sulpicians at Saint Mary's—joined by three more some days later—were signatories of the "Statement of Dissent." After meeting with Paul Purta and John Dede, the president of the seminary, Shehan met with the dissenters on 25 August. The Sulpicians had explained the basis of their action in a letter to Shehan, but he wished to receive assurance that nothing contrary to *Humanae Vitae* would be taught at the seminary. The meeting concluded with full agreement that the professors would provide their students with the official teaching, but in the event a question arose as to the content of the "Statement of Dissent" they could respond truthfully without hesitation. Hence, both the cardinal and the professors appeared moderately satisfied with the results of this meeting.[11] Shehan, who viewed the dissent movement as symbolic of a deep cultural crisis of faith, was a very loyal Sulpician alumnus, but subsequent to this crisis relations between the diocese and Saint Mary's never achieved a level beyond formal cordiality until Robert Leavitt was appointed president-rector in 1980, long after Shehan had retired.

Saint Mary's needed episcopal support during these years. The national character of Saint Mary's and Sulpician ownership of the institution made the seminary unique. During the early 1970s some students and faculty were perceived as wild dissidents by those who cherished traditional forms of clerical decorum as symbolic of spirituality as well as by moderates who feared such behavior would discredit the reformed seminary. Saint Mary's image among many bishops suffered during this period; many today consider that this condition could have been avoided had there been a local bishop to articulate the generally nonextremist character of the seminary. Since his appointment in 1974, Archbishop William D. Borders has been very supportive of Saint Mary's; indeed he has frequently praised the Sulpician seminary for its excellent preparation for priests to live in the modern world.

Meanwhile, on the Pacific coast, James Laubacher succeeded Paul Purta as rector of Saint Patrick's Seminary. As an alumnus of the seminary of San Francisco, Laubacher was well known in the archdiocese. Reform and renewal were well under way by the time of his appointment in 1967. During the first two years of his administration the faculty established a faculty-student committee responsible for the spiritual, academic, and social aspects of priestly formation. It also created a theology senate composed of administrative staff, faculty, and students and responsible for passing upon committee reports and for dealing with policy issues. During these years the seminary's deacon program evolved from parish assignment in the summer and on weekends to one in which the deacon spent roughly three-fourths of his fourth year in the parish and the remaining fourth in the classroom. Archbishop Joseph McGucken was not sympathetic to these changes and was particularly critical of the deacon program, which Laubacher defended by referring to the documents on priestly formation passed by Vatican Council II and by the NCCB. Laubacher was also active in the archdiocesan priests' senate, which assumed a liberal position on the question of the ordinary's authority on pastoral assignments.[12]

By 1970 polarization between the archbishop and his seminary reached such a level of intensity that McGucken asked the NCCB to establish an ad hoc investigating committee to visit Saint Patrick's and report on its general condition in light of the bishops' program on priestly formation. Although the committee was favorably impressed with the academic character and the religious life of the seminary, including the deacon program, its recommendation included the appointments of a spiritual director and of a vicar for the seminary who would act as a liaison between faculty and bishops.[13]

Because the visitation of January 1971 was initiated without any prior consultation of the administration or faculty, it seems to have exacerbated tensions. James Laubacher resigned in the spring of 1971, and Melvin Farrell became rector. Laubacher's tenure as rector was riddled with controversy as well as personal disappointment. He seems to have been deeply frustrated in his inability to persuade traditionalists to understand the need for renewal and reform; moreover, many of his old classmates from Saint Patrick's felt that he had betrayed them. In August of 1971, the bishops of the province met with Farrell and later submitted a "bishops' paper," portions of which the faculty considered to be in violation of the NCCB program on priestly formation, as well as a repudiation of the report of the visitation committee.

Polarization intensified during the remainder of the academic year of 1971–1972, with a majority of the Sulpician faculty advocating the society's withdrawal from the seminary if some episcopal support was not forthcoming. Purta, the provincial council, and the provincial assembly, which met that summer (1972), wished to avoid the imminent break. Because Purta had the confidence of McGucken and of the province, the Sulpicians managed to maintain a hold on the seminary during this crisis.[14] By the end of the next academic year most of the Sulpicians at Saint Patrick's were replaced by a faculty free from the wounds of polarization. Joseph Bonadio was appointed rector, and he, together with his newly assigned confreres, began to heal the rupture between the archbishop and his seminary.

The story of the society's experience in San Francisco illustrates the general struggle between the transformationists and the preservationists within the church in the United States. Each side interprets the conciliar and NCCB documents on priestly formation in light of their own general perspective on the role of the seminary in the life of the church. In his article on Archbishop McGucken's controversial new cathedral, constructed during this period of polarization, James Gaffey points out that the social-reform prophets challenged his symbol of the institutional church on the grounds that the expenditure violated the principle of social justice in conciliar decrees and encyclicals of John XXIII and Paul VI.[15] Hence, the story of the conflict between the Sulpicians and Archbishop McGucken was but one aspect of a much more general confrontation.

The Sulpicians at Saint John's Seminary in Plymouth also found themselves caught in the grips of polarization. Because Saint John's was a provincial seminary governed by a board of five bishops, including Cardinal John Dearden, the situation at Plymouth was very complicated. According to the available documentation, by 1970 the majority of the bishops of Michigan had lost confidence in the Sulpicians because the faculty held too much authority on matters involving the general direction of the seminary and some faculty members were believed to be too radical. Addison Wright, Saint John's rector and a highly regarded scripture scholar, was closely identified with the faculty. Paul Purta was unable to restore the board's confidence in the seminary, and during negotiations for the regular renewal of the contract with the society the board proposed that it appoint a non-Sulpician rector from the archdiocese of Detroit who would have, as in a Roman-style seminary, final internal authority. With this proposed arrangement the board of bishops could assert direct authority over the seminary. Since specific Sulpician faculty members had alienated some of the bishops and since the province and the seminary had adopted due-process procedures for appointments to the faculty, the proposal for a non-Sulpician rector was also perceived as a way of controlling the composition of the faculty. The bishops viewed their proposal as a reasonable compromise, but because it would undercut the Sulpician system, Purta, the provincial council, and the Sulpician faculty at Saint John's withdrew the society from Saint John's at the end of the academic year 1970–1971.[16] Relations between the society and Cardinal Dearden remained amicable throughout this crisis. In retrospect, Saint John's appears to have been the casualty of a conflict of authority, but in those days of polarization, the Sulpician system appeared to the bishops as fostering an excessive degree of faculty and student autonomy. To the Sulpicians the system represented not only tradition but also contemporary principles of collegiality and subsidiarity.

The Sulpician seminaries in Seattle experienced a similar crisis of authority during the early 1970s that involved the intervention of Archbishop Thomas Connolly in the internal affairs of the seminary. Connolly directly disciplined a student involved in a public incident without going through the due-process procedures of the institution. In defense of those procedures the students at Saint Thomas's went on strike, and this exacerbated the tension. After several sessions of negotiations involving students, faculty, administration, the provincial, and the archbishop, the multifaceted conflict was resolved. That same year, 1971, the chapel of Saint Thomas's Seminary became the center for Saint John Vianney parish, staffed by Sulpicians.[17]

When Raymond G. Hunthausen became archbishop of Seattle (1975), negotiations were initiated for the transfer of ownership of Saint Edward's Seminary (then limited to high-school students) from the Sulpicians to the archdiocese; the transfer was effected in August 1976. That previous spring low enrollments, high costs, and the general trend away from residential preparatory seminaries led the archdiocese to close Saint Edward's. (The Sulpicians had withdrawn from the high-school seminary at Mountain View, California, the previous year.) In the spring of 1977 Archbishop Hunthausen closed Saint

Thomas's theologate and college, not only because of low enrollment, but also because he wanted to incorporate formation of priests into a general ministry training. Although several Sulpicians were directly involved in the preparation of this new program, the provincial council considered the closing of Saint Thomas's precipitous.[18] (The new program has not received final approval by Rome; the seminarians for the archdiocese of Seattle are assigned to various seminaries, with the majority at Theological College.) During the same spring that witnessed the closing of Saint Thomas's, Saint Mary's Seminary College closed after eight years at the Catonsville site.[19] After consultation with the provincial committee for research and planning, the board of trustees felt that low enrollments and high costs compelled them to close the institution. In the Provincial Bulletin of October 1976, the provincial council listed several items under the heading of self-criticism that indicate the toll of ten years of almost continuous crises:

> Still a forest, confusing; no focus, goals need precision.
> More positive leadership. What does that mean?
> Not acting from our goals consciously enough, just responding.
> Still falling apart, fragmenting . . .
> Signs of some encouraging steps to cohesiveness.[20]

In April 1977, Paul Purta announced his resignation, brought about by the strains of office; after a year's graduate study he withdrew from the society and in 1980 withdrew from priestly ministry.[21] This first modern provincial streamlined the governance structures and promoted the Sulpician principle of collegiality and subsidiarity within the general postconciliar spirit of reform and renewal. While Purta was no radical, he was frequently called upon to defend radical confreres. In a crisis he was the consummate diplomat. Active on several committees of priestly formation, he had the confidence of many members of the hierarchy. Perhaps, in a sense, his administration reflected the evolution from the idealism of the 1960s to the skeptical realism of the 1970s. According to his reflections on his administration, Purta regretted that the demands of his office prevented him from exerting a spiritual influence on the province. He also states that "a collegial and consultative style [had] so developed that it often submerged my personal views on issues to the point where some could justly criticize [my] lack of directness and direction."[21]

Upon the resignation of Purta, Edward Frazer, the first consultor, became acting administrator of the province and was elected provincial at the assembly of 1978. A priest from the diocese of Great Falls, Montana, Frazer was educated at the Seattle seminary and served as vice-rector of the philosophy seminary at Paca Street (1968–1969) and rector of Theological College (1971–1976). Ordained in 1961, his perspective was profoundly influenced by the spirit of Vatican II. A creative person with a flair for artistic expression, Frazer was also a very professional executive of the province. He rationalized the administrative staff: he appointed Joseph Reynolds, a layman who had had charge of the staff work since 1969, to the newly created office of administrative assistant; he upgraded the office of provincial secretary to a full-time position and appointed William J. Lee, former president of Saint Mary's Seminary and University at Roland Park, to that office; Louis Reitz was appointed provincial treasurer and, because Frazer had initiated an annual audit of the financial records of the province, the treasurer's office was modernized. In 1977 Purta had appointed James Harkness, a former provincial administrator of the Franciscans, associate director of research and planning; Frazer appointed him director, and then in 1982 he was appointed director of personnel services for the province.

Frazer's top priority was to restore the morale of the province. From 1971 to 1977, Sulpician institutions dropped from eleven to four; student enrollment in the eleven seminaries was 1,408 in 1971, while in 1977 the figure for the four seminaries was 578; twenty-five Sulpicians left the active ministry; seventeen left the society to do pastoral work in local dioceses. Frazer met the challenge of demoralization by making personal visitations to the houses. He was particularly concerned with the ways in which poor morale affects the relationships with bishops. With the support of the provincial council, Frazer strongly supported those rectors who were able to lead their faculty and students along a course of moderation and represent to the bishops the strengths of the Sulpician spirit; in short he aimed to deradicalize the Sulpician image by placing a cap upon the urge for continued seminary reform. The following rectors represent the move to moderation: Howard Bleichner at Saint Patrick's, Gerald Brown at the college seminary at Mountain View, Albert Giaquinto and since July 1986 Laurence Terrien at Theological College, and Robert Leavitt at Saint Mary's Seminary and University. The appointment of Leavitt, who was received into the society concurrent with the appointment, was, according to Frazer, one of the most significant events of his provincialship. Just thirty-eight when he was appointed president-rector (the two offices were united for the first time) in 1980, Leavitt is a forceful and imaginative leader who appeals to both the traditionalists and liberals and who is a realist on the need to accommodate to the current conservative trends in the church.

During Frazer's provincialship (1978-1984), U.S. membership went from 136 to 111; 11 new members entered, 15 died, 18 returned to their dioceses, and 2 left the priesthood. Many of the Sulpicians who returned to their dioceses did so because they were involved in minor seminary work that the society had abandoned except for the college seminary in Mountain View, California.

The major institutional development during this period was the 1982 transfer of the Sulpician Institute of Continuing Education (I.C.E.) from its original residence at the Jesuit School of Theology, Berkeley, to Saint Mary's Seminary in Baltimore. During the period of 1983–1985, the Vatican visitations teams evaluated the programs at each of the Sulpician institutions—Saint Mary's, Theological College, Saint Patrick's, and Saint Joseph's College Seminary at Mountain View, California. Although the reports of these visitations are confidential, the experience appeared to be very positive and resulted in a restoration of self-confidence throughout the province. Because Sulpician seminaries had incorporated women into the programs of spiritual direction (in 1969 at Theological College), many Sulpicians were disappointed to discover that the revised Code of Canon Law (1983) prohibited women as well as nonordained religious from serving as spiritual directors in seminaries; it stipulated that candidates for the priesthood must have priests for spiritual direction.

Edward Frazer's provincialship was a period of enormous energy aimed at the restoration of morale, continuous spiritual renewal, encouragement of professional growth (particularly in the areas of faculty publications), and the recruitment and formation of Sulpician candidates. In anticipation of the bicentennial of the Sulpicians in the United States (1991), Purta appointed Vincent Eaton archivist of the province. In 1982, Frazer commissioned this history and placed the province's renewal within the context of the historical charisms of the society. In this process he was encouraged by superiors general Constant Bouchaud and Raymond Deville. Although Frazer relied upon the modern structures of staff and committees, most of the energy flowed from his own commitment. Hence, it did not come as a surprise when he announced in late 1984 that he did not want to be reelected at the next meeting of the provincial assembly in January of 1985.[22] Frazer is currently assistant director to Eugene Konkel at the Vatican II Institute of Continuing Education at Saint Patrick's Seminary, where each year approximately seventy priests participate in 2 three-month periods of spiritual renewal and intellectual growth.

Gerald L. Brown, Frazer's successor, is a priest of the archdiocese of San Francisco, trained at Sulpician seminaries from high school through the theologate at Saint Patrick's. He taught at Saint Edward's and Saint Thomas's seminaries in Seattle and was responsible for transferring the pastoral program at Theological College to the Catholic University of America. He served on the provincial council and its planning committee, which established the research and planning office in 1976, and was elected once again to the provincial council in 1982.

From 1978 to the time of his election as provincial he was rector of the college seminary at Mountain View. For his general contribution to U.S. seminary education, the NCEA presented him with the Loras Lane Award at its 1986 meeting in Anaheim, California. In 1986, Brown defined the role of the Sulpicians in the American Church of the year 2000.

> I see a new priesthood emerging in the Church. . . . In my judgment, priesthood will continue to evolve from a one-to-one ministry as its primary focus to a ministry much like that of the local bishop . . . a ministry marked by a concern for unity and coordination, faithfulness to the tradition, sensitivity to the wider Church and world, and commitment to peace and justice. His ministry will be primarily one of animation, education, and celebration. In union with the bishop, he will stimulate service and ministries among the people. . . . For almost 200 years, the Society of St. Sulpice has been training priests for the American Church. Currently, we have on our provincial address list over 12,000 living alumni residing in every state of the Union. . . . As we look to the future, we know that we need to be in close dialogue with the bishops who, in our tradition, are the pastoral leaders of our seminaries. Together, we need to build seminaries sensitive to a shifting American Catholic population, to the values of social justice and peace, and to the needs to the third world. At the same time, seminaries need to develop spiritual leaders capable of adaptation and conversion as we face the needs of a changing church and priesthood. If we are to fulfill our charism of "renewing the church through the renewal of its priests," then, we need to grow in numbers as a community. We need new candidates committed to the church and its future. Some of these candidates must come from black, Hispanic, and Asian backgrounds in order to help us meet the needs of a multi-cultural church.[23]

Post–Vatican II Catholic culture has been in continuous flux, a condition that disturbs the preservationists and excites the transformationists. The Sulpician provincials, like most people of sincere reflection, are both disturbed and excited. In terms of their perceptions of the role of the Sulpicians in the United States, however, they are in the transformationist tradition established by Louis Deluol, Alphonse Magnien, and John Hogan, as they view Saint Sulpice at the crossroads of the Catholic church in America.

II

Tradition and transformation are the *leitmotifs* in the story of the Sulpicians in the United States as well as in the society's overall history. For nearly 350 years the Sulpicians have been dedicated to the religious formation and intellectual development of those aspiring to the priesthood. In the process they have been models and spiritual directors to their seminarians and to their alumni priests and bishops. The unique interaction between Saint-Sulpice and the French episcopacy and between religion and French culture was imprinted upon the Sulpician character. Similar to the way in which the superior of Saint-Sulpice was more influential than many French prelates, so too the superior of Saint Mary's perceived his role as central to the ecclesiastical life of the new nation. Hence, no matter how small the society, the Sulpician presence in the American church was of paramount significance precisely because of the community's tradition as shapers of religious culture.

As I have emphasized, their moderate Gallicanism prompted the Sulpicians to identify strongly with the national church. Isaac Hecker, John Ireland, and others articulated in various ways what they perceived as the movement of the Holy Spirit within the cultural condition of American religious freedom. Each of them sensed that the church in the United States was entering a new era in which the dynamic of Catholicism and American culture would form a new transformationist synthesis. Sulpicians absorbed this transformationist élan into their traditional role as makers of religious culture, and with their particularist ecclesiology they profoundly influenced the articulation and direction of this synthesis.

Their attachment to this ideal caused such men as Alphonse Magnien and John Hogan to become leading figures in the progressive ecclesiological and intellectual movements of American Catholic culture. Thus to say that Edward Frazer and Gerald Brown were in the transformationist tradition of Deluol, Magnien, and Hogan is to place them at the center of the salient thematic pattern in the history of Saint Sulpice in America—a pattern that is inherently workable for the future because it entails the creative interaction between religion and culture.

Appendix A

Chronology of Events in the U.S. Province

Prepared by John W. Bowen, S.S., Provincial Archivist

1790   In September, at a meeting held in England, Bishop John Carroll of Baltimore and Charles Nagot agree to initiate Sulpician presence in the United States.

1791   On 10 July, Nagot, three other priests, and five students arrive in Baltimore to open Saint Mary's Seminary.

1798   After missionary work in Illinois country, Gabriel Richard begins thirty-four years of labor among the people of Detroit.

1799   William DuBourg opens a "French academy" at Saint Mary's Seminary that later develops into Saint Mary's College for lay students.

1805   On 19 January, William DuBourg obtains a state charter for Saint Mary's College from the Maryland legislature.

1806   On 15 August, Charles Nagot opens a minor seminary at Pigeon Hill, Pennsylvania, for the sons of German farmers.

1808   On 16 June, John Carroll dedicates the chapel of Saint Mary's, designed by Maximilian Godefroy, to serve the seminary, the college, and a parish of French-speaking refugees.

On the same day, Mrs. Elizabeth Ann Seton arrives in Baltimore from New York to open a girls' school, which gives rise, in the next year, to the Sisters of Saint Joseph (at present the Daughters of Charity).

Benedict Joseph Flaget, of Saint Mary's faculty, is appointed first bishop of Bardstown (later Louisville), which he serves for forty years.

1809   Mount Saint Mary's College at Emmitsburg, Maryland, is opened by John Dubois; students from Pigeon Hill are transferred to Emmitsburg.

1810   Charles Nagot resigns as superior; John Tessier takes his place.

1812   John B. David, while in Kentucky with Bishop Benedict Flaget, founds the Sisters of Charity of Nazareth.

1815   William DuBourg is appointed bishop of Louisiana and the Floridas (later New Orleans); in 1826, DuBourg becomes bishop of Montauban, France.

1817   Ambrose Maréchal of Saint Mary's Seminary faculty becomes archbishop of Baltimore, serving until his death in 1828.

John B. David is appointed auxiliary bishop of Bardstown.

1822   On 1 May, at the request of Archbishop Maréchal, the Holy See elevates Saint Mary's College to a pontifical university.

1823   Gabriel Richard is elected delegate to the U.S. Congress from the Territory of Michigan.

1826   On 8 January, after a long series of negotiations, Mount Saint Mary's College is officially stricken from the list of Sulpician houses.

John Dubois, founder of Mount Saint Mary's College, is appointed bishop of New York, where he serves until 1842.

1829   On 2 July, the Oblate Sisters of Providence, the first black religious community in the United States, is founded by Mother Mary Lange, the first superior, and James H. Joubert of Saint Mary's College.

1830   Charles Carroll of Carrollton gives property for a minor seminary and has it chartered by the Maryland legislature.

1834   Samuel Eccleston, Sulpician president of Saint Mary's College, becomes archbishop of Baltimore; he serves until his death in 1851.

Guy I. Chabrat, serving in Kentucky with Bishop Flaget, becomes Flaget's coadjutor. Chabrat resigns in 1846 and returns to France.

Simon Bruté, of Mount Saint Mary's College, becomes the first bishop of Vincennes, Indiana, which he serves until his death in 1839.

1840   On 15 December, John Chanche, Sulpician president of Saint Mary's College, is named first bishop of Natchez, Mississippi.

1848   Archbishop Eccleston succeeds in opening Saint Charles' College, near Ellicott City, Maryland, under the direction of Oliver Jenkins.

1849   Étienne Michel Faillon and Constant Guitter begin a visitation of Sulpician houses in the United States. Louis Deluol is recalled to France. François Lhomme becomes superior.

1852   In July, Saint Mary's College closes, resulting in the transfer of its students to Loyola College, the Jesuit college founded in the same year.

1857   Augustine Verot, former faculty member of Saint Mary's College, is made vicar apostolic of Florida. He later becomes bishop of Savannah, then of Saint Augustine.

1860   On 27 October, after asking to resign as superior, François Lhomme dies and is replaced by Joseph Paul Dubreul.

1867   James McCallen becomes the first alumnus of Saint Charles' College and the first American in twenty-five years to join the society.

1878   On 11 February, the new Saint Mary's Seminary building on Paca Street in Baltimore opens.

On 20 April, Joseph Dubreul dies. Alphonse Magnien becomes the new superior in Baltimore.

1884   At the request of Archbishop John Williams of Boston, the Sulpicians undertake the direction of the new Saint John's Seminary, Brighton, Massachusetts.

In November and December, Saint Mary's Seminary hosts the Third Plenary Council of Baltimore.

1896   At the request of Archbishop Michael A. Corrigan, the Sulpicians take charge of the new Saint Joseph's Seminary, Dunwoodie, New York.

1898   At the request of Archbishop Patrick Riordan of San Francisco, the Sulpicians assume the direction of Saint Patrick's Seminary, Menlo Park, California.

1901   Saint Austin's College, a house of studies for Sulpician candidates, opens at the Catholic University of America in Washington, D.C.

1902   Alphonse Magnien retires (the summer before his death). Edward
       R. Dyer succeeds Magnien as superior in Baltimore.

1903   On 20 July, Edward Dyer becomes the first (and only) vicar-
       general for the U.S. Sulpicians.

1906   In January, five of the six Sulpicians at Saint Joseph's, Dunwoodie,
       withdraw from the society; henceforth the seminary is staffed by
       New York priests.

       On 18 April, Saint Patrick's Seminary, Menlo Park, is damaged in
       the San Francisco earthquake; operations continue during the
       rebuilding.

1911   On 16 March, Saint Charles' College burns to the ground with no
       loss of life. The college reopens at Catonsville, Maryland, three
       weeks later.

       In June, Archbishop William H. O'Connell of Boston expels the
       Sulpicians from the seminary in Brighton.

       On 17 September, the first American Solitude begins at Saint
       Austin's College under the direction of Francis Havey.

1917   The Sulpician Seminary, Washington, D.C., opens for Sulpician
       candidates and for students in their final year of priestly training.

1921   After papal approval of the Sulpician constitutions, Edward Dyer
       is appointed the first American provincial.

       The Solitude resumes in a house on the grounds of Saint Charles'
       College, where it continues until 1940.

1924   The minor-seminary division of Saint Patrick's Seminary, Menlo
       Park, is transferred to the new Saint Joseph's College in Mountain
       View, California.

1925   After Edward Dyer's death, John Fenlon is appointed provincial.

1929   After a million-dollar fund-raising drive led by Archbishop
       Michael Curley of Baltimore, Saint Mary's Seminary opens its
       theologate in Roland Park, Maryland; the department of philos-
       ophy remains at the Paca Street building until 1969.

1931   On 19 September, at the invitation of Bishop Edward O'Dea of
       Seattle, Saint Edward's Seminary opens its minor seminary for
       the Pacific Northwest; the major seminary opens four years later.

1940   In response to a 1937 request from the Vatican's Sacred
       Congregation of Seminaries and Universities, the Sulpician
       Seminary in Washington, D.C. becomes the Theological College
       of the Catholic University of America.

1941   The first of seven solitudes begins at Saint Mary's Seminary at
       Paca Street.

A major celebration of the 300th anniversary of the founding of the society and the 150th anniversary of the Sulpicians' arrival in Baltimore is held.

1943   After the death of John Fenlon, John Lardner is elected interim provincial. After the end of World War II, the new superior general, Pierre Boisard, confirms Lardner as provincial.

1946   At the invitation of Bishop James Sweeney of Honolulu, the Sulpicians open Saint Stephen's Seminary, a minor seminary, at Kaneohe, Hawaii.

1948   John Lardner dies suddenly; Lloyd McDonald is appointed U.S. provincial.

1949   Under the auspices of Cardinal Edward Mooney of Detroit and the Michigan bishops, the Sulpicians open Saint John's Provincial Seminary in Plymouth, Michigan.

1952   As a result of a 1931 agreement with Archbishop John Floersh of Louisville, Kentucky, the Sulpicians open Saint Thomas' Seminary, a minor seminary, there.

1955   The first of ten solitudes is conducted at the Dohme estate, adjacent to Saint Mary's Seminary, Roland Park.

1958   Thanks to Archbishop Thomas Connolly's leadership, Saint Thomas the Apostle Major Seminary opens on property adjacent to the minor seminary in Seattle.

1965   Four members of the province begin preparations to assist the Canadian province in staffing Latin American seminaries. One member is eventually dispatched to Samoa and another to Africa.

1967   Lloyd McDonald resigns as provincial; the Provincial Assembly elects Paul Purta, the first provincial to be elected rather than appointed.

1968   With the encouragement of Cardinal Lawrence Shehan of Baltimore and the Right Reverend Harry Lee Doll, Episcopal bishop of Maryland, the Ecumenical Institute is founded at Saint Mary's Seminary, Roland Park.

        Saint Patrick's College, Menlo Park, and Saint Joseph's College, Mountain View, unite under a new administration at the Mountain View campus.

1969   The high-school department of Saint Charles' College closes; its junior college unites with the philosophy department of Saint Mary's Seminary to become Saint Mary's Seminary College, Catonsville.

1970   Saint Thomas's Seminary, Louisville, closes.

1971   Saint Charles's Villa, Catonsville, Maryland, opens in February as the province's main retirement center.

Sulpicians withdraw from Saint John's Provincial Seminary and are replaced by the diocesan priests of Michigan.

The chapel of Saint Thomas's Seminary, Kenmore, Washington, begins serving as the center for Saint John Vianney parish, staffed by Sulpicians until 1984.

1972   All U.S. Sulpician records begin to be consolidated at the Sulpician Archives, Baltimore, located at Saint Mary's Seminary College.

1974   First Renewal Session of the U.S. province is held at Saint Patrick's Seminary, Menlo Park, with almost all the membership present.

1975   The Paca Street building of Saint Mary's Seminary is demolished, the grounds converted into a city park, and the former convent renovated into Saint Mary's Residence.

The province withdraws from responsibility for the high-school department of Saint Joseph's College, Mountain View.

On 14 September, Mother Elizabeth Ann Seton, who had begun her work in Baltimore at Old Saint Mary's, is canonized.

1976   Saint Edward's Seminary, Kenmore, closes at the school year's end.

Sulpicians begin to participate in the Institute for Continuing Education at Berkeley, California.

1977   Saint Thomas's Seminary, Kenmore, closes both college and theologate.

Saint Mary's Seminary College, Baltimore, closes after eight years on the Catonsville site.

Paul Purta resigns as provincial; Edward Frazer is elected to complete the term. Frazer is reelected two years later.

The Sulpician Formation Community at Berkeley is inaugurated. Later it acquires its own house, named Vaugirard.

Joseph A. Ferrario, former member of the American province, is named auxiliary bishop of Honolulu; in 1982 he becomes ordinary.

1981   With the erection of the new diocese of San Jose, Saint Patrick's College, Mountain View, resumes the name Saint Joseph's College after thirteen years.

1982   The former Saint Charles' College (Saint Mary's Seminary College) is sold and converted into the Charlestown Retirement Community.

1985   Gerald Brown is elected to succeed Edward Frazer as provincial.

Appendix B

Priests of Saint Sulpice Who Have Served in the United States

Following is a list of 439 members (322 of them born in the United States) of the Society of Saint Sulpice who have worked in what became the American province of the Sulpicians. Two, Pierre Coupey and Jean Tiphaigne, were lost at sea on their way to their assignments. One, Michael Gorey, died during his Solitude year. Dates are dates of birth and death. The symbol * indicates members who have withdrawn from the society. The symbol † indicates members or former members who have become bishops.

André, Gabriel (1848–1931
Arand, Louis A. (b. 1892)
Arbez, Edward P. (1881–1967)
*Atkinson, J. Bruce (b. 1932)
*Atzert, Edward P. (b. 1912)
Aycock, Robert E. Lee (1891–1977)
Ayrinhac, Henri J. (1867–1930)
Babad, Pierre (1763–1846)
Baisnée, Jules A. (1879–1970)
Baron, Michel (b. 1914)
Barre, Michael L. (b. 1943)
Barrett, John D. M. (1895–1957)
*Barrett, Robert F. (b. 1950)

*Basso, Richard (b. 1937)
Bast, Victor A. (1883–1937)
Bazinet, John L. (1900–1963)
Beaulieu, Adrian G. (b. 1953)
Becker, Charles J. (b. 1924)
Bender, Lawrence A. (b. 1924)
Berkeley, Charles C. (1874–1914)
Bernard, L. Adhemar (1855–1940)
Bernhard, Aloysius (1904–1969)
Besnard, Leo M. (1859–1925)
Bioletti, Nizier (1871–1916)
Bitterman, John L. (b. 1942)
Blanc, François R. (1828–1860)

Blanc, Philip J. (1876–1948)
Blanchette, Melvin (b. 1940)
Bleichner, Howard P. (b. 1937)
*Bombardier, Gerald W. (b. 1946)
Bonadio, Joseph J. (b. 1937)
Boone, Charles E. (1876–1924)
Bougie, Pierre (b. 1940)
Bowen, John W. (b. 1924)
Boyer, Arsenius (1852–1939)
Branderis, Herman (1893–1963)
Braun, William A. (1918–1964)
Braye, Paul M. J. (1851–1926)
Brennan, James H. (b. 1905)
Brianceau, Henri L. (1874–1950)
Brown, Gerald L. (b. 1938)
Brown, Lawrence A. (1881–1958)
Brown, Raymond E. (b. 1928)
*Browne, J. Patrick (b. 1941)
Brulé, Réné J. (1872–1941)
Bruneau, Joseph (1866–1933)
*†Bruté de Remur, Simon (1779–1839)
*Burke, Henry R. (b. 1911)
Burke, Patrick F. (1887–1924)
*Burns, James M. (b. 1930)
Buttner, Michael T. (b. 1946)
*Calegari, Pierre J. (b. 1932)
Callaghan, James (1850–1901)
Callahan, Robert T. (b. 1919)
Campbell, James T. (1906–1973)
Canfield, John J. (b. 1915)
*Caringella, Paul (b. 1939)
*Castelot, John J. (b. 1916)
Cawley, John M. (1913–1957)
Cerny, Edward A. (1890–1962)
†Chabrat, Guy I. (1787–1868)
†Chanche, John J. (1795–1852)
Chapon, Pierre P. (1837–1915)
Chapuis, Henri (1830–1909)
Cheneau, August M. (1859–1908)
Chicoisneau, John B. (1737–1818)
Chirico, Peter F. (b. 1927)
*Chochol, Ronald C. (b. 1937)
Chudzinski, Frederick V. (b. 1910)
Ciquard, François R. (1754–1824)
Clapin, George C. (1857–1929)
*Clark, Thomas R. (b. 1936)
Coleman, Gerald D. (b. 1942)
Colin, F. Louis (1835–1902)

Collins, Joseph B. (1897–1975)
Connaghan, Eugene P. (1906–1946)
*Connelly, Edward C. (b. 1933)
Connerton, Francis R. (1908–1968)
Connolly, Bernard P. (1891–1932)
Connolly, Edward A. (1904–1961)
Connor, Raymond J. (1951–1984)
Cope, Edward T. (1910–1987)
*Cormier, Edmond (b. 1933)
Coupey, Pierre (?–c. 1811)
Coyle, Edward F. (1878–1954)
*Crisman, William H. (b. 1942)
Cronan, Edward P. (1913–1978)
Cronin, John F. (b. 1908)
Cronin, Paul J. (1922–1981)
Crowley, Cale J. (b. 1943)
Cullinan, Richard P. (1913–1977)
Cuoq, Jean A. (1821–1898)
Cuyler, Cornelius M. (1904–1976)
Cwiekowski, Frederick J. (b. 1936)
*Damphoux, Edward (1788–1860)
*Dannemiller, J. Lawrence (b. 1925)
†David, John B. (1761–1841)
*Dede, John F. (b. 1922)
Deguire, Pierre (1833–1895)
de la Croze, Matthew A. (1866–1916)
Deluol, Louis R. (1787–1858)
Denis, Pierre P. (1820–1903)
*Desmond, John T. (b. 1926)
*Des Rosiers, Denis A. (b. 1943)
Dilhet, Jean (1753–1811)
Dillon, Charles P. (b. 1914)
*DiNardo, Ramon A. (b. 1916)
Dinneen, Michael F. (1860–1941)
Dissez, Paulin F. (1828–1908)
*Donovan, John F. (b. 1942)
Doran, John J. (1872–1939)
Dorvaux, Jean E. (1859–1931)
Dougherty, John M. (1904–1977)
Doyle, Thomas (b. 1926)
*Driscoll, Harry A. (b. 1903)
*Driscoll, James F. (1859–1922)
*†Dubois, Jean (1764–1842)
*†DuBourg, Louis William (1766–1833)
Dubreul, Joseph P. (1814–1878)
*Duchaine, Maurice C. (b. 1932)
Duffy, Daniel P. (1864–1929)
Dujarié, Julien H. (1832–1875)

Dukehart, C. Henry (b. 1917)
Dukehart, J. Cyril (1905–1960)
Dumont, Francis L. M. (1838–1915)
Dumont, Paul C. (1857–1893)
*Dunne, John J. (b. 1937)
Dwyer, William F. (1895–1960)
Dyer, Edward Randall (1854–1925)
Dyer, Paul R. (1894–1949)
Eaton, Vincent M. (b. 1915)
*Ebert, John W. (b. 1926)
†Eccleston, Samuel (1801–1851)
*Eddy, Corbin T. (b. 1942)
Elder, Alexis J. (1791–1871)
Eno, Robert B. (b. 1936)
Evers, Robert T. (b. 1931)
*Falcone, John C. (1927–1980)
*Falk, Charles (1899–1971)
Farrell, John J. (1869–1942)
Farrell, Melvin L. (1930–1986)
Fenlon, John F. (1873–1943)
Fenn, Lyman A. (1901–1985)
*†Ferrario, Joseph A. (b. 1926)
Ferté, H. Stanislaus (1821–1895)
*Fitzgerald, Thomas F. (1897–1954)
Fives, Daniel C. (b. 1905)
†Flaget, Benedict J. (1763–1850)
Flammant, Alphonse (1824–1864)
*Fletcher, William J. (b. 1918)
Flynn, William J. (b. 1933)
*Foisy, Leonard R. (b. 1930)
Fonteneau, August S. (1841–1905)
*Forest, Eugene (1851–?)
Forster, Andrew A. (b. 1914)
*Foudy, Denis D. (b. 1917)
Franey, John T. (b. 1911)
Frazer, Edward J. (b. 1935)
Fredericks, James L. (b. 1951)
Fredet, Pierre (1801–1856)
*Gallitzin, Demetrius A. (1770–1840)
*Galvin, John J. (1907–1962)
Garnier, Antoine (1762–1845)
Garrouteigt, Henri (1875–1965)
Gavin, Robert V. (b. 1927)
*Gendreau, Alfred J. (b. 1911)
Genovese, Paul F. (b. 1919)
*Gervais, J. Marie (1829–?)
Giaquinto, Albert C. (b. 1923)
*Gietzin, Albin J. (b. 1924)

*Gigot, Francis E. (1859–1920)
Giguere, Robert J. (b. 1917)
Gilgan, Edward A. (1873–1944)
Gleason, George A. (1887–1955)
Glendon, Lowell M. (b. 1935)
Godon, Eugene (1868–1938)
Gorey, Michael J. (1897–1928)
*Gorman, James C. (b. 1942)
Gratto, R. Leon (1900–1959)
Gray, Peter W. (b. 1953)
*Greenalch, John H. (b. 1938)
*Gregoire, Paul L. (b. 1929)
Guilbaud, Sebastian (1836–1912)
Gula, Richard M. (b. 1947)
Gustafson, G. Joseph (1910–1970)
Haggerty, Thomas F. (1902–1987)
Hamon, Pierre M. (1844–1890)
Harent, Joseph (1755–1818)
Harig, George L. (1868–1940)
Harrigan, Eugene F. (1889–1936)
Hartgen, William E. (b. 1934)
Harvey, James J. (1900–1953)
Haug, Joseph M. (1851–1929)
Havey, Francis P. (1864–1945)
Healy, James J. (b. 1921)
*Helminiak, Daniel A. (b. 1942)
Hemelt, Theodore M. (1890–1976)
*Hendricks, Joseph M. (b. 1947)
Hesler, Raymond F. (b. 1909)
Hester, David P. (b. 1948)
Hickey, John F. (1789–1869)
*Hill, William F. (b. 1920)
Hoey, George W. (1880–1947)
Hogan, Edward J. (1914–1986)
Hogan, John B. (1829–1901)
Hogue, Charles D. (1863–1928)
*Holland, Timothy P. (1873–1948)
*Holstein, Roland H. (1939–1985)
*Horn, Joseph A. (b. 1933)
Horning, Joseph L. (1907–1976)
Hoskyns, John H. (1808–1837)
Hurst, Thomas R. (b. 1947)
Jenkins, Oliver L. (1813–1869)
Jepson, John J. (1882–1951)
*Johnson, Timothy K. (b. 1945)
Joubert, James Hector (1777–1843)
Jouvenet, Antoine C. (1863–1899)
Judge, Charles J. (1846–1909)

*Kalkman, Richard G. (b. 1930)
*Kaulbach, Ernest N. (b. 1935)
*Kazista, Francis G. (b. 1936)
Keane, Philip S. (b. 1941)
*Kelmartin, John J. (b. 1924)
Kerin, Charles A. (1905–1982)
*Kerney, Nicholas F. (1787–1841)
Klaphecke, Paul W. (1875–1950)
*Knepper, Daniel J. (b. 1944)
*Knight, Edward (1806–1862)
Knuff, Justin E. (b. 1915)
Konkel, Eugene J. (b. 1931)
Kortendick, James J. (1907–1986)
*Kraemer, Eugene J. (1895–1950)
Krisak, Anthony F. (b. 1949)
Kselman, John S. (b. 1940)
Kunkel, Francis W. (1870–1951)
Ky, Joseph T. (b. 1929)
*Lardner, Gerald V. (b. 1941)
Lardner, John J. (1893–1948)
*Larkin, John (1801–1858)
Larrivee, Leo J. (b. 1951)
Laubacher, James A. (1908–1987)
*Law, Joseph A. (b. 1924)
Leavitt, Robert F. (b. 1942)
Le Blanc, Paul J. (1898–1932)
Lee, William J. (b. 1922)
Leigh, Thomas R. (1920–1974)
Lequerré, Urbain E. (1836–1877)
Levadoux, Michel (1746–1815)
Levatois, Andrew L. (1871–1948)
*Leveille, Roland E. (b. 1931)
Lhomme, François (1794–1860)
*Linehan, David A. (b. 1930)
Linehan, James C. (b. 1902)
Linn, John F. (1900–1975)
Lobo, Anthony F. (b. 1936)
*Loffredo, Peter J. (b. 1944)
*Loney, Norman G. (b. 1924)
Lothamer, James W. (b. 1942)
*Loughran, Terence L. (b. 1932)
*Lowell, James W. (b. 1933)
MacDonough, Richard B. (b. 1935)
*MacKay, Charles R. (b. 1935)
Magner, James (1899–1980)
Magnien, Alphonse (1837–1902)
Mahar, John D. (1899–1974)
Maher, Daniel E. (1858–1906)

*Mahon, Peter F. (1867–c. 1934)
*Mahoney, John R. (1862–1951)
Marcetteau, Benjamin F. (1877–1958)
†Maréchal, Ambrose (1768–1828)
Marre, Victor H. M. (1847–1900)
Martin, Joseph C. (b. 1924)
Martin, Narcisse L. (1845–1923)
Mattingly, John F. (b. 1923)
*Maynard, Frederick J. (1902–1965)
*McAllister, Joseph B. (b. 1906)
McAndrew, Miles M. (1900–1966)
McBrearity, Gerald D. (b. 1947)
McCallen, James (1847–1912)
*McCarthy, Walter J. (1904–1968)
McCorkle, John A. (1909–1977)
McCormick, John P. (1904–1981)
*McCormick, Patrick J. (b. 1938)
McDonald, Lloyd P. (1896–1968)
McDonald, Raymond J. (1905–1960)
McDonald, William J. (1910–1941)
*McDonnell, Francis E. (b. 1927)
McDonough, John S. (1894–1977)
McHugh, Alonzo J (1891–1955)
McHugh, J. Carroll (b. 1913)
McKenny, Francis X. (1860–1917)
McManus, John Paul (1913–1986)
McMurry, John E. (b. 1931)
McMurry, Vincent D. (b. 1924)
Meil, Lucien F. (1870–1919)
Menu, John B. (1821–1888)
*Mercier, Adrian G. (b. 1931)
*Meyer, Clayton S. (b. 1939)
Meyer, Raymond B. (1907–1985)
*Milholland, W. Carroll (1884–1944)
*Miller, Edward D. (b. 1939)
*Millet, Albert H. L. (1873–1933)
*Minelli, Peter A. (b. 1937)
*Mohan, Robert P. (b. 1920)
Morris, William S. (b. 1905)
*Mulka, Arthur L. (b. 1930)
Mulligan, Thomas C. (1892–1960)
*Murphy, William R. (b. 1917)
Nagot, F. Charles (1734–1816)
*Nainfa, John A. (1878–1938)
Neiswanger, David L. (1924–1982)
Nevins, Joseph V. (1884–1979)
Nicolaus, Eugene T. (1913–1973)
Noonan, Carroll J. (1903–1981)

Norris, Frank B. (b. 1925)
Oberle, G. Vincent (1905-1982)
*O'Brien, Roger G. (b. 1935)
O'Connor, Thomas E. (1909-1984)
O'Connor, William V. (1887-1968)
*O'Kane, Brian J. (b. 1931)
O'Keeffe, William T. (b. 1920)
Olivier, John H. (b. 1920)
O'Neil, Maurice L. (b. 1931)
O'Neill, John J. (b. 1909)
O'Neill, Michael J. (1910-1969)
Orban, Alexis J. (1850-1915)
*O'Shea, William J. (b. 1913)
Ott, George E. (1893-1984)
Ouvrard, Jean M. (1881-1946)
Palin d'Abonville, Clement F.
   (1838-1897)
Parent, Joseph T. (1836-1912)
*Parke, James E. (b. 1939)
Peltier, Alexander M. (1867-1940)
Perkosky, Francis J. (1928-1962)
*Peterson, Casimir M. (b. 1921)
*Piot, Bertrand S. (1808-1882)
*Pluchon, Hippolyte (1865-1944)
*Power, John (1874-1961)
Power, Thomas F. (1888-1954)
*Purta, Paul P. (b. 1927)
*Putsche, Elmer J. (b. 1921)
*Queenan, William J. (b. 1935)
Quinn, John B. (1899-1969)
Randanne, Jean B. (1793-1864)
*Raymond, Gilbert (1809-1889)
Redden, Pierce F. (1900-1962)
*Redmond, Richard X. (b. 1928)
Redon, John M. (1873-1955)
*Reilly, Bartholomew M. (1909-1977)
Reilly, Wendell Stephen (1875-1950)
Reitz, Louis M. (b. 1929)
Rex, Charles B. (1856-1897)
Richard, Gabriel (1767-1832)
Riddlemoser, Joseph (1899-1978)
Rincé, Louis M. (1836-1869)
*Rivard, Joseph (1898-1972)
Rock, Francis J. (1896-1975)
Roinard, Eugene (1859-1905)
Rothureau, Mathurin (1851-1935)
Roux, Pierre F. (1850-1930)
Rouxel, Hyacinthe F. (1830-1899)

*Ruane, Joseph (1904-1983)
*Ruggeri, Michael A. (b. 1944)
Ruskowski, Leo F. (b. 1907)
Russell, Robert L. (b. 1929)
Sage, Carleton M. (b. 1904)
Saupin, Eugene L. (1872-1956)
*Schaefers, Francis J. (b. 1905)
Schindler, Thomas F. (b. 1941)
*Schmitz, Edwin F. (b. 1928)
Schmitz, Walter J. (b. 1907)
Schneider, Edwin J. (1899-1974)
Schrantz, Charles B. (1845-1934)
Schwalbach, J. Emerle (1886-1914)
Selner, John C. (b. 1904)
Serieys, Adrien A. (1850-1908)
*Shea, John M. (b. 1934)
*Shea, Maurice F. (b. 1930)
Sheehan, Michael J. (1901-1981)
Sheehy, William J. (1893-1962)
Spencer, James P. (1900-1959)
*Stallings, Albert T. (b. 1908)
*Stanks, Thomas D. (b. 1930)
*Stanley, Gerald F. (b. 1937)
*Stasker, R. Louis (b. 1939)
*Statnick, Roger A. (b. 1947)
*Strain, Eugene R. (b. 1927)
*Strange, J. Donald (b. 1907)
Strange, J. Michael (b. 1939)
Sullivan, Daniel D. (1904-1984)
Sullivan, John R. (1907-1984)
*Sullivan, J. Vincent (b. 1913)
*Talbot, Albert Donat (1898-1962)
Tanquerey, Adolphe A. (1854-1932)
Taylor, Lawrence V. (1912-1980)
Tennelly, J. Benjamin (1890-1981)
Terrien, Lawrence B. (b. 1946)
Tessier, Jean (1758-1840)
Thayer, David D. (b. 1949)
Thielemann, William A. (b. 1916)
Thirlkel, John H. (b. 1919)
*Thompson, William M. (b. 1943)
*Tiernan, Joseph J. (b. 1944)
*Tierney, John J. (b. 1910)
Tiphaigne, Jean F. (1779-c. 1811)
Trainer, Charles P. (1895-1947)
Tucker, James S. (b. 1943)
Turner, Robert L. (b. 1934)
*Tuscher, Joseph F. (1878-1941)

Twamley, John H. (1894–1971)
Ulshafer, Thomas R. (b. 1944)
Urique, P. Albert (1857–1925)
*Van Antwerp, Eugene I. (b. 1917)
*†Verot, Augustine (1805–1876)
Vieban, Anthony (1872–1944)
Viger, George E. (1839–1908)
Vignon, Marc (1841–1900)
*Voirdye, Charles (1819–1880)
Vuibert, Arsenius J. B. (1840–1926)
Wagner, Edward J. (1902–1964)
*Wakeham, Richard K. (1848–1914)
Wall, Frederick H. (1888–1916)
Walsh, Eugene A. (b. 1911)
*Walter, George I. (1907–1970)
Ward, John A. (b. 1914)
Waznak, Robert P. (b. 1938)
Webster, Royal B. (1879–1962)
Welch, J. Paul (b. 1912)
Wheeler, Michael F. (1796–1832)

White, Joseph L. (b. 1905)
Whitford, George J. (1905–1956)
*Wingate, Carl E. (b. 1939)
Witherup, Ronald D. (b. 1950)
*Wohinc, Karl R. (b. 1937)
*Wood, Thomas O. (b. 1923)
Wright, Addison G. (b. 1932)
*Xaupi, Honoré X. (1787–1869)
*Zenk, Joseph P. (b. 1936)
*Zoph, John L. (b. 1908)

As of spring 1987 there were five candidates for membership in the society: M. Stephen Barrett (b. 1931), John C. Kemper (b. 1957), Peter P. Kenny (b. 1950), Luis F. Martinez (b. 1949), and Richard Pelkey (b. 1952).

Notes

Abbreviations

AAB	Archives of the Archdiocese of Baltimore
AABO	Archives of the Archdiocese of Boston
AAC	Archives of the Archdiocese of Cincinnati
AAD	Archives of the Archdiocese of Detroit
AANY	Archives of the Archdiocese of New York
AAS	Archives of the Archdiocese of Seattle
AASL	Archives of the Archdiocese of Saint Louis
AASP	Archives of the Archdiocese of Saint Paul
ACQR	*American Catholic Quarterly Review*
ACUA	Archives of the Catholic University of America
ADR	Archives of the Diocese of Richmond
AER	*American Ecclesiastical Review*
AMSM	Archives of Mount Saint Mary's College
APF	Archives of the Paulist Fathers
ASCN	Archives of the Sisters of Charity of Nazareth
AUND	Archives of the University of Notre Dame
J.C.P.	*The John Carroll Papers*, 3 volumes, edited by Thomas O'Brien Hanley, S. J. (Notre Dame, Ind., 1976)
OSA	Oblate Sisters' Archives
SAB	Sulpician Archives of Baltimore
SAP	Sulpician Archives of Paris
STP	Saint Patrick's Seminary, Historical Files

Prologue

1. Carl J. Friedrich, *The Age of the Baroque* (New York, 1952), 44–45.
2. The following is a brief bibliography of works on the life and spirituality of Jean-Jacques Olier. Gilles Chaillot, "Critères pour la formation spir-

ituelle des pasteurs: La tradition pédagogique heritée de M. Olier," *Bulletin de Saint-Sulpice* 4 (1978): 15–23; "La pédagogie spirituelle de M. Olier d'après ses Mémoires," *Bulletin de Saint-Sulpice* 2 (1976): 27–64; "Les premières leçons de l'expérience mystique de Monsieur Olier," *Bulletin du comité des études* 40 (December 1962): 501–543; "Monsieur Olier éducateur spirituelle des pasteurs d'après les sources principales du Traité des Saints Ordres," *Bulletin de Saint-Sulpice* 4 (1978): 205–238; Michel Dupuy, *Se laisser a l'esprit: L'itinéraire spirituel de Jean-Jacques Olier,*" (Paris, 1982); Michel Dupuy and Irénée Noye, "Jean-Jacques Olier," *Bulletin de Saint-Sulpice* 8 (1982): 19–41; Frederick Faber, *Growth in Holiness* (Baltimore, 1855); Étienne-Michel Faillon, *Vie de M. Olier*, 3d ed., 3 vols (Paris, 1873); Jean Gautier, "Les étapes mystiques de M. Olier," *Vie spirituelle* 13 (March 1926): 665–684; Lowell Glendon, "Jean-Jacques Olier's Shifting Attitude toward the Human," *Bulletin de Saint-Sulpice* 5 (1979): 43–49; and "Jean-Jacques Olier's View of the Spiritual Potential of Human Nature" (Ph.D. diss., Fordham University, 1983); H.J. Icard, *Doctrine de M. Olier* (Paris, 1889); Timothy Johnson, "Jean-Jacques Olier: Spiritual Director," *Bulletin de Saint-Sulpice* 6 (1980): 287–310; Frederick Monier, *Vie de Jean-Jacques Olier* (Paris, 1914); Irénée Noye, "Recherches sur quelques éditions de Monsieur Olier," *Bulletin du comité des études* 2 (April–June 1957): 12–19; Pierre Pourrat, *Father Olier: Founder of Saint-Sulpice*, trans. W.S. Reilly (Baltimore, 1932); Sacred Congregation of Rites, "Jean-Jacques Olier: Positio super revisione scriptorum" (Rome: Propagation of the Faith, 1899); Eugene Walsh, *The Priesthood in the Writings of the French School: Bérulle, De Condren, Olier* (Washington, D.C. 1949).

3. Edward Healy Thompson, *The Life of Jean-Jacques Olier* (London, 1886), 11.
4. Ibid., 19.
5. Ibid., 43.
6. C.V. Wedgewood, *Richelieu and the French Monarchy* (New York, 1962), 18.
7. Thompson, 78. See also Dupuy, 193.
8. For a comprehensive view of Salesian piety, see Francis Vincent, "The Spirituality of St. Francis DeSales," *Some Schools of Catholic Spirituality*, ed. Jean Gautier (New York, 1959), 49–75.
9. Henri Daniel-Rops, *The Church in the Seventeenth Century* (London, 1963), 24.
10. Quoted by Pierre Coste, C.M., *The Life and Work of St. Vincent dePaul* (Westminster, Maryland, 1952), 1:245.
11. Ibid., 1:246–247.
12. Quoted by Daniel-Rops, 20.
13. H. L. Sidney Lear, *The Revival of Priestly Life in France* (London, 1878), 49.
14. Henri Brémond, *A Literary History of Religious Thought in France* (London, 1936), 3:275.
15. Ibid., 368. See also Dupuy, 34.
16. Brémond, 3:383.
17. Dupuy, 69–107.
18. Quoted by Jean Gautier, "Oratorian Spirituality," in *Some Schools of Catholic Spirituality*, 332.
19. Lowell M. Glendon, S.S., "Jean-Jacques Olier's View of the Spiritual Potential of Human Nature," 147, n. 20.
20. Quoted by Brémond, 3:386.
21. Thompson, 133.

22. Pierre Boisard, P.S.S., *La compagnie de Saint-Sulpice: Trois siècles d'histoire* (Paris, 1959), 1:7.
23. Thompson, 292–306.
24. Quoted by Walsh, xii.
25. Ibid., 42.
26. Gautier, "Oratorian Spirituality," 296.
27. Thompson, 253–263.
28. Quoted by Daniel-Rops, 343.
29. Alexander Sedgwick, *Jansenism in Seventeenth-Century France, Voices from the Wilderness* (Charlottsville, VA, 1977), 47–75.
30. James A. O'Donohue, "Tridentine Seminary Legislation: Its Source and its Foundation" (Ph.D. diss., Louvain, 1957), 98–120.
31. John Tracy Ellis, *Essays in Seminary Education* (Notre Dame, Indiana, 1967), 38–39.
32. Ibid., 39.
33. Daniel-Rops, 71.
34. Coste, 1:257–259.
35. Quoted by Coste, 1:259.
36. Daniel-Rops, 75.
37. Quoted by Thompson, 131.
38. Thompson, 318.
39. Ibid.
40. Quoted by Lear, 298–299.
41. Quoted by Pourrat, 162.
42. Quoted by Gautier, "Oratorian Spirituality," 309.
43. Quoted by Walsh, 78.
44. Ibid., 85–86.
45. Quoted by Thompson, 445.
46. Ibid., 450.
47. Louis Bouyer, *Introduction to Spirituality*, trans. Mary Perkins Ryan (New York, 1961), 84–85.
48. Daniel-Rops, 34.
49. Quoted by Daniel-Rops, 342–343.
50. Sedgewick, 51–54.
51. Quoted by Thompson, 350.
52. Ibid.
53. Brémond, 278–288.
54. Thompson, 486–492.
55. Quoted by Walsh, 113–114.
56. Thompson, 501–502.
57. Quoted by Thompson, 499.
58. Henry d'Antin de Vaillac, "Les constitutions de la compagnie de Saint-Sulpice" (Ph.D. diss., Institut Catholique de Paris, 1965), 41.
59. Gautier, "Oratorian Spirituality," 316.
60. Quoted by Thompson, 501.
61. Dupuy and Noye, 8, 39–42.
62. Maurice A. Roche, S.M., *Saint Vincent dePaul and the Formation of Clerics* (Freiburg, 1964), 119–142.
63. Thompson, 544–554.

64. D'Antin de Vaillac, 1:66.

65. Quoted by Lyman A. Fenn, S.S., *Examens for Seminarians and Priests* (Baltimore, 1960), viii.

66. Ibid.

67. Louis Tronson, P.S.S., *Examination of Conscience upon Special Subjects* (London, 1870), 206.

68. Ibid., 207.

69. Ibid., 244.

70. Ibid. For further insights into Tronson's ideas on the priesthood, see Louis Tronson, *Conferences for Ecclesiastical Students and Religious* (London, 1878) and Jean Delumeau, *Catholicism between Luther and Voltaire: A New View of the Counter-Reformation* (Philadelphia, 1977), 44.

71. Quoted by John B. Wolf, *The Emergence of the Great Powers* (New York, 1955), 212.

72. Boisard, 61.

73. R. R. Palmer, *Catholics and Unbelievers* (Princeton, New Jersey, 1939), 14.

74. Ibid., 13.

75. John McManners, *French Ecclesiastical Society under the Ancien Regime* (Manchester, England, 1970), 137.

76. Ibid, 13. The *Nouvelles ecclésiastiques* labeled the Sulpicians as "leaders of a Molinist conspiracy," which for a Jansenist was synonymous to a Satanic conspiracy. Louis de Molino (c. 1590), a Spanish Jesuit, developed a very liberal notion of grace that has been labeled "semi-pelagian" and that the Jansenists considered to be a gross form of heresy. See Daniel-Rops, 371–373.

77. Quoted by Delumeau, 33–34.

78. John Carroll Futrell, S.J., "Discovering the Founder's Charism," *The Way*, Supplement no. 14 (Autumn 1971): 62.

Chapter 1

1. Pierre Boisard, *La compagnie de Saint-Sulpice: Trois siècles d'histoire* (Paris, 1959), 1:182–183. For biographical information on Emery see Jean-Edme-August Gosselin, *Vie de M. Emery*, 2 vols. (Paris, 1862); Jean Leflon, *Monsieur Emery*, 2 vols. (Paris, 1945); and Elie Meric, *Histoire de M. Emery et de l'église de France pendant la Revolution*, 2 vols. (Paris, 1885).

2. John McManners, *French Ecclesiastical Society under the Ancien Regime* (Manchester, England, 1970), 137.

3. Leflon, 1:20–28.

4. Ibid., 27.

5. Ibid., 47–56. Also see l'Abbe Migne, ed., *Œuvres complètes de M. Emery* (Paris, 1857), 945–1358 (hereafter cited as *Œuvres*).

6. R. R. Palmer, *Catholics and Unbelievers* (Princeton, New Jersey), 89.

7. Quoted from "A Superior of Pre-Revolutionary Days," *The Voice* (December 1932). The article is contained in *The Voice of History*, Vincent M. Eaton, S.S., ed. *The Voice of History* may be found in Sulpician Archives Baltimore (hereafter cited as SAB).

8. Alec Vidler, *Prophecy and Papacy* (London, 1954), 76.

9. *Œuvres*, 12–383.

10. Leflon, 1:61–70.

11. McManners, 138.

12. Palmer, 14.

13. Adrien Dansette, *Religious History of Modern France* (New York, 1961), 1:13.

14. SAB, "Souvenirs d'Edward Mondésir," *The Voice* (October 1931): 22 (hereafter cited as *Souvenirs de Mondésir*).

15. Quoted by Dansette, 1:13.

16. Ibid., 7.

17. Robert Belaney, *Massacre at the Carmes in 1792* (London, 1855).

18. Leflon, 1:282–285.

19. John McManners, *The French Revolution and the Church* (London, 1969), 148.

20. John McGovern, O.P., "The Gallipolis Colony in Ohio: 1788–1793," *Records of the American Catholic Historical Society* 37 (1926): 29–72.

21. Joseph William Ruane, *The Beginning of the Society of St. Sulpice in the United States 1791–1829* (Baltimore, 1935), 21.

22. Dugnani to Carroll, 24 August 1790. Thomas O'Brien Hanley, S.J., *The John Carroll Papers* (Notre Dame, Indiana, 1976), 1:22 (hereafter cited as *J.C.P.*).

23. Carroll to Plowden, 2 September 1790, Ibid., 1:454.

24. Carroll to Emery, Ibid., 1:462.

25. Answers to Francis Nagot, [14–18] September 1790, Ibid., 1:462–463.

26. Ibid.

27. Carroll to Dugnani, 19 September 1790, Ibid., 1:463–464.

28. Carroll to Plowden, 25 September 1790, Ibid., 1:466.

29. Carroll to Emery, 11 March 1791, Ibid., 1:498.

30. Carroll to Nagot, 11 March 1791, Ibid., 1:494.

31. A manuscript copy of Nagot's Life of Olier is in Record Group 1, Box 16, SAB.

32. Quoted by Ruane, 28.

33. *Souvenirs de Mondésir*, SAB.

34. *The Diary of Jean-Marie Tessier*, SAB (hereafter cited as *Tessier Diary*).

35. *Souvenirs de Mondésir*, SAB.

36. Ibid.

37. *The Memoirs of Chateaubriand* (New York, 1902), 1:181–182, 195–197.

38. Jacques-André Emery, "Counsels and Rules of Conduct for the Priests of the Seminary of St. Sulpice," quoted in their entirety by Ruane, 222–224. The original is in SAB.

39. Ibid., 222.

40. Ibid., 223.

41. Ibid., 224.

42. Ibid., 223.

43. Ibid., 224.

44. John M. Daley, S.J., *Georgetown University; Origin and Early Years* (Washington, D.C., 1957), vii.

45. Carroll to Antonelli, 23 April 1792, *J.C.P.*, 2:27.

46. Register, Saint Mary's Seminary, 1:2, SAB. See also "Sulpician Involvement in Educational Projects in the See and Province of Baltimore," by Vincent Eaton, S.S., *U.S. Catholic Historian* 2 (1982): 70–72.

47. James Hennesey, S.J., *American Catholics* (New York, 1981), 80.

48. *History of St. Patrick's Parish* (Baltimore, 1952), 17–22.

49. Ruane, 68.

50. Thomas Hughes, S.J., *The History of the Society of Jesus in North America, Colonial and Federal* (Cleveland, 1908), 1.1:746.

51. Carroll to the Clergy, 28 January 1793, *J.C.P.*, 2:79–80.

52. Ibid.

53. Ruane, 73.

54. Ibid., 80. See also Record Group 1, Box 16, Bohemia Plantation Papers, SAB.

55. Ibid., 86.

56. Carroll to Plowden, 20 October 1798, *J.C.P.*, 2:248. See also Daley, 98–99; Daley acknowledges DuBourg's accomplishments, but he does not place anti-DuBourg sentiment within the conflict over Bohemian Manor.

57. Registre du résultat des assemblées du séminaire commencé en September, 1791, 12, SAB (hereafter cited as Registre). See also Ruane, 81.

58. Registre, 14, SAB.

59. Ruane, 84.

60. John Gilmary Shea, *History of Georgetown University* (Washington, D.C., 1891), 29.

61. Quoted in "The Early History of Georgetown University" *College Journal* 6 (March 1878), 62, Archives of Georgetown University. Also see Daley, 100–101. For a general history of the Jesuits, see Gerald P. Fogarty, Joseph Durkin, and R. Emmett Curran, *The Maryland Jesuits, 1634–1833* (Baltimore, 1976).

62. Ruane, 40–42.

63. *The Epoques of Jean-Marie Tessier* (1796), SAB.

64. Ruane, 97–103; also see James Joseph Kortendick, S.S., *The History of St. Mary's College, Baltimore, 1799–1852* (M.A. thesis, Catholic University of America, 1941), 9, and Dorothy Mackay Gwynn, "Dangers of Subversion in an American Education: A French View," *The Catholic Historial Review*, 29 (April 1953): 28–35.

65. Ruane, 105.

66. Ibid., 106.

67. Emery to Carroll, 9 August 1800, SAB.

68. Registre, 26 April 1800, SAB.

69. Carroll to Nagot, August 1800, *J.C.P.*, 2:313.

70. Carroll to Plowden, 3 September 1800, Ibid., 2:318.

71. Carroll to Emery, 6 January 1801, Ibid., 2:343.

72. Registre, 3 October 1800, SAB.

73. Quoted by Ruane, 48.

74. Carroll to Emery, 6 January 1801, *J.C.P.*, 2:343–344.

75. Quoted by Ruane, 113.

76. Ibid.

77. Registre, 2 October 1801, SAB.

78. Ibid., 31 October 1801.

79. Ibid., 21 December 1801.

80. Quoted by Ruane, 51.

81. Ibid., 113–114.
82. Ibid., 51.
83. Ibid., 51–52.
84. Ibid., 49–50.
85. Ibid., 53.
86. Ibid.
87. Kortendick, 17.
88. Emery to DuBourg, 4 September 1803, Record Group 3, Box 17, SAB.
89. Emery to DuBourg, 26 February 1804, Record Group 3, Box 17, SAB.
90. Emery to DuBourg, 16 January 1806, Record Group 3, Box 17, SAB.
91. Ibid.
92. Kortendick, 21–22.
93. Emery to DuBourg, 16 January 1806, Record Group 3, Box 17, SAB.
94. Quoted by Ruane, 54.

Chapter 2

1. Pierre Boisard, *La compagnie de Saint-Sulpice: Trois siècles d'histoire* (Paris, 1959), 1:82.
2. S. L. Emery, "Jacques-André Emery," *American Catholic Quarterly* (March 1897): 611–615.
3. Georges Goyau, "Concordat," *The Catholic Encyclopedia* (New York, 1908), 4:200.
4. C. S. Phillips, *The Church in France* (New York, 1936), 2:5.
5. This translation of the Gallican Articles is in Phillips, 5; also see Aimé Georges Martimort, *Le Gallicanisme* (Paris, 1973); Alec Vidler, *The Church in an Age of Revolution* (London, 1971); J. Leflon, *Le crise révolutionnaire* (Paris, 1959); and Hans Maier, *Revolution and Church* (Notre Dame, Indiana, 1969).
6. Quoted by Adrien Dansette, *Religious History of France* (New York, 1961) 1:155.
7. Ibid., 1:159–160.
8. Boisard, 1:184.
9. J. Calvert, "Claude Fleury" in *Catholicisme, hier-au jourd'hui-demain* (Paris, 1956), 4:1343.
10. Joseph P. Chinnici, O.F.M., *The English Catholic Enlightenment, John Lingard and the Cisalpine Movement, 1780–1850* (Shepherdstown, West Virginia, 1980), 109.
11. Ibid.
12. Leflon, "Jacques-André Emery" in *Catholicisme*, 4:47.
13. George Goyau, "Joseph Fesch," *The Catholic Encyclopedia* (New York, 1909), 6:601.
14. Leflon, "Jacques-André Emery," 47.
15. S. L. Emery, 617.
16. Ibid.; also see Boisard, 1:207–108.
17. S. L. Emery, 617.
18. Ibid., 620.
19. Ibid., 622–623.
20. Ibid., 623–627.

21. Quoted by Boisard, 1:210; also see S. L. Emery, 628.

22. Boisard, 1:210–211.

23. Ibid., 216.

24. Alec Vidler, *Prophecy and Papacy; A Study of Lamennais, The Church and Revolution,* (London, 1954), 49. For the friendship see Sister Mary Salesia Godecker, *Simon Brute de Remur* (Saint Meinrad, Indiana, 1931).

25. Vidler, 44–46.

26. Ibid., 54.

27. Ibid.

28. Ibid., 55.

29. Ibid.

30. Boyer's pamphlet was not published under his name but under "Professor de Théologie, Directeur de Séminaire." The following title reveals its polemical character: *Antidote contre les aphorismes de M.F.D.L.M.,* (Paris, 1826). For Lamennais's response, see Louis Bertrand, *Bibliothèque Sulpicienne où histoire littéraire de la Compagnie de Saint-Sulpice* (Paris, 1900), 2:145.

31. Vidler, 76.

32. Quoted by Vidler, 77; also see Bertrand, 146.

33. Vidler, 86.

34. Ibid., 87–88.

35. Quoted by Vidler, 85.

36. For analyses of Lamennais's liberalism, see C. S. Phillips, *The Church in France* (London, 1929), 1:230–258; Bernard Reardon, *Liberalism and Tradition* (London, 1975), 62–112; and Vidler, 152–220.

37. Vidler, 205.

38. Pierre-Denis Boyer, *Défense de l'ordre social contre carbonarisme moderne* (Paris, 1835); also see Bertrand, 147.

39. Vidler, 164.

40. Jean Soulcie, P.S.S. "La Formation des clercs au séminaire Saint-Irenée de Lyon de 1659–1905" (Ph.D., diss., Faculty of Canon Law of the University of Lyon, 1955), 211–218.

Chapter 3

1. Robert T. Handy, *A Christian America: Protestant Hopes and Historical Realities* (New York, 1971) 27–64. James Hennesey, S.J., *American Catholics* (New York, 1981), 9–88. Martin E. Marty, *Righteous Empire: The Protestant Experience in America* (New York, 1970).

2. Hennesey, 65.

3. Quoted by Hennesey, 68.

4. "An Address to the Roman Catholics of the United States of America by a Catholic Clergyman, Fall, 1784" in Thomas O'Brien Hanley, S.J., J.C.P., 1:105–106.

5. Ibid.

6. Joseph P. Chinnici, O.F.M., *The English Catholic Enlightenment, John Lingard and the Cisalpine Movement* (Shepherdtown, Virginia, 1980), 95. Also see John Tracy Ellis, *Perspectives in American Catholicism* (Baltimore, 1963), 93–100; Peter Guilday, *Life and Times of John Carroll* (Westminster, Maryland, 1954);

Annabelle M. Melville, *John Gilmary Shea, History of the Catholic Church in the United States; Life and Times of Archbishop Carroll* (New York, 1888).

7. Levadoux to Carroll, 10 September 1796, 4E2, Archives of the Archdiocese of Baltimore (hereafter cited as AAB).

8. Levadoux to Carroll, 9 February 1797, 4T5, AAB.

9. Michael Levadoux, S.S., *Eulogy on George Washington*, ed. and trans. Edward B. Ham (Ann Arbor, Michigan), 17–19.

10. Levadoux to Carroll, 1 March 1797, 4T6, AAB. See also George Paré, *The Catholic Church in Detroit* (Detroit, 1951), 268–277.

11. "Funeral Eulogy of John Carroll," *J.C.P.*, 2:294.

12. "To the Clergy on George Washington," *J.C.P.*, 2:296.

13. Ibid.

14. Charles F. Nagot, "Rule of Life for the Seminary," Record Group 1, Box 17, SAB.

15. Ibid. See also Ruane, 89.

16. Tessier to Emery, March 1811 Sulpician Archives Paris (hereafter cited as SAP).

17. John Tracy Ellis, "Catholics and the Intellectual Life," in *Catholicism in America*, ed. Philip Gleason (Notre Dame, Indiana, 1970), 119.

18. Carroll to Garnier, 15 April 1805, *J.C.P.* 2:476.

19. Carroll to Plowden, 10 January 1808, *J.C.P.* 3:36.

20. Carroll to Garnier, 15 April 1805, *J.C.P.* 2:476.

21. William Harvey Hunter, Jr., ed., *The Architecture of Baltimore, a Pictoral History* (Baltimore, 1953), 39–42.

22. Ibid., 40.

23. Ellin M. Kelly, ed., *Numerous Chairs, A Chronicle of Elizabeth Bayley Seton and Her Spiritual Daughters* (Evansville, Indiana, 1981) 116.

24. Ibid, 114.

25. Ibid, 117.

26. Ibid, 118.

27. Joseph F. Dirvin, C.M., *Mrs. Seton, Foundress of the American Sisters of Charity* (New York, 1967) 218.

28. Ibid, 225.

29. Quoted by Joseph William Ruane, *The Beginnings of the Society of St. Sulpice in the United States* (Baltimore, 1935), 224.

30. "Trappists," Notes of Wendell S. Reilly, S.S., Record Group 1, Box 8, SAB. See also Jean Dilhet, *État de l'église catholique or diocèse du etats-unis de l'Amérique septentrionale* (Washington, D.C.), 76.

31. Quoted in "Pigeon Hill," *Borromean* 13 (November 1947): 6.

32. Carroll to Maréchal, 7 February 1808, *J.C.P.*, 3:42–44.

33. Quoted by Ruane, 161.

34. Richard Shaw, *John Dubois: Founding Father* (New York, 1983), 7–9.

35. Ibid, 16.

36. Quoted by Ruane, 166.

37. Quoted by Ruane, 232.

38. Ibid

39. Annabelle M. Melville, *Elizabeth Bayley Seton, 1774–1821* (New York, 1951; reprint, 1976), 221.

40. Ellin B. Kelley, 31–32.

41. Carroll to Garnier, 29 April 1806, *J.C.P.*, 2:513.

42. Melville, 220.

43. Carroll to Seton, 21 September 1811, *J.C.P.*, 3:156.

44. Theodore Maynard, *The Reed and the Rock* (New York, 1942).

45. Carroll to Tessier, 13 September 1812, *J.C.P.*, 3:199–200.

46. Ibid.

47. Quoted by Melville, 295.

48. Quoted in James Roosevelt Bayley's *Memoirs of Bishop Bruté* (New York, 1861), 44.

49. For a detailed analysis of the Dubois-Sulpician struggle see Joseph William Ruane, *The Beginnings of the Society of St. Sulpice in the United States*, (Baltimore, 1935), 158–186; Richard Shaw, *John Dubois: Founding Father*, (New York, 1983); Mary M. Meline and Edward F.X. McSweeney, *The Story of the Mountain, Mount St. Mary's College and Seminary* (Emmitsburg, 1911).

50. Dubois to Garnier, 11 November 1821, Archives Mount Saint Mary's College (hereafter cited as AMSM).

51. Pise to Bruté, 23 July 1824, AMSM.

52. Dubois to Tessier, 15 February 1829, AMSM.

53. Charles G. Herbermann, *The Sulpicians in the United States* (New York, 1916), 143–61. Sr. Romana Mattingly, *The Catholic Church on the Kentucky Frontier, 1795–1812* (Washington, D.C., 1936). J. Herman Schauinger, *Cathedrals in the Wilderness* (Milwaukee, 1952). M. J. Spalding, *Sketches in the Life and Times and Character of the Rt. Rev. Benedict Joseph Flaget* (Louisville, 1852). Robert Trisco, *The Holy See and the Nascent Church in the Middle Western United States, 1826–1850* (Rome, 1962). Ben J. B. Webb, *The Anatomy of Catholicity in Kentucky* (Louisville, 1884).

54. Carroll to Di Pietro, 17 June 1807, *J.C.P.*, 3:27.

55. Carroll to Garnier, 14 August 1809, *J.C.P.*, 3:90.

56. David to Bruté, 8 June 1811, Sulpician Papers (English translation), Archives University of Notre Dame (hereafter cited as AUND).

57. Quoted by Sr. Columba Fox, *The Life of the Right Reverend John Baptist Mary David* (New York, 1929), 47.

58. J. Herman Schauinger, *Stephen T. Badin, Priest in the Wilderness* (Milwaukee, 1956). Victor F. O'Daniel, O.P., *The Dominican Province of St. Joseph* (New York, 1942).

59. "Bishop Flaget's Report of the Diocese of Bardstown to Pius VII, April 10, 1815," trans. V. F. O'Daniel, O.P., *Catholic Historical Review* 1 (October 1915): 314.

60. *The Metropolitan Catholic Almanac and Laity's Directory* (Baltimore, 1850), 81.

61. "Bishop Flaget's Report. . . ," 316.

62. William J. Howlett, *St. Thomas Seminary* (Saint Louis, 1906), 70.

63. David to Rosati, 18 November 1823, Archives Archdiocese of Saint Louis (hereafter cited as AASL), copy and English translation, Archives of the Sisters of Charity of Nazareth, Nazareth, Kentucky.

64. Flaget to Bruté, 25 January 1815, Francis Clark Papers, AUND.

65. Ibid.

66. Flaget to Garnier, 8 April 1816, copy, Record Group 24, Box 6, SAB.

67. Ibid.

68. Columba Fox, 67–75.

69. Mary Charles Bryce, O.S.B., *Pride of Place; The Role of Bishops in the Development of Catechesis in the United States* (Washington, D.C., 1984), 41–42.

70. Flaget to Garnier, 15 April 1818, copy, Record Group 24, Box 6, SAB.

71. Flaget to Garnier, 16 October 1829, Record Group 24, Box 6, SAB.

72. Annabelle M. Melville, "Some Aspects of Bishop DuBourg's Return to France," in *Studies in Catholic History in Honor of John Tracy Ellis*, ed. Nelson H. Minnick, Robert B. Eno, S.S., and Robert F. Trisco (Wilmington, Delaware, 1985), 88–90.

73. Flaget to Rosati, 1 April 1834, Francis Clark Papers, AUND, original in AASL.

74. Flaget to Rosati, 8 August 1834, AUND. See also Theodore Maynard, *The Reed and the Rock, Portrait of Simon Bruté*, (New York, 1942), and James Roosevelt Bayley, *Frontier Bishop* (Huntington, Indiana, 1971).

75. Boisard, 43, 62, 68, 96, 109, 286; also see George Paré, *The Catholic Church in Detroit* (Detroit, 1951), 47–58, and Vincent M. Eaton, "The Montreal Seminary," unpublished MS, SAB.

76. Hennesey, 111.

77. Dilhet, 119–129.

78. Quoted by Frank B. Woodford and Albert Hyma, *Gabriel Richard* (Detroit, 1958), 67–68.

79. Ibid, 65.

80. Ibid, 107.

81. Ibid, 112–116; also see Paré, 327–351.

82. Richard to Rosati, 24 November 1823, AASL.

83. Hennesey, 130.

84. Herberman, 169.

85. Finbar Kenneally, O.F.M., *United States Documents in the Propaganda Fide Archives, A Calendar*, (Washington, D.C., 1974), first series, 5:312–313.

Chapter 4

1. Carroll to Plowden, 27 January 1812, in Thomas O'Brien Hanley, S.J., *J.C.P.*, 3:175.

2. Quoted by Peter Guilday, *The Life and Times of John Carroll* (New York, 1922), 755.

3. Carroll to Maréchal, 30 April 1806, *J.C.P.*, 2:513.

4. Quoted by Ronin John Murtha, O.S.B., *The Life of the Most Reverend Ambrose Maréchal, Third Archbishop of Baltimore, 1768–1828.* (Ph.D. diss., The Catholic University of America, 1965), 22.

5. Carroll to Litta, 5 January 1815, *J.C.P.*, 3:303.

6. Annabelle M. Melville, *Jean Lefebvre de Cheverus* (Milwaukee, 1958).

7. For analysis of Neale's life see James Hennesey, S.J., "First American Foreign Missionary. Leonard Neale in Guyana," *Records of the American Catholic Historical Society of Philadelphia* 83 (1972): 82–86 and M. Bernatta Brislen, O.S.F., "The Episcopacy of Leonard Neale, Second Archbishop of Baltimore," *Historical Records and Studies* 34 (1945): 20–111.

8. Deluol Diary, 25 January 1824, trans. Alfred Gendreau, Record Group 1, Box 1, SAB

9. Murtha, 241–291.

10. Louis Arand, S.S., to Vincent M. Eaton, S.S., in "The Early Years of Sulpician Activity in the United States: Relations with the Jesuits," *Bulletin de St. Sulpice* 4 (1978): 252.

11. For analysis of the trustee system see Patrick Casey, "The Laity's Understanding of the Trustee System, 1785–1855," *The Catholic Historical Review* 64 (July 1978): 367.

12. Thomas T. McAvoy, *A History of the Catholic Church in the United States*, (Notre Dame, Indiana, 1969), 92–102.

13. "Archbishop Maréchal's Report to Propaganda, October 16, 1818," in *Documents of American Catholic History*, ed. John Tracy Ellis (Milwaukee, 1956), 216–223.

14. Quoted by Murtha, 168.

15. James Hennesey, *American Catholics*, (New York, 1981), 114.

16. Flaget to Bruté, 1 June 1827, Archives of the Sisters of Charity of Nazareth (hereafter cited as ASCN).

17. Ibid.

18. Deluol Diary, 21 October 1821, Record Group 1, Box 1, SAB.

19. Quoted by Columba E. Halsey, O.S.B., "The Life of Samuel Eccleston, Fifth Archbishop of Baltimore," *Records of the American Catholic Historical Society of Philadelphia* 70 (1965): 81–82.

20. Patrick Carey, *Immigrant Bishop: John England's Adoption of Irish Catholicism to American Republicanism* (New York, 1982). Also see Andrew M. Greeley, *The Catholic Experience* (New York, 1967), 63–101.

21. Matthew Leo Panczyk, "James Whitfield, Fourth Archbishop of Baltimore, The Episcopal Years: 1828–1834," *Records of the American Catholic Historical Society of Philadelphia* 75 (1965): 222–251.

22. Peter Guilday, *The Life and Times of John England* (New York, 1927), 2:122–123.

23. Peter Guilday, *A History of the Councils of Baltimore* (New York, 1932), 81–99.

24. Whitfield to Garnier, 17 October 1829, Sulpician Archives of Paris (hereafter cited as SAP), dossier U.S.A.; see also Record Group 24, Box 8, SAB, copy.

25. Quoted by Guilday, *Life and Times of John England*, 2:490–491.

26. Quoted by Panczyk, 27.

27. Quoted by Guilday, *Life and Times of John England*, 2:261.

28. Panczyk, 33.

29. Deluol Diary, 29 October 1833, Record Group 1, Box 1, SAB.

30. Quoted by Guilday, *Life and Times of John England*, 2:441.

31. Ibid., 1:489.

32. Quoted by Ella M. E. Flick, "John England," *Records of the American Catholic Historical Society of Philadelphia*, 32 (1927): 374.

33. Quoted by Guilday, *Life and Times of John England*, 2:537.

34. Chanche to Eccleston, 1 August 1833, 24M4, Archives Archdiocese of Baltimore (hereafter cited as AAB).

35. Deluol Diary, 1 April 1828, Record Group 1, Box 1, SAB.

36. Ibid, January 18, 1822.

37. Deluol to Carrière, 21 July 1833, Record Group 24, Box 9, SAB.

Chapter 5

1. Visitation 1829, SAB.
2. Jean-Marie Tessier, *Epoques*, SAB.
3. Oblates' Diary, 27 October 1827, Oblate Sisters' Archives (hereafter cited as OSA). This diary was recorded by Joubert from 1827 to his death in November 1843.
4. Matthew Leo Panczyk, "James Whitfield, Fourth Archbishop of Baltimore, the Episcopal Years: 1828–1834." *Records of the American Catholic Historical Society of Philadelphia.*
5. Oblates' Diary, March 1828 OSA. For a general history of the Oblate Sisters see Grace M. Sherwood, *The Oblates' One Hundred and One Years* (New York, 1931); also see Joseph B. Code, "Negro Sisterhoods in the United States," *America* 8 January 1938: 318–319.
6. Deluol Diary, 2 July 1829, Record Group 1, Box 1, SAB.
7. Oblates' Diary, 5 June 1829, OSA.
8. Ibid., 21 October 1829 and 3 November 1829, OSA.
9. Peter Guilday, *The Life and Times of John England* (New York, 1927), 2:151–161.
10. Oblates' Diary, 8 October 1834, OSA.
11. Cyprian Davis, O.S.B., "Black Catholics in the Nineteenth Century," *U. S. Catholic Historian* 5 (1986): 1–10.
12. *Catholic Almanac for 1847* (Baltimore, 1847), 69.
13. Deluol Diary, 16 May 1822, Record Group 1, Box 1, SAB.
14. Ibid., 26 February 1826.
15. Eccleston to Garnier, 12 September 1828, Visites et Rapports, SAP.
16. Ibid., The Baltimore Community to Garnier, 15 July 1828.
17. Ibid., Joubert to Garnier, c. July 1828.
18. Garnier to Eccleston, April 1828, 24Y9, AAB.
19. Deluol Diary, 18 November 1828, Record Group 1, Box 1, SAB.
20. Minutes of the Visitation of 1829, 35–37. Since my research, Alfred Gendreau has provided the archives with his English translation of this *Process-Verbal.*
21. Ibid., 38.
22. Ibid.
23. Ibid., 39–40.
24. Ibid., 82–83.
25. Ibid., 86.
26. Deluol Diary, 10 September 1829, Record Group 1, Box 1, SAB.
27. Wheeler to Garnier, 17 October 1829, Record Group 24, Box 7, SAB.
28. Wheeler to Garnier, 3 October 1831.
29. Joubert to Garnier, n.d., c. 1 October 1829, Visites et Rapports, SAP.
30. *Catologue of Saint Mary's College, 1833–34*, SAB.
31. Deluol Diary, 24 July and 18 August 1843, Record Group 1, Box 1, SAB. See also Columba E. Halsey, O.S.B., "The Life of Samuel Eccleston, Fifth Archbishop of Baltimore," *Records of the American Historical Society of Philadelphia* (1965), 94, 96–103.
32. Ibid., Deluol Diary, 24 August 1843.
33. Ibid., 19 April 1845.
34. John Peter Marschall, "Francis Patrick Kenrick, 1851–1863, The Baltimore Years" (Ph.D. diss., The Catholic University of America, 1965), 30.

35. *Golden Jubilee of St. Charles' College, 1848–1898* (Baltimore, 1898), 16.
36. Ibid.
37. Deluol's "Thoughts on Closing St. Mary's College and Opening St. Charles' College—1837," Record Group 1, Box 13, SAB.
38. Ibid.
39. *Golden Jubilee*, 23.
40. Quoted by James Joseph Kortendick, S.S., *The History of St. Mary's College, Baltimore 1799–1852* (M.A. thesis, The Catholic University of America, 1942), 111–112.
41. Ibid., 110–121.
42. Ibid., 123–29.
43. Deluol Diary, 28 February 1848, Record Group 1, Box 1, SAB.
44. Ibid., 1 March 1848.
45. Ibid., 26 September 1848.
46. Jenkins to Eccleston, 29 September 1848, copy, 12C2, SAP.
47. Ibid.
48. Quoted in "Years of Waiting," *The Borromean 14*, (1948): 32.
49. Quoted in *Golden Jubilee*, 28.
50. Louis Branchereau, S.S., *Vie de M. deCourson* (Paris, 1879) 555.
51. Fredet to deCourson, 24 May 1849, Visites et Rapports, SAP.
52. Quoted by Michael V. Gannon, *Rebel Bishop, The Life and Era of Augustin Vérot* (Milwaukee, 1964), 12.
53. Deluol to deCourson, 12 August 1849, Record Group 24, Box 9, SAB.
54. Deluol to deCourson, 27 October 1849.
55. Eccleston to deCourson, 9 August 1849, 24-0-13, AAB.
56. Quoted in Deluol Diary, 4 November 1849, Record Group 1, Box 1, SAB.
57. Deluol to Eccleston, 29 November 1849, 24013, AAB.
58. Deluol to Elder, 13 September 1850, Record Group 3, Box 1, SAB.
59. Vérot to Carrière, 7 January 1851, Record Group 24, Box 8, SAB.
60. Vérot to Carrière, 11 September 1851.
61. Deluol to Isaac Hecker, 20 October 1857, Archives of the Paulist Fathers (hereafter cited as APF).

Chapter 6

1. John Peter Marschall, "Francis Patrick Kenrick, 1851–1863: The Baltimore Years" (Ph.D. diss., The Catholic University of America, 1965). See also Hugh J. Nolan, *The Most Reverend Francis Patrick Kenrick, Third Bishop of Philadelphia* (Philadelphia, 1948). For the immigrant church see Jay P. Dolan, *The American Catholic Experience* (New York, 1985), 127–321, and *The Immigrant Church: New York's Irish and German Catholics* (Baltimore, 1975), 34.
2. Ibid., 37.
3. Deluol Diary, 16 November 1951, Record Group 1, Box 1, SAB.
4. Whitfield to Nicholas Wiseman, a sermon, 6 June 1833. Quoted by Thomas T. McAvoy, *A History of the Catholic Church in America* (Notre Dame, Indiana, 1969), 130.
5. Deluol to Lhomme, 21 September 1851, Record Group 5, Box 11, SAB.
6. Lhomme Diary, 10 October 1851, Record Group 52, Box 2, SAB.

7. Marschall, 126.
8. James Joseph Kortendick, S.S., "The History of St. Mary's College, Baltimore, 1799–1852" (M.A. thesis, The Catholic University of America, 1942); also see *The Metropolitan Catholic Almanac 1853* (Baltimore, 1853), 65.
9. Kortendick, 29–31.
10. Peter Guilday, *A History of the Councils of Baltimore* (New York, 1932), 173–180.
11. Ibid., 183.
12. *The Metropolitan Catholic Almanac* (Baltimore, 1852), 69, 257.
13. Saint Mary's Seminary Registration Book, 1850–59, SAB.
14. Lhomme Diary, 27 May 1853, Record Group 52, Box 2, SAB.
15. Marschall, 166.
16. Hughes to Bacon, n.d., 1859, Hughes Papers, Archives of the Archdiocese of New York (hereafter cited as AANY).
17. Charles George Herbermann, *Historical Sketch of St. Joseph's Seminary, Troy, New York* (New York, 1905), 7–22.
18. For an introduction to nativism and anti-Catholicism see Ray Allen Billington, *The Protestant Crusade, A Study of the Origins of American Nativism* (New York, 1938). J. Humphrey Desmond, *The Know-nothing Party: A Sketch* (Washington, D.C., 1904). John Higham, *Strangers in the Land: Patterns of American Nativism* (New York, 1965). Carroll Noonan, S.S., *Nativism in Connecticut* (Washington, D.C., 1938).
19. William DuBourg, *The Sons of St. Dominic: A Dialogue between a Protestant and a Catholic* (Baltimore, n.d.). This was a polemical pamphlet in defense of Catholicism against antipopery sentiment in the Baltimore Presbyterian community.
20. Deluol Diary, Record Group 1, Box 1, SAB.
21. James Hennesey, *American Catholics* (New York, 1981), 122–127.
22. James F. Connelly, *The Visit of Archbishop Gaetano Bedini* (Rome, 1960), 131.
23. Lhomme Diary, 16 January 1854, Record Group 52, Box 2, SAB.
24. Ibid., 7 January 1852.
25. Connelly, 132.
26. Thomas Spalding, *Martin John Spalding: American Churchman* (Washington, D.C., 1973), 63–64.
27. Robert F. McNamara, *The American College in Rome* (Rochester, New York, 1956), 3ff. Also see John D. Sauter, *The American College in Louvain* (Louvain, 1959).
28. Quoted by Marschall, 282–283, n.38.
29. Charles George Herbermann, *The Sulpicians in the United States* (New York, 1916), 296–301.
30. Ibid., 245.
31. *Golden Jubilee*, 28.
32. Ibid., 32–36.
33. "Oliver Lawrence Jenkins, S.S.," *The Borromean* 14, (1948): 12–14.
34. Dubreul to Carrière, 13 October 1858, Carrière Papers, SAP.
35. Ibid., 185.
36. "Joseph Dubreul," an obituary, 14 May 1878 in *American Necrology of the Society St. Sulpice*, ed. Vincent Eaton, S.S., (Baltimore, 1983), 59.
37. "Sulpician Specialty," *The Voice* 19 (November 1941): 10–11.

38. Marschall, 349. Also see Michael V. Gannon, *Rebel Bishop, The Life and Era of Augustin Vérot* (Milwaukee, 1964) 35–49.
39. Quoted by Marschall, 332.
40. Deluol to Dear Madam (a granddaughter of Charles Carroll) n.d., ca. 1840, Record Group 24, Box 9, SAB.
41. Quoted in "Sixty Years a Priest," *The Voice* 3 (February, 1926): 14–15.
42. Dubreul Diary, 4 July 1863, Record Group 52, Box 2, SAB.
43. Ibid., 11 July 1863.
44. Spalding, 149–155.
45. Spalding to Dubreul, 14 April 1864, Record Group 5, Box 10, SAB.
46. Dubreul Diary, 24 October 1864, Record Group 52, Box 2, SAB.
47. Spalding to Caval, 1 February 1866, Spalding Letterbook, 725–726 AAB; copy of same, Record Group 5, Box 10, SAB.
48. Ibid., Spalding to Kenrick, 2 February 1866.
49. Kenrick to Spalding, 6 February 1866, 34-N-21, AAB.
50. Dubreul-Spalding Correspondence. "Memorandum for the Seminary of St. Sulpice," 7 March 1866, Record Group 5, Box 10, SAB. Also see Spalding, 182–184.
51. Caval to Spalding, 7 April 1866, unclassified, AAB.
52. Dubreul-Spalding Correspondence, Record Group 5, Box 10, SAB.
53. Ibid., Dubreul to Spalding, 27 July 1866.
54. McCaffrey to Spalding, 28 August 1866, 35-C-12, AAB.
55. Ibid., 15 November 1867.
56. Registration Book of St. Mary's Seminary 1866–69, *1791–1891 Memorial Volume of the Centenary of St. Mary's Seminary* (Baltimore, 1891), 56, SAB.
57. Spalding to Dubreul, 19 June 1866, Record Group 5, Box 10, SAB.
58. Dubreul to Spalding, n.d. c. June 1866, Record Group 5, Box 10, SAB.
59. Sister M. Hildegard Yaeger, C.S.C., *The Life of James Roosevelt Bayley, First Bishop of Newark and Eighth Archbishop of Baltimore* (Washington, D.C., 1847), 446–447.

Chapter 7

1. "Alphonse Magnien," *American Necrology of the Society of St. Sulpice*, ed. Vincent Eaton, S.S. (Baltimore, 1983), 119–126.
2. For an introduction to liberal Catholicism in France see: Roger Aubert, *Le pontificat de Pie IX* (Paris, 1952); Yves M.-J. Congar, *Vrae et fausse: Réforme dans l'église* (Paris, 1950); Jean Leflon *La crise révolutionnaire 1789–1846* (Paris, 1949); C. S. Philips, *The Church in France 1789–1848* (London, 1929); Bernard Reardon, *Liberalism and Tradition: Aspects of Catholic Thought in Nineteenth-Century France* (London, 1975); and Alec R. Vidler, *Prophecy and Papacy, A Study of Lamennais, The Church and Revolution* (London, 1954).
3. C. S. Philips, *The Church in France 1848–1907* (London, 1966), 1.
4. Ibid., 2:36–39.
5. Roger Aubert, "Monsignor Dupanloup et le syllabus, in *Revue d'histoire ecclésiastique* 51 (1956): 79–142.
6. Yves M.J. Congar, "Gallicanisme" in *Hier-aujourdi-demain* (Paris, 1956), 4:1735.

7. Rogert Aubert, "Géographie ecclésiologique au XIXème siècle," in M. Nedoncelle, ed., *Ecclésiologie XIXème siècle* (Paris, 1960), 47.
8. Adrien Dansette, *Religious History of Modern France* (New York, 1961), 1:301.
9. Deluol Diary, 31 December 1852, Record Group 1, Box 1, SAB.
10. Boisard, *La compagnie de Saint Sulpice: Trois siècles d'histoire* (Paris, 1959), 2:452.
11. Jean-Marie Palanque, *Catholiques libéraux et Gallicans en France face au concile du Vatican 1867-1870* (Aix-en-Provence, 1962), 65.
12. Boisard, 1:369-374.
13. Correspondence between A. Captier and E. Captier, 1860s, 16C, SAP.
14. Bernard Reardon, 164-167; also see Boisard, 1:370-371.
15. Boisard, 2:425, 488.
16. Gamon, *Vie de Faillon* (Paris, 1977), 315-367.
17. Cuthbert Butler, *The Vatican Council* (London, 1930), 259. For background on this council see Frederick Cwiekowski, S.S., *The English Bishops and the First Vatican Council* (Louvain, 1971); James Hennessey, S.J., *The First Council of the Vatican* (New York, 1963); and J. M. R. Tillard, O.P., *The Bishop of Rome* (Wilmington, Delaware, 1983).
18. Franzelin Ponenza, October 1883, acta 252 (1883), 1088-1089, Archives of the Sacred Congregation for the Propagation of the Faith.
19. Roger Aubert, "Résumé des discussions," in Nedoncelle, 375.
20. L'Abbé J. E. Darras, L'Abbé J. Bareille, continuée par Mgr J. Fèvre, *Histoire de l'église* (Paris, 1885), 37:404. For background on this conflict see Boisard 2:486-487.
21. Henri Icard, P.S.S., *Observations sur quelques pages de la continuation de l'histoire* (Paris, 1886); also see Icard's defense of the Sulpician way of life, *Traditions de St. Sulpice* (Paris, 1886).
22. Darras, et al., *Histoire de l'église* (Paris, 1886), 40:619-639. Fèvre's rejoinder to Icard is in the "note finale."
23. Henri Icard, P.S.S., *Observations sur quelques pages d'une histoire de l'église relative à la compagnie de St. Sulpice: Lettres du plusieurs éveques, brief du Saint-Père* (Paris, 1887).
24. For background on Americanism see Robert D. Cross, *The Emergence of Liberal Catholicism* (Cambridge, Massachusetts, 1958); R. Emmett Curran, S.J., *Michael Augustine Corrigan and the Shaping of Conservative Catholicism in America* (New York, 1978); Dorothy Dohen, *Nationalism and American Catholicism*, (New York, 1967); John Tracy Ellis, *James Cardinal Gibbons, 1834-1921*, (Milwaukee, 1952), vols. 1 and 2; Gerald P. Fogarty, S.J., *The Vatican and the Americanist Crisis* (Rome, 1974), and *The Vatican and the American Hierarchy* (Stuttgart, 1982); Andrew M. Greeley, *The Catholic Experience* (New York, 1967); James Hennesey, S.J., *American Catholics* (New York, 1982), 184-203; Thomas McAvoy, *The Great Crisis in American Catholic History* (Chicago, 1957); James J. Moynihan, *The Life of Archbishop Ireland* (New York, 1953); William Leroy Portier, "Providential Nation: An Historical Theological Study of Isaac Hecker's Americanism" (Ph.D. diss. University of Toronto, Saint Michael's College, Canada, 1980); also by Portier, "Isaac Hecker and *Testem Benevolentiae*" in *Hecker Studies*, ed. John Farina (New York, 1983); Margaret Mary Reher, "The Church and the Kingdom of God in America: The Ecclesiology of the Americanists" (Ph.D. diss. Fordham University, 1972) and "Leo XIII and

Americanism" in *Theological Studies* 34 (1973): 679–689; and Thomas E. Wangler, "The Ecclesiology of John Ireland," (Ph.D. diss., Marquette University, 1968).

25. Albert Houtin, *L'américanism* (Paris, 1904), 80–81.

26. Ireland to Magnien, 17 March 1892, Record Group 6, Box 3, SAB. For the Faribault-Stillwater school controversy see Fogarty, *The Vatican and the Americanist Crisis*, 63–80. James H. Moynihan, *The Life of Archbishop Ireland* (New York, 1953); and Daniel F. Reilly, *The School Controversy* (Washington, D.C., 1943). The *Civiltà* attacked the Baltimore Sulpicians for their support of Ireland's arrangement with the public schools of Faribault-Stillwater, *Civiltà Cattolica* 15.7 (1893), 160.

27. Magnien to Ireland, 31 March 1892, Archives of the Diocese of Richmond (hereafter cited as ADR), microfilm copy at the Archives of the Catholic University of America.

28. Magnien to O'Connell, 3 August 1892, ADR.

29. Ireland to O'Connell, 3 August 1893, Archives of the Archdiocese of Saint Paul (hereafter cited as AASP).

30. Magnien to Ireland, 26 March 1895, AASP.

31. O'Connell to Ireland, 21 January 1897, AASP.

32. Same to same, 12 August 1897, AASP.

33. Same to same, 5 September 1897, AASP.

34. Magnien to O'Connell, 27 September 1897, AASP.

35. Walter Elliot, *The Life of Father Hecker* (New York, 1897), and Vincent F. Holden, *The Yankee Paul* (Milwaukee, 1968).

36. O'Connell to Klein, 13 January 1898, Americanism File, Archives of the Paulist Fathers (hereafter cited as APF). Also see Felix Klein, *Americanism, Phantom Heresy* (Atchison, Kansas, 1951), 100.

37. Gerald P. Fogarty, S.J., *The Vatican and the Americanist Crisis*, 264–266. O'Connell's defense of the separation of church and state was rationalized in the thesis-hypothesis construction popularized by Dupanloup in his acceptance of the Syllabus of Errors. Roger Aubert, "Monsignor Dupanloup et le Syllabus" in *Revue d'histoire ecclésiastique* 51 (1956): 79–142.

38. Magnien to O'Connell, 27 September 1897, ADR.

39. Klein, 68.

40. Magnien to O'Connell, 6 December 1897, ADR.

41. Same to same, 4 March 1898, ADR.

42. Klein to O'Connell, 14 May 1898, ADR. See also Charles Maignen, *Études sur l'Américanisme; Le pere Hecker, est-il un saint?* (Rome, 1899).

43. Quoted by Klein, 171.

44. Ibid., 170.

45. Magnien to O'Connell, 18 October 1898, ADR.

46. *Testem Benevolentiae*, quoted in Klein, 314.

47. Magnien to Ireland, 9 March 1899, ADR.

48. Ireland to O'Connell, 28 November 1902, ADR.

49. Ireland to Edward Dyer, S.S., 24 December 1902, quoted in *Very Reverend A.L. Magnien, A Memorial* (Baltimore, 1903), 84.

50. Fogarty, *The Vatican and the Americanist Crisis*, and Wangler, "The Ecclesiology of John Ireland."

51. For background on Modernism see, Albert Houtin, *L'americanisme* (Paris, 1904) and *Histoire du modernisme catholique* (Paris, 1913); Lester R. Kurtz, *The Politics of Heresy: The Modernist Crisis in Roman Catholicism* (Los Angeles, (1986); Thomas Michael Loome, *Liberal Catholicism, Reform Catholicism, Modernism, A Contribution to a New Orientation in Modernist Research* (Mainz, 1979); Michele Ranchetti, *The Catholic Modernists* (London, 1969); Margaret Mary Reher, "Americanism and Modernism Continuity and Discontinuity" in *U. S. Catholic Historian* 1 (1981), 87–103; Alec Vidler, *The Modernist Movement in the Roman Catholic Church: Its Origins and Outcome* (Cambridge, England, 1934); and Michael de Vito, *The New York Review*, 1905 to 1908 (New York, 1977). Other general works on Modernism include Gabriel Daly, OSA, *Transcendence and Immanence, a Study in Catholic Modernism and Integralism,* (Oxford, 1980); Michael V. Gannon, "Before and After Modernism: The Intellectual Isolation of the American Priest," in *The Catholic Priest in the United States: Historical Investigations,* ed. John Tracy Ellis (Collegeville, Minnesota, 1971), 293–384; René Marlé, *Au coeur de la crise moderniste* (Paris, 1960); and Émile Poulat, *Histoire, dogme et critique dans la crise moderniste* (Paris, 1960), and *Intégrisme et catholicisme intégral: Unréseau secret international antimoderniste La "Sapinière," 1909–1921,* (Paris, 1969); Bernard Reardon, *Roman Catholic Modernism* (London, 1970).

52. Historian Irenée Noye, the Sulpician archivist of Saint-Sulpice in Paris, reports of a letter Hogan received from a confrere in Le Puy in which he expresses his hope that the publication of the encyclical *Quanta Cura* would not oblige Hogan to change his principles and that he would remain Catholic and liberal.

53. For Hogan's influence upon his students see Albert Houtin, *Un prêtre symboliste; Marcel Hebert, 1851–1916* (Paris, 1925), 22, 27–34, 36–45; Émile Poulat, *Histoire, dogme et critique dans la crise moderniste* (Tournai, 1979), 471; and Alec Vidler, *A Variety of Catholic Modernists* (Cambridge, England, 1970), 65. For Hogan's visits with Newman see Charles Stephen Dessain and Thomas Gornal, eds. *The Letters and Diaries of John Henry Newman* (Oxford, 1973), 24:332.

54. Hogan-Hewit Correspondence, 1883–1884, APF.

55. Diary of John B. Hogan, Record Group 9, Box 6, SAB.

56. Donna Merwick, *Boston's Priests* (Cambridge, Massachusetts, 1973).

57. John B. Hogan, *Daily Thoughts for Priests* (Boston, 1899).

58. E.I. Mignot, "Introduction," in John B. Hogan, *Les études du clergé* (Paris, 1901), 3.

59. Patrick J. Ahern, *The Catholic University of America, 1887–1896, The Rectorship of John J. Keane* (Washington, D.C., 1948), 29, 38–40.

60. Ibid., 55–56.

61. "The Abbe Hogan" in *The Voice of History,* ed. Vincent Eaton, S.S. 3.13.

62. Felix Klein, *The Land of the Strenuous Life* (Chicago, 1905), 54.

63. "Charles Rex," *The Voice of History,* 3.13.

64. Hogan-O'Connell Correspondence, 1892–1899, ADR.

65. Elliot to Klein, 14 February 1898, Americanism File, APF. See also Klein, *Phantom Heresy,* 97.

66. Hogan to Deshon, 28 February 1899, APF.

67. Cross, 41–42.
68. Quoted by Felix Klein, *Phantom Heresy*, 248–249; Georges Périés, a bitter anti-Americanist, lashes out at Hogan's bold insinuations against the papacy, included in this article in the *Boston Globe;* see Saint-Clement, (pseudonym for Périés), *La liquidation du consortium américaniste* (Paris, 1899), 63–65. This is a pamphlet published by *Revue canonique* found in Hecker Pamphlets, Archives of the Catholic University of America.
69. Hogan's bibliography includes *Clerical Studies* (Boston, 1899), which was first published as a series of articles in the *American Ecclesiastical Review* (hereafter cited as AÈR), 1891–1899. Some of his other articles include: "Christian Faith and Modern Science," *American Catholic Quarterly Review* (hereafter ACQR) 22 (1897): 383–398; "The Miraculous in Church History," ACQR 23 (1898): 383–398; "Priests and People in France," ACQR 24 (1899): 123–136; "Penitential Discipline in the Early Church," ACQR 25 (1900): 417–437.
70. Houtin, *L'américanisme*, 81.
71. James J. Burtchael, CSC, *Catholic Theories of Biblical Inspiration Since 1810, A Review and Critique* (Cambridge, England, 1969), 4–5.
72. Hogan to Hewit, 23 February 1885, APF.
73. Same to same, 11 April 1885, APF.
74. Johannes Weiss, *Jesus' Proclamation of the Kingdom of God* (Philadelphia, 1971).
75. Hogan to Hewit, 25 February 1885, APF.
76. Burtchael, 220–225.
77. D'Hulst to Hogan, 14 December 1893, Record Group 9, Box 5A, SAB.
78. D'Hulst to Hogan, 7 May 1893, Record Group 9, Box 5A, SAB.
79. Hogan to Rex, November 1893, Record Group 4, Box 36, SAB.
80. Loisy to Hogan, 21 December 1893, Record Group 9, Box 5A, SAB.
81. Hogan to Rex, 13 December 1893, Record Group 4, Box 36, SAB.
82. Same to same, 10 January 1894, Record Group 4, Box 36, SAB.
83. Hogan to Loisy, 18 April 1898, Bibliotheque Nationale, Papiers Loisy, 21 Lettres Adressée à Loisy 15654 F 382.
84. J. Healy, O. CARM. "George Tyrrell and Christ," *Downside Review* 103 (1 January 1985): 50–55.
85. See footnote 83.
86. John B. Hogan, *Clerical Studies* (Boston, 1898), 473.
87. Ibid., 477–478.
88. Ibid., 480.
89. Ibid., 191.
90. "Clerical Studies," *Catholic World* 68 (1898): 280.
91. Hogan to O'Connell, 20 July 1900, ADR.
92. Alfred Loisy, *Memoirs pour servir à l'histoire religieuse de notre temps*, (Paris, 1931), 2:47–48.
93. "John B. Hogan," in *American Necrology*, 107–110.
94. Loisy to von Hügel, 25 November 1901, quoted by Loisy, *Memoirs*, 2:73.
95. Alfred Loisy, "Chronique biblique," *Revue d'histoire et de littérature religieuses*, 7 (1902): 262.
96. Hogan, *Clerical Studies*, 33, *Les études du clergé*, 60.
97. Alfred Loisy, *My Duel With the Vatican; The Autobiography of a Catholic Modernist* (New York, 1968), 212–224.

98. Magnien to O'Connell, 4 March 1898, ADR.

99. Klein, xvi-xvii.

Chapter 8

1. Magnien Diary, 27 September 1878, Record Group 52, Box 2, SAB.
2. Ibid., 21 November 1878.
3. John Tracy Ellis, "Episcopal Vision in 1884 and Thereafter," *U.S. Catholic Historian* 4 (1985): 197.
4. Magnien Diary, 9 November 1884, Record Group 52, Box 2, SAB.
5. Magnien's report to Superior General Captier, SAP.
6. Hogan Diary, 19 November 1884, Record Group 9, Box 4, SAB.
7. Ibid., 22 November 1884.
8. Ibid.
9. Ibid., 23 November 1882.
10. "A Plan of Studies for the Direction of Those Institutions Which Educate Youth for the Priesthood," Record Group 6, Box 2, SAB.
11. Faculty Minutebook, "Visite du Grand Séminaire Saint-Marie Baltimore," 25 and 26 June 1886, 3. English translation by Alfred Gendreau.
12. Ibid., 2-4.
13. Ibid. 19.
14. Jean Gautier, P.S.S., "Nécrologie M. Adolphe Tanquerey," *Bulletin des anciens élèves de St. Sulpice 33* (15 May 1932): 397-408.
15. Caval-Dubreul correspondence. Record Group 5, Box 9, SAB.
16. Gerald P. Fogarty, *The Vatican and the Americanist Crisis: Denis J. O'Connell, American Agent in Rome* (Rome, 1974).
17. Magnien report to the superior general, 1893-1894, Record Group 6, Box 2, SAB.
18. Ibid.
19. Ibid.
20. Faculty Meeting Minutebook, "Visitation of M. Captier, May 1896," 122.
21. Ibid., 120.
22. Ibid., 121.
23. Ibid., 123.
24. See Slattery to O'Connell, 10 November, 1899, ADR.
25. William Portier, "John R. Slattery's Vision for the Evangelization of American Blacks," *U.S. Catholic Historian* 5 (February 1986): 19-44.
26. Josephite Archives, see the Slattery-Dissez correspondence.
27. Ibid.
28. Stephen Ochs, "The Ordeal of the Black Priest," *U.S. Catholic Historian* 5 (February, 1986): 45-66.
29. Ireland to John R. Slattery, 14 April 1888, 7-B-9, Josephite Archives.
30. Portier, 20.
31. "Biographie de J.R. Slattery," 135, Les Papiers Houtin HAF 15741-42, Bibliothèque Nationale. Houtin referred to this as a biography, but because it was composed in the first person, it is actually Slattery's autobiography from which Houtin may have planned to write a biography. I am grateful to Professor William Portier for providing me with a copy of portions of this autobiography.

32. Saint John's Seminary, Brighton Faculty Minutebook, "Visitation, 4 June 1886," 23ff. Archives Archdiocese of Boston (hereafter cited as AABo).
33. Ibid., 26.
34. Wakeham to Rex, 21 December 1894, Record Group 4, Box 36, SAB.
35. Rex to Magnien, 13 February 1880, Record Group 6, Box 3, SAB.
36. Hogan to Rex, 13 February 1890, Record Group 24, Box 36, SAB.
37. Wakeham to Dyer, 4 March 1894, Record Group 10, Box 22, SAB.
38. John Sebastian McDonough, S.S., "Saint Patrick's Seminary, Menlo Park, California, 1898–1948" (privately circulated MS, 1948) 1–122, SAB.
39. Dyer to Rex, 19 May 1892, Record Group 10, Box 23, SAB.
40. Same to same, 1 December 1893.
41. Same to same, 13 February 1894.
42. Same to same, 29 July 1894.
43. Magnien to Dyer, 6 July 1894, Record Group 10, Box 21, SAB.
44. Ibid.
45. Dyer to Rex, 30 August 1894, Record Group 10, Box 23, SAB.
46. Faculty Minutebrook, Saint Mary's Seminary, "Visitation," 16 May 1896, 109, SAB.
47. Ibid., 110.
48. *Visites et Rapports, Circular Letter of Arthur Jules Captier,* with a commentary by Alphonse Magnien, SAP.
49. Ibid.
50. Ibid.
51. Ibid.
52. Fenlon to Dyer, 23 September 1899, Record Group 10, Box 19, SAB.
53. Narcisse Amable Troie, S.S., "Notes sur divers subjets concernant le séminaire de Montreal" (unpublished ms.), 37–42, Sulpician Archives Montreal.
54. Boisard, 2:640–642.
55. Lebas to Dyer, 16 August 1902, Record Group 10, Box 21, SAB.
56. John W. Bowen, S.S., *Statistical Survey of the Sulpicians* (1903), SAB.

Chapter 9

1. Arthur Scanlon, *St. Joseph's Seminary, Dunwoodie, New York* (New York, 1922), 74–75. Also see Corrigan to Icard, 24 April 1891, 15C3, SAP. Captier to Corrigan, 13 January 1896, G11, Archdiocese of New York (hereafter cited as AANY).
2. For an excellent analysis of Corrigan's role in the American church see Robert Emmett Curran, S.J., *Michael Augustine Corrigan and the Shaping of Conservative Catholicism in America, 1878–1902* (New York, 1978). Also see Philip Gleason, *The Conservative Reformers: German-American Catholics and the Social Order* (Notre Dame, 1968).
3. Robert Emmett Curran, S.J., "Prelude to Americanism; the New York Accademia and Clerical Radicalism in the Late Nineteenth Century," *Church History* 47 (1978): 48–75.
4. Corrigan to Rex, 30 January 1896, Record Group 4, Box 36, SAB. Copy in Rex's handwriting.
5. Rex to Corrigan, 7 February 1896, CI2, AANY.

6. Consultors' Minutebook 1 April 1896, AANY. I am indebted to R. Emmett Curran, S.J., for providing me with copies of these minutes, which have been inaccessible in recent years.
7. Ibid.
8. Corrigan to Rex, 4 March 1896, G6, AANY.
9. Rex to Corrigan, 22 June 1896, G11, AANY.
10. Dyer to Corrigan, 7 June 1896, G11, AANY.
11. Same to same, 8 July 1896.
12. Scanlon, 83.
13. Faculty Minutebook, 17 September 1896, AANY.
14. House Diary, Saint Joseph's Seminary, 2:47, AANY.
15. Ibid., 3:22.
16. E. R. Dyer, S.S., "Organization of Classes and Studies in the Seminary," *American Ecclesiastical Review* 23 (1 October 1900): 37–42.
17. Faculty Minutebook, 27 April 1899, AANY.
18. Ibid., 7, 11, and 12 December 1897.
19. Dyer to Paul deFoville, 7 September 1897, Record Group 10, Box 15, SAB.
20. Same to same, 29 March 1898.
21. Joseph Bruneau, S.S., "Recent Contributions to Biblical Theology," *American Ecclesiastical Review*, 20 (October 1899): 271–280.
22. Joseph Bruneau, *Harmony of the Gospels* (New York, 1898), preface, n.p.
23. Michael DeVito, *The New York Review, 1905–1908* (New York, 1977), 25–27.
24. James P. Duffy, "Does Theology Serve Religion," *American Ecclesiastical Review* 20 (1901): 372–390.
25. Dyer to deFoville, 21 March 1899, Record Group 10, Box 15, SAB.
26. John R. Slattery, "The Workings of Modernism," *Journal of Theology* 13 (October 1909): 571.
27. Driscoll to Hyvernat, 20 April 1893, Hyvernat Papers, Archives of the Catholic University of America (hereafter cited as ACUA).
28. Driscoll to Dyer, 3 September 1901, Record Group 10, Box 19, SAB.
29. Ibid.
30. Ibid.
31. Circular Letter of the Superior General, 1901, Record Group 24, Box 4, SAB.
32. Driscoll to Dyer, 26 February 1902, Record Group 10, Box 14, SAB.
33. Same to same, 11 April 1902.
34. Gigot material, Record Group 10, Box 19, SAB.
35. Ibid.
36. Driscoll to Houtin, 31 May 1902, Papiers Houtin no. 15699, 436–437, Bibliothèque Nationale.
37. Same to same, 10 December 1902.
38. Driscoll to Loisy, 11 December 1903, Papiers Loisy 21, no. 15652, 189–191, Bibliotheque Nationale.
39. "Report of the Committee on Education," 3 February 1902, Minutes of the Trustees 12 (1901–1902), 196, Archives of Columbia University.
40. Michael V. Gannon, "Before and After Modernism: The Intellectual Isolation of the Modern Priest." John Tracy Ellis, ed., *The Catholic Priest in the United States* (Washington, D.C., 1971), 330.
41. U. S. Vicariate Minutebook, 8 September 1903, 2, SAB.

42. Ibid.

43. Faculty Minutebook, September 1904, AANY.

44. Roger Aubert, *The Church in a Secularized Society* (New York, 1978), 76, 81. John McManners, *Church and State in France 1870–1914* (London, 1972).

45. Émile Poulat, *Intégrisme et catholicisme intégral: un réseau secret international anti-moderniste: "La Sapinière," 1909–1921* (Tournai, 1969).

46. Driscoll to Dyer, 11 January 1905, Record Group 8, Box 1, SAB.

47. Dyer to Driscoll, 18 January 1905, Record Group 8, Box 1, SAB.

48. Driscoll to Dyer, 26 January 1905, Record Group 8, Box 1, SAB.

49. Dyer to Driscoll, 29 January 1905, Record Group 8, Box 1, SAB.

50. Edward Dyer, *Dunwoodie* (a privately circulated, bound volume, 1906), 53, SAB. This work contains many letters and Dyer's Commentary on the crisis at Dunwoodie.

51. Wakeham to Dyer, 5 February 1905, Record Group 10, Box 22, SAB.

52. Dyer to Wakeham, 14 February 1905, Record Group 10, Box 22, SAB.

53. "Compte-rendu de réunion des consulteurs du 1904–1912," 26 March 1905, 26–27, SAP.

54. *Dunwoodie,* 57–58, SAB.

55. *The New York Review* 1 (1905–1906).

56. *Dunwoodie,* 58–59, SAB.

57. Ibid., 59–60.

58. Ibid., 57.

59. Ibid., 60–61.

60. Ibid., 62–63.

61. Ibid., 63–80.

62. Ibid., 70–78.

63. Ibid., 84–86.

64. Driscoll, *A Statement of the Facts and Circumstances that Led to the Withdrawal of the Dunwoodie Seminary from the Society of St. Sulpice,* Record Group 8, Box 1, SAB.

65. Ibid., 1–5.

66. Ibid., 8–10.

67. Ibid., 10–11.

68. Ibid., 13–15.

69. *Dunwoodie,* 143, SAB.

70. Copy of *The Transcript,* 16 February 1906, Record Group 8, Box 1, SAB.

71. DeVito, 276–282.

72. "Compte-rendu . . . ," 111, SAP.

Chapter 10

1. James P. Gaffey, *Citizen of No Mean City: Patrick Riordan of San Francisco* (Wilmington, 1976), 14–16.

2. Ibid., 97.

3. John Sebastian McDonough, "St. Patrick's Seminary Menlo Park 1898–1948," (privately circulated MS, 1948), 162–164, SAB.

4. Riordan to Magnien, 21 May 1899, Record Group 38, Box 2, SAB.

5. Doran to Dyer, 16 December 1903, Record Group 10, Box 5, SAB.

6. Gaffey, 101.

7. McDonough, 193, SAB.
8. "Process Verbal Assemblies 1912–1920," 8 June 1912, 4, SAP.
9. Gaffey, 245–255, and McDonough, 204–208.
10. Gaffey, 102.
11. Ibid., 329–346.
12. For Riordan's involvement in the opposition to O'Connell see Ibid., 347–359, and James P. Gaffey, "The Changing of the Guard; The Rise of Cardinal O'Connell of Boston," *The Catholic Historical Review* 59 (July 1973): 225–244.
13. Gaffey, "The Changing of the Guard," 329–330.
14. Ibid., 331.
15. Ibid., 337.
16. Ibid., 335–336.
17. Maher to Dyer, 31 January 1985, Record Group 10, Box 1, SAB.
18. William Henry O'Connell, *Recollections of Seventy Years* (Boston, 1934), 55–64. Also see Dorothy G. Wyman, *Cardinal O'Connell of Boston: A Biography of William Henry O'Connell, 1859–1944* (New York, 1955) and Joseph M. White, "St. John's Seminary and the Transition of American Catholic Seminaries, 1884–1910," *Seminaries in Dialogue* (Fall 1984): 6–10.
19. Reminescences of M. Vuibert, 5 January 1919, Record Group 9, Box 6, SAB.
20. Havey's notes on Saint John's Seminary, Brighton, Record Group 9, Box 6, SAB.
21. Ibid.
22. Ibid.
23. Ibid.
24. John E. Sexton and Arthur J. Riley, *History of St. John's Seminary, Brighton* (Boston, 1945), 15. Also see Robert E. Sullivan, "Beneficial Relations: Toward a Social History of the Diocesan Priests of Boston, 1875–1944," in *Catholic Boston: Studies in Religion and Community,* eds., Robert E. Sullivan and James O'Toole (Boston, 1985), 201–238.
25. Dyer-Hertzog and Dyer-Garriguet Correspondence, Record Group 10, Box 20, SAB. Also Chapon to Hertzog, 18 February 1909, 18C3, SAP.
26. Hertzog to Dyer, 17 April 1909, Record Group 10, Box 20, SAB.
27. Same to same, 16 June 1909.
28. Same to same, 23 November 1909.
29. *The Pilot* newspaper cutting, Record Group 10, Box 15, SAB. Also see Herzog to Garriguet, 20 February 1910, 18C3, SAP.
30. O'Connell to Merry del Val, 24 February 1910, O'Connell Papers, AABo.
31. Falconio to Gibbons, 8 March 1910, 108D2, AAB.
32. Bruneau to Gibbons, 13 March 1910, 108D5, AAB.
33. Ibid.
34. Gibbons to del Val, 15 March 1910, copy, 108D8, AAB.
35. Urique to Garriguet, 19 May 1910, 18C3, SAP. The letter is a copy of the minutes of this meeting of the Council of the U.S. Vicariate, 19 May 1910.
36. Ibid.
37. Hertzog to Garriguet, c. June 1910, 18C3, SAP.
38. Same to same, 13 June 1910.

39. Same to same, 18 June 1910.
40. "Agreement Reached by R.C. Archbishop of Boston and Superior General of Sulpicians, September 29, 1910," Seminary Files, AABo.
41. *Entrevue avec Mgr. l'archeveque de Boston*, 29 September 1910, Record Group 9, Box 6, SAB.
42. "Agreement . . . ," Seminary Files, AABo.
43. Francis Havey's Notes on the Meeting of 29 September 1910, Record Group 9, Box 6, SAB.
44. Ibid.
45. Ibid.
46. O'Connell to Garriguet, 21 October 1910, Record Group 9, Box 6, SAB.
47. Garriguet to O'Connell, copy, n.d., c. 15 November 1910, Record Group 9, Box 6, SAB.
48. O'Connell to Bisletti, 4 May 1933, O'Connell Papers 13.5. AABO.
49. Ireland to Walsh, 19 September 1914, Record Group 9, Box 6, SAB.
50. Gerald P. Fogarty, *The Vatican and the American Hierarchy* (Stuttgart, 1982), 205.
51. "Greatest Alumnus of Boston College," *The Pilot* 83 (23 March 1912): 1.
52. "Cardinal Gibbons Lauds Fathers of St. Sulpice," newspaper cutting from the *Catholic Review*, Record Group 4, Box 10, SAB.
53. John J. Tierney, *Historical Sketch of St. Charles' College, 1848-1948* (Baltimore, 1948), 29-35, SAB.

Chapter 11

1. Michael J. Gannon, "Before and After Modernism, the Intellectual Isolation of the Modern Priest," in *The Catholic Priest in the United States: Historical Investigations*, ed. John Tracy Ellis (Collegeville, Minnesota, 1971), 293-384.
2. For the history of the Catholic University of America see John Tracy Ellis, *The Formative Years of the Catholic University of America* (Washington, D.C., 1946); Patrick Henry Ahern, *The Catholic University of America; The Rectorship of John J. Keane* (Washington, D.C., 1948); Peter E. Hogan, *The Catholic University of America, 1896-1903; The Rectorship of Thomas J. Conaty* (Washington, D.C., 1949); and Colman Barry, OSB, *The Catholic University of America, 1903-1909; The Rectorship of Denis J. O'Connell* (Washington, D.C., 1950).
3. Edward Dyer, see chap. 9, n. 16. See also Peter F. Hogan, 68-74.
4. Colman Barry, O.S.B., 214-18.
5. Ibid., 123-125.
6. Record Group 12, Box 1, SAB.
7. Shahan to Dyer, 19 June 1909, Record Group 10, Box 23, SAB.
8. Oblate Case, Record Group 12, Box 1, SAB.
9. Quoted in Dyer to Garriguet, 24 November 1916, Record Group 10, Box 20, SAB.
10. Dyer to Gibbons, 24 November 1916, Record Group 10, Box 20, SAB.
11. Faculty Minutebook, Saint Mary's Seminary, 15, SAB.
12. Ibid.
13. Philip Sheridan, "Father Dyer as a Teacher," *The Voice* 3 (December 1925): 8.
14. "Reasons for the Plan We Follow at the Washington Seminary," Record Group 10, Box 20, SAB.

15. Dyer to Garriguet, 30 March 1922, Record Group 10, Box 7, SAB.
16. Ibid.
17. Pierre Boisard, P.S.S., *La compagnie de Saint-Sulpice; Trois siècles d'histoire* (Paris, 1962), 2:710–711. See also Henri d'Antin de Vaillac, "Les constitutions de la compagnie de Saint-Sulpice" (J.C.D. diss., Institut Catholique de Paris, 1965), 2:395–397.
18. De Vaillac, 2:382–390. See also Garriguet, Circular Letter on the Sulpician Constitutions, 22 January 1922, Record Group 24, Box 4, SAB.
19. De Vaillac, 2:387.
20. Garriguet, Circular Letter on the General Chapter of 1922, Record Group 24, Box 4, SAB.
21. Boisard, 2:710–711.
22. Henri Cheramy to Joseph Ducher, 9 March 1924, 18C3, SAP. For background on the condemnation of the *Manuel biblique*, see Jean Levie, S.J., *The Bible, Word of God in Words of Men* (New York, 1961), 124.
23. DeLai to O'Connell, c. 25 December 1923, O'Connell Papers, AABO.
24. Faculty Minutebook, Saint Mary's Seminary, 4 February 1924, 202, SAB.
25. Vieban to Garriguet, n.d., 18C3, SAP.
26. Faculty Minutebook, Saint Mary's Seminary, 13 November 1922, 173, SAB.
27. Ibid., 18 September 1923, 189–190.
28. Visitation Letters (U.S.), Minutes of the Visitation of Verdier, Record Group 24, Box 1, SAB.
29. "Saint Charles' College Visitation, 1923," Record Group 24, Box 8, SAB.
30. Ibid.
31. Ibid.
32. *Saint Charles' College Catalogue, 1923–24*, SAB.
33. *Saint Mary's Seminary Catalogue, 1923–24*, SAB.
34. Curley to Pastor, 4 April 1923, 18C3, SAP. See also Archdiocese of Saint Paul file copy, Record Group 38, Box 2, SAB.
35. Dyer to Dowling, 18 April 1918, Record Group 38, Box 1, SAB.
36. Garriguet, "Edward Dyer" in *American Necrology of the Society of Saint Sulpice*, ed. Vincent Eaton, S.S., 212–215, SAB.

Chapter 12

1. "Father Fenlon, An Introduction," *The Voice* 3 (January 1926): 1.
2. Ibid.
3. Magnien to O'Connell, n.d. (c. September 1898), ADR.
4. Fenlon to Dyer, 23 September 1899, Record Group 10, Box 19, SAB.
5. "Father Fenlon, An Introduction," 6.
6. The following articles by Fenlon appeared in the *Catholic World*: "A Word for the Old Testament" (April 1907); "Methodist Pioneers in Rome" (May 1910); and "General Convention of the Episcopalian Church" (February 1911 and January 1914).
7. Christopher J. Kauffman, *Faith and Fraternalism, The History of the Knights of Columbus, 1882–1982* (New York, 1982), 190–227. Also see John Tracy Ellis, *The Life of James Cardinal Gibbons* (Milwaukee, 1951), 2:240–259. Gerald P. Fogarty, *The Vatican and the American Hierarchy from 1870–1965* (Stuttgart,

1982), 207–213. Elizabeth McKeown, "The National Bishops' Conference," *The Catholic Review* 65 (October 1980): 565–583.

8. Dyer to Russell, 4 December 1917, Record Group 10, Box 23, SAB.
9. McKeown, 574–575.
10. Fogarty, 215.
11. Ibid., 220–221. John B. Sheerin, *Never Look Back: The Career and Concerns of John J. Burke* (New York, 1975), 64–69.
12. Quoted by Sheerin, 69.
13. Ibid., 70.
14. "Petition of the Seven Bishops of the Administrative Committee of the National Catholic Welfare Council to His Holiness Pope Pius XI," 25 April 1922 (in printed, typed, and handwritten form), 3, Record Group 13, Box 9, SAB.
15. Sheerin, 72.
16. Quoted by Fogarty, 223.
17. Ibid., 227.
18. Walsh to "My dear Bishop" (a fellow suffragan bishop of Boston), May 1921, Record Group 9, Box 6, SAB. Louis Walsh presented his documentary evidence on O'Connell to the Sulpicians, a gift that he must have viewed as a source of some consolation for their eviction from Brighton.
19. Ibid.
20. Ibid., Walsh et al. to O'Connell, November 1921.
21. John Tracy Ellis, *Catholic Bishops: A Memoir* (Wilmington, Delaware, 1983), 73.
22. Walsh to Pius XI, n.d., c. February 1924, Record Group 9, Box 6, SAB.
23. John F. Fenlon, *The Voice* 14 (February 1937), 23.
24. Paulist File, Record Group 23, Box 7, SAB.
25. Robert E. Sheridan, M.M., *Collected Letters of Thomas Frederick Price*, M.M. (Maryknoll, New York, 1981).
26. The General Council Minutebook, 28 August 1933, Maryknoll Archives, acknowledged Bruneau's contribution on the day the Sulpician died. James A. Walsh was also close to André, a Sulpician who taught at Brighton but was transferred back to France. See the André-Walsh Correspondence in the Maryknoll Archives.
27. Minutes of the Provincial Council, 31 May 1923, SAB.
28. Dyer to Hoban (then auxiliary bishop of Chicago), 14 May 1925, Record Group 37, Box 3, SAB.
29. The Saint Camillus Association, Record Group 14, Box 10, SAB.
30. "Alumni Hold Annual Meeting," *The Voice* 6 (November 1929): 10–11.
31. Christie to Dyer, 18 August 1917, Record Group 17, Box 1, SAB.
32. Ibid., Dyer to Christie, 28 August 1917.
33. F.P. Havey's Notes on the Seattle Seminary, September 1927, Record Group 17, Box 5, SAB.
34. Minutes of the Provincial Council, 1 May 1927, SAB.
35. Ibid.
36. F.P. Havey's Notes, SAB.
37. Fumasoni-Biondi to Fenlon, 1 June 1928, Record Group 17, Box 1, SAB.
38. Ibid.

39. Minutes of the Provincial Council, 3 September 1929, SAB.
40. Contract between Sulpicians and the diocese of Seattle, Record Group 17, Box 1, SAB.
41. Thomas O. Wood, s.s., "A History of St. Edward's Seminary," *The Harvester* 18 (17 October 1956): 20–21.
42. Mulligan to Fenlon, 26 January 1932, Record Group 17, Box 2, SAB.
43. Ibid., Fenlon to Mulligan.
44. Wood, 42–43.
45. Shaughnessy to Mulligan, 27 March 1937, Record Group 17, Box 1, SAB.
46. Ibid. (see also Shaughnessy-Mulligan and Shaughnessy-Fenlon Correspondence of 1938–1941). Also see Shaughnessy-Fenlon correspondence, 1938–1941, Archives of Archdiocese of Seattle (hereafter cited as AAS).
47. Minutes of the Provincial Council, 12 January 1926, SAB.
48. Ibid.
49. Ibid.
50. Quoted by Joseph M. White, "Archbishop John T. McNicholas and the Pontifical Commission of the Catholic University of America, 1934–1950," 4. Paper presented at the meeting of the American Catholic Historical Association, John Carroll University, Cleveland, Ohio, 18 April 1986.
51. Corrigan to McNicholas, 30 June 1937, McNicholas Papers, Archives of the Archdiocese of Cincinnati (hereafter cited as AAC).
52. Ibid., Cicognani to McNicholas, 17 February 1937.
53. Ibid., McNicholas to Cicognani, 23 February 1937.
54. Ibid.
55. Ibid.
56. Ibid. Corrigan to McNicholas, 23 March 1937.
57. Fenlon to Boisard, 5 May 1938, extract Record Group 13, Box 1A, SAB.
58. Minutes of the Provincial Council, 19 July 1937, SAB.
59. Ibid., June 1938.
60. Minutes of the Visitation to the Sulpician Seminary, 11 and 12 April 1938, Record Group 12, Box 6, SAB.
61. Ibid.
62. Ibid.
63. Fenlon to Cassidy, 25 September 1937, Record Group 12, Box 6, SAB.
64. "Sulpician Seminary," Fenlon to Cheramy, 27 February 1939, Record Group 13, Box 1A, SAB.
65. Ibid.
66. Minutes of the Provincial Council, 25 March 1938, SAB.
67. John J. Mitty, "Hidden in God," *The Voice* 19 (December 1941); 30.
68. Minutes of the Provincial Council, 12 September 1942, SAB.
69. Ibid., 13 January 1939.
70. Ibid., 13 September 1936.

Chapter 13

1. For background on this period see Sydney E. Ahlstrom, *A Religious History of the American People* (New Haven, 1972), 503–527; *The Catholic Priest in the United States: Sociological Investigations* (Washington, D.C., 1972); Jay P. Dolan, *The*

American Catholic Experience (New York, 1985), 406–454; John Tracy Ellis, *American Catholicism* (Chicago, 1969); Philip Gleason, "The Crisis of American-ization" in *Contemporary Catholicism in the United States* ed. Philip Gleason (Notre Dame, Indiana, 1969); Andrew Greeley, *The American Catholic* (New York, 1977); James Hennesey, S.J., *American Catholics* (New York, 1981), 307–331; Eugene C. Kennedy and Victor J. Heckler, *The Catholic Priest in the United States: Psychological Investigations* (Washington, D.C., 1972); Thomas T. McAvoy, C.S.C., *A History of the Catholic Church in the United States* (Notre Dame, Indiana, 1969), 451–468; National Opinion Research Center, *The Catholic Priest in the United States: Historical Investigations* (Collegeville, Minnesota, 1971); and Walter J. Ong, S.J., *Catholicism at the Crossroads: Religious-Secular Encounters in the Modern World* (New York, 1959).

2. Michael V. Gannon, "Before and After Modernism: The Intellectual Isola-tion of the American Priest" *The Catholic Priest in the United States: Historical Investigations* (Collegeville, Minnesota, 1971), 360–362.

3. The following essays from the 1950s point to the reforms of the 1960s. John Courtney Murray, S.J., "America's Four Conspiracies"; Walter J. Ong, S.J., "The Religious-Secular Dialogue"; Gustav Weigel, S.J., "The Present Embarrassment of the Church," in *Religion in America* ed. John Cogley (New York, 1959), 12–41; 170–207; 224–243.

4. Provincial Council Minutebook, 5 November 1944, SAB.

5. Ibid., 24 March 1946.

6. Mark Brasher, "St. Stephen's," *Hawaii Catholic Herald* (22 March 1985): 6.

7. Saint Stephen's Seminary: Official Diary of Fathers Linn and Cullinan, 1946–1949, 1, Record Group 32, Box 1, SAB.

8. Ibid., 125. See also Cullinan to Lardner, 1 October 1946, Record Group 32, Box 1.

9. Joseph A. Ferrario's Report on Saint Stephen's Seminary, April 1970, Record Group 32, Box 1, SAB.

10. Gerald P. Fogarty, S.J., *The Vatican and the Hierarchy from 1870 to 1965* (Stuttgart, 1982), 242, 251–252.

11. Provincial Council Minutebook, 12 June 1945, SAB. At this same meeting it was noted that Bishop Ready of Columbus, Ohio, had asked for three or four Sulpicians to help with his minor seminary. "The Bishop would like us to take charge of this seminary, but feels that it is too soon to make such a radical change, inasmuch as we are not well known in the diocese of Columbus." The request is somewhat vague. No action is taken at this meeting.

12. Ibid., 25 May 1947.

13. Lardner to Mooney, 19 July 1945, Record Group 28, Box 1, SAB.

14. Ibid., Contract between Provincial and Dioceses, copy, Saint John's Provin-cial Seminary, Detroit. Also see Mooney to Cicognani, 9 August 1947, and Mooney to Lardner, 11 September 1947, Box 6, Folder 8, Archives of the Archdiocese of Detroit (hereafter cited as AAD).

15. Lardner to Mooney, 17 September 1947, Record Group 28, Box 1, SAB.

16. "John J. Lardner, Provincial of Sulpician Fathers, Stricken Fatally," *The Catholic Review* 12 (8 October 1948): 1.

17. "He Adopted the Rule of the Saints," *The Catholic Review* 12 (5 October 1948): 14.
18. Lyman A. Fenn, s.s., "Michigan Milestone," *The Voice* 27 (January 1949): 6–9, 25.
19. Provincial Council Minutebook, 14 September 1948, SAB.
20. Provincial Visitation Saint John's, Plymouth, 29 May–1 June 1950, Record Group 16, Box 6, SAB.
21. Provincial Council Minutebook, January 1930, SAB.
22. Ibid., 5 June 1948.
23. Ibid., 21 November 1948.
24. Ibid., 12 March 1949.
25. Ibid., 5 April 1949.
26. Ibid., 29 May 1949. Floersh to McDonald, 28 May 1949. This letter was inserted into the council minutebook.
27. Ibid., 30 April 1950.
28. Council Minutebook, 30 November 1953, SAB.
29. Boxes 2 and 3 in Record Group 11, SAB, contain several documents on the Solitude in the United States.
30. Ibid.
31. Circular Letter of Lloyd McDonald, 5 March 1959, Record Group 16, Box 2, SAB.
32. Ibid.
33. Saint John's Provincial Seminary, Faculty Minutebook, 14 November 1958, Record Group 19, Box 1, SAB.
34. James Michael Lee, "Educational Problems I," in *Seminary Education in a Time of Change*, eds. James Michael Lee and Louis J. Putz (Notre Dame, 1965), 106.
35. Frank B. Norris, "The Lord Incarnate" *The Voice* 34 (December 1956): 5–7, 23–26. Raymond E. Brown, "Priest and King" *The Voice* 34 (December 1956): 18–9, 22–23.
36. Eugene A. Walsh, "Father Olier and the French School of Spirituality" *The Voice* 34 (March 1957): 14–17, 28–30.
37. David Stanley, "Rudolph Bultmann," *The Voice* 34 (April 1957): 11–14, 28–30.
38. "Catholic Bible Week, 1958," *The Voice* 35 (April 1958): 15–17.
39. James A. Laubacher, s.s., *Dogma and the Development of Dogma in the Writings of George Tyrrell* (Louvain, 1939).
40. McDonald to Sullivan, 14 May 1956, AAS. A copy of Laubacher's untitled proposal accompanied this letter.
41. Ibid., 106.
42. Lawrence Cardinal Shehan, *A Blessing of Years* (Notre Dame, Indiana, 1982), 30–52.
43. Ibid., 150–151.
44. McCormick to McDonald, 9 November 1962, Record Group 16, Box 11, SAB.
45. Sullivan to McDonald, 23 November 1962, Record Group 16, Box 6A, SAB.
46. Ibid.

47. Ibid.
48. Purta to McDonald, 24 August 1964, Record Group 16, Box 3, SAB. Ibid., McDonald to Purta, 16 January 1965.
49. Frank B. Norris, "The 'De Ecclesia' Tract in the Seminary," in *Apostolic Renewal in the Seminary in Vatican Council II* (New York, 1965), 94.
50. Eugene A. Walsh, "Liturgy and Apostolate," Ibid., 210–223.
51. Louis J. Putz, C.S.C., "Religious Education and Seminary Studies," in *Contemporary Catholicism in the United States*, ed. Philip Gleason (Notre Dame, Indiana, 1969), 239–267. Also see Stafford Poole, C.M., *Seminary in Crisis* (New York, 1965).
52. Minutebook, Saint John's Seminary, 4 April 1965, Record Group 19, Box 1, SAB.
53. Ibid., May 1965.
54. Ibid., 18 September 1963.
55. Archbishop Gabriel Garrone, "The Seminary in the Light of the Council," *The Voice* 44 (Winter 1966): 4–6.
56. John Tracy Ellis, "The Seminary Today," Ibid., 10.
57. Kennedy and Hickler, 1.
58. Lyman A. Fenn, "Lloyd P. McDonald, S.S., Sulpician Provincial, 1948–1967," *The Voice* 45 (Winter 1967): 8–9. Joseph J. Tiernan, "Very Rev. Paul P. Purta," *The Voice* 46 (Autumn 1967): 2–4.

Epilogue

1. James Hitchcock, *The Decline and Fall of Radical Catholicism* (New York, 1971).
2. Provincial Council Bulletin, 1967–1974, Record Group 23, Box 1, SAB.
3. Purta-McGucken Correspondence, 1965–1967, Saint Patrick's Seminary, Historical Files (hereafter cited as STP).
4. Ibid., 1970.
5. Documents Related to the Ecumenical Institute, Record Group 46, Box 1, SAB.
6. Paca Street Joins Saint Charles', Provincial Council Bulletins, 1969, Record Group 23, Box 1, SAB.
7. Ibid., 1969–1970.
8. Provincial Council Minutes, 1970, Record Group 23, Box 19, SAB.
9. Ibid.
10. Lawrence Cardinal Shehan, *A Blessing of Years* (Notre Dame, Indiana, 1981).
11. Ibid.
12. Faculty Minutes, 1967–1971, and Laubacher-Purta and Laubacher-McGucken Correspondence, 1967–1971, STP.
13. Saint Patrick's Seminary and the Archdiocese of San Francisco—Report of the Bishops' Committee on Priestly Formation Concerning Visitation . . . , 11–14 January 1971, Record Group 7, Box 1, SAB.
14. Farrell-Purta Correspondence, 1971–1972, Record Group 7, Box 1, SAB.
15. James P. Gaffey, "The Anatomy of Transaction: Cathedral Building and Social Justice in San Francisco, 1964–1971," *The Catholic Historical Review* 70 (January 1984): 45–73.
16. Provincial Council Meeting, 13–15 March 1971, and Paul Purta's Proposed

Official Letter of Response to Bishops of Michigan, n.d., Record Group 23, Box 19A, SAB.

17. Provincial Council Supplementary Documents, January–March 1970. Purta-Connolly Correspondence and various documents on the crisis, Saint Thomas Seminary, Record Group 23, Box 19, SAB.
18. Purta-Hunthausen Correspondence, 1976–1977, AAS.
19. Provincial Council Bulletins, 1977, Record Group 23, Box 1, SAB.
20. Ibid., October 1976.
21. Purta to the Members of the American Province, Record Group 56, Box 9, SAB. See also Purta to Lee, 13 January 1987, Record Group 56, Box 9, SAB.
22. This story of Frazer's provincialate was gleaned from interviews with him, William Lee, and John Bowen and from the documents of the General Assembly, December 1985, located in the current files, Sulpician Provincial House.
23. Gerald P. Brown, "The Vocation Shortage: A New Perspective," in *Update— 1986*, Record Group 58, Box 1, SAB.